Washington, DC

timeout.com

Time Out Guides Ltd
Universal House
251 Tottenham Court Road
London W1T 7AB
United Kingdom
Tel: +44 (0)20 7813 3000
Fax: +44 (0)20 7813 6001
Email: guides@timeout.com
www.timeout.com

Published by Time Out Guides Ltd, a wholly owned subsidiary of Time Out Group Ltd.
Time Out and the Time Out logo are trademarks of Time Out Group Ltd.

© Time Out Group Ltd 2011
Previous editions 1999, 2001, 2004, 2007.

10 9 8 7 6 5 4 3 2 1

This edition first published in Great Britain in 2011 by Ebury Publishing.
A Random House Group Company
20 Vauxhall Bridge Road, London SW1V 2SA

Random House Australia Pty Ltd 20 Alfred Street, Milsons Point, Sydney, New South Wales 2061, Australia

Random House New Zealand Ltd 18 Poland Road, Glenfield, Auckland 10, New Zealand

Random House South Africa (Pty) Ltd Isle of Houghton, Corner Boundary Road & Carse O'Gowrie, Houghton 2198, South Africa

Random House UK Limited Reg. No. 954009

Distributed in the US and Latin America by Publishers Group West (1-510-809-3700)
Distributed in Canada by Publishers Group Canada (1-800-747-8147)

For further distribution details, see www.timeout.com.

ISBN: 978-1-84670-122-1

A CIP catalogue record for this book is available from the British Library.

Printed and bound by Firmengruppe APPL, aprinta druck, Wemding, Germany.

The Random House Group Limited supports The Forest Stewardship Council (FSC), the leading international forest certification organisation. All our titles that are printed on Greenpeace approved FSC certified paper carry the FSC logo. Our paper procurement policy can be found at www.randomhouse.co.uk/environment.

Time Out carbon-offsets its flights with Trees for Cities (www.treesforcities.org).

Contents

In Context 15

History 16
Washington Today 29
Architecture 34

Sights 41

Monumental Center 42
DC Neighborhoods 64
Arlington & Alexandria 88

Consume 93

Hotels 94
Restaurants 111
Bars 134
Shops & Services 143

Arts & Entertainment 163

Calendar 164
Children 169
Film 172
Galleries 175
Gay & Lesbian 181
Music 185

Nightlife 194
Sport & Fitness 197
Theater 202

Escapes & Excursions 209

Escapes & Excursions 210

Directory 221

Getting Around 222
Resources A-Z 226
Further Reference 234
Index 235
Advertisers' Index 242

Maps 243

Escapes & Excursions 245
DC Overview 246
DC Neighborhoods: NW
  & Upper NW 248
DC Neighborhoods: NW & NE 250
Monumental Center/
  DC Neighborhoods 252
Street Index 254
Metro Map 256

Introduction

Washington DC began life as a planned capital, a monumental entity that harked back to Ancient Greece, a worthy center for a fledgling democracy. Its rational layout remains, along with a collection of neo-classical buildings (although not the original White House and Capitol building, both destroyed by the British in the 1812-14 War). At its heart is the National Mall, with the Capitol at one end, the Lincoln Memorial at the other. Today, the Mall is ringed by the nation's museums, world-class collections of art and artifacts, free to view. The buildings add to the resonance of 'Washington' as a concept: a hallowed space to some, the root of all liberal, big-government evil to others. But while the monuments are a reminder that this is a government town, DC is not one of those planned capitals that doesn't quite make it in its own right. Step just a few blocks away from the Mall and you will discover a different, engaging and independent city: in fact, fewer than 20 per cent of the area's workers are government employees.

If non-monumental Washington's recent history has a theme, it's regeneration. From a mid 20th-century slump, exacerbated by damage caused by riots following the assassination of Martin Luther King in 1968, Washington has been reborn, with dozens of new residential buildings springing up in remade neighborhoods and a continuing process of gentrification. In the face of nationwide recession, Washington is doing pretty well. It hasn't been a bonanza for all, however. The new urbanites, along with the area's other prosperous inhabitants, who live principally in the suburbs, have very different lives from the working-class, mainly African-American residents on the city's east side. The urban-urban and urban-suburban divide is very real but, nevertheless, DC's education and income levels are now above the United States average, and increasing. So it's not surprising that today Washington has excellent restaurants, with some of the nation's best chefs making a mark. The theater scene is vibrant and DC has a musical heritage all of its own. Add in those great museums, and the fact that much of the city is easily accessible using the clean and efficient Metrorail service, and you'll discover a city that is highly rewarding to visit. *Ros Sales, Editor*

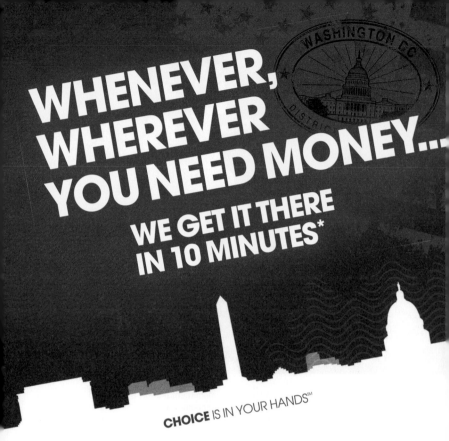

WHENEVER, WHEREVER YOU NEED MONEY...

WE GET IT THERE IN 10 MINUTES*

CHOICE IS IN YOUR HANDS℠

1. Arrange for the person sending the money to visit a MoneyGram agent near them. After sending the money, they will give you a reference number.

2. Find your nearest MoneyGram agent at **www.moneygram.com** or anywhere you see the MoneyGram sign.

3. Give the reference number and your ID** to the MoneyGram agent.

4. Fill out the simple form or pick up the MoneyGram phone to receive your money.

MoneyGram.

1-800-MONEYGRAM® MONEYGRAM.COM

Washington, DC, In Brief

IN CONTEXT

Our In Context section examines the development of Washington from planned government center to modern city, tracing its journey through civil war, civil rights and political change, and taking stock of the economic success of Washington today. We also look at the built environment and how layers of neo-gothic and modernist buildings have added to DC's distinctive neo-classical skyline.

▶ *For more, see pp16-40.*

SIGHTS

The monumental core, centred on the National Mall, surrounded by national museums, is at the heart of the city. This is where you'll find the White House, Capitol, Supreme Court and other buildings of state. Beyond, we cover the city's varied neighborhoods, from wealthy Dupont Circle to a regenerated Downtown and the entertainment hub of U Street.

▶ *For more, see pp42-91.*

CONSUME

Washington's restaurants are many and varied, from upmarket establishments with big-name chefs to modest Ethioipian eateries. Bars range from old-school joints known for political deal-making to sophisticated cocktail bars and down-home dives. We cover the best of both, along with a rundown on the city's best shops and its outstanding hotels, from the historic to the stylishly contemporary.

▶ *For more, see pp94-161.*

ARTS & ENTERTAINMENT

The city has a vibrant arts scene, with nationally recognised theater and art, and a distinctive music culture. It is matched by performance spaces ranging from gleaming new theaters to the national institution of the Kennedy Center to tiny rock venues. Many of the city's museums also host cultural events. In the world of sport, DC now has its own ballpark, Nationals Park.

▶ *For more, see pp164-208.*

ESCAPES & EXCURSIONS

There's something worth seeing in nearly every direction out of Washington. To the north is Baltimore, a gritty port city where regeneration is making a mark. At the heart of Chesapeake Bay is the historic town of Annapolis, while in Virginia there is stupendous scenery in the Shenandoah Valley. The state is also the location of the well-preserved homes of some of the nation's early presidents.

▶ *For more, see pp210-220.*

Washington, DC, in 48 Hrs

Day 1 Museums and Monuments

8.30AM Start your day by roaming the halls of power at the **US Capitol** (*see p58*). The underground visitor center features exhibits on the history of US lawmakers and the building itself. To arrange a free hour-long tour of the rest of the Capitol building, book online in advance.

10.30AM Stroll along the National Mall to the **National Gallery of Art** (*see p47*), which has one of the best art collections in the US. You'll find works by da Vinci, Rembrandt, Vermeer and others in the West Building and contemporary artists such as Lichtenstein and Pollock in the East Building. The gift shop is great for unusual souvenirs.

1.30PM Next, head outside to the National Gallery's Sculpture Garden, where you can grab a bite to eat at the **Pavillion Cafe** and sit near the huge fountain – its pool doubles as a skating rink in winter – and enjoy some of DC's best people-watching.

3PM Time for a trip through the **National Portrait Gallery** (*see p70*). Stop to admire the undulating steel-and-glass roof of the enclosed courtyard, a great place for an afternoon pick-me-up. Then take a quick walk through the collections – the special exhibits often offer an interesting perspective on American history and culture.

6.30PM Penn Quarter – the neighborhood surrounding the Portrait Gallery – happens to be Washington's best restaurant district. **Central** (*see p118*) is a modern French bistro, with upscale takes on traditional staples like fried chicken. For something slightly less expensive, try the Mediterranean small plates at **Zaytinya** (*see p117*).

8.30PM Take in one of the best views in Washington from the roof terrace at **POV** (*see p134*) at the W Hotel, where you can look out on the White House (and see the snipers on the roof) while sipping a cocktail. Just make sure to call ahead – reservations are required.

NAVIGATING THE CITY

Washington is great for walking, with a wealth of attractions packed close together. The Metro system is efficient, but it doesn't go everywhere. To fill in the gaps, the city has launched a highly successful new bus service. Called the Circulator, its six color-coded routes run frequently to parts of town that draw lots of tourists.

The Capital Bikeshare program lets you pick up a bike at any of the 110 stations around town and drop it off at any other. One-day memberships cost $5, plus hourly rates for bike usage.

The streets are laid out on a grid, with numbered streets running north–south and lettered streets going east–west in alphabetical order. Beyond W Street, the roads have two-syllable names in alphabetical order (Belmont, Chapin), then three-syllable names (Albemarle, Buchanan). Avenues named after states cut through the city on diagonals. Washington is divided into four quadrants (Northwest,

Day 2 From Antiques to Half-Smokes

9AM Start your morning with coffee and a croissant at **Patisserie Poupon** (*see p131*), a tiny French bakery popular with wealthy Georgetowners. From here, shop your way down Wisconsin Avenue – lined with interesting antiques shops and boutiques – to M Street, Georgetown's other main drag, where you'll find name-brand stores like Coach and Kate Spade.

1PM There's no shortage of good lunch spots in Georgetown. Try the crusty wood-fired pizzas at **Pizzeria Paradiso** (*see p124*), or, if the weather's nice, grab something at **Dean and Deluca** (*see p153*), a gourmet market, and sit outside.

2.30PM Take a short afternoon stroll along the **C&O Canal** (*see p80*), which once ran from Georgetown all the way to Cumberland, Maryland – 185 miles to the west. Then head up to the grounds of **Dumbarton Oaks** (*see p80*), a mansion with 53 acres of gorgeous gardens.

6PM Visit the **Kennedy Center** (*see p65*), the city's premiere performing arts venue, for a free performance at the Millennium Stage. While some of the concerts are good, the real draw is the lovely view of the Potomac River from the Kennedy Center's terrace.

7.30PM For dinner, take a taxi to the fashionable Logan Circle/U Street area, where scores of new restaurants have opened in recent years. Try **Estadio** (*see p127*) for authentic Spanish tapas or **Cork** (*see p127*), a cozy wine bar that serves excellent small plates. Or for a downscale, yet quintesssential, DC experience, try **Ben's Chili Bowl** (*see p128*), a long-established landmark known for its half-smokes – thick, spicy sausages.

9.30PM After dinner, there's time to catch some music at one of the many nearby clubs such as **Twins Jazz** (*see p189*), **U Street Music Hall** (*see p196*), the **9:30 Club** or the **Black Cat** (for both, *see p186*).

Northeast, Southwest, and Southeast, with Northwest being by far the largest). The numbered streets count up from the US Capitol Building on both the east and west sides. The letter streets do the same from the north and south. That means, for example, that there are two 1st Streets – one to the east of the Capitol and one to the west. To get to the right place, you often have to specify the quadrant. H Street, NW is very different from H Street, NE.

SEEING THE SIGHTS
Most of Washington's attractions are free for visitors and open seven days a week.

PACKAGE DEALS
One of Washington's most appealing features is that most of its major museums are free, and therefore city package deals are not needed. For Metro travel, you may find it worth your while to buy one of various passes that are available (*see p224*).

Washington, DC, in Profile

MONUMENTAL CENTER

The city's center has the **National Mall** at its
heart, with the **Capitol** at one end, the **Lincoln
Memorial** at the other, and the **Washington
Monument** somewhere in the middle. The
White House is slightly to the north. The Mall
is also home to other national monuments,
including the **Vietnam Veterans Memorial** and
the **National World War II Memorial**. Around

the Mall are various museums of the Smithsonian Institution, among them the **National
Gallery of Art** and the **National Air & Space Museum**. All are free to visit.
▶ *For more, see pp42-63.*

DC NEIGHBORHOODS: NORTHWEST

The largest of the city's four quadrants,
bisected north to south by Rock Creek
Park, Northwest is also the most affluent.
Foggy Bottom is home to the Kennedy
Center. To the west, across Rock Creek,
Georgetown has tranquil residential steets
lined with historic homes. **Downtown** has
experienced a radical regeneration over the
last 15 years or so, and, along with its neighbor, **Penn Quarter**, now houses many bars and
restaurants as well as a couple of major museums. **U Street/14th Street Corridor**, to the
north, another regenerated area, is also an entertainment hub. **Dupont Circle**, to the west
of U Street, is home to many embassies as well as restaurants, bars, shops and galleries.
▶ *For more, see pp64-80.*

DC NEIGHBORHOODS:
UPPER NORTHWEST

This affluent sector lies north of Georgetown.
Rock Creek Park, 1,750 acres of forest,
lies north to south along its eastern side.
The extensive **National Zoo** is in the
Woodley Park neighborhood. To the west,
Washington National Cathedral is the
second-largest place of worship in the US.
▶ *For more, see pp80-81.*

DC NEIGHBORHOODS: NORTHEAST

In the south of the area, bordering on Capitol
Hill, **H Street, NE** has undergone a revival in
recent years and is now a popular nightlife
area. Elsewhere, much of the quadrant
remains deprived. However, it's also notable
for a couple of peaceful areas of greenery:
the **United States National Arboretum** and
Kenilworth Aquatic Gardens.
▶ *For more, see pp84-85.*

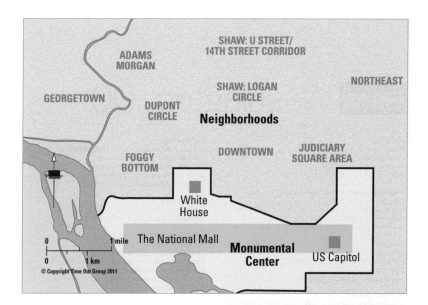

ADAMS MORGAN

SHAW: U STREET/ 14TH STREET CORRIDOR

GEORGETOWN

DUPONT CIRCLE

SHAW: LOGAN CIRCLE

NORTHEAST

Neighborhoods

FOGGY BOTTOM

DOWNTOWN

JUDICIARY SQUARE AREA

White House

0   1 mile

0   1 km

© Copyright Time Out Group 2011

The National Mall

Monumental Center

US Capitol

DC NEIGHBORHOODS: SOUTHEAST

'Southeast' often refers to some of the city's rougher neighborhoods, across the Anacostia River and far from the center of town. However, the quadrant also includes half of **Capitol Hill**, a genteel neighborhood that has the popular Eastern Market food market as its hub. South of Capitol Hill, the once-dodgy tract by the Washington Navy Yard is the site of DC's new ballpark, **Nationals Park**.
▶ For more, see pp86-87.

DC NEIGHBORHOODS: SOUTHWEST

Southwest is the smallest quadrant, much of it blighted by a 1950s attempt at urban renewal. However, it is beginning to reap the benefits of the new Nationals ballpark nearby in Southeast. A gleaming new theater for **Arena Stage** is its brightest spot.
▶ For more, see p87.

ARLINGTON AND ALEXANDRIA

Arlington, over the Potomac in Virginia, is home to the national institutions of Arlington National Cemetery and the Pentagon. Further south along the river, Old Town Alexandria was estabished in the mid 18th century as a port; many of its historic homes have been preserved.
▶ For more, see pp88-91.

TimeOut Washington, DC

Editorial
Editor Ros Sales
Listings Editor Cathryn Connolly
Proofreader Tamsin Shelton
Indexes William Crow, Jess Fleming

Managing Director Peter Fiennes
Editorial Director Ruth Jarvis
Business Manager Dan Allen
Editorial Manager Holly Pick
Assistant Management Accountant Ija Krasnikova

Design
Art Director Scott Moore
Art Editor Pinelope Kourmouzoglou
Senior Designer Kei Ishimaru
Group Commercial Designer Jodi Sher

Picture Desk
Picture Editor Jael Marschner
Acting Deputy Picture Editor Liz Leahy
Picture Desk Assistant/Researcher Ben Rowe

Advertising
New Business & Commercial Director Mark Phillips
International Advertising Manager Kasimir Berger
International Sales Executive Charlie Sokol
Advertising Sales (Washington, DC) Kimberly Mallory

Marketing
**Sales & Marketing Director, North America
& Latin America** Lisa Levinson
Senior Publishing Brand Manager Luthfa Begum
Group Commercial Art Director Anthony Huggins
Marketing Co-ordinator Alana Benton

Production
Group Production Manager Brendan McKeown
Production Controller Katie Mulhern

Time Out Group
Director & Founder Tony Elliott
Chief Executive Officer David King
Group Financial Director Paul Rakkar
Group General Manager/Director Nichola Coulthard
Time Out Communications Ltd MD David Pepper
Time Out International Ltd MD Cathy Runciman
Time Out Magazine Ltd Publisher/MD Mark Elliott
Group Commercial Director Graeme Tottle
Group IT Director Simon Chappell

Contributors
History Mark Jenkins (*The Star-Spangled Banner* Ros Sales). **Washington Today** Mark Jenkins. **Architecture** Mark Jenkins. **Sightseeing** Steve Ackerman, Ros Sales. **Hotels** Kelly DiNardo, Denise Kersten, Ros Sales (*Small Treats, Beak a Sweat* Kelly di Nardo). **Restaurants** Denise Kersten, Amanda McClements, Caroline Schweiter (*Meals on Wheels, Power Points* Amanda McClements). **Bars** Cathy Alter, Sophie Gilbert. **Shopping & Services** Brad McKee, Caroline Schweiter (*Biagio Fine Chocolate* Caroline Schweiter). **Calendar** Trey Graham. **Film** Mark Jenkins. **Galleries** Jessica Dawson. **Music** Christopher Porter, Mark Jenkins. **Nightlife** Mark Jenkins. **Sport & Fitness** Cathryn Connolly. **Theatre** Trey Graham. **Escapes & Excursions** Cathryn Connolly.

Maps john@jsgraphics.co.uk

Front Cover Photograph: Getty Images
Back Cover Photographs: Songquan Deng; Elan Fleisher

Photography by Elan Fleisher except: pages 3, 68 courtesy of the Smithsonian American Art Museum; pages 5, 10 (bottom left), 30, 79, 85, 93, 111, 113, 117, 120, 126, 132, 141, 143, 149, 155, 156, 159, 186, 189 Susana Raab; pages 7 (top left), 11 (top), 119, 123, 129, 205 Washington DC Tourism; page 7 (centre) Darko Zagar; page 7 (bottom right) S. Borisov; pages 7 (bottom left), 185, 192, 195 John Shore/www.johnshorephoto.com; pages 8, 10 (top right), 41 Songquan Deng; pages 10 (top left), 40 James P. Blair/Newseum; pages 11 (centre), 206 Nick Lehoux; pages 16, 25 Getty Images; page 19 trappy76; page 20 Smithsonian Institution Photo; page 21 courtesy of National Museum of American History; page 28 Rex Features; page 34 Kim Seidl; page 44 Olivier Le Queinic; page 56 kropic1; page 59 SFC; page 69 Tim Hursley; page 102 (top) Gaszton Gal; page 102 (bottom) Paul Morigi; pages 164, 181 courtesy Metro Weekly; page 165 Rena Schild; page 167 Vsevolod33; page 194 Mark Maskell/Panorama Productions; pages 202, 203 Joan Marcus; page 209 Brendan Reals; page 215 Quantabeh; page 221 Katherine Welles.

The following photographs were provided by featured establishments/artists: pages 61, 74, 75, 94, 95, 96, 101, 104, 105, 107, 110, 134, 135, 138, 139, 163, 170, 172, 177, 178, 183, 201.

About the Guide

GETTING AROUND

The back of the book contains street maps of Washington, DC, as well as overview maps of the city and its surroundings. The maps start on page 245; on them are marked the locations of hotels (❶), restaurants and cafés (❶), and pubs and bars (❶). The majority of businesses listed in this guide are located in the areas we've mapped; the grid-square references in the listings refer to these maps.

THE ESSENTIALS

For practical information, including visas, disabled access, emergency numbers, lost property, useful websites and local transport, please see the Directory. It begins on page 222.

THE LISTINGS

Addresses, phone numbers, websites, transport information, hours and prices are all included in our listings, as are selected other facilities. All were checked and correct at press time. However, business owners can alter their arrangements at any time, and fluctuating economic conditions can cause prices to change rapidly.

The very best venues in the city, the must-sees and must-dos in every category we cover, have been marked with a red star (★). In the Sights chapters, we've also marked venues with free admission with a FREE symbol.

PHONE NUMBERS

The area code for Washington, DC is 202. You don't need to use this when calling from within DC: simply dial the last seven digits of the number listed (though you will still get through if you dial the full code). The code is needed for calls to and from Virginia and Maryland, or for long-distance calls within the US. Codes vary for Virginia and Maryland numbers; they are included in listings for this guide.

From outside the US, dial your country's international access code or a plus symbol, followed by the US country code (1) and the ten-digit number as listed in the guide. So to reach the International Spy Museum, for example, dial + 1-202 393 7798. For more on phones, *see p232*.

FEEDBACK

We welcome feedback on this guide, both on the venues we've included and on any other locations that you'd like to see featured in future editions. Please email us at guides@timeout.com.

Time Out Guides

Founded in 1968, Time Out has grown from humble beginnings into the leading resource for anyone wanting to know what's happening in the world's greatest cities. Alongside our influential weeklies in London, New York and Chicago, we publish more than 20 magazines in cities as varied as Beijing and Beirut; a range of travel books, with the City Guides now joined by the newer Shortlist series; and an information-packed website. The company remains proudly independent, still owned by Tony Elliott four decades after he launched *Time Out London*.

Written by local experts and illustrated with original photography, our books also retain their independence. No business has been featured because it has advertised, and all restaurants and bars are visited and reviewed anonymously.

ABOUT THE EDITOR

Ros Sales studied in Washington, DC, and has edited various city guides for Time Out. A full list of the book's contributors can be found opposite. We've also included details of our writers in selected chapters through the guide.

Offset your
flight with
Trees for Cities
and make your
trip mean
something for
years to come

www.treesforcities.org/offset

Trees for Cities
Charity registration number 1032154

In Context

Vietnam Veterans Memorial. *See p52.*

History	16
Profile: the Star-Spangled Banner	20
Going Underground	24
Washington Today	29
Architecture	34

History

It began with a plan.

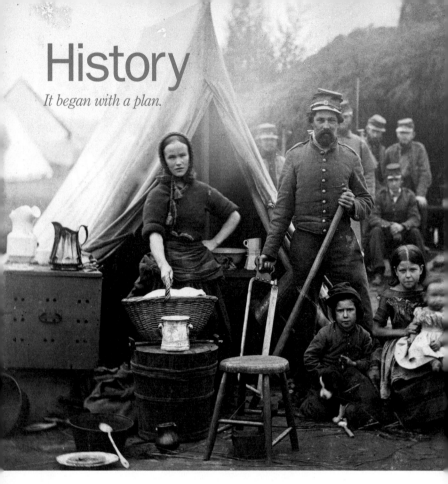

Symbolically, Washington is the heart of American democracy. More than 200 years after its founding, however, democracy for its own residents is only partial: DC's citizens can participate in presidential elections, but have no voting representation in the US Congress. This awkward circumstance is rooted in the city's founding, which was a political compromise between Northern and Southern states. The Revolutionary War left the North with substantial debts that it pressed the new federal government to assume. In exchange, the Northerners abandoned their hopes of locating the government in a large Northern city such as New York or Philadelphia, each of which served as capital for a time. Instead, they agreed to construct a new city on the border between North and South. The actual choice was left to President George Washington, who chose a spot less than 20 miles from his Virginia plantation, Mount Vernon.

'The Civil War transformed Washington from a sleepy part-time capital into the command center of an energized country.'

THE NEW CAPITAL

The first president was not the first person to recognize that the confluence of the Potomac and Anacostia rivers was a natural crossroads. The area was an Indian meeting place a millennium before the Federal City was conceived. ('Potomac' may mean 'place where people trade' in the Algonquin language.) Still, the people who lived in the area when Europeans first arrived in the early 17th century left little besides place names.

Within the new city were two port towns that had been founded around 1750: Georgetown on the Maryland side and Alexandria in Virginia. Both were incorporated into the new District of Columbia, a diamond-shaped 100-square-mile precinct that took 70 square miles from Maryland and 30 from Virginia.

But the new capital, which came to be known as Washington, would be built from scratch on land that was originally mostly farmland or forest – contrary to the popular belief that the city is built on a swamp. Washington hired a former member of his army staff, Pierre-Charles L'Enfant, to design the new city.

Construction of the White House and Capitol began in 1792-93, but neither was finished when John Adams, the country's second president, arrived in 1800. Adams and other members of the new government were but the first to notice the gap between the grandeur of L'Enfant's baroque street plan and the reality: a muddy frontier town of a mere 14,000 inhabitants, most of them living in Georgetown and Alexandria.

After 1801, residents of the District of Columbia lost their right to vote in Maryland or Virginia. The Constitution specified that Congress alone would control 'the federal district', although it's unclear that the document's drafters actually intended to disenfranchise the District's residents. The city of Washington was incorporated, with an elected city council and mayor appointed by the president. In 1820, the city's residents were allowed to elect the mayor as well. This was the first of the many tinkerings with the local form of government that were to follow.

What progress had been made in creating the new capital was largely undone during the War of 1812. In 1814, after defeating local resistance at the Battle of Bladensburg, British troops marched unopposed into the city and burned most of the significant buildings. President Madison fled the White House for the **Octagon** (*see p65*), the nearby home of Colonel John Tayloe. It was there that he ratified the Treaty of Ghent, which ended the war. Among the things destroyed by the British was the original collection of the Library of Congress, which didn't yet have its own building; former president Thomas Jefferson had sold the nation his library as the basis for a new collection.

After the War of 1812 established American sovereignty, European guests began to arrive to inspect the new capital. They were unimpressed. Visiting in 1842, Charles Dickens provided the most withering sobriquet for pre-Civil War Washington: 'the city of magnificent intentions'. It was another Englishman, however, who made the greatest impact on the city in this period. In 1829, James Smithson, a professor of chemistry at Oxford who had never even visited the United States, left his estate to the new nation for the founding of an educational institution. Congress was so bewildered by this bequest that it didn't act on it for more than a decade, but the Smithsonian Institution was finally founded in 1846. Its original building opened in 1855.

While the Smithsonian laid one of the earliest foundations for Washington's contemporary position as an information hub, the city showed few signs of becoming a centre of commerce. In an attempt to increase trade, the Chesapeake & Ohio Canal was built, paralleling the Potomac River for 185 miles to Cumberland, Maryland. Ground was broken in 1828, and the canal's Georgetown terminus opened in 1840. The canal continued to operate into the early 20th century, but its importance was soon diminished by the Baltimore & Ohio Railroad, the country's first railway, which began operation in 1830 and arrived in Washington in 1835.

The other event of this period that had long-term significance for Washington was the 1846 retrocession to Virginia of the southern third of the District; this area now encompasses Arlington County and part of the city of Alexandria. Among the grievances of the area's residents was Congress's refusal to loan money to construct a Virginia-side canal connecting Alexandria to the west. The Virginia state government was more inclined to support the project than Congress, which has always been reluctant to spend money on people without any voting representatives in the Capitol. (The canal project was ultimately reduced to an aqueduct connecting Alexandria to the C&O Canal.) An underlying issue, however, was some Virginians' anticipation that Congress would soon restrict the slave trade in the District.

AFRICAN-AMERICAN CITY

From its founding, Washington had a large African-American population. By 1800, around one-quarter of the city's population was African-American, and most of those were slaves. By 1840, the ratio of white to black was similar, but there were almost twice as many free blacks as slaves. Free blacks and runaway slaves arrived in Washington to escape the horrors of life on Southern plantations, and quickly set up institutions to help their compatriots. Washington became a more attractive destination in 1850, when Congress did ban slave trading (but not slavery itself). A year before Abraham Lincoln's 1863 Emancipation Proclamation, Congress abolished slavery in the District.

Despite the presence of some relatively prosperous free blacks, Washington was hardly a safe haven for former slaves. African-Americans were sometimes kidnapped off the city's streets and sold into slavery, the papers certifying their free status having been destroyed by their captors. Those who escaped this fate still had to live under the onerous 'black codes' adopted by Congress from the laws of Virginia and Maryland. These restricted African-Americans' property ownership, employment and trades, public meetings and even use of profane language. Being arrested for an infraction of these laws could result in a permanent loss of liberty, since jail wardens were authorised to sell their black prisoners to pay the cost of their incarceration.

CIVIL WAR CONSEQUENCES

The Civil War transformed Washington from a sleepy part-time capital into the command center of an energized country – the first (but not the last) time that a national crisis actually benefited the city. New residents flooded into town, and such DC inhabitants as photographer Matthew Brady became nationally known for their war work. Among the new Washingtonians was poet Walt Whitman, who initially came to care for his wounded brother and then became a volunteer at the makeshift hospitals in the converted Patent Office and Washington Armory. (Whitman remained in the city for 12 years, working as a clerk at various federal agencies; he was fired from the Bureau of Indian Affairs when the new secretary of interior deemed *Leaves of Grass* to violate 'the rules of decorum & propriety prescribed by a Christian Civilization'.)

Several Civil War battles were fought near Washington, notably the two engagements at Manassas, now a local commuter-rail stop. A string of forts was built to protect the District, but only one saw action: Fort Stevens, site of an 1864 skirmish. The city's most significant war-related incident, the 1865 assassination of President Lincoln at Ford's Theatre, actually occurred five days after the South surrendered.

IN CONTEXT

Lincoln Memorial.

Following the end of the war, a Congress dominated by 'radical Republicans' made some efforts to atone for the sins of slavery. The Freedman's Bureau was established to help former slaves make the transition to freedom and in 1867 Howard University was chartered for African-American students. All adult male residents of Washington were granted local suffrage in 1866, and 9,800 white and 8,200 'colored' men registered to vote.

Yet Congress did not address Washingtonians' lack of Congressional representation. In 1871, it reclassified the city as a territory, but quieted the latest round of rumors that it intended to move the capital west by authorizing the construction of the massive State, War & Navy Departments Building directly west of the White House. A prominent local real-estate developer, Alexander Shepherd, was appointed to the territory's Board of Public Works, which he soon dominated. 'Boss' Shepherd began an ambitious program of street grading and paving, sewer building and tree planting, transforming the city but also unfortunately quickly bankrupting it.

Only three years after establishing the territorial government, Congress abandoned it, putting the city under the control of three presidentially appointed commissioners. Local voting rights were eliminated, a move that one local newspaper welcomed as ending the 'curse' of African-American suffrage. President Grant, still a Shepherd supporter, nominated the 'Boss' to be one of the three new commissioners, but the Senate wouldn't confirm him. In 1876, Shepherd moved to Mexico, leaving behind a city that was beginning to look something like modern Washington.

The next major round of civic improvements was inspired in 1881 by severe flooding. A land-reclamation and flood-control project built Hains Point and West Potomac Park, quite literally creating the ground that would become the home of such Washington landmarks as the Lincoln and Jefferson Memorials. That same year, President Garfield was shot at the Baltimore & Potomac Railroad station (now the site of the National Gallery of Art) by a disgruntled job-seeker. Garfield died two months later in New Jersey, where he had been taken for the supposedly rehabilitative effect of the sea air.

Profile The Star-Spangled Banner

A song and a flag.

In 1814, the fledgling American nation was in crisis. Only 30-odd years after its hard-won independence, the British were back, this time for a war with origins mainly in international trade and the desire of the young nation to prove itself. In August of that year, Americans learned that British troops had burned down the White House and Capitol building – a major blow. Then the British set their sights on Baltimore, a vital seaport, where Fort McHenry stood guard over the harbor. On 13 September a battle began; the British would bombard the fort with rockets and bombs for 25 hours.

Meanwhile, lawyer Francis Scott Key was aboard a boat some miles out to sea. As dawn came at the battle's end, he looked towards land and was just able to make out an American flag flying over the fort. The fort had not been lost. He returned home full of hope and joy, inspired to write a song (or, to be

ON VIEW
The restored flag is on display in a special, climate-controlled chamber in the **National Museum of American History** (*see p49*).

accurate, song lyrics) and the rest – as they say – is history.

This is a familiar story to Americans, but now they – and the rest of the world – can see the flag that inspired the song that was to become the American national anthem, preserved in in an exhibition that follows its journey both as physical artifact and national symbol.

The garrison flag, measuring a huge 30 by 42 feet, was made by professional flag-maker Mary Pickersgill, her teenage daughter and nieces, and a 13-year-old African American indentured servant named Grace Wisher. After the battle, the flag stayed in the possession of the commander of Fort McHenry and his family for 90 years. Snippets, including one of the 15 original stars, were given away from time to time as patriotic keepsakes.

The fact that the owners thought nothing of cutting pieces off the flag perhaps demonstrates that, while Key's song caused some early stirrings of a patriotic attachment to the flag – both this particular flag

and 'the flag' in general – its status as a real symbol, with emotional resonance and to be treated with reverence, took a while to develop. In the early 19th century flags were official emblems with little cultural significance. It was by giving the flag a name and telling a story that Francis Scott Key began the process of turning it into an evocative symbol of national identity.

However, it wasn't until the next national crisis, the Civil War, that the flag's full symbolism was realised. It's probably no coincidence that the song caught on during this period too – by the end of the war, most Americans would have heard it, and in the 1890s the military began to use the tune for ceremonial occasions. By 1907, when it was lent to the Smithsonian, the flag had gone from personal keepsake to national treasure. The loan became a gift a few years later, but it wasn't until 1931 that 'the Star-Spangled Banner' was declared the official national anthem of the United States of America.

IN CONTEXT

Following Shepherd's modernisation of the city, many improvement projects were undertaken. The Washington Monument was finally finished in 1885, and electric streetcars began operation in 1888, opening the areas beyond Boundary Street (now Florida Avenue) to development. In 1889, the National Zoological Park was founded in Rock Creek Park, which was officially established the following year.

NEW CENTURY AND THE NEW DEAL

Washington's 1900 centennial brought major plans to remake the city. Under the influence of the City Beautiful movement, the Congressionally chartered McMillan Commission proposed restoring the primacy of the oft-ignored L'Enfant Plan and developing the neglected Mall and nearby areas along the river. Some of the city's poorest and most dangerous neighborhoods were to be removed to create a grand greensward, and such unseemly intrusions as the Baltimore & Potomac station were to be banished from the Mall. The result of the latter dictum was Union Station, which upon its 1908 opening consolidated the city's several downtown railroad stations on a site north of the Capitol. In 1910, the Fine Arts Commission was established to ensure the aesthetic worthiness of new federal structures, and an act was passed to limit the height of buildings.

A practical challenge to the McMillan Plan came with World War I, which prompted another Washington building boom. Dozens of 'temporary' structures were erected, including some built on the western part of the Mall. Many of these buildings were used not only during that war but for World War II as well. The last of them was torn down in 1971 and part of the space they occupied became Constitution Gardens, which opened in 1976.

The large numbers of sailors and soldiers demobilized in Washington after World War I are often cited as one of the root causes of the terrible race riots that convulsed the city in the summer of 1919. Nine people were killed in the worst disturbance, which began after false rumors spread that a black man had raped a white woman. Much of the violence spread from the Navy Yard into the predominantly African-American neighbourhoods nearby in Southwest.

Race relations were strained by the riots, but they were precarious even before them. Most of the advances for African-Americans in the post-Civil War era had been turned back by the early 20th century; President Woodrow Wilson, hailed as a visionary in foreign policy, was a reactionary on matters of race. Federal government agencies were rigidly segregated, as were most of the capital's public facilities – although its libraries, trolleys and buses, and baseball stadium (but not the teams that played there) were integrated.

In 1922, when the **Lincoln Memorial** (see p46) opened, the man who freed the slaves was commemorated by a racially segregated crowd; Tuskegee Institute president Robert Moten, an official invitee, was ushered to the negro section. Three years later, 25,000 hooded Ku Klux Klansmen marched down Pennsylvania Avenue, although the founding of a local Klan chapter drew little support. In 1926, the local superior court upheld the legality of voluntary covenants that were designed to prevent black people from buying property in predominantly white neighborhoods.

Women won the vote in 1920, although not if they were DC residents. Meanwhile, separate and unequal African-American Washington boomed, with the Harlem Renaissance mirrored on U Street, known as the Great Black Way. The Howard and other theaters frequently presented such performers as Ella Fitzgerald, Eubie Blake and Washington native Duke Ellington. The city's African-American neighbourhoods were swelled by dispossessed Cotton Belt agricultural workers, and the Depression was soon to send more Southern blacks to town.

In central Washington, the work begun by the McMillan Commission continued. Beginning in 1926, the construction of the Federal Triangle displaced the city's Chinatown and one of its roughest neighbourhoods, 'Murder Bay', while creating

'When Roosevelt's New Deal created new programs and jobs, Washington again benefited from national adversity.'

an area of monumental federal office buildings unified by their Beaux Arts style. Other events boosted the capital's national prestige: in 1924 and 1925, the Washington Senators baseball team made the first two of three trips to the World Series. (They won only in 1924, and disappeared altogether in 1973.) In 1927, the first Cherry Blossom Festival was held, calling attention to the city's new ornamental riverfront.

The Depression soon ended the major civic improvement projects and made Washington the focus for a different sort of national attention. In 1931, a group called the Hunger Marchers arrived in the city; they were followed by some 20,000 jobless World War I veterans who became known as the Bonus Army. They encamped at various places around the city, sometimes with their families, waiting for Congress to pass legislation awarding them back pay. Eventually, troops under the command of General Douglas MacArthur dispersed the camps with bayonets and tear gas. During this action four people were killed, two of them young children.

In 1932, Franklin D Roosevelt was elected president. When his New Deal created new programs and jobs, Washington again benefited from national adversity. Local construction crews began to work once more, erecting the **National Archives** (*see p60*) and the **Supreme Court** (*see p57*), both finished in 1935. Meanwhile, some of the president's cabinet members and top advisers discovered Georgetown, which fitted the 1930s vogue for the colonial style; the old port town, which then had a large African-American population, became the first Washington neighborhood to go down the road towards gentrification.

The New Dealers took a more liberal stand on racial issues. Although Roosevelt was reluctant to antagonize segregationists with major changes, he did sometimes invite black leaders to receptions – and black musicians to perform – at the White House. In 1939, when the Daughters of the American Revolution refused to let famed African-American contralto Marian Anderson perform at the group's Constitution Hall, Secretary of the Interior Harold Ickes immediately approved a concert at the Lincoln Memorial. Anderson performed there for an integrated crowd of 75,000.

World War II added to the city's bustle, as thousands of workers and volunteers arrived to further the war effort. National Airport opened in 1941, and the **Pentagon** (*see p90*), still the nation's largest federal office building, was rapidly constructed for the military command. (The Pentagon was built with separate bathrooms for white and black employees, but after FDR protested, signs distinguishing the facilities were never added to the doors.) Also opening in this period were two less martial structures, the **Jefferson Memorial** (*see p46*) and the **National Gallery of Art** (*see p47*). The arts kept a low profile for the remainder of the war, however, as such institutions as Dumbarton Oaks were requisitioned by wartime agencies.

Despite fears of a post-war depression, the city continued to boom in the late 1940s. As the Korean War began, the 1950 census put the District's population at 800,000, its highest point. Washington's new position as an imperial capital was emphasized by a series of controversial hearings on alleged Communist infiltration of the federal government. There were also two attacks by Puerto Rican nationalists: gunmen tried to shoot their way into Blair House to kill President Truman (he was living at the property, normally used for visiting dignitaries, during renovations to the White House). And then, soon after, attackers wounded five Congressmen on the floor of the House of Representatives.

IN CONTEXT

In the 1950s, suburbanization began to transform the land around Washington, most of it farms or woodland. Aided by new highways and federally guaranteed home mortgages, residential developments grew rapidly in the inner suburbs, followed by commercial development. Congress authorized the Interstate Highway System and supported plans for an extensive system of urban freeways for Washington that would destroy neighbourhoods and overwhelm the proportions of L'Enfant's plan.

The automobile, petroleum and rubber interests that worked quietly to destroy public transit systems in other American cities had no need for such subtlety in DC, which still had no elected local government. Corporate envoys influenced law makers to eliminate trolleys in favour of 'modern' cars and buses. Under Congressional pressure, streetcar lines were abandoned throughout the decade, with the final routes cut in 1962. While the suburbs grew, Congress turned again to remaking embarrassing examples of poverty in the vicinity of the Capitol. Thousands of working-class inhabitants were displaced from Southwest Washington in a process called 'urban renewal'. (Critics called it 'urban removal'.) Southwest also became a focus for federal development, with massive new headquarters buildings erected near the new L'Enfant Plaza.

RIGHTS AND RIOTS
The city's white population began to decline precipitously in 1954, after the Supreme Court outlawed racial segregation. While many jurisdictions resisted the ruling, Washington quickly came into compliance. It was soon a majority black city, with a poverty rate that mortified federal officials. Under Presidents John F Kennedy and Lyndon Johnson, the capital became both the symbolic focus and a conspicuous test case of the civil rights movement and the 'war on poverty'.

In 1963, Martin Luther King Jr led a 200,000-person March for Jobs and Freedom to Washington, and delivered his 'I have a dream' speech at the Lincoln Memorial. Neither race relations nor inner-city economies improved significantly in the mid 1960s, and some feared the capital would soon experience the same sort of riots that had already scarred other major cities. Upon the 1968 assassination of Martin Luther King Jr, Washington and other cities erupted in flames. Twelve people were killed as rioters burned many small businesses in predominantly black sections of the city.

Congress had already made tentative steps toward enfranchizing Washington residents. In 1961, a Constitutional amendment gave Washington residents the right to vote in presidential elections, and in 1967, Congress restored the mayor and council system of government, but with all officials appointed by the president. Despite post-1968 fears that Washington would explode again, progress in establishing an elected local government was slow. Finally, in 1975, Walter Washington became the city's first elected mayor of the 20th century and its first African-American one.

The 'Free DC' battle for local voting rights was rooted in, and interconnected with, the larger civil rights movement. Many of the city's first elected officials – notably Marion Barry, who began the first of four terms as mayor in 1979 – were civil rights veterans. Almost as important, however, was the anti-freeway campaign. An ad hoc citizens' group managed to stop most of the proposed highways through the city. Protests halted a planned freeway bridge across the Potomac River, and the slogan 'white men's roads through black men's homes' halted an eight-lane thoroughfare through Upper Northeast.

Local activists preferred a mostly underground rapid-rail system, which had already been discussed for half a century. Congress funded the system that would become the Metro, but influential Congressmen held up financing until residents also accepted the freeway system. They never did, and the Metro finally opened its first section in 1976. *See also p25* **Going Underground**.

In the 1970s, Washington served as a backdrop for several national struggles, notably the one over the Vietnam War. President Richard Nixon, who recognized his local unpopularity, stressed 'law and order' – considered code words for racial fears – and painted the majority-black city as the nation's 'crime capital'. Then five burglars

Martin Luther King at the Lincoln Memorial, 1963.

Going Underground

DC's Metrorail system has helped shape the modern city.

Just like the authorities in other US cities, Congress in the mid 20th century was subject to lobbying from business interests determined to destroy public transport and make way for the car. However, this wasn't the end for transit in DC, and Congress funded a study for an underground system. A plan released in 1965 called for a 25-mile system, less than a quarter of the size of today's Metrorail network. The concept grew over time, and became entwined with the bitter fight over building freeways through the city center. Eventually local protests managed to stop the decimation of the city by freeways, and the money earmarked for roads was transferred to Metro. Groundbreaking came in December 1969, with the first short section – from Farragut North to Rhode Island Avenue – inaugurated in March 1976.

Today, Washington's Metrorail carries almost 800,000 passengers on a typical weekday, making it the second busiest urban rail system in the country, after New York's. The connection is somewhat ironic, since Metrorail was planned from the beginning to be the antithesis of New York's subway, which had a reputation for being dirty, noisy,

unreliable and crime-ridden. Even the name 'Metro' was chosen to avoid scary New York subway connotations and evoke Paris or Montreal instead. Metro authorities are still proud to make the comparison: notices reinforce the rule against eating or drinking on the system, explaining how successful the Metro is at keeping mice and rats at bay, unlike 'certain other systems'. Trains are clean. Stations are well-maintained and uniform in appearance. When Metro was being planned, only four US cities had heavy-rail lines: New York, Chicago, Philadelphia and Cleveland. New York's was the best known, but all had similar reputations – and they weren't good. So Metro's planners decided to build a system that would appear – and be – clean, airy and safe.

They enlisted Chicago architect Harry Weese, who designed vaulted stations to combine the utility of poured-concrete forms with a suggestion of Washington's iconic domes. Clear sightlines were emphasized, and places for potential attackers to hide were mini-mized; video surveillance added to the sense that Metro was wide open, without the secret crannies of older systems. Not every aspect of Weese's

working indirectly for Nixon were arrested during a break-in at the Democratic National Committee campaign headquarters in the Watergate office building, and 'Watergate' gradually became synonymous with Washington and the corruption of the political system. Nixon resigned the presidency in 1974.

The city's reputation was supposed to be bolstered by the 1976 celebration of the nation's bicentennial, but most people skipped the party, perhaps frightened by reports of crowds that never materialized. Still, the year saw the opening of the **National Air & Space Museum** (*see p46*), which soon became the country's most popular museum.

The following year, members of a small black Islamic group, the Hanafi Muslims, seized the District Building, the B'Nai Brith Building and the Washington Islamic Center in a protest against an obscure film depicting the prophet Mohammed. In the attack on the District Building, the headquarters of the mayor and the city council, a journalist was killed and councilman Marion Barry was wounded.

Faced with pressure from the DC statehood movement, in 1978 Congress passed a Constitutional amendment that would have given the District voting representation

design was hailed. He intentionally kept the stations dim, saying that he wanted people to know they were underground; some passengers who tried to read complained that the ambience was altogether too cave-like. The heavy reliance on escalators became a problem as the system aged and mechanical systems began to fail more frequently. Bad maintenance of the system was blamed for a 2009 crash that killed nine people.

Overall, though, Weese's design has proved both elegant and functional. Metro's crime rate remains low, with most infractions committed not in stations or on trains but in parking lots and garages. An expansion is currently under way. The Dulles Corridor Metrorail project will give Dulles International Airport, to the west of DC, a Metro station. The new line will have 30 new stations, many of them shared with the Blue and Orange lines. It will run from Route 772 in the west to Stadium-Armory in the east. From Dulles, the new line will run through Tysons Corner, with four stops in the area, before reaching Falls Church. The full line is expected to be completed in 2016.

in both the House and the Senate. The amendment was ratified by only 16 of the necessary 35 states, however, and it expired in 1985.

In 1981, Ronald Reagan became president and, that same year, survived an assassination attempt outside the Washington Hilton Hotel. Reagan was ideologically opposed to big government and temperamentally averse to Washington. Nonetheless, after surviving the major recession of Reagan's first term, the region enjoyed a building boom, as new office buildings rose in both the city and its suburbs, especially Virginia. Tenants of the latter were known as 'Beltway bandits', after their proximity to the circumferential highway completed in 1964, which has become the main street of Washington's suburbs; many of them were government contractors who enjoyed the Reagan administration's large military build-up.

Although the city benefited from the tax revenues flowing from the new developments, Barry spent much of the money on assuring his political invulnerability. Years of rumors about the mayor's nocturnal activities were validated in 1990 when Barry was arrested after being videotaped smoking crack. Many Barry supporters were ,

Barack and Michelle Obama.

by the FBI sting, however, charging entrapment. When brought to trial,
Barry was convicted of only a misdemeanour, making him eligible for office at
the end of his jail term.

DC IN THE 1990S AND 2000S

The city's white population has grown in recent years, while middle-class blacks have
departed. The 2005 census put DC's population at 582,000, a figure that surely
undercounts the illegal immigrants, many of whom fled Central America in the 1980s.
Among Washington's foreign-born recent arrivals, Latinos are the fastest-growing group.
The tension between these new residents and the city's predominantly black police
force erupted in 1991, with two days of anti-police rioting in the Mount Pleasant,
Adams Morgan and Columbia Heights neighborhoods.

Barry did indeed run again in 1994, winning re-election in a vote polarized along
racial and class lines. He showed little interest in the job, however, and Congress
had no patience for the notorious mayor. With revenues diminished by the early
1990s real-estate slump, the city was at great fiscal risk. Congress took advantage
of the crisis to seize control of the city, putting a financial control board in charge
of most municipal business.

When Barry was replaced by the sober, low-key Anthony Williams in 1999,
Congressional leaders backed off. The pro-business Williams antagonized many
residents, but his administration met the requirement to produce three years of
balanced budgets, thus causing the financial control board to disappear in 2001.

On September 11 of that year, a hijacked airliner smashed into the Pentagon in
nearby Virginia, killing 184. Although overshadowed by the much greater death toll in
New York, the Pentagon attack – and the likelihood that a fourth plane was supposed
to hit the Capitol or the White House – put the federal government on high alert,
where it essentially remains. Security was tightened, barriers went up around federal
buildings, and permanent new crowd-control methods were hastily put in place.

Meanwhile, many inner-city neighborhoods, such as Columbia Heights, continue to
gentrify as Washington escapes the worst of the recession. A new ballpark, Nationals
Park, opened in Southwest Washington in 2008. And the eyes of the world were on
Washington once again in 2009 for the inauguration of the country's first African-
American president, Barack Obama, in January of that year.

Washington Today

DC's growth bucks economic trends, but the city still has no political clout.

Mark Jenkins writes for the Washington Post, NPR.org and Blurt, and runs the website reeldc.com.

While most of the USA struggles to overcome the damage done by Wall Street's 2008 tumble, Washington is very nearly a boom town. As of late 2010, the region's unemployment rate is almost four points lower than the national one. Restaurants and shops from around the world are acquiring DC locations, seeking a chunk of the city's 'recession-proof' economy. Washington office rents are now the highest in the nation, topping New York's (albeit by less than 50 cents per square foot). Visitors from other affluent, globalized major cities may feel right at home. They can grab a snack at outlets of London's Pret a Manger or Brussels' Le Pain Quotidien, eat at a branch of New York's PJ Clarke's or make the scene at an outpost of Paris's Buddha Bar. They'll find dozens of new residential buildings in such recently remade neighborhoods as NoMa (a Manhattan-style tag for 'North of Massachusetts Avenue') and Logan Circle. And they'll brush shoulders with lawyers, scientists and other professionals in a region dubbed 'Nerdopolis' for having the nation's highest percentage of college-educated residents.

As always in Washington, however, the bounty is not equally distributed. The area's most prosperous inhabitants live principally in the suburbs, and might as well be on a different planet from the working-class, principally African-American residents on the city's east side. In fact, the current unemployment rate for DC alone is higher than the national rate.

The contrast between city and suburbs in the Washington region – which encompasses much of Maryland and Virginia and bits of West Virginia, Pennsylvania and Delaware – has long been striking. It reflects the legacy of American racism and anti-urban policies, but also DC's lack of political clout. Officially, Washington is a 'federal enclave', and its 600,000 residents send no voting representatives to the US Congress. This powerlessness makes DC easy to ignore and safe to impugn, by liberals and conservatives alike. In their time, Presidents Nixon and Reagan frequently denigrated the city. These days, President Obama uses much of the same anti-Washington rhetoric once employed by his Republican predecessors.

Not all the old epithets still apply, however. No one has called Washington the country's 'murder capital' in years. Following national trends, the city's infamous homicide rate has declined dramatically since its 1991 peak of 489 per annum. The year 2010 saw 131 slayings. Another outdated term is 'Chocolate City', coined back in the 1970s when Washington was 70 per cent African-American. Today, the figure is about 50 per cent, a change that in part reflects migration to the suburbs (especially neighboring Prince George's County, Maryland, the first US suburban county to become majority black). Recently, Washington has been the fastest-growing city on the East Coast, which is attributed to a solid job market and a modest baby boom. Many of the adult new arrivals are white, Latino or Asian, and there's also a new sort of African-American in the mix: DC now has the US's largest population of Ethiopians and Eritreans.

CHANGING NEIGHBORHOODS, POLITICAL CONTROVERSY

The transformation is evident in many neighborhoods that were predominantly poor and neglected just a decade or two ago. While change has come slowly to the city's eastern-most precincts, areas along Metro's center-city Green Line are rapidly gentrifying. The

H Street.

most dramatic transformation is in Columbia Heights, a neighborhood whose stretch of 14th Street was scarred by the riots following Martin Luther King's 1968 assassination. After decades of inaction, this is now a lively shopping district, with hundreds of new housing units overlooking such mainstream retailers as Target and Best Buy.

Gentrification remains controversial, and the battle lines over Washington's future were revealed yet again by the 2010 mayoral race. One-term mayor Adrian Fenty was defeated by City Council Chairman Vincent Gray, whose political base is east of the Anacostia, the river that divides most of the city from some of its poorest precincts. Both candidates are black, but the *Washington Post*, which strongly backed Fenty, tried to depict the election in inflammatory racial terms. Gray, they warned, would drag DC back to the bad old days personified by former mayor Marion Barry, who will always be better known for his FBI crack-smoking bust than his political acumen. (Barry is more than a symbol of the past, by the way; he's still on the city council.)

Yet Fenty didn't lose simply because he was the candidate of the upscale, mostly white gentrifiers who are strongly resented in some quarters. The former mayor's reign was characterized by secretiveness, arrogance and hastiness. The highly competitive Fenty, who trained conspicuously for triathlons, bragged that he got things accomplished 'as fast as humanly possible'. But often those things were left half-complete. A stroll through Washington will reveal plenty of unfinished business. The city now boasts the largest bicycle-sharing program in the US, Capital Bikeshare. But it also has the remnants of a previous scheme, Smartbike, that failed because it was too small to be practical for most potential users. The city rushed into Smartbike without much planning, and the effect was simply to delay the introduction of a viable system.

MOVING TOO FAST?

The Fenty administration also hurried into building a streetcar system, whose first two lines are scheduled to begin operation in 2012. The under-construction segments, which will run on the city's east side, are intended more to encourage real-estate development than as a form of transportation. As currently planned, the streetcars will connect poorly to the rest of the city's transit system. It sounds like Smartbike all over again.

Undue speed is also implicated – along with the near-collapse of the country's banking system – in the number of empty lots around town, some in prominent locations. A massive mixed-use project, dubbed CityCenter, is planned for the site of the former convention center, demolished back in 2004. This four-square-block complex is meant to compensate for the ill-considered uprooting of the city's downtown shopping district during redevelopment in the 1980s and '90s, but its groundbreaking remains on hold.

In 2008, the city government hailed the new (if consistently losing) baseball team, the Washington Nationals, by opening a $611 million stadium in the Navy Yard area. Forecasting an immediate building boom, redevelopment officials drove businesses and residents from the district. A few office and residential buildings subsequently arose, but the neighborhood today is mostly empty. Fans can see a baseball game or patronize one of several fast-food eateries, but there's little else to do in the renamed 'Capitol Riverfront' area, which by now was supposed to be a bustling entertainment district.

The DC political culture that prides itself on quick decisions is also notorious for ignoring projects once they're completed. Such shopping complexes as Georgetown Park and the Shops at National Place were allowed to wither, and the central library (the city's only Mies van der Rohe building) was only recently renewed after deteriorating for decades. But the area's most infamous case of neglect involves a different sort of real estate: the Metrorail system.

PROBLEMS WITH METRO

Metro was once hailed as the nation's best urban rail system, with a design that combined practicality and grace. But squabbling local jurisdictions kept underfunding the system, and the quality of both management and maintenance declined. This slump

IN CONTEXT

'*The victory went to the Republicans, who have a long history of tormenting DC.*'

culminated in a June 2009 Red Line collision that killed nine people, by far the worst disaster in Metrorail's 34 years of operation. Even after the crash, Metro management has been slow to improve inadequate systems and procedures, in part because the 2008 recession caused financial shortfalls for the transit agency and the local governments that fund it.

Metrorail remains the nation's second busiest rapid-rail system, after New York's MTA. (This is noteworthy because New York is the largest US metro area, while Washington is ranked eighth.) But Metro's ridership growth stalled after a large fare increase in mid 2010, and the system's reliability continues to be shaky. One problem is that the transit agency's former general manager, who resigned after the 2009 crash, gutted its planning department. Construction of a 23-mile extension to Washington Dulles International Airport – set to open in two phases, in 2013 and 2016 – is being supervised by the Metropolitan Washington Airports Authority, not Metro.

COMMUTING CONUNDRUM

Metro's high ridership reflects the fact that Washington is, by American standards, a geographically small city: only 68 square miles. Most of the region's nearly six million people live outside the District, and suburban workers swell DC's weekday daytime population to nearly twice its night-time residency – by far the biggest such increase in the US. As of 2009, Washington was officially the nation's 27th largest city, but at noon on any given Wednesday, it's (unofficially) the tenth biggest.

Despite DC's longtime reputation as a 'government town', fewer than 20 per cent of area workers toil for the feds. Of course, many of the area's leading industries are linked to the federal presence: defence contractors serve the Pentagon, biotech labs are offshoots of the National Institutes of Health, and telecom and satellite companies originally wanted to be just a local call away from the Federal Communications Commission. The area's many internet-related businesses, still thriving despite the decline of such once-dominant firms as AOL, took root here because the internet began as a military project.

The area also has some major businesses with no direct federal ties, notably in the hotel industry. Marriott International, which began with a single root-beer stand in Columbia Heights, is now one of the world's leading hoteliers. Marriott's influence was shown in 2009, when its chief rival, Hilton Hotels, announced it was relocating from southern California to the DC suburbs. The company's new home will be in Tysons Corner, the sprawling Virginia pile-up of malls and office parks that has grown into the region's second 'downtown'. (Plans are now under way to make Tysons more 'urban', and that Metrorail extension to Dulles Airport will include four stops in the area.)

The growth in suburban employment has fueled an increase in reverse commuting, which also contributes to gentrification. A new generation of urban-living enthusiasts has been moving to the city, despite having jobs in its suburbs. The long-term effect is likely to be a further blurring of the differences between Washington and the upscale jurisdictions that surround it. Seven of the nation's ten richest counties are in the Washington area, so the District always looks a little shabby by comparison. Yet DC's income and education levels are well above the American average, and – unlike in many distressed American cities – are increasing.

The new urbanites have moved mostly to Washington's diverse city-center neighborhoods, where they live alongside first-generation immigrants and people whose families have been here for generations. (Contrary to legend, there actually *are* native-born

Washingtonians.) Gays and lesbians, estimated at eight per cent of DC's population, play a significant role. Two of the city council's 13 members are gay, and in 2010 Washington became one of the first American 'states' to legalize same-sex marriage.

TAXATION WITHOUT REPRESENTATION

Washington isn't a state, of course. Although it's treated as one in most federal legislation, the District lacks the autonomy granted to the 50 states. Ultimate control of DC's laws and finances rests with the US Congress, which can overturn any local legislation and must approve the city's annual budget. (Yet city residents pay federal taxes, unlike people who live in such US territories as Guam and Puerto Rico.)

Because of the city's unique political dependence, the most important 2010 election for DC residents was probably not the mayoral race, but the battle for control of the US House of Representatives. The victory went to the Republicans, who have a long history of tormenting DC, partly to score ideological points and partly just because they can. Congressional Republicans have often interfered in the city's education policies – they want the city to fund private and religious schools – and HIV-AIDS programs. Revoking the gay-marriage law may also be on the Republican agenda.

The most heated issue is likely to be gun control. The Republican-dominated Supreme Court already overturned part of DC's Firearms Control Regulation Act in 2008, ruling some of its restrictions unconstitutional. Pro-gun activists want to go further, essentially gutting the DC law. The Democratic-controlled US Senate may resist, but some Democrats are as inclined as Republicans to obey the dictates of the National Rifle Association, one of the country's most powerful lobbying groups.

In addition to Congressional meddling, Washington is constrained by a severely limited tax base. More than half of the city's land is exempt from property taxes because it belongs to the federal government or universities, religious institutions and other non-profit organizations. In addition, the federal law that gave DC limited autonomy forbids its government to tax the income of non-residents, who earn about 60 per cent of the wages paid in the city. Suburbanites pay income tax only to the jurisdictions in which they live, not to the one in which they work. (Most large American cities tax non-resident workers.)

Yet federal control of DC is not universally begrudged. Some residents are happy with the status quo, and would prefer not to see what would happen if Washington became independent of Congress, either through Constitutional amendment or outright statehood. Take the city's federally imposed height limitation, which prevents buildings of more than 15 storeys. Real-estate developers and their political allies chafe at this restriction, but many Washingtonians would rather preserve the city's distinctive low-rise skyline.

THE FORTIFIED CITY

Even people with no stake in the periodic strife between DC and Congress can't help but notice how federal concerns shape the city's life. The power of such state-security agencies as the Secret Service is evident from the closed streets around the White House and the US Capitol, and the barriers (some masquerading as planters) that surround federal buildings.

The lockdown began after the 1995 bombing of a federal building in Oklahoma, and Washington became even more fortified after the September 11, 2001 attacks. A new headquarters for the Bureau of Alcohol, Tobacco and Firearms was built behind a huge circular battlement, and a visitors' entrance for the Capitol ballooned into an underground complex that went wildly over budget. Recently, the National Park Service proposed adding massive redoubts and underground-only access to the Washington Monument.

Barricading the gentle, grassy slope that leads to the monument seems pointless, especially since the Washington area has not suffered a major terrorist attack in almost a decade. But this is a city of bureaucrats, and bureaucrats like to cover themselves. It's also a city of contradictions, and a plan to imprison a national symbol of liberty is hardly the strangest of them.

IN CONTEXT

Architecture

Built from a neo-classical base.

TEXT: MARK JENKINS

Despite some forays into modernism, architecture in Washington remains at heart about neo-classicism. DC's two best-known buildings, the Capitol and the White House, symbolize American government and, specifically, Congress and the President. They also exemplify the city's dedication to a formal, low-rise style at odds with most American cities.

Although Washington was the first major Western capital designed from scratch, it never occurred to its creators to build a city free of classical precedents. Such founding fathers as Thomas Jefferson (an avid, if self-educated, architect) insisted on architectural styles that recalled democratic Athens and republican Rome. George Washington hired Pierre-Charles L'Enfant to design a baroque street plan, which became known as the L'Enfant Plan. The plan is a rectangular street grid with broad diagonal avenues radiating from ceremonial circles and squares and from two essential structures, the White House and the Capitol. Washington also mandated that the new capital's structures be built of brick, marble and stone, thus giving a sense of permanence to a city – and a country – that in its early days seemed a bit wobbly.

FIRST BUILDINGS

The city's oldest buildings actually precede Washington's founding. The river ports of Georgetown and Alexandria existed prior to their incorporation into the District of Columbia, and they contain most of the area's examples of 18th-century architecture. The city's only surviving pre-Revolutionary War structure is Georgetown's **Old Stone House** (3051 M Street, NW, 1-202 426 6851), a modest 1765 cottage with a pleasant garden.

Georgetown may have the feel of a colonial-era village, but most of its structures date from the 19th and early 20th centuries. Many are Victorian, but some are in the Federal style, a common early 19th-century American mode that adds classical elements like columns, pediments and porticoes to vernacular structures usually made of brick or wood.

Across the river in the Old Town district of Alexandria, which was once but is no longer part of DC, there are some larger pre-Revolutionary structures, including **Carlyle House** and **Christ Church** (for both, *see 89*), a Georgian-style edifice where George Washington was a vestryman. Like Georgetown, however, most of Old Town is of 19th- and 20th-century vintage.

Further south is George Washington's plantation, **Mount Vernon** (*see p216* **Presidential Homes**), now a museum about the first president and the life of colonial-era gentry. This Georgian estate (including a dozen outbuildings) is one of the finest extant examples of an 18th-century American plantation. Next to Arlington National Cemetery is **Arlington House** (also known as the Lee-Custis House), a neo-classical mansion that was once the home of another Virginia aristocrat, Confederate general Robert E Lee.

Washington's two most metonymic structures, the White House and the Capitol, were both first occupied in 1800 and have been substantially remodelled and expanded since. James Hoban was the original architect of the **White House** (*see p55*), but Thomas Jefferson, who lost the competition to design what was originally called simply the President's House, tinkered with the plans while in residence during 1801-09; the most significant additions were new monumental north and south porticoes, designed in 1807 by Benjamin Latrobe but not built until the 1820s. Many additions followed, with some of the more recent ones (for offices and security equipment) out of sight. The structure apparently got its current name after it was whitewashed to cover the damage that resulted from being burned in 1814 by British troops, although the sandstone façade was first whitewashed in 1797 while still under construction.

The **US Capitol** (*see p58*), at the center of the city's grid, has grown dramatically from William Thornton's modest original design. Since the cornerstone was laid in 1793, virtually every visible part of the structure has been replaced, from the dome to the east and west façades. The last major renovation of the exterior was done in 1987; the most recent update has been the construction of a new underground visitor center. Despite its grander scale, the Capitol remains true to the original neo-classical conception, with Corinthian columns making the case that the building is a temple to democracy.

Other buildings that survive from the Federal period are less august, although one of them takes a singular form. Built in 1800 as the city home of the prosperous Tayloe family, the **Octagon** (*see p65*) gives a distinctive shape to the Federal style. Actually a hexagon with a semi-circular portico, the house was designed by Capitol architect Thornton. Both the **Sewall-Belmont House** (144 Constitution Avenue, NE) and **Dumbarton Oaks** (*see p80*) are fine examples of the Federal style, although they've been much altered since they were built in, respectively, 1790 and 1801. (The earliest part of Sewall-Belmont House dates to about 1750.) Dumbarton Oaks is most notable for its elegant gardens and its scenic location on the edge of Rock Creek Park. All three structures are now museums.

IN CONTEXT

Washington's first business district developed around the intersection of Pennsylvania Avenue and Seventh Street, NW, and there are still some examples of pre-Civil War vernacular architecture in this area. The buildings near the intersections of Seventh Street with Indiana Avenue, E Street and H Street in nearby Chinatown all offer examples of the period. Also noteworthy is the 500 block of Tenth Street, NW, whose most imposing structure is the 1863 **Ford's Theatre** (*see p70*), site of Abraham Lincoln's assassination.

The government buildings erected in the first half of the 19th century generally adhered to the Greek Revival style, which modelled itself on such Athenian edifices as the Parthenon, rediscovered by European architects in the mid 18th century. Two of these structures, the **Patent Office** and the **Tariff Commission Building** (part of which also functioned as the General Post Office), face each other at Seventh and F Streets, NW. Both are early examples of the city's official style – also known in the US and especially in DC as neo-Grec – and both were designed at least in part by Robert Mills, best known for the Washington Monument. In 2002, the long-neglected Tariff Building became the Hotel Monaco. The Patent Office, home to the National Portrait Gallery and the Smithsonian American Art Museum, reopened in July 2006 after extensive renovations.

Mills also designed the **US Treasury Building** (15th Street and Pennsylvania Avenue, NW), with its 466-foot Ionic colonnade along 15th Street. In the first major divergence from the L'Enfant Plan, this edifice was placed directly east of the White House, thus blocking the symbolic vista between the building and the Capitol. Construction began in 1836 and wasn't completed until 1871, but that's speedy compared to the progress of Mills's **Washington Monument** (*see p52*). Started in 1845, it was completed (after a 20-year break due to lack of funds) in 1884. The highest structure in the world at its completion, the 600-foot monument is unusually stark by the standards of 19th-century Washington architecture. That's because the colonnaded base of Mills's plan was never built, leaving only a tower modelled on an Egyptian obelisk. Other notable examples of the pre-Civil War era are **St John's Church** (1525 H Street, NW, 1-202 347 8766), designed in 1816 by Benjamin Latrobe, the architect of the Capitol's first expansion, but subsequently much altered; **Old City Hall** (now occupied by Superior District Court offices, Fourth and F Streets, NW); and the

Arts & Industries Building

'Now the National Building Museum, the structure was based on Rome's Palazzo Farnese, but is twice the size.'

modest but elegant Georgetown **Custom House & Post Office** (1221 31st Street, NW), derived from Italian Renaissance *palazzi* and typical of small US government buildings of the period.

AFTER THE CIVIL WAR

The more exuberant styles that came after the Civil War are presaged by the first **Smithsonian Institution** building (1000 Jefferson Drive, SW), designed by James Renwick in 1846. Its red sandstone suits the turreted neo-medieval style, which has earned it the nickname the Castle. Fifteen years later, Renwick designed the original building of the **Corcoran Gallery** (now the Renwick Gallery, *see p54*). Modelled on the Louvre, it is the first major French-inspired building in the US. The Renwick is a compatible neighbor to a more extravagant Second Empire structure, the **Eisenhower Office Building** (17th Street & Pennsylvania Avenue, NW, 1-202 395 5895). The lavish interior of the structure, originally the State, War and Navy Building, is open to tours by appointment on Saturdays. After the war, Adolf Cluss designed the **Arts & Industries Building** on the Mall (1881, *see p43*), also in red-brick neo-Gothic style and part of the Smithsonian. The building fell into decline in the early 2000s but is currently under restoration.

The Civil War led directly to the construction of the **Pension Building** (Fifth & F Streets, NW), designed by Montgomery Meigs in 1882 to house the agency that paid stipends to veterans and their families. Now the **National Building Museum** (*see p76*), the structure was based on Rome's Palazzo Farnese, but is twice the size. Outside is a frieze that depicts advancing Union Army troops; inside is an impressive courtyard, featuring the world's largest Corinthian columns. The atrium was once essential to one of the building's marvels, its highly efficient passive ventilation system, now supplanted by air-conditioning.

The Eisenhower Building and the Pension Building were disparaged by both classicists and modernists, who often proposed razing them. Equally unpopular was the **Old Post Office** (1100 Pennsylvania Avenue, NW, 1-202 289 4224), which now houses shops, restaurants and offices. The 1899 building is an example of the Romanesque Revival, which adapted the rounded arches, dramatic massing and grand vaults of 11th- and 12th-century Northern European cathedrals. The structure contrasts strongly with its Federal Triangle neighbors, all built in a more sedate style in the 1920s, and was threatened with demolition in the 1920s and again in the 1960s.

Second Empire, Romanesque Revival and other ornate styles are still well represented in the Logan Circle, Dupont Circle, Sheridan Circle and Kalorama Triangle areas. Many palatial homes were built in these areas in the late 19th and early 20th centuries, and some survive as embassies, museums and private clubs. Among those open to the public are the **Phillips Collection** (*see p77*) and **Anderson House** (2118 Massachusetts Avenue, NW, 1-202 785 2040), home to the Society of the Cincinnati, a group founded by Revolutionary War veterans. The survival of the **Heurich Mansion** (1307 New Hampshire Avenue, NW, 1-202 429 1894), a Victorian house museum that was once home to a German-born beer mogul, is now in question.

One of the city's most remarkable architectural fantasies is the **Scottish Rite Temple** (1733 16th Street, NW, 1-202 232 3579), finished in 1915 and modelled on the mausoleum at Halicarnassus, one of the seven wonders of the ancient world.

IN CONTEXT

It was designed by John Russell Pope, later the architect of some of the city's most prominent buildings. His work includes the **National Archives** (*see p60*), the neo-classical temple that holds the country's most fundamental documents.

The Archives is the tallest structure erected during Washington's first large urban renewal project, which during the 1920s converted one of the city's most notorious precincts into the government office district known as the Federal Triangle. The Triangle's massive structures provided the headquarters for most of the executive-branch departments, and reiterated the federal government's preference for classicism. The project, which stretches from Sixth to 15th Streets between Pennsylvania and Constitution Avenues, NW, was interrupted by the Depression, and its completion was then debated for 50 years. Finally the government committed to a design for the final structure, the **Ronald Reagan Building** (14th Street & Pennsylvania Avenue, NW), a hulking mediocrity that opened in 1998. It too is in classical drag, albeit with some tricky angles to show that it's the work of the prominent architectural firm of Pei Cobb Freed.

Pope went on to design several more neo-classical temples, including the 1941 original (now called West) building of the **National Gallery of Art** (*see p47*) and the 1943 **Jefferson Memorial** (*see p46*). The latter is partially derived from Rome's Pantheon, while its 1922 predecessor, the **Lincoln Memorial** (*see p46*), is modelled on Athens' Parthenon.

These contemplative edifices' bustling cousin is **Union Station** (*see p59*), the 1908 structure whose Daniel Burnham design borrows from two Roman landmarks, the Arch of Constantine and the Baths of Diocletian. Dramatically remodelled before reopening in 1988, the building's interior still features many of its original architectural details – including statues of centurions whose nudity is hidden only by shields – but now incorporates shops, eateries and a cinema. Most of the train-related functions have been moved to an undistinguished new hall to the rear.

Other notable neo-classical structures of the period are the 1928 **Freer Gallery of Art** (*see p44*) and the 1932 **Folger Shakespeare Library** (*see p57*), an example of Paul Cret's art deco-influenced 'stripped classicism'.

THE ARRIVAL OF MODERNISM

Modernism reached Washington after World War II, but couldn't get comfortable. One dilemma was (and is) the city's Height Limitation Act, which bans skyscrapers. Various subterfuges have been employed to get an extra storey here or there, but no 'inhabitable' space is allowed to go above the 150-foot limit.

In the 1950s, modernist notions of design and planning were applied to an urban-renewal project, the New Southwest, with awkward results. Modernism also guided the nearby **L'Enfant Plaza**, a mammoth office, hotel and retail complex (bordered by Independence Avenue, Ninth Street and various freeway approaches); its masterplan was the first of several bad Washington designs by IM Pei, later one of the namesakes of Pei Cobb Freed. This ironically named assault on the L'Enfant Plan was followed by many stark, bleak buildings in Southwest, most of which were rented to the federal government.

In the 1960s and '70s, modernist architects designed some of the city's least popular structures, including the **J Edgar Hoover FBI Building** (*see p72*), a brutalist concrete fortress finished in 1972. Perhaps more damaging to the style's reputation, however, was the profusion of mediocre office buildings in the 'New Downtown' along K Street and Connecticut Avenue, NW. Built with little consideration for Washington's distinctive street plan and without strategies for adapting the Bauhaus-derived American skyscraper style to the city's height limitation rules, these blank-walled knock-offs look like New York office blocks inexplicably stunted at the 12th floor.

Most of these buildings were designed by local architects, but nationally renowned modernists and postmodernists have also done work in Washington, including Marcel

IN CONTEXT

National Gallery
of Art East Building.

Breuer's 1976 precast concrete **Hubert H Humphrey Building** (2nd Street & Independence Avenue, SW). Mies van der Rohe's 1972 black-box **Martin Luther King Jr Memorial Library** (*see p71*) has recently been listed on the National Register of Historic Places.

One of modernism's local successes is actually far from the District: **Washington Dulles International Airport**, designed by Eero Saarinen in 1962 and now being expanded in accord with his widely imitated gull-wing scheme. Others include IM Pei's 1978 **National Gallery of Art East Building** (*see p47*) and Harry Weese's **Metro** system, which applies the same architectural motifs to all its stations. The latter two designs succeed in part because they're sensitive to their Washington context: the East Building's overlapping triangles play off the trapezoidal plot created by the L'Enfant street plan, while Metro's coffered vaults are simply an extreme example of stripped classicism. For more on the history of the Metro, *see p24* **Going Underground**.

The city's response to modernism is rooted in Georgetown, with its Federal-style structures, which became a fashionable neighborhood when it began to be gentrified in the '30s, and **Lafayette Square**, which is surrounded by Federal-period houses. In the '60s, when demand for federal office space grew dramatically, replacing these houses with new office buildings was proposed. The eventual compromise was to erect two large structures just off the square, John Carl Warneke's 1969 **New Executive Office Building** (722 Jackson Place, NW) and **Court of Claims Building** (717 Madison Place, NW), which would defer to their older neighbors in form and material, if not in size.

These 'background buildings' set a precedent for design in the city's older districts; several local firms came to specialize in contextual postmodern structures that often incorporated façades of existing buildings. Examples include Shalom Baranes's remake of the **Army-Navy Club** (901 17th Street, NW) and Hartman-Cox's **1001 Pennsylvania Avenue, NW**, both finished in 1987. Such 'façadomies' were widely criticised, especially when the new construction dwarfed the historic component; one conspicuous example of this is **Red Lion Row** (2000 Pennsylvania Avenue, NW). Yet the technique continues to be employed, with new examples along 7th, 10th and F Streets, NW.

The city's historicist architects are still influential, but no one style currently dominates. An updated, less dogmatic modernism is showcased in such structures as Kohn Pederson Fox's asymmetrical, vaguely industrial 1997 **World Bank** headquarters (1818 H Street, NW, 1-202 473 1806, tours by appointment), and Mikko Heikkinen and Markku Komonen's 1994 **Embassy of Finland** (3301 Massachusetts Avenue, NW, 1-202 298 5824, tours by appointment), which features a trellis façade, dramatic atrium and glass-wall overlook of Rock Creek Park. Such glass curtains are back in favour, notably in the sail-shaped exterior of Graham Gund Architects' near-triangular 2004 headquarters for the **National Association of Realtors** (500 New Jersey Avenue, NW).

On the Mall, 2004 brought a new example of neo-classicism, as well as a novel piece of contextual architecture. Friedrich St Florian's **World War II Memorial** (*see p51*) is an imperial-style shrine with a circular array of pillars and arches tucked into the vista between the Washington Monument and the Lincoln Memorial. In contrast, the **Museum of the American Indian** (*see p50*), adapted from a design by Douglas Cardinal, is clad in multi-hued limestone with a rough façade to suggest Southwestern mesas.

At the Reynolds Center, joint home of both the **National Portait Gallery** and the **Smithsonian American Art Museum** (*see p68* **Profile**), Norman Foster's curving glass canopy in the building's central courtyard – forming the Kogod Courtyard, opened in 2007 – adds a contemporary, organic dimension to the building's Greek Revival architecture. Pokshek Partnership, the architects of the **Newseum** (*see p74* **Profile**), opened in 2008, designed a building composed of three rectilinear volumes, one behind the other, with a rectangular glass window running most of the height of the Pennylvania Avenue façade, allowing passersby to view the museum's atrium inside. Very different, but also attracting praise from architectural critics, Arena Stage's new theater, the **Mead Center for the American Theater** (*see p206* **Crystal Palaces**), by Vancouver-based Bing Thom, is flowing and curvaceous, with vast wooden exterior columns and a glass frontage.

Newseum.

Sights

Lincoln Memorial. *See p46.*

The Monumental Center	**42**
The Smithsonian	45
Mall Stories	51
Walk The Road to the White House	54
Treasure Rooms	61

DC Neighborhoods	**64**
Adolf Cluss's Capital	66
Profile National Portrait Gallery/Smithsonian American Art Museum	68
Profile Newseum	74
U Street Highlights	79
Walk Georgetown	81
A Taste of H Street	84

| **Arlington & Alexandria** | **88** |

The Monumental Center

Monuments, museums and the Mall.

The Monumental Center is the neo-classical heart of picture-postcard Washington, centered on a long swathe of green – the National Mall – which is crowned by the Capitol at its eastern end. The center's distinctive look is a result of George Washington's wish that his new nation have a suitably imposing capital – and for a man of his era, a classical style that referenced Athenian democracy was the way to achieve this. He hired Pierre-Charles L'Enfant to design the fledgling city. The L'Enfant Plan consisted of a grid system; superimposed on this were

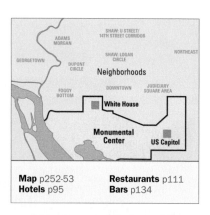

Map p252-53 **Restaurants** p111
Hotels p95 **Bars** p134

broad diagonal avenues radiating from ceremonial squares and circles, and from the Capitol and White House. And given that the one thing a government is good at doing is producing plans, sure enough in 1902 another scheme – the McMillan Plan – reinterpreted L'Enfant's original vision. Now, more than a century later, the National Capital Planning Commission referees continual development debates over the quasi-sacred space of the Mall and its immediate surrounds.

THE MALL & TIDAL BASIN
The Mall from west to east

The western boundary of the mall centres on the **Lincoln Memorial**, in front of the long Reflecting Pool. Beyond rises the needle of the Washington Monument and, finally, at the eastern end of the Mall, the Capitol, two miles away. The previously uncluttered vista between the Lincoln and Washington monuments was interrupted in 2004 by the new **National World War II Memorial**.

Starting south-east of the Lincoln Memorial, across the Tidal Basin, the circular **Jefferson Memorial** commemorates the third US president and author of the Declaration of Independence. Tucked just south is a monument to Jefferson's friend, the local

Revolutionary-era thinker **George Mason**, portrayed relaxing on a bench with his ever-present books.

The **Franklin Delano Roosevelt Memorial** enlivens West Potomac Park, across the cherry tree-rimmed Tidal Basin, which has paddleboats for rent. Nearby, a memorial to civil rights leader **Martin Luther King** is under construction. The memorial will feature a statue of King, and a wall of quotations from his writings and speeches. It is hoped to unveil the monument in 2011. It was from the Lincoln Memorial that King delivered his famous 'I have a dream' speech four decades ago.

Two war monuments flank Lincoln's. To the north-east is the V-shaped black wedge of the **Vietnam Veterans Memorial**; to the south-east is the evocative **Korean War Veterans Memorial**. Walking east past Constitution

Gardens on the Mall's northern border, you first encounter the **National World War II Memorial**. Next is the starkly impressive **Washington Monument**, honoring the 'father of his country', who selected this site for its capital.

To the north spreads the Ellipse, formally the President's Park South. It contains the **Boy Scout Memorial**, in Socialist Realist style, and the **First Division Memorial**, an 80-foot monument to the soldiers of the First Division of the US Army. Atop is a gilded bronze Victory. On the north of the Ellipse is the **Zero Milestone**, from which distances from the capital are measured.

The Washington Monument overlooks museumland. Nearest to it, on the Mall's north side, is the **National Museum of American History**. The turreted red fortress, guarded by a carousel, is the **Smithsonian Castle**, which houses an information center and the crypt for Smithsonian benefactor, Englishman James Smithson.

Clustered about are the palazzo-like **Freer Gallery** (Asian art); its younger sibling, the subterranean **Arthur M Sackler Gallery**; the Sackler's twin, the **National Museum of African Art**; and the neo-Gothic **Arts & Industries Building**, currently under renovation. Further along are the doughnut-shaped **Hirshshorn Museum & Sculpture Garden**; the modernist, glass and marble of the **National Air & Space Museum** – the world's most visited museum; and the organic, curving structure of the **National Museum of the American Indian**.

On the north side of the Mall, the space between 14th and 15th Streets is designated for an African American museum, now raising construction funds, while the **National Museum of American History** and the **National Museum of Natural History** are between 14th and Ninth Streets. An adjacent sculpture garden's pool becomes an ice rink in winter. Next in line, the neo-classical **National Gallery of Art** connects to the angular geometry of its **East Building**.

On the far side of the Capitol Reflecting Pool, at the foot of Capitol Hill, stands a sprawling sculptural group that features an equestrian

vstatue of Ulysses S Grant, the triumphant Union general, modeled after the Victor Emmanuel memorial in Rome. Crowning the hill is the United States **Capitol**, whose dome Lincoln insisted be finished during the Civil War as a symbol of the Union's durability.

FREE Arthur M Sackler Gallery (S)

1050 Independence Avenue, SW, between 11th & 12th Streets (1-202 633 4880, www.asia.si.edu). Smithsonian Metro. **Open** *July-mid Aug* 10am-5.30pm daily. **Admission** free. **Map** p252 J7.

Opened in 1987, the Sackler contains some of the most important holdings of Asian art in the world. It has more flexibility than its neighbor, the Freer Gallery (*see p44*), whose mandate forbids the exhibition of anything from outside its collection. The Sackler does international loan exhibitions of Asian art, from ancient to contemporary. Connected to the Freer by an underground passageway, the Sackler was built up around a 1,000-piece Asian art gift from Dr Arthur M Sackler.

Visitors enter through architects Shepley Bulfinch Richardson and Abbott's first-floor granite pavilion (a similar pavilion, by the same firm, is at the National Museum of African Art). You then head below ground into a maze of overlapping bridges and long passageways that give the feel of an ancient temple. Artifacts on permanent display include pieces from China – such as lacquered tropical hardwood Ming-style furniture and a late 17th-century Qing dynasty rosewood armchair. More than 100 ancient Chinese jades and bronzes are also back on view in two reinstalled galleries after nearly a decade, the first phase of the Freer's effort to renovate and reinstall its entire suite of Chinese galleries over the next few years. Elsewhere, there's sculpture from South and Southeast Asia, including 12th-century Hindu temple sculpture and fifth-century BC Jainist religious figures.

▶ *For children's activities at the museum, see p171.*

FREE Franklin Delano Roosevelt Memorial

Off West Basin Drive, SW, at the Tidal Basin (1-202 426 6841, www.nps.gov/fdrm). Smithsonian Metro. **Map** p252 G7.

FDR, who led the country through the Great Depression and World War II, was the only president to be elected four times. Despite Roosevelt's preference for a simple desk-sized memorial slab (still in place outside the National Archives), in 1997 designer Lawrence Halprin created an epic monument here. The four 'galleries' combine waterfalls, giant stones engraved with memorable quotations and sculptures (including a statue of Eleanor Roosevelt, the first First Lady to be honored in a national memorial). Disabled advocates objected that the original, somewhat dyspeptic statue of the polio-stricken president only hinted that he used a wheelchair. A second, jauntier FDR, with wheels in full view, joined the display in 2000.

SIGHTS

INSIDE TRACK
SUMMER HOURS

Most Smithsonian museums have summer hours, which are decided annually by individual museums. Check the websites, or ask at the **Information Center** (*see p45*) for details.

FREE Freer Gallery of Art (S)

Jefferson Drive, SW, at 12th Street (1-202 633 4880, www.asia.si.edu). Smithsonian Metro. **Open** 10am-5.30pm daily. **Admission** free. **Map** p252 J7.

When Detroit business magnate Charles Lang Freer (1854-1919) began collecting the works of American painter James McNeill Whistler in the 1880s, the artist encouraged him to collect Asian art while on his travels to the Middle and Far East. Freer did so, amassing Neolithic Chinese pottery, Japanese screens and Hindu temple sculpture, along with works by 19th-century American painters – including over 1,300 works by Whistler. A room interior, the *Peacock Room*, painted by Whistler in 1876-77, is probably the gallery's best-known piece.

In 1904, Freer offered his collection to the Smithsonian, which commissioned this dignified, grey granite, Renaissance palazzo-style building from architect Charles Adam Platt to house the collection; it opened in 1923. The collection's mandate precludes any lending of its 26,500-piece holdings, which are rotated regularly on display. Occasional special exhibitions are small but smart. An underground passage connects the Freer to the neighbouring Sackler Gallery.

▶ *For more on the Peacock Room, see p61* **Treasure Rooms**.
▶ *For films at the Freer, see p174.*

Jefferson Memorial.
See p46.

★ FREE Hirshhorn Museum & Sculpture Garden (S)

Independence Avenue, SW, at 7th Street (1-202 633 4674, http://hirshhorn.si.edu). L'Enfant Plaza Metro. **Open** *Museum* 10am-5.30m daily. *Plaza* 7.30am-5.30pm daily. *Sculpture Garden* 7.30am-dusk daily. **Admission** free. **Map** p253 J7.

This spectacular, aggressively modern cylindrical building by Skidmore, Owings and Merrill enlivens the predominantly neo-classical architecture lining the Mall. The purpose of the structure, which was completed in 1974, was to house self-made Wall Street millionaire Joseph Hirshhorn's collection of 20th-century painting and sculpture. The museum now presents art in a range of media, including works on paper, painting, installation, photography, sculpture, digital and video art. SOM's chief architect, Gordon Bunshaft, has created a three-story hollow concrete drum supported on four curvilinear piers. In keeping with the modernist tradition, there is no ceremonial entrance, only a utilitarian revolving door (strictly speaking there are two, but usually only one is in use).

Third-level galleries house works from the permanent collection. These include a significant Giacometti collection, the largest public collection of works by Thomas Eakins outside the artist's native Philadelphia, works by Arshile Gorky and Clyfford Still and a pair of Willem de Kooning's rare 'door paintings' (the museum has the largest public collection of his work in the world).

On the second level are rotating exhibitions. These might explore the work of a particular artist, or a theme: ColorForms presents works, dating from the 1960s to the present, which share 'a mesmerizing blend of saturated color and abstract form'. Pieces shown include Olafur Eliasson's *Round Rainbow* (2005), a gallery of early '60s dot paintings by Larry Poons, and Richard Serra's works on paper *Morro Bay* (1991) and *Balance* (1972). Among other recent exhibitions have been solos by Belgian Hans Op de Beeck and Argentinian Guillermo Kuitca.

The basement galleries house large-scale installations, often recent acquisitions, and rotating video programs in the museum's 'Black Box'. The museum also offers the well-regarded Directions series, spotlighting unusual or cutting-edge artists.

The Sculpture Garden is located on the side of the gallery facing the National Mall, across Jefferson Drive. It has works by Rodin, Matisse, Koons, Calder and more, set amid green space and a reflecting pool.
▶ *For films at the National Gallery, see p174.*

SIGHTS

The Smithsonian

The institution behind the city's big museums.

SIGHTS

Founded by wealthy British chemist and mineralogist James Smithson (1765-1829), who – rather bizarrely, as he never visited the US – conferred his fortune on the United States government, the Smithsonian Institution was created by an act of Congress in 1846. Smithson requested that it be an institution promoting research and the dispersal of academic knowledge.

Architect James Renwick designed the first building, known as the **Castle** because its combination of late Romanesque and early Gothic styles included signature turrets, on a prime piece of national real estate on the verdant Mall. Completed in 1855, the Castle now serves as the Smithsonian Information Center and administrative hub – and should be the first port of call for any visitor. The Victorian red-brick Arts & Industries Building, designed as the Smithsonian's first hall devoted solely to exhibitions, was added in 1881 (it is currently under renovation). Over the years, collections shown here became large enough to warrant their own buildings. After the creation of the National Zoo in 1890, Congress began the steady erection of museums lining the Mall, beginning with the Museum of Natural History in 1910. From 1923 to 1993, 11 new museums entered the Smithsonian portfolio, most of them holding fine art.

Today the Smithsonian owns more than 140 million objects (plus a further 128 million in its libraries and archive collections), covering everything from ancient Chinese pottery to dinosaurs, Italian Renaissance painting to moon landings, so you're bound to find at least one collection that interests you.

INFORMATION

There is one central phone number – 1-202 357 2700 – where you can get information on all the Smithsonian's museums. The website – www.si.edu – is also useful and has links to individual museum websites.

Smithsonian Access, a brochure detailing the disabled facilities at the museums, is available at each museum – or call 1-202 786 2942. If you need to arrange special facilities you should call the museum two weeks in advance.

Smithsonian Institution museums are marked with an **(S)** in our listings.

Smithsonian Information Center

Smithsonian Institution Building (The Castle), 1000 Jefferson Drive, SW, between Seventh & 12th Streets, The Mall & Tidal Basin (1-202 357 2700, 24hr recorded information 1-202 357 2020, www.si.edu). Smithsonian Metro. **Open** *8.30am-5.30pm daily.* **Map** *p252 J7.*

SIGHTS

FREE Jefferson Memorial

Southern end of 15th Street, SW, at the Tidal Basin & East Basin Drive (1-202 426 6841, www.nps.gov/thje). Smithsonian Metro. **Map** p252 H8.

FDR promoted this 1942 shrine to the founder of his Democratic Party, balancing that to the Republicans' icon, Lincoln. Roosevelt liked it so much he had trees cleared so he could see it from the Oval Office. In 2006, the Park Service imposed a fee on commercial wedding-party photographers, whose newlywed clients covet the backdrop.

John Russell Pope designed an adaptation (sneered at by some as 'Jefferson's muffin') of the Roman Pantheon that the architect Jefferson so admired. It echoes the president's designs for his home, Monticello, and for his rotunda at the University of Virginia. The Georgia marble walls surrounding Jefferson's 19ft likeness are inscribed with his enduring words. Alas, the 92-word quote from the Declaration of Independence contains 11 spelling mistakes and other inaccuracies. *Photo p44.*

FREE Korean War Veterans Memorial

The Mall, SW, just south of Reflecting Pool, at Daniel French Drive & Independence Avenue (1-202 426 6841, www.nps.gov/kwvm). Smithsonian Metro. **Map** p252 G7.

This monument, which honors the 12 million Americans who fought in the bloody 'police action' to prevent Communist takeover of South Korea, features 19 battle-clad, seven-foot soldiers slogging across a V-shaped field towards a distant US flag. Their finely detailed faces reflect the fatigue and pain of battle, while bulky packs show beneath their ponchos. Reflected in the polished granite wall, these 19 become 38 – in reference to the 38th parallel separating North and South Korea. Unlike the wall at the Vietnam Veterans Memorial, this shows a subtle mural sandblasted into rock, a photo-montage of the support troops – drivers and medics, nurses and chaplains.

★ FREE Lincoln Memorial

The Mall, 23rd Street, NW, between Henry Bacon Drive & Daniel French Drive (1-202 426 6841, www.nps.gov/linc). Smithsonian or Foggy Bottom-GWU Metro. **Map** p252 F7.

Despite its appearance on the penny and the $5 bill, the Lincoln Memorial is perhaps most recognizable as the site of historic demonstrations. In 1939, when

---

INSIDE TRACK **EARLY BIRD**

The **Smithsonian Information Center** at the Castle (*see p45*) opens at 8.30am, an hour and a half ahead of the museums, so get there early and you'll have plenty of time to plan your day's schedule.

---

the Daughters of the American Revolution barred the African-American contralto Marian Anderson from singing in their Constitution Hall, she performed for more than 75,000 people from these steps. It was here that Martin Luther King delivered his 'I have a dream' speech in 1963. Just a few months later, President Lyndon Johnson led candle-carrying crowds in ceremonies concluding national mourning for John F Kennedy. Half a century of debate followed Lincoln's assassination in 1865 before Henry Bacon's classical design was chosen in 1911 (over proposals ranging from a triumphal arch to a memorial highway from Washington to Gettysburg).

The 'cage' surrounding Lincoln has one Doric column representing each of the 36 states in the Union at the time of his death, their names inscribed above. The 19ft marble statue of Lincoln himself, by Daniel Chester French, peers out over the Reflecting Pool, his facial expression seeming to change at different times of day. Cut into the wall to the left of the entrance is Lincoln's Gettysburg Address; to the right is his second inaugural address.

FREE National Air & Space Museum (S)

6th Street & Independence Avenue, SW (1-202 633 1000, www.nasm.si.edu). L'Enfant Plaza Metro. **Open** *Sept-May* 10am-5.30pm daily. *June-Aug* 9am-5.30pm daily. **Admission** *Museum* free. *Planetarium* $8; $7-$7.50 reductions. **Credit** AmEx, MC, V. **Map** p253 J7.

Air & Space tops visitors' to-do list, year in, year out. The imposing Tennessee marble modernist block, by Hellmuth, Obata and Kassabaum, incorporates three skylit, double-height galleries, which house missiles, aircraft and space stations. In the central Milestones of Flight hall, towering US Pershing-II and Soviet SS-20 nuclear missiles stand next to the popular moon rock station, where visitors can stroke a lunar sample acquired on the 1972 Apollo 17 mission. The 1903 Wright Flyer – the first piloted craft to maintain controlled, sustained flight (if only for a few seconds) – and Charles Lindbergh's Spirit of St Louis are both suspended here.

Permanent exhibitions in the museum detail the history of jet aviation and satellite communications. Updates acknowledge contemporary information technology, but most of the collection's low-tech presentation maintains the quaint optimism of the early space age. A bevy of hands-on exhibits appeal to children, who line up to pilot a full-size Cessna aircraft in the How Things Fly exhibit or to walk through the research lab in the Skylab Space Station. The Albert Einstein Planetarium offers half-hour multimedia presentations about stars and outer space; the Langley Theater shows IMAX films on air and space flight. After an exhausting mission, pick up some freeze-dried space food in the gift shop.

The museum's annex, the Steven F Udvar-Hazy Center, named after its major donor, opened in Chantilly, Virginia, in December 2003. Its hangar-like halls hold the restored Enola Gay, the shimmer-

National Air &
Space Museum.

ing B-29 that dropped the first atomic bomb, and the space shuttle Enterprise, among other large-scale treasures. A shuttle bus service makes a round trip between the two outposts several times a day (tickets cost $15 for the round trip, and you're strongly advised to book in advance by calling 1-202 633 4629).
Other locations Steven F Udvar-Hazy Center, 14390 Air & Space Museum Parkway, Chantilly, VA (1-703 572 4118).

★ FREE National Gallery of Art
West Building *Constitution Avenue, NW, between 4th & 7th Streets.*
East Building *Constitution Avenue & 4th Street, NW (1-202 737 4215, www.nga.gov). Archives-Navy Memorial, Judiciary Square or Smithsonian Metro.* **Both Open** 10am-5pm Mon-Sat; 11am-6pm Sun. **Admission** free. **Map** p253 J6.

Pittsburgh investment banker and industrialist Andrew Mellon was born the son of a poor Irish immigrant but went on to serve as US Treasury secretary from 1921 to 1932. In 1941 he presented the National Gallery's West Building as a gift to the nation. Mellon's son, Paul, created the gallery's East Building in 1978. Mellon junior, who had donated over 900 artworks during his lifetime, bequeathed $75 million and 100 paintings – including works by Monet, Renoir and Cézanne – on his death in 1999.

In designing the Tennessee marble West Building, architect John Russell Pope borrowed motifs from the temple architecture of the Roman Pantheon. The white marble stairs at the Constitution Avenue entrance lead to the main-floor rotunda, with its impressive green Italian marble floors and columns around a bubbling fountain encircled by fragrant flora and greenery. On this

level, galleries lead off the building's 782ft longitudinal spine. The ground level houses galleries as well as a gift shop and garden court café. An underground concourse has a cafeteria, another shop and a moving walkway that connects the West Building to the skylit, IM Pei-designed East Building.
West Building
The West Building's skylit main floor covers European and American art from the 13th to the early 20th centuries. Exhibits begin in gallery 1 with Italian Gothic works 1270-1360, among them Giotto's seminal *Madonna and Child*. Pre- to high Renaissance Italian works represent a large proportion of the collection; highlights include Leonardo da Vinci's almond-eyed portrait of *Ginevra de' Benci* (gallery 6), Botticelli's *Adoration of the Magi*. Giovanni Bellini and Titian's *Feast of the Gods* commands Gallery 17, to the north of the West Garden Court.

Late medieval Flemish highlights include Jan Van Eyck's *Annunciation* (gallery 39). Unmistakeable among the Netherlandish works 1485-1590 in gallery 41 is Hieronymus Bosch's *Death and the Miser*.

Spanish, Dutch, Flemish, French and German works of the 17th century also have a large presence (galleries 29-34, 36, 37, 42-51). Among them are works by Vermeer (*Woman Holding a Balance*, in gallery 50A) and Rembrandt's 1659 self-portrait, with his intense gaze, in gallery 48.

On the east side of the Rotunda, there's 18th- and 19th-century Spanish painting (gallery 52), including Goya's *The Marquesa de Pontejos*. Highlights among the French paintings of a similar era in galleries 53-56 include work by Jean Simeon Chardin in gallery 53 and Jacques-Louis David's *The Emperor Napoleon in his Study at the Tuileries* (gallery 56). British landscapes by Turner and Constable are in gallery 57,

National Gallery. See p47.

among them Turner's *Keelmen Heaving Coals by Moonlight*, while gallery 58 is devoted to portraits by Gainsborough and Reynolds. Galleries 60-60B and 62-71 are the American rooms. Among the works are naive paintings in gallery 63, immense and idealized 19th-century landscapes, such as Thomas Cole's *A View of the Mountain Pass Called the Notch of the White Mountains* (gallery 64). George Catlin's distinctive American Indian portraits are in gallery 65. American Impressionism 1860-1925, in gallery 70, includes John Singer Sargent's *Repose*. Early 20th-century American painting in gallery 71 includes Edward Hopper's *Cape Cod Evening*. Galleries 80-93 feature 19th-century French work.

Downstairs, the West Wing sculpture galleries, which occupy the entire north-west quadrant of the building's ground floor, now register 24,000sq ft divided into 22 galleries, following a major expansion in 2002. More than 900 works are on view, including masterpieces from the Middle Ages to the early 20th century. Visitors entering from the museum's 6th Street entrance encounter works by Auguste Rodin and Augustus Saint-Gaudens. From there, they move in reverse chronological order from the 19th century to the Middle Ages, with detours into a pair of galleries housing early modern sculpture. Highlights of the collection include Leone Battista Alberti's bronze *Self-Portrait* plaque (c1435); Honoré Daumier's entire bronze sculptural oeuvre, including all 36 of his caricatures of French government officials, and the world's largest collection of Edgar Degas original wax and mixed-media sculptures.

The Micro Gallery, just inside the West Building's main-floor Mall entrance, has 15 individual cubicles with touch-screen color monitors where visitors can learn more about individual works, movements, artists and the precise location of each work. Conservation techniques are also explained.

The concourse tunnel to the East Building takes you on a moving walkway through what seems like a fantastic journey through the Milky Way; swathes of starry lights seem to ebb and flow above you. Called *Multiverse*, the installation is the work of American artist Leo Villareal.

East Building

The East Building's triple-height, skylit atrium is dominated by Alexander Calder's 32ft by 81ft aluminum and steel mobile. The gallery's small but strong collection of modern and contemporary art includes several must-sees on view in the concourse-level galleries. Don't miss Barnett Newman's minimalist *Stations of the Cross*, a 15-panel installation of monochromatic paintings that ring the walls of a dedicated room (gallery 29A). Salvador Dali's *Sacrament of the Last Supper* hangs in the mezzanine elevator lobby. The East Building devotes much of its space to temporary exhibitions.

Sculpture Garden

The gallery opened a sculpture garden in 1998 on a six-acre square across Seventh Street from the West Building. Designed by Philadelphia landscape architect Laurie Olin, the garden's circular fountain bubbles in summer, and is transformed into an ice rink in winter. Among trees are Louise Bourgeois' 10ft bronze cast *Spider*, whose spindly legs span 24ft, Sol LeWitt's 15ft-high concrete *Four-Sided Pyramid*, and Tony Smith's stout *Moondog*.

FREE **National Museum of African Art (S)**
950 Independence Avenue, SW, between 7th & 12th Streets (1-202 633 4600, www.nmafasi.edu). Smithsonian Metro. **Open** 10am-5.30pm daily. **Admission** free. **Map** p252 J7.

This museum's entrance pavilion, designed by Shepley Bulfinch Richardson and Abbott, lies across the amazing Enid Haupt Garden from its twin, the Sackler *(see p43)*. The primary focus of the collection, which opened in 1987, is ancient and contemporary work from sub-Saharan Africa,

INSIDE TRACK
AFRICAN AMERICAN MUSEUM

Groundbreaking for the **National Museum of African American History & Culture**, on the north side of the Mall, between 14th and 15th Streets, is scheduled for 2012. Until the museum opens, the **National Museum of American History** (*see right*) hosts the museum's collections on its second floor.

although it also collects arts from other African areas, including a particularly strong array of royal Benin art. Temporary shows present a wide variety of African visual arts, including sculptures, textiles, ceramics and photos. Contemporary art surveys are also included in the museum's roster.

★ FREE National Museum of American History (S)
Constitution Avenue, NW, at 14th Street, NW (1-202 633 1000, www.americanhistory.si.edu). **Open** 10am-5.30pm daily. **Admission** free. **Map** p252 H6. **Map** p252 H6.

Reopened in November 2008 after a lengthy renovation, the National Museum of American History now features a central atrium, a grand staircase, ten-foot artefact walls on the first and second floors, as well as a dedicated Star-Spangled Banner gallery and a new gallery for the Lemelson Center for the Study of Invention and Innovation. The exhibitions cover several broad themes: American wars and politics; entertainment, sport and music; American lives; American ideals; transport and technology; and science and innovation.

On the first floor East, America on the Move chronicles the changing ways Americans have got around a large country and how different modes of transport have transformed the nation. Exhibits include a Southern Railways locomotive, all 199 tons of it, along with a reconstructed 1920s railway station. Also examined is the domination of cars over public transport and how this enabled the suburbanisation of America. Over on the first floor West is a very different display: the entire kitchen (plus contents) of America's best-known chef, Julia Childs. She donated the kitchen from her Massachusetts home to the Smithsonian in 2001. Also on the first floor West, Hot Spots of Invention looks at how creative people came together to make MIT a center of invention during World War II. And the new Lemelson Hall of Invention has highly interactive and engaging activities for children, while its Invention at Play section looks at how inventors also use 'play', creativity and problem-solving skills to come up with products.

First Ladies, on the second floor, has inaugural ball gowns from many presidents' wives, with pride of place given to Michelle Obama's 2009 dress. The American Presidency exhibition, meanwhile, has more than 900 objects bringing to life the role of the president in American life.

Treasures of Popular Culture, on the third floor West, includes such famous objects as Michael Jackson's hat and Kermit the Frog. A small adjacent exhibition, 1939, explores how Americans used entertainment to distract themselves in a difficult era; among the exhibits are Dorothy's red shoes from *The Wizard of Oz*. On the third floor East, The Price of Freedom examines America at war, covering conflicts from colonial days until the Cold War and its aftermath. The Vietnam War section is the most striking: a lounge installation comes with a couch

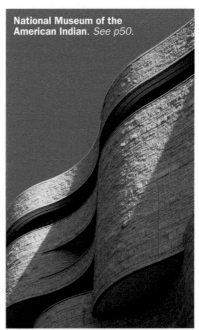

National Museum of the American Indian. *See p50.*

SIGHTS

INSIDE TRACK
AMERICAN INDIAN DISHES

The cafeteria at the **National Museum of the American Indian** (*see below*) serves traditional Native dishes from around the continent.

and 1970s wallpaper; a TV plays continuous footage on the war and its ramifications, from an early feature in which President Eisenhower outlines the Domino Theory to coverage revealing the gradual loss of purpose and discipline among the troops, violence at the 1968 Democratic Convention and the killings at Kent State University in 1970. A Vietnam-era Huey helicopter is also among the exhibits.

But perhaps the museum's most memorable exhibits are the landmark objects scattered throughout, identifying the themes of the exhibitions in their surrounding area. Dumbo the Elephant identifies the sports and entertainment section; the actual 1960 lunch counter where students began the Greensboro sit-in indicates the American Ideals section, while the John Bull locomotive is placed in the transport and technology area.

▶ *For more on the Star-Spangled Banner,* *see p20* **Profile**.

★ FREE **National Museum of the American Indian (S)**
Independence Avenue & 4th Street, SW (1-202 633 1000, www.nmai.si.edu). L'Enfant Plaza Metro. **Open** 10am-5.30pm daily. **Admission** free. **Map** p253 J7.

Dedicated to America's colonised and historically abused indigenous people, the National Museum of the American Indian marks the latest addition to the Mall's museum ring. The structure was designed by a Native American team; the building is as much a part of the message as the exhibits. The details are extraordinary: dramatic, Kasota limestone-clad undulating walls resemble a wind-carved mesa; the museum's main entrance plaza plots the star configurations on 28 November 1989, the date that federal legislation was introduced to create the museum; fountains enliven outdoor walkways.

Visitors enter at the dramatic Potomac Hall rotunda, with its soaring 120ft stepped dome. The museum's permanent collection, exhibited on the third and fourth floors, orbits around thousands of works assembled at the turn of the 20th century by wealthy New Yorker George Gustav Heye, including intricate wood and stone carvings, hides and 18th-century materials from the Great Lakes region. Collections also include a substantial array of items from the Caribbean, Central and South America, including a dramatic quantity of gold, and the individual and non-stereotypical portraits of George Caitlin.

Native history from a native perspective is a theme of much of the rest of the material on show. Our Peoples looks at how contact changed the world, bringing disease, guns, Bibles and foreign governments to native peoples, and exporting corn, tobacco and chocolate. It focuses on eight tribes, from the Blackfeet of Montana to the Ka'apor of Brazil. Our Universes explores native cosmologies and traditions, including the Day of the Dead, which was eventually assimilated into Christian tradition. Our Lives looks at life and identities in the 21st century through the experiences of eight communities. A contempo-

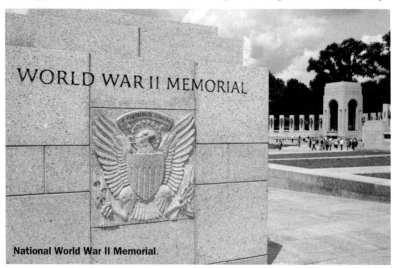

National World War II Memorial.

rary art collection is based around four broad themes: cultural memory and resistance; landscape and place; personal memory and identity; and history and the contemporary urban experience. *Photo p49*.
► *For the museum's unusual cafeteria, see left* **Inside Track**.

★ FREE **National Museum of Natural History (S)**
10th Street & Constitution Avenue, NW (1-202 633 1000/www.mnh.si.edu). Smithsonian Metro.
Open 10am-5.30pm daily. **Admission** free.
Map p252 J6.
The gem at the heart of the Museum of Natural History is a state-of-the-art IMAX cinema and an 80,000sq ft brushed steel and granite Discovery Center housing a cafeteria and exhibition space. The rotunda, too, is an impressive structure, dominated by an eight-ton African elephant. A renovation in the late 1990s added chrome- and halogen-filled galleries; more recently, in late 2003, the museum's restored west wing opened its glistening, 25,000sq ft Kenneth E Behring Hall featuring interactive displays alongside 274 taxidermied critters striking dramatic poses. The gem and mineral collection attracts gawking spectators, who ring two-deep the very well-guarded 45.52-carat cut blue Hope Diamond – currently in a temporary setting voted for online. The Hall of Human Origins tells the story of evolution, examining scientific evidence and providing striking representations of early humans. The museum is a real magnet for children: its Dinosaur Hall has an assortment of fierce-looking dinosaur skeletons and a 3.4-billion-year-old stromatolite; tarantulas and other live arthropods ripe for petting inhabit the Insect Zoo. The museum celebrated its centenary in 2010.

FREE **National World War II Memorial**
The Mall, 17th Street, from Independence to Constitution Avenues (1-202 426 6841, www.wwiimemorial.com). Smithsonian or Farragut West Metro. **Map** p252 G6/7.
Dedicated in 2004, the monument that honors America's 'Greatest Generation' is a grandiose affair on a 7.4-acre plot. Designed by Friedrich St Florian, it is a granite-heavy space dominated by the central Rainbow Pool set between two 43ft triumphal arches, representing the Atlantic and Pacific theatres of war. Fifty-six wreath-crowned pillars represent the US states and territories (including the Philippines), while a bronze Freedom Wall displays 4,000 gold stars, each signifying 100 war dead. The ceremonial entrance, descending from 17th Street,

Mall Stories

Many of the nation's big moments have been played out here.

For most of the 19th century the area that is now the Mall was a swampy tract of land appropriated by stockyards, a railroad station and 'the most active and importune squatters'. But in 1902 the McMillan Commission revisited L'Enfant's vision of a grand *allée* stretching from the Capitol to the Washington Monument, then for good measure extended it for an extra mile of land reclaimed from the Potomac to where the Lincoln Memorial now stands.

Over the decades the area took on a role not only as a space for public celebrations but as the theater for great national events. Here, at the Lincoln Memorial, Martin Luther King delivered his 'I have a dream' speech in 1963 (on the same site as Marian Anderson's dramatic Easter recital of 1939). In 1979, Pope John Paul II celebrated mass here. And in 1981, the site of the presidential inauguration was moved from the East Front of the Capitol to the West, adding further gravitas to the grounds.

And, of course, the Mall is famous as the site of demonstrations, among them the anti-Vietnam War protests of the 1960s and '70s, the 'tractorcades' of discontented farmers in the late 1970s, the Million Man marchers in the '90s and, most recently, those organized by the Tea Party movement.

Its growing ceremonial status has put pressure on the Mall as groups vie for a share of the turf. Revolutionary War thinker George Mason nabbed a spot by the Jefferson Memorial, while a nearby swatch by the Tidal Basin awaits a Dr King monument. A memorial to the two presidents Adams and a new museum, the National Museum of African American History & Culture, have also been approved. Conservative campaigners have pressed for a Ronald Reagan memorial square in the center of the Mall, while partisans of other causes covet many surrounding patches of ground.

The National World War II Memorial, opened in 2004, also proved controversial. Some criticized the design as backward-looking and grandiose, others deplored the interruption of the Mall's grand open sweep between the Capitol and Lincoln Memorial.

When it comes to the National Mall, never was the phrase 'watch this space' more literally spoken.

passes bas-reliefs depicting events of the global conflict. A Circle of Remembrance garden off to the side fosters quiet reflection. A visitor kiosk and restrooms clutter the periphery.

The memorial attracted controversy, partly due to its location (boggy enough to require pumping and breaking the sweep of the Mall), and partly its heavy neo-classical design, which prompted Der Spiegel to quip that it looked as if Hitler had won. However, the memorial's apologia is engraved in granite at the 17th Street entrance, saying why those who defended freedom during World War II fully deserve their place between the heroes of the 18th (Washington) and 19th (Lincoln) centuries. To partly preserve the open vista, the memorial was sunk below street level.

FREE Vietnam Veterans Memorial

West Potomac Park, just north of the Reflecting Pool, at Henry Bacon Drive & Constitution Avenue, NW (1-202 462 6841, www.nps.gov/vive). Foggy Bottom or Smithsonian Metro. **Map** p252 G6.

Despite initial controversy, the somber black granite walls of the Vietnam Veterans Memorial have become a shrine, with pilgrims coming to touch the more than 58,000 names, make pencil rubbings and leave flowers, letters and flags. In 1981, 21-year-old Yale University senior Maya Ying Lin won the nationwide competition with this striking abstract design – two walls, each just over 246ft long – angled to enfold the Washington Monument and the Lincoln Memorial in a symbolic embrace. Political pressures forced later additions: first, a flagpole, then a sculpture by Frederick Hart of three Vietnam GIs. In 1993 came the Vietnam Women's Memorial, a sculpture group inspired by Michelangelo's *Pietà*. Happily, these additions were placed harmoniously.

Names on the wall appear in the chronological order that they became casualties. To descend gradually past the thousands of names to the nadir, then slowly emerge, is to follow symbolically America's journey into an increasingly ferocious war, only to try to 'wind it down' over years. It can be a genuinely touching experience.

FREE Washington Monument

The Mall, between 15th & 17th Streets, & Constitution & Independence Avenues (1-202 426 6841, www.nps.gov/wamo). Smithsonian Metro. **Open** *June-Sept* 9am-10pm daily. *Oct-May* 9am-5pm daily (last tour 4.45pm). **Admission** free, but ticket required. **Map** p252 H7.

The Washington Monument was completed in 1884, 101 years after Congress authorized it. It rises in a straight line between the Capitol and the Lincoln Memorial, but is off-center between the White House and the Jefferson Memorial because the original site was too marshy for its bulk. Private funding ran out in the 1850s, when only the stump of the obelisk had been erected. Building resumed in 1876, producing a slight change in the color of the marble

Washington Monument.

about a third of the way up. The 555ft monument – the tallest free-standing masonry structure in the world – was capped with solid aluminum, then a rare material.

Timed tickets for same-day visits are available for free from the 15th Street kiosk, which opens at 8.30am. During summer, lines can form by 7am. You can book in advance by calling National Park reservations on 1-877 444 6777 for an admin fee of $1.50 per ticket.

South of the monument, a cast-iron plate near the light box conceals an underground 162in miniature of the monument, measuring the rate at which the big version is sinking into the ground: around a quarter-inch every 30 years.

THE WHITE HOUSE & AROUND

Set above the Ellipse to the north of the Mall, the **White House** opens up the rectangular dynamic of the Mall with north–south sightlines to the Washington Monument and Jefferson Memorial. Directly north of it is the park named for the Marquis de Lafayette, hero of the American Revolution. Workers and tourists fill its benches at lunchtime; a round-the-clock anti-nuclear protest has camped here continuously since 1981, and various eccentrics choose this spot to try and get their message to the American people. The stretch of Pennsylvania Avenue between the park and the White House is reserved for the use of pedestrians only due to security considerations.

Though the park is named after Lafayette, its most prominent statue – the hero on the horse in the middle – is Andrew Jackson at the Battle of New Orleans in 1815. This was the first equestrian statue cast in the US at the time of its unveiling in 1853. His four companions are European luminaries of the American Revolution: Lafayette, Comte de Rochambeau, General Kosciusko and Baron von Steuben.

Every president since James Madison has attended at least one service at the mellow yellow St John's Episcopal Church north of the park at 16th and H Streets. A brass plate at pew 54 marks the place reserved for them.

TV news-watchers might recognize the green awning across Jackson Place to the west of the square: this is **Blair House** (1660 Pennsylvania Avenue, NW), where visiting heads of state bunk. Next door, at Pennsylvania and 17th Street, is the **Renwick Gallery** – an 1859 building in the French Second Empire mode, named after its architect, James Renwick. Part of the Smithsonian, it commonly features 20th-century crafts. Lately, its opulent Grand Salon has replicated period exhibits – like that of George Caitlin's Indian Gallery – of the kind local grandee William Wilson Corcoran built this place to display. These contrast with the contemporary American exhibits featured elsewhere. At the end of the 19th century, the original collection moved three blocks south into the purpose-built **Corcoran Museum of Art**, the Beaux Arts building on the south-west corner of 17th and E Streets. Just west of it, toward Foggy Bottom, is the **Octagon** (*see p65*).

Decatur House, at 748 Jackson Place, was home to naval hero Stephen Decatur, as well as French, British and Russian diplomats, and 19th-century statesmen Henry Clay and Martin Van Buren. Across the square, at H Street and Madison Place, is the Dolley Madison House (closed to the public), home of the widowed but effervescent First Lady until her death.

Bookending Lafayette Square are the New Executive Office Building on the west and the US Court of Claims opposite, tucked behind historic edifices. West of the White House is the **Dwight**

D Eisenhower Executive Office Building, aka the Old Executive Office Building (OEOB). With its 900 Doric columns and French Empire bombast, this was the largest office building in the world in 1888, housing the entire State, War and Navy departments.

The Treasury, the third-oldest federal office building in Washington, interrupts Pennsylvania Avenue because the ornery President Jackson, exasperated at endless debate, declared, 'Put it there!' Symbolically close is a cluster of solid-looking banks and former banks, vestiges of the old financial district, once known as 'Washington's Wall Street', now the 15th Street Financial Historic District.

Corcoran Museum of Art

500 17th Street, NW, between New York Avenue & E Street (1-202 639 1700/www.corcoran.org). Farragut West Metro. **Open** 10am-5pm Wed, Fri-Sun; 10am-9pm Thur. **Admission** $10; $8 reductions; free under-12s. **Credit** AmEx, MC, V. **Map** p252 G6.

When District financier William Wilson Corcoran's collection outgrew its original space (now the Renwick Gallery, *see p54*), gallery trustees engaged architect Ernest Flagg to design its current Beaux Arts building, which opened in 1897. Despite significant bequests that added the minor Renoirs and Pissarros that now grace the wood-paneled Clark Landing, the Corcoran's strength remains its 19th-century American paintings, featuring landscapes of the American West by Albert Bierstadt, Frederick Church and Winslow Homer. Church's mammoth oil, *Niagara*, and Bierstadt's *Mount Corcoran* capture Americans' awe of the Western landscape.

The museum's 6,000 pieces also include contemporary art, photography, prints, drawings and sculpture. Notable displays include the Evans-Tibbs collection of African-American art and drawings by John Singer Sargent. Visitors looking for contemporary work will find it on view in special exhibitions; for example, Washington Color and Light presented works by artists associated with the Washington Color School and their contemporaries.

Decatur House

748 Jackson Place, NW, at H Street (1-202 842 0920, www.decaturhouse.org). Farragut West Metro. **Open** *Guided tours* every hr, 10.15am-4.15pm Mon-Sat; 12.15-3.15pm Sun. **Admission** $5. **Credit** AmEx, MC, V. **Map p252** H5.

Admiral Nelson declared Stephen Decatur 'the greatest hero of the age' for his 1804 raids crippling the 'Barbary' pirates. Decatur uttered the famous toast, 'my country, right or wrong', but he died in a needless duel in 1820. The property, a square three-story townhouse constructed with red brick in Federal style, was designed by architect Benjamin Henry Latrobe for Decatur in 1818. The permanent collection comprises furniture, textiles, art and ceramics of the period.

INSIDE TRACK
VIETNAM VETS REMEMBERED

Authorities at the **Vietnam Veterans Memorial** (*see left*) are in talks with the Smithsonian about staging an exhibition using the many and varied mementos to those killed in the war that have been left at the memorial.

FREE Renwick Gallery of the Smithsonian American Art Museum (S)
17th Street & Pennsylvania Avenue, NW (1-202 633 2850, http://americanart.si.edu/renwick/ renwick_about.cfm). Farragut North or Farragut West Metro. **Open** 10am-5.30pm daily. **Admission** free. **Map** p252 G5.
This mansarded building, modeled on the Louvre, was built across from the White House in 1859 by architect James Renwick to house the art collection of financier and philanthropist William Wilson Corcoran. The space soon became too small for the displays, and it changed hands several times before opening in 1972 as the Smithsonian's craft museum. The exhibition of 20th-century American crafts – defined as objects created from materials associated with trades and industries, such as clay, glass, metal and fiber – often showcases striking work. In the

---

Walk The Road to the White House

In the footsteps of presidents.

In 1977, the newly elected Jimmy Carter walked the traditional inauguration parade route up Pennsylvania Avenue from the Capitol to the White House, and most of his successors have followed suit, popping out of the limo for at least a few token steps. It's an interesting route to follow, the core of old Washington.

Its nickname of 'America's Main Street' is not particularly apt: this ceremonial thoroughfare is anything but homey. Passing the ornate little **Peace Monument** at 1st Street and the Capitol Reflecting Pool, the walker encounters on his left IM Pei's angular **East Wing** of the National Gallery (*see p47*), with its neo-classical predecessor just beyond. To the right is the 'Watergate Courthouse' known from the Nixon-era scandals, now sporting a jazzy new east wing of its own.

Just beyond, the **Canadian Embassy** justifies its special location by architecturally echoing the city's monumental motifs. A gallery inside the building displays Canadian artworks. Adjoining rises the

Newseum (*see p74*) – a striking rectangular structure housing a museum dedicated to journalism and free speech.

At 6th Street begins the Federal Triangle, a cluster of heavy neo-classical government offices begun in the 1920s. Some of the buildings here recycle an old look, with vintage store façades fronting pricey offices. The venerable National Council of Negro Women occupies what locals still call the Apex Building, once home to Apex Liquor store. The building's eastern extension takes in the one-time studio of Matthew Brady, photographer of Lincoln and Civil War scenes.

Across 7th Street and to the south looms the National Achives, with the *Lone Sailor* statue marking the **US Navy Memorial**. An equestrian statue of General WS Hancock, a combat hero who lost the presidential election of 1880 by about 1,000 votes, is grander than that of President Garfield (1st & Maryland, SW), who beat him.

The sterility of the 900 block stems from FBI director J Edgar Hoover's vetoing

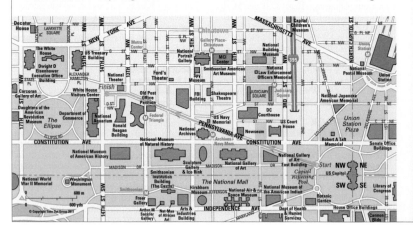

mansion's refurbished Grand Salon picture gallery, paintings that exemplify the taste of wealthy late 19th-century collectors hang in gilt frames stacked two and three high; works on view rotate regularly. Temporary exhibitions, which are held downstairs, survey artistic movements or artists. Gaman: art from the Japanese internment camps, with poignant pieces made from whatever the internees had to hand, featured recently.

of plans for shops at the front of the FBI building on security grounds. The avenue resumes its character at 11th Street, with the old *Washington Star* newspaper building. The **Old Post Office** tower disrupts the Federal Triangle façade with Romanesque impudence. Its tourist pavilion struggles along, but an ascent of the tower offers a truly impressive panorama. West lies the **Ronald Reagan Building & International Trade Center**, DC's first federal building designed for both government and private use. It engulfs the John A Wilson Building (1909), DC's city hall, usually called by its previous name, the District Building. The statue outside depicts Alexander 'Boss' Shepherd, who oversaw a large building program after the Civil War to prevent the government moving to St Louis, spending $20 million when only $10 million had been approved. Shepherd then prudently relocated himself to Mexico.

Across is **Freedom Plaza**, with L'Enfant's city plan etched into the pavements, alongside sometimes arch comments by historic visitors such as Charles Dickens. Polish-Americans ensured that the incongruous statue of Revolutionary hero Casimir Pulaski held its longtime ground. The **National Theatre** (*see p203*) has thrived here since 1835.

On to the legendary **Willard Hotel** (*see p97*), the grand 1902 incarnation of the hostelry where statesmen plotted and partied and Julia Ward Howe wrote 'The Battle Hymn of the Republic'. Featuring a popular ice rink in winter, **Pershing Park** to the south commemorates American campaigns of World War I. The Avenue doglegs around the Treasury, passing the **White House**, where we end our walk, then resuming for a pleasant mile to Georgetown.

FREE White House

1600 Pennsylvania Avenue, NW, between 15th & 17th Streets (1-202 456 7041, www.white house.gov). McPherson Square Metro. **Open** *Tours* 7.30-11am Tue-Thur; 7.30am-noon Fri; 7.30am-1pm Sat. Booking essential, at least 30 days in advance; see review. *Visitors' center* 7.30am-4pm daily. **Admission** free. **Map** p252 H6.

Part showplace, part workplace, the White House is sometimes called 'the people's house'. Indeed, until the 20th century the public could walk freely in and the grounds remained open until World War II. Today, those visiting the Executive Mansion simply get to peek at a scant eight rooms out of the house's 132, and with little time to linger (the tour can take as little as 20 minutes). The public tour is self-guided (though highly regimented) and there's not much in the way of interpretation, but the nation proudly clings to keeping its leader's residence open to the public.

To arrange a tour, US citizens should contact their senator or representative. Visitors with foreign passports should contact their nation's embassy. Tours may be scheduled up to six months in advance and must be scheduled no fewer than 30 days in advance.

Finished in 1800, the White House has been home to every US president except George Washington. Early presidents lived and worked above the shop. In 1902, Teddy Roosevelt added the East Gallery and the West Wing, which grew to include today's renowned Oval Office.

Each new First Lady can furnish the White House as she pleases: Jacqueline Kennedy, for example, replaced the B Altman department store furniture and frilly florals of her predecessors, the Trumans and Eisenhowers, with understated blues and whites. Her overall refurbishment of the White House restored many historic furnishings and artworks to the rooms. Her tour on national television was a triumph. Each president, meanwhile, imposes his character on the Oval Office, bringing in favorite furniture and personal selections from the White House art collection.

There are also offices for around 200 executive branch staffers, and recreational facilities, including a cinema, tennis courts, putting green, bowling alley and, courtesy of the elder George Bush, a horseshoe pitch. All told, there are 32 bathrooms, 413 doors, three elevators, seven staircases and a staff of more than 100, including florists, carpenters and cooks.

On the tour, you may get a look in the China Room, the pantry for presidential crockery. Don't miss Nancy Reagan's $952-per-setting red-rimmed china, which sparked a controversy about conspicuous consumption – as had Mrs Lincoln's previously.

Up the marble stairs, visitors enter the cavernous East Room, which holds the sole item from the original White House: the 1797 portrait of George Washington that Dolley Madison rescued just before the British burned the place down on 24 August 1814. The East Room is the ceremonial room where

SIGHTS

seven presidents have lain in state – and where Abigail Adams, wife of the second president, John, hung her laundry. At 3,200sq ft, the space could hold the average American home.

Next is the Green Room, once Jefferson's dining room, and where James Madison did his politicking after Dolley had liquored up important guests in the Red Room, the tour's next stop, decorated as an American Empire parlor of 1810-30. It was here that Mary Todd Lincoln held a seance to contact her dead sons and where President Grant and his former generals refought the Civil War on the carpet using salt shakers and nut dishes as troops.

The color naming scheme continues in the Blue Room – although it actually has yellow walls. The furnishings here, the traditional home of the White House Christmas tree, were ordered in 1817 by President Monroe. Last stop: the cream and gold State Dining Rooms, which can seat up to 140. Then you're out the door.

Visitors can repair to the White House Visitors' Center, in the dignified former search room of the Patent Office, at 15th and E Streets, NW, which has historical displays and even living history re-enactments. In some ways, the new arrangements tell visitors more than the old walk-throughs ever did.

Alternatively, you can stop at the White House Historical Association offices (740 Jackson Place, NW, on the west side of Lafayette Park, 1-202 737 8292, www.whitehousehistory.org, open 9am-4pm Mon-Fri) to pick up an extensive guide to the mansion, a CD-ROM, or the definitive books by official historian William Seale.

THE CAPITOL & AROUND

An angry senator once scolded President Lincoln that his administration was on the road to hell – in fact, just a mile from it. Lincoln shot back that that was almost exactly the distance from the White House to the Capitol. The Legislative Branch on the east end of Pennsylvania Avenue balances the Executive on the west.

Standing at the east end of the Mall is the commanding presence of the **United States Capitol**. Achieving both dignity and grace from every angle – though the walk along the Mall via the Capitol Reflecting Pool and its ducks shouldn't be missed – the Capitol rises elegantly to the occasion.

The **United States Botanic Garden** at the foot of the Capitol employs high-tech climate controls to replicate the home climate of flora from around the globe. Its highlight is the central rainforest room, equipped with a catwalk affording palm tree-top views. This glass palace houses tropical and subtropical plants, cacti, ferns, palm trees, shrubs and flowers, including its hallmark 500 varieties of orchid.

North of the Capitol, the grounds extend towards **Union Station**. Downhill is a carillon dedicated to conservative 'Mr Republican', Ohio senator Robert A Taft, son of a president and perennial aspirant himself.

Around the Capitol throbs a civic city of Congressional office buildings (the Senate's to the north, the House's to the south). In its

White House. See p55.

eastern lee are the decorous **Supreme Court** and the lavish **Library of Congress**. Beside the art deco Adams Building annex is the incomparable **Folger Shakespeare Library**. Books here are available only to scholars, but the Elizabethan Garden and the museum reward public visits.

Adjoining the Senate offices is the **Sewall-Belmont House** (144 Constitution Avenue, NE; *see p35*), a three-story Federal Period mansion, with a museum detailing women's suffrage struggles.

FREE Folger Shakespeare Library

201 East Capitol Street, SE, between 2nd & 3rd Streets (1-202 544 4600, www.folger.edu). Capitol South or Union Station Metro. **Open** 10am-5pm Mon-Sat. *Reading Room* 8.45am-4.45pm Mon-Sat. *Guided tours* 11am Mon-Fri; 9am-noon, 1-4.30pm Sat. **Admission** free. **Map** p253 L7.

The marble façade sports bas-relief scenes from Shakespeare's plays. Inside is the world's largest collection of the his works, including the 79-volume First Folio collection. Standard Oil chairman Henry Clay Folger, who fell in love with Shakespeare after hearing Ralph Waldo Emerson lecture on him, endowed the lot. Other items include musical instruments, costumes and films, as well as 27,000 paintings, drawings and prints. Open during the library's annual celebration of Shakespeare's birthday in April, the Reading Room has a copy of a bust of the Bard from Stratford's Trinity Church and a stained-glass window of the Seven Ages of Man as described in *As You Like It*.
► *The intimate theater at the Folger (see p204) is a replica of one from the Elizabethan era.*

FREE Library of Congress

Visitors' Center, Jefferson Building, First Street & Independence Avenue, SE (1-202 707 9779, www.loc.gov). Capitol South Metro. **Open** *Thomas Jefferson Building* 8.30am-4.30pm Mon-Sat. *James Madison Building* 8.30am-9.30pm Mon-Fri. *John Adams Building* 8.30am-9.30pm Mon, Wed, Thur; 8.30am-5pm Tue, Fri, Sat. *Guided tours* 10.30am, 11.30am, 1.30pm, 2.30pm, 3.30pm Mon-Fri; 10.30am, 11.30am, 1.30pm, 2.30pm Sat. **Admission** free. **Map** p252 L7.

The national library of the US, the Library of Congress is the world's largest. Its three buildings hold some 100 million items – including the papers of 23 US presidents – along 535 miles of bookshelves. Contrary to popular notion, the library does not have a copy of every book ever printed, but its heaving shelves are still spectacular.

To get to grips with the place, it's best to start with the 20-minute film in the ground-floor visitors' center, excerpted from a TV documentary, which provides a clear picture of the place's scope and size. An even better option is to join a guided tour.

The original library was crammed into the Capitol. Ransacked by the British in 1814, it revived

when president-scholar Thomas Jefferson offered his collection of 6,487 books. The Thomas Jefferson Building – the main one – was finished in 1897 and splendidly restored upon its centennial. Based on the Paris Opera House, the Library has granite walls supporting an octagonal dome, which rises to 160ft above the spectacular Main Reading Room. Gloriously gaudy mosaics, frescos and statues overwhelm the visitor with a gush of 19th-century high culture.

The Main Reading Room has classical marble archways and great plaster figures of disciplines (Philosophy, Religion, Art, History – all women) flanked by bronze images of their mortal instruments (Plato, Moses, Homer, Shakespeare – all men).

The library hosts several long-term exhibitions, all with an interactive focus. Hope for America: Performers, Politics and Pop Culture draws on papers, jokes, films and TV programs from comedian Bob Hope, and examines the careers of Hope and other entertainers who chose to involve themselves with the political issues of their day. Exploring the Early Americas uses material from the Jay I Kislak collection to look at indigenous cultures and the consequences of contact with European settlers. Creating the United States looks at the nation's founding documents and examines how they emerged. An interactive display looks at source documents and traces the crafting of the language. Also on display are the library's collection of Bibles and Thomas Jefferson's collection of books and manuscripts.

The James Madison Building, opened in 1980, encloses an area greater than 35 football fields. It houses the copyright office, manuscript room, film and TV viewing rooms and the incredible photography collections. Diagonally opposite is the 1939 John Adams Building, which contains the Science and Business reading rooms.

Anyone with photo ID can obtain a research card within about ten minutes. You can't wander all the shelves yourself: a librarian will dig out your selected text. The library catalog is also available online at www.lcweb.loc.gov, though many of the old card-catalogue entries are found only in their original drawers.

FREE Supreme Court

1st Street & Maryland Avenue, NW (1-202 479 3211/www.supremecourtus.gov). Capitol South or Union Station Metro. **Open** 9am-4.30pm Mon-Fri. **Map** p253 L6.

The ultimate judicial and constitutional authority, the United States Supreme Court pays homage in its architecture to the rule of law. Justices are appointed for life, and their temple reflects their eminence. Designed by Cass Gilbert in the 1930s, its classical façade incorporates Corinthian columns supporting a pediment decorated with bas-reliefs representing Liberty, Law, Order and a crew of historical lawgivers. The sober style conceals whimsy in the shape

SIGHTS

of sculpted turtles lurking to express the 'deliberate pace' of judicial deliberations. There are also ferocious lions – enough said.

You can tour the building any time. Visitors enter from the plaza doors, on either side of the main steps. The ground level has a cafeteria, an introductory video show, a gift shop and changing exhibitions. The cathedral-like entrance hall daunts one into hushed tones. The courtroom, with its heavy burgundy velvet draperies and marble pillars, is where the nine judges hear around 120 of the more than 6,500 cases submitted each year. The black-robed figures appear as the court marshal announces 'Oyez! Oyez! Oyez!' and sit in seats of varying height, handcrafted to their personal preferences. Goose-quill pens still grace the lawyers' tables, for tradition's sake.

When the court is in session, from October to April, visitors can see cases argued on Mondays, Tuesdays and Wednesdays from 10am to 3pm. Two lines form in the plaza in front of the building: one for those who want to hear the whole argument (better be there by 8am), and the 'three-minute line', for those who just want a peek. Seating for whole-argument visitors is at 9.30am; three-minute visitors are admitted from 10am. In May and June, 'opinions' are handed down usually on Tuesdays and Wednesdays. Check the newspapers' Supreme Court calendars to see what cases are scheduled. Celebrated cases draw massive queues. Courtroom lectures are available daily. On days that the Court is not sitting, they are hourly, on the half-hour, beginning at 9.30 a.m. with a final lecture at 3.30 p.m. When the Court is in session, lectures take place only after Court adjourns for the day.

FREE United States Botanic Garden

245 1st Street, at Maryland Avenue (1-202 225 8333, www.usbg.gov). Federal Center SW Metro. **Open** 10am-5pm daily. **Admission** free. **Map** p253 K7.

In 1842, the Navy's Wilkes Expedition returned from exploring Fiji and South America, showering Congress with a cornucopia of exotic flora. The present conservatory was erected in 1930 and recently modernised with state-of-the-art climate controls and a coconut-level catwalk around the central rainforest.

The conservatory displays 4,000 plants, including endangered species. Themed displays feature the desert and the oasis, plant adaptations and the primeval garden. The orchid collection is a particular delight. Across Independence Avenue, Bartholdi Park displays plants thriving in Washington's climate, ranged around an alluring fountain created by Bartholdi, sculptor of the Statue of Liberty. The new National Garden aims to be a showcase for 'unusual, useful, and ornamental plants that grow well in the mid-Atlantic region'.

★ FREE United States Capitol

Capitol Hill, between Constitution & Independence Avenues (recorded tour information 1-202 225 6827, www.aoc.gov). Capitol South or Union Station Metro. **Open** *Guided tours* 8.30am-4.30pm Mon-Sat (last ticket 3.30pm); must be booked in advance (see below). **Admission** free. **Map** p253 K7.

French architect Major Pierre-Charles L'Enfant, hired by President Washington to plan the federal city, selected Capitol Hill – a plateau, actually – as 'a pedestal waiting for a monument'. Indeed it was. In 1793, George Washington and an entourage of local masons laid the building's long-lost cornerstone, then celebrated by barbecuing a 500-pound ox. Thirty-one years later, despite a fire, a shortage of funds and the War of 1812, the structure was complete. But as the Union grew, so did the number of legislators. By 1850, architects projected the Capitol would have to double its size. In 1857, they added wings for the Senate (north) and the House of Representatives (south). An iron dome (a 600-gallon paint job each year makes it look like marble) replaced the wooden one in 1865.

Today, as well as being a landmark of neo-classical architecture, the Capitol – which has 540 rooms, 658 windows (108 in the dome alone) and 850 doorways – is something like a small city. As well as the 535 elected lawmakers, an estimated 20,000 workers toil each day among the six buildings (not including the Capitol itself) – all connected by tunnels – that make up the complex. A US flag flies over the Senate and House wings when either is in session; and at night a lantern glows in the Capitol dome.

United States Botanic Garden.

United States Capitol.

Tickets for a Capitol tour are free but must be obtained online in advance; you'll be assigned a time (it's usually possible to secure a slot within a day or two). Entrance is through the new Emancipation Hall underground visitor center. Once inside you will also be able to obtain a pass for the House and Senate floors. Visits begin with an orientation film. The highlight of the short tour is the Rotunda, its dome containing nine million tons of iron. On its ceiling is a massive fresco by Constantino Brumidi, consisting of a portrait of the nation's first president rising to the heavens flanked by allegorical figures of Liberty and Authority, Victory and Fame. They are surrounded by maidens representing the original 13 colonies. Around the walls are other paintings, with figures depicting elements in American life such as commerce and agriculture; in these scenes mythological gods and goddesses interact with historical figures. The National Statuary Hall was originally the chamber of the House of Representatives, but it outgrew the room, moving to a new chamber, and the room was devoted to statuary. Each state was invited to contribute two statues to honor individuals significant to their state; these are displayed throughout the Capitol and in the visitor center.

UNION STATION & AROUND

Daniel Burnham's Beaux Arts-style **Union Station** is a monument to the railroad age. The Thurgood Marshall Judiciary Building east of Union Station complements the former City Post Office – now the **National Postal Museum** – also built by Burnham, to present

an elegant urban vista. In front of the trio, the flags of all the US states and territories are ranged around the central Columbus Memorial Fountain (1912).

The neighborhood around Union Station was once a shantytown of Irish railroad labourers, who christened their marshy abode 'Swampoodle' after its swamps and puddles.

FREE National Postal Museum (S)
2 Massachusetts Avenue, NE, at 1st Street (1-202 633 5555/http://postalmuseum.si.edu). Union Station Metro. **Open** 10am-5.30pm daily. **Admission** free. **Map** p253 L6.
Audio-visual and interactive presentations in this family-friendly museum detail the invention and history of stamps, the postal service, the role of letters as a means of communication (including letters to and from soldiers during wartime), and stamp collecting. The frequent special exhibitions aren't likely to bowl over serious philatelists. They should head to the museum's huge library and research center.
▶ *For children's activities at the museum, see p170.*

FREE Union Station
40 Massachusetts Avenue, NE, at Delaware Avenue (1-202 298-1908, www.unionstation dc.com). Metro Union Station. **Open** *Station* 24hrs daily. *Shops* 10am-9pm Mon-Sat; noon-6pm Sun. **Map** p253 K/L 5/6.
Built in 1908, Union Station grandiosely reflects its inspiration – the Baths of Diocletian in Rome. Envisioning the most splendid terminal in the country, architect Daniel 'make no small plans' Burnham lavished the building with amenities,

including a nursery, a swimming pool and even a mortuary for defunct out-of-towners. The Main Hall is a huge rectangular space, with a 96ft barrel-vaulted ceiling and a balcony with 36 sculptures of Roman legionnaires.

The station languished when rail travel declined. The President's Room, reserved for chief executives welcoming incoming dignitaries such as King George VI and Haile Selassie, is now a restaurant. In 1953, a decidedly non-stop express train bound for Eisenhower's inauguration smashed into the crowded concourse; incredibly, nobody was killed. Two decades later, a deliberate but also disastrous hole was sunk in the Great Hall to make way for the multi-screen video set-up of an ill-conceived (and short-lived) visitors' center. At this stage, despite its lingering grandeur, the station seemed doomed to the wrecking ball.

But in 1988 a painstaking $165-million restoration program was begun, during which time entertainment came into play. There are now shops, amusements and eateries of all sorts, and even a multi-screen cinema. Rents are high and some of the shops have failed, but successors always seem to come along and more sales per square foot move through the shops here than any other DC mall. It's easy to forget that the marble and gilt palace's main function is still as a railway station – with lines to New York, Chicago, Miami and New Orleans, as well as the suburbs – though the crowds at rush hour will bring you back to your senses.

▶ *For shops at Union Station, see p144.*

THE FEDERAL TRIANGLE

The nine-block-long triangle of monolithic federal buildings wedged between Pennsylvania Avenue, NW, and the Mall is known as the Federal Triangle. The government bulldozed the whole district in the 1920s, claiming 'eminent domain' (the right of compulsory purchase), and today the Federal Triangle is the ballpark for the heavy hitters of the government machine, housing some 28,000 office workers. The triangle is both a labyrinth and a fortress. Security is tight, and visitors usually end up asking about six different people before finally making it to their destination. Wags call it the Bermuda Triangle.

All but three of the buildings in the Triangle were built between 1927 and 1938 as massive Beaux Arts limestone structures, complete with high-minded inscriptions, to house various federal agencies, such as the Departments of Commerce and Justice, and the **National Archives**. The Internal Revenue Service headquarters are inscribed with the words of former justice Oliver Wendell Holmes: 'Taxes are what we pay for a civilized society'. The three exceptions are the John Wilson (District) Building (the city hall, on the corner of 14th

and E Streets), the Ronald Reagan Building and the **Old Post Office**. Once sneered at as the 'old tooth' and slated for demolition, the latter now sports a tourist mall and a brilliant view from the top of its 315ft tower.

Built in the 1990s, the **Ronald Reagan Building & International Trade Center** (on 14th Street, opposite the Department of Commerce) is the most expensive building ever constructed in the US for federal use, at a cost of over $700 million.

In the basement of the Department of Commerce is an unexpected novelty: the National Aquarium of Washington DC, an old-fashioned exhibit that affords a closer look at sea creatures than many more modern aquaria.

FREE National Archives
Constitution Avenue, NW, between 7th & 9th Streets (1-866 272 6272, www.archives.gov). Archives-Navy Memorial Metro. **Open** 9am-5pm Mon, Tue, Sat; 9am-9pm Wed, Thur, Fri. **Admission** free. **Map** p253 J6.

The vast collection of the National Archive & Record Administration (NARA) represents the physical record of the birth and growth of a nation in original documents, maps, photos, recordings, films and a miscellany of objects. The catalog resonates with national iconography and historical gravitas (and pathos): it includes the Louisiana Purchase, maps of Lewis and Clark's explorations, the Japanese World War II surrender document, the gun that shot JFK, the Watergate tapes and documents of national identity, among them the Declaration of Independence, Constitution and Bill of Rights (collectively known as the Charters of Freedom). Nearby is one of the original copies of the Magna Carta.

The building that houses them was opened in 1935 and designed to harmonize with existing DC landmarks – in other words, it's neo-classical in style. In a city of monumental architecture the most distinctive features are the bronze doors at the Constitution Avenue entrance. Each weighs six and a half tons and is 38ft high and 11in thick. Though security is their main function, they also remind the visitor of the importance of the contents. The main attraction is the Rotunda, where the original Charters of Freedom are mounted, triptych-like, in a glass case at the center of a roped-off horseshoe containing other key documents. A renovation completed in 2003 protecting them with high-tech gizmos proved itself in 2006 when the building flooded. A semi-circular gallery running behind the Rotunda stages temporary exhibitions drawn from the vast collections. Research access (photo ID required) is via the door on Pennsylvania Avenue. A free shuttle bus connects to Archives II in College Park, Maryland, for collections housed there, including all post-World War II files.

Treasure Rooms

Some rooms in the city's art museums are as extraordinary as the paintings.

Peacock Room.

SALON DORÉ AT THE CORCORAN GALLERY OF ART

The 18th-century neo-classical Salon Doré – transported from the Hôtel de Clermont in Paris, complete with gilded and mirrored paneling decorated with garlands, Corinthian pilasters and trophy panels – is a feast for the eyes. Given to the museum by industrialist and US senator William A Clark (1839-1925), the room was removed from its original location in aristocratic Faubourg Saint-Germain and brought to New York, where it was installed in Clark's Fifth Avenue mansion. For the Corcoran Gallery, *see p53.*

MUSIC ROOM AT THE PHILLIPS COLLECTION

Duncan Phillips' luxuriant 1897 mansion holds a special treat: a dark, enveloping Music Room with spectacular oak wainscoting and ceiling coffers. The room originally functioned as Duncan and his brother James' recreation room – and a very sophisticated rec room indeed. Later, it was converted to a recital space, playing host to Sunday afternoon concerts, beginning in 1941. Today, the room continues to host Sunday concerts from October to May. For the Phillips Collection, *see p77.*

PEACOCK ROOM AT THE FREER GALLERY OF ART

Whistler's deep green and gilt Peacock Room was purchased by Detroit business magnate Charles Lang Freer in 1904. The 1876-77 dining room was transported wholesale from British shipowner Frederick R Leyland's London townhouse. Whistler covered the ceiling with a gold leaf and peacock feather pattern, and added gilded shelving and painted wooden shutters with immense plumed peacocks. His Japanese-influenced canvas, *The Princess from the Land of Porcelain*, presides over the room. For the Freer Gallery of Art, *see p44.*

DINING ROOM AT HILLWOOD MUSEUM AND GARDENS

This sumptuous room, covered in 18th-century French oak panels, hosted some of Washington's most lavish dinner parties. Though today the dining table is set with spectacular displays of porcelain, silver and glassware, once a year these are removed and the gorgeous table uncovered. Spanning 28 feet, the piece features around 70 types of minerals and marbles set into its surface in glorious stylized floral motifs. For Hillwood Museum and Gardens, *see p84.*

FREE Old Post Office

*1100 Pennsylvania Avenue, NW, between 11th &
12th Streets (1-202 606 8691/www.nps.gov/opot).
Federal Triangle Metro.* **Open** *June-Aug* 9am-8pm
Mon-Wed, Thur-Sat; 9am-7pm Thur; 10am-6pm
Sun. *Sept-May* 9am-5pm Mon-Sat; 10am-6pm Sun.
Last tours 15mins before closing time.
Admission free. **Map** p252 J6.

Washington's best views may be from the
Washington Monument, but from here you get to
see the Monument itself. It's a 47-second ride to the
ninth floor; you then change to another elevator
bound for the 12th, and top, floor. The 270ft observation level allows visitors an awe-inspiring view
of the city and surrounding area.

THE NORTHWEST RECTANGLE

The Northwest Rectangle is not an official
appellation, but it's sometimes used to describe
the rectangle of federal buildings west of the
Ellipse and south of E Street that roughly
mirrors the Federal Triangle to the east. It's
really just part of Foggy Bottom (*see p64*), an
industrial immigrant area in the 19th century,
but any original character that the area has
retained emerges only further north.

In this southern part, it's grandiose federal
anonymity all the way. From west to east, the
buildings of interest are the **State
Department**, whose opulent reception rooms
can be toured by arrangement; then, dropping
down to Constitution Avenue, the American
Pharmaceutical Association, the National
Academy of Sciences, with its invitingly
climbable statue of Einstein, the Federal Reserve
Board and the Organization of American States
(OAS). Behind the OAS art gallery annex is the
Department of the Interior, housing in its
museum examples of Native American arts,
with authentic goods for sale in its craft shop.
Attempting to improve its PR, the **IMF Center**
– scene of an annual siege by anti-globalization
protesters – offers displays explaining
international finance.

FREE Department of the Interior Museum

*1849 C Street, NW, between 18th & 19th Streets
(1-202 208 4743, www.doi.gov/interiormuseum).
Farragut West Metro.* **Open** currently closed for
renovations. **Admission** free. **Map** p252 G6.

The Department of the Interior's exhibits are a hotchpotch of Indian arts and crafts: Pueblo drums; Apache
basketwork; Cheyenne arrows that a soldier plucked
from dying buffalos at Fort Sill Indian Territory
(Oklahoma) in 1868. You can also see early land boun-
ties and exhibits about endangered species, complete
with shoes made from crocodile skin. The gift shop,
one of Washington's best-kept secrets, is over 60 years
old and contains wares from 40 Indian tribes, from
Navajo folk art to Alaskan ivory. Note that tours are

by reservation only and that photo ID is required. The
museum is currently closed for renovation.

**FREE State Department Diplomatic
Reception Rooms**

*C & 22nd Streets, NW (1-202 647 3241/
www.state.gov/www/about_state/diprooms/index.ht
ml). Foggy Bottom-GWU Metro.* **Guided tours**
9.30am, 10.30am, 2.45pm Mon-Fri. **Admission**
free. **Map** p252 G6.

When the State Department was finished in 1951,
the wife of the secretary of state wept when con-
fronted with the chrome, glass-and-concrete walls
and tasteless furniture. Today, the diplomatic reception rooms, fit to receive foreign dignitaries, are
dubbed Washington's best-kept secret – a delight
for serious art- and antiques-lovers. They contain
national masterpieces from 1740 to 1825, valued at
some \$90 million. Among the collection are
Chippendale pieces; the English Sheraton desk on
which the Treaty of Paris was signed in 1783, ending
the Revolutionary War; and a table-desk used by
Thomas Jefferson. There are also some none-too-
exciting exhibits in the lobby on the history of the
State Department, which is the oldest of the cabinet
departments. Note that you can only visit by guided
tour, for which reservations are required (call or
book on https://receptiontours.state.gov).

SOUTH OF THE MALL

To the south of the Mall lie mostly nondescript
federal buildings (Federal Aviation
Administration, Transportation Department and
so on). The principal exceptions are the **United
States Holocaust Memorial Museum** and
the **Bureau of Engraving & Printing**, where
the greenback is printed. Both are to the west
near the Tidal Basin.

To the east, L'Enfant Plaza is ironically
named, considering that it's supposed to honor
the man whose city plan made Washington so
stately – it's a barren expanse of ground.

FREE Bureau of Engraving & Printing

*14th Street, SW, at C Street (1-202 874 2330,
www.moneyfactory.com). Smithsonian Metro.*
Open *Visitor Center* Sept-Mar 8.30am-3.30pm
Mon-Fri. Apr-Aug 8.30am-7pm Mon-Fri. *Tours*
Sept-Mar every 15mins 9-10.45 am, 12.30-2pm
Mon-Fri. Apr-Aug 9-10.45am, 12.30-3.45pm,
5-7pm Mon-Fri. **Admission** free. **Map** p252 H6.

As the sign says, 'The Buck Starts Here!'. The printing in the title refers to hard currency: this is where
the dollar bill is born. The 40-minute guided tour
provides a glimpse into the printing, cutting and
stacking of the 37 million banknotes produced daily.
It's all done behind the thickest of plate glass, with
scads of security. In the off-season (September to the
end of March) you should be able to go in with a minimal wait; lines form at the visitors' entrance on 14th

Street. In summer, you'll need a timed ticket, given out from 8am from the booth just outside in Raoul Wallenberg Place. You'll probably have to queue, and tickets are usually gone by 9am. Alternatively, US citizens can contact their senator or congressman for access to special tours.

★ FREE United States Holocaust Memorial Museum

100 Raoul Wallenberg Place, SW, at 14th Street (1-202 488 0400/www.ushmm.org). Smithsonian Metro. **Open** 10am-5.20pm daily. Closed Yom Kippur. Timed passes required for main exhibition Mar-Aug, available from 10am on day of visit or book online ($1 per pass) or on 1-877 808 7466 for additional fee. **Admission** free, except for online or phone bookings (see above). **Map** p252 H7.

Since its opening in 1993, the Holocaust Museum has attracted legions of visitors to its permanent exhibition, the Holocaust. The three-floor exhibition, containing over 900 artifacts, many video screens and four theaters showing archive footage and survivor testimony, presents a chronological history of the Nazi holocaust. On the top level, Nazi Assault covers the rise of Hitler and Nazism in the mid 1930s; the incarceration of Jews in ghettos and their murder – along with gypsies and many others – in death camps in the 1940s is the focus of Final Solution on the third floor; on the second floor, Last Chapter covers Allied liberation and subsequent war-crime trials. Visitors travel to the exhibition in a steel-clad freight elevator that deposits them into an environment of unparalleled sobriety. Themes, such as murder of the handicapped, Nazi eugenics, resistance, and so on, are comprehensively covered. The photo- and text-intensive accounts of events and atrocities unfold dispassionately, but objects and symbols make powerful impressions: thousands of camp victims' shoes piled in a heap personalize the losses.

While the main exhibition is suitable for children of 11 and over only, a specially designed children's exhibition, Daniel's Story, at ground level, is suitable for children of eight and over and teaches about the holocaust through the story of one boy. Other, changing, exhibitions have included an examination of *The Protocols of the Elders of Zion* and State of Deception: the Power of Nazi Propaganda. The museum also attempts to highlight recent genocides and genocide prevention through the installation *From Memory To Action: Meeting The Challenge of Genocide* in the museum's Wexner Center, and through other programs and initiatives.

The building (designed by Pei Cobb Freed) incorporates red brick and slate-grey steel girders and catwalks, echoing death camp architecture; within the permanent exhibition, skylit zones alternate with claustrophobic darkness. Notable artworks include a Richard Serra sculpture and graceful Ellsworth Kelly and Sol LeWitt canvases.

United States Holocaust Memorial Museum

SIGHTS

DC Neighborhoods

Beyond the monuments is a city where people live, work and play.

Beyond the monumental core of the Mall is a real, rather quirky city, full of distinctive and interesting neighborhoods, populated by people rather than institutions and made more from brick than marble. If there is a theme to this other Washington's history over the last few decades, it has been one of regeneration, as areas such as Downtown, U Street and – more recently – H Street have pulled themselves out of decline and regained the vibrancy and economic pulling power that they once had.

The city is divided into quadrants, taking the Capitol – slightly east of center – as its nexus, and we follow these divisions below.

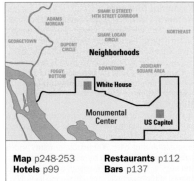

Neighborhoods

Map p248-253   **Restaurants** p112
Hotels p99   **Bars** p137

Northwest

Northwest is the most affluent quadrant. It is roughly bisected from south to north by Rock Creek Park. The Northwest section of this chapter starts with the neighborhoods nearest the Monumental Center, heads north and then west to Rock Creek Park, Georgetown and further suburbs.

FOGGY BOTTOM

West and south-west of the White House down to the Potomac River, Foggy Bottom takes its name from its original, marshy riverside location. That the name is so well known in the US is due largely to the Department of State, which moved into the Truman Building (2201 C Street, NW) in 1950. The immigrant settlers who once worked in the factories wouldn't recognize the area's current hauteur. A historic district on the National Registry since 1987 because of the design of its rowhouses, these days Foggy Bottom is home to highly transient foreign service workers, federal appointees, college students and performing artists – along with older long-term residents.

Near the dock where the US government first arrived in its muddy new capital in 1800, the white marble box of the John F Kennedy

Center for the Performing Arts (known as the **Kennedy Center**, *see below*) rises above the river. North of the Kennedy Center lie the swirling contours of the **Watergate** complex (at 26th Street & Virginia Avenue, NW), site of the eponymous 1972 burglary that unraveled Richard Nixon's presidency. Shops and delis line its courtyard. The humble Howard Johnson motel across the street, from where Tricky Dick's 'plumbers' monitored the break-in, is now a George Washington University dorm.

At Virginia and New Hampshire Avenues, a statue of Mexican president Benito Juarez points symbolically towards the distant

---

INSIDE TRACK CITY TRAILS

Cultural Tourism DC's **neighborhood heritage trails** are a great way to get the best out of exploring the city's diverse neighborhoods. You'll spot the trails' information boards as you walk around town. Each combines stories, historic photos, and maps. In addition, Audio Journeys are available for the Downtown Heritage Trail and the Greater U Street Heritage Trail. See www.culturaltourismdc.org.

Watergate.

monument to George Washington, who inspired him. Above Virginia Avenue, Foggy Bottom seeps from monumental into urban Washington. Although many of the neighborhood's characteristic tiny townhouses were bulldozed to make way for the notoriously expansionist George Washington University, some neat pockets – such as the area between New Hampshire Avenue and K Street – survive.

The **Octagon** was President James Madison's refuge for seven months after the British invaders torched the executive mansion in 1814. The **Arts Club of Washington** (2017 I Street, NW) was home to his successor, James Monroe, until the charred mansion was rebuilt.

Around Pennsylvania Avenue, Foggy Bottom frequently succumbs to 'façadism', token retention of the fronts of historic buildings to satisfy preservation rules, with massive modern structures ballooning behind. The blatant Mexican Chancery (1911 Pennsylvania Avenue, NW) and slightly subtler Red Lion Row (2000 Pennsylvania Avenue, NW) are prime examples. The Spanish Chancery on Washington Circle is subtler still, and more stylish.

North of Pennsylvania Avenue, the 'New Downtown' to the west of Farragut Square is the haunt of the 'K Street lawyer' lobbyists. Despite the fall of freespending lobbyist Jack Abramoff in 2006, lots of cash is still spent on entertaining. Expense-account hangouts still aren't cheap.

Kennedy Center

2700 F Street, NW, at New Hampshire Avenue & Rock Creek Parkway (1-800 444 1324, 1-202 467 4600, www.kennedy-center.org). Foggy Bottom-GWU

Metro. **Open** 10am-11pm daily. *Guided tours* every 10mns 10am-5pm Mon-Fri; 10am-1pm Sat, Sun. **Map** p252 F6.

Festooned with decorative gifts from many nations and some wonderful 20th-century works of art, 'Ken Cen' is as much a spectacle as the shows it presents, with its six theatres and concert halls, three rooftop restaurants and great views from the open-air terrace. Free concerts (6pm daily) liven up the Millennium Stage, and there are free 45-minute guided tours (call 1-202 416 8340 or walk-ins welcome; visit the Tour Desk on Level A) . Parking is inadequate when several shows are playing at once – better to walk or take the free shuttle bus from the Foggy Bottom-GWU Metro stop.

▶ *For the Kennedy Center as a performance venue, see p190. For children's activities, see p171.*

The Octagon

1799 New York Avenue, NW, at 18th Street (1-202 638 3221, http://archfoundation.org). Farragut West or Farragut North Metro. **Open** Currently closed for renovation. **Map** p252 G6.

Designed for its odd-shaped lot by Dr William Thornton, first architect of the Capitol, this elegant brick mansion was completed in 1800. The aristocratic Tayloes offered it to a fellow Virginian, President Madison, when he was made homeless by the 1814 White House fire. More like a pregnant hexagon than an octagon, the house – reputedly haunted – is a gem of light and proportion. The related American Institute of Architects headquarters are next door; hence the Octagon hosts topical architectural exhibitions as well as Madison-era furnishings – including the desk where Madison signed

SIGHTS

Adolf Cluss's Capital

The architect who added red brick to Washington's palette.

Architect Adolf Cluss (1825-1905) emerged from obscurity as a draughtsman at the Navy Yard to become the prime mover in redesigning the city in the wake of the Civil War. With a background in engineering, Cluss was able to move into architecture, favouring brick made from the city's clay soil and obsessing over light, ventilation and fire safety. His great opportunity came in 1871, when the Territory of the District of Columbia was formed under Alexander 'Boss' Shepherd, with a programme to turn the tawdry town into 'a capital worthy of a republic'. As the city's chief engineer, Cluss plunged into giving Washington what would become its characteristic look, planning 'tree boxes' of greenery between the streets and the sidewalks, ceding homeowners tax-free front yards, with freedom to extend bay windows into that space, and designing public and private buildings on a human scale.

Few would have realised that the makeover of the post-Civil War capital was actually in the hands of a communist. Born in Heilbrunn, Wurrtemberg, Cluss had led the Communist League of Mainz during the 1848 revolution, coming as Marx's personal agent to Washington, where he ran the Communist League, USA from his Navy Yard office. He prospered and married,

experiencing social mobility unlikely in Europe, finally telling Marx that communism wouldn't work here. But his early social philosophy remained a major influence on his urban planning.

Even after the spendthrift Shepherd regime collapsed in scandal in 1874, Cluss continued to leave his mark through many churches, private homes, public buildings, and Washington's first apartment house. Most are gone, because they centred on old Downtown, where office blocks claimed the sites of Cluss's winsome, eclectic Rundbogenstil works. We list those that remain below.

● **Sumner School** (1872) 17th & M Streets, NW (202 442-6060). The first public high school for African Americans, now the DC Public School Museum and Archives.

● **Masonic Temple** (1869) 910 F Street, NW. The building has thrived as a restaurant and offices. Across the street, the National Portrait Gallery reopened in 2006 drawing acclaim for its interiors, which Cluss redesigned after a fire. (He also restored the Smithsonian's Castle Building interiors after another conflagration.)

SIGHTS

Eastern Market.

Sumner School.

● **Calvary Baptist Church** (1864, 1869) 777 Eighth Street, NW. In 2004 Cluss's unique steeple, which had been blown down by a 1913 hurricane, was replaced with a replica.

● **Eastern Market** (1873) 7th and C Streets, SE. Now meticulously restored to its former glory, following a fire in 2007.

● **Alexandria, Virginia City Hall** (1873) 301 King Street. It retains the original Cluss look on the Cameron Street side only.

● **Franklin School** (1869) 13th and K Streets, NW. The building won contemporary design acclaim as far away as England and Argentina.

● **Arts & Industries Building** (1881, 900 Jefferson Drive, SW). Regarded as Cluss's mid-Mall masterpiece, it became the centre of controversy when the Smithsonian Institution left the premises, pleading that the handsome but deteriorating roof it had long neglected was too costly to fix. The building is now on the National Trust for Historic Preservation's list of top ten endangered buildings.

the Treaty of Ghent in 1815, ending the war between the US and Britain. The museum was closed for renovation at the time of writing.

DOWNTOWN

Once a bustling city hub, synonymous with F Street's theatres, restaurants and department stores, the Downtown area slumped in the 1960s as shoppers began to prefer suburban malls; and it virtually keeled over after the 1968 riots tarnished it as unsafe. In 1985 the Hecht Company – whose original Downtown store at 7th Street had been vandalised during the riots – reopened at 12th and G Streets, the first freestanding department store built in an American downtown in four decades. It was later bought out by **Macy's** (*see p143*), which still trades on the site. In 1997 the **Verizon Center** (*see p72*) opened, pushing a revival that has totally transformed the area into a safe restaurant, entertainment and retail district.

An influx of law firms spawned such power-lunch hangouts as DC Coast at K and 14th Streets and Oceanaire Seafood Room (for both, *see p116*) at F and 12th. At Franklin Square (14th & I Streets, NW), strip clubs long ago gave way to offices, which chip in to maintain the park. Even the statue facing 14th Street – of Irishman John Barry, Father of the US Navy – got its purloined sword restored.

National Theatre (1321 Pennsylvania Avenue, NW, *see p203*) flourishes as an independent theater, while the **Warner Theatre** (at 13th & E Streets, NW, *see p193*) reflects a thorough restoration. At 511 Tenth Street, NW, is **Ford's Theatre** (*see p70*). Still a functioning theatre, its main claim to fame is as the site of Lincoln's assassination.

The **National Press Club** (14th & F Streets, NW), opened in 1924, still draws reporters, and sponsors speeches by newsmakers, foreign and domestic. The *Washington Post* is at 1150 15th Street, NW. One block west is the home of the **National Geographic Society**.

The **Russian Embassy** (1125 16th Street, NW, between L & M Streets) was a wedding gift for the daughter of sleeping-car tycoon George Pullman; the gushy palazzo became the embassy of Tsarist Russia in 1917. With US recognition in 1934, the USSR moved in, planting hammer-and-sickle motifs amid the gilt cherubs adorning the walls. The red flag finally came down in 1991. This Russian Embassy was only the ceremonial appendage of the working compound on Wisconsin Avenue at Calvert Street. In 2001 it came to light that US spies had burrowed a surveillance tunnel under the latter building.

SIGHTS

Profile National Portrait Gallery/ Smithsonian American Art Museum

A dilapidated landmark building reborn.

By the late 1990s, the former Patent Office building in Downtown was in a sad state of disrepair. One of the finest examples of Greek Revival architecture in the city, the original, Robert Mills-designed, south wing opened in 1840 and was the site of President Lincoln's inaugural ball in 1865. Three other wings were added later, each facing a central courtyard. Two museums – American Art and Portraiture – were housed here from 1968. But in 2000, beset with problems, the once-magnificent building was closed for careful renovation. Gifts allowed for the building of an auditorium, constructed beneath the courtyard. Two large elms there suffered from Dutch elm disease and had to be removed, and what had been a grassy area was paved over. Another gift allowed for the covering of the courtyard with a glass canopy designed by Norman Foster. This created the Kogod Courtyard, a pleasantly airy space rendered slightly dour by the grey stone of its surrounding walls. The buildings that surround the courtyard are once again home to the two museums, each accessible from the other, each telling the story of America from a different perspective.

The **National Portrait Gallery** features people who played a role in the shaping of the nation and its culture, with figures as diverse as Pocahontas and Juliette Gordon Low, founder of the US Girl Scouts. Presidents are gathered in the America's Presidents section on the second floor. Among the portraits is Gilbert Stuart's seminal 'Lansdowne' portrait of George Washington. Other paintings feature the Bushes, father and son, in separate portraits side by side. A TV plays excerpts from epoch-making presidential speeches, Kennedy's 'ask not what your country can do for you', and Reagan's 'Mr Gorbachev, tear down that wall' among them.

On the first (ground) floor, until July 2011, Americans Now allows observers to wonder who will still be famous in a hundred years time. One person who probably will be is Barack Obama: the iconic *Hope* poster, by Shepard Fairey, is here.

Alongside the magnificently re-created grand hall on the third floor is 20th-Century Americans. Andy Warhol's iconic *Marilyn* is here, alongside a striking kitsch-classical *Elvis* by Ralph W Cowan, looming huge over a rural scene with Gracelands in the background, as well as serious figures such as Hillary Clinton.

The theme of art as a window on America continues in the **American Art Museum**. On the second floor is American Art Through 1940, a chronological collection that reflects America's changing self-image. In the 19th and early 20th centuries, the West was a distant and intriguing place and the frontier a big concept in the national mindset, so artists sought to bring them to the viewing public. Huge,

idealised and stylised visions of an almost supernatural landscape were the speciality of Albert Bierstadt, and nothing came bigger or more idealised than his *Among the Sierra Nevada, California*, which was actually painted in Rome. George Catlin, meanwhile, had a very different mission: to record disappearing tribal cultures. Contrary to his own prevailing culture, he sought to portray native people not as savages but as individuals and his moving portraits are a testament to this.

Contemporary art and art since 1945 is on the third floor, with work from leading artists, such as Frank Kline's *Merce C*, a dynamic representation in black and white of dancer Merce Cunningham. Perhaps the most striking exhibit here is Nam June Paik's huge neon map, *Electronic Superhighway: Continental US, Alaska, Hawaii*. This floor is also

home to the Lunder Conservation Center, which allows the public to see the work of conservation staff, and the Luce Foundation Center for American Art, the first public study and art storage center in Washington, wtih more than 3,300 works from the permanent collection on display. Interactive kiosks provide detailed information.

Back down on the first (ground) floor, American Experience draws on the collections to explore themes of land, frontier, cities, monuments and ideals. Here, Edward Hopper's *Cape Cod Morning* shows a woman looking out of a window; she seems to have spotted something we can't see, and the picture hints at anxiety and isolation. And Georgia O'Keefe's *Manhattan* is a series of dynamic geometrical shapes reaching skywards, their sharp lines contrasting with flowers floating in the sky.

MORE PORTRAITS
Other examples of George Catlin's portraits of Native Americans can be seen in the **National Museum of the American Indian** (*see p50*).

Sixteenth Street is also notable for its procession of handsome houses of worship, which line it all the way to Maryland, and its Renaissance-style **Meridian Hill Park** (aka Malcolm X Park), adorned with cascading waterfalls and a statue of Joan of Arc. The former Greyhound bus terminal at 12th Street and New York Avenue used to be a wino magnet. Now its streamlined façade, treasured by Washington's ardent art deco devotees, fronts an office building complementing its lines. Street-level tenants include restaurants and bars. In 1987, the **National Museum of Women in the Arts** redeemed a dignified 80-year-old Renaissance Revival Masonic lodge that had become a cinema.

The gigantic **Convention Center** north of Mount Vernon Square replaced a drab, punier predecessor at Ninth Street and New York Avenue. On the square itself, the old wedding-cake Carnegie Library housed the failed City Museum of Washington, DC. The successor **Martin Luther King Jr Memorial Library** is a late design of Bauhaus guru Mies van der Rohe.

The **Smithsonian American Art Museum** and the **National Portrait Gallery** (see p68 **Profile**), which split the historic Patent Office building at 7th and F Streets, reopened in 2006 to acclaim after six years' restoration – the building has been renamed the Donald W Reynolds Center for American Art and Portraiture . Across 7th Street looms the **Verizon Center**, the huge venue for basketball, hockey, concerts and horse shows that did so much to revive the neighborhood. The explosive revival it triggered along 7th Street, and the accompanying escalating rents, blew some old Chinese businesses out of Chinatown. Although their names may be written in Chinese characters, chains like Legal Sea Foods and even Hooters don't quite pass chopstick muster. Gaudy chinoiserie still obscures some quite old house façades; Wok-'n'-Roll restaurant (604 H Street, NW,

1-202 347 4656) occupies Mary Surratt's boarding house, where in 1865 John Wilkes Booth's co-conspirators plotted Abe Lincoln's doom. Texan barbecues and Irish bars now thrive within sight of the world's largest **Chinese arch** (over H Street, at 7th Street), given by the People's Republic of China. When a hefty chunk of the arch broke away a few years ago, local Taiwanese rejoiced in a perceived omen. DC's Chinese population has largely dispersed to the suburbs, but Chinatown remains the community's spiritual centre and site of celebrations at Chinese New Year.

Nearby houses of worship testify to Washington's immigrant past, particularly **St Mary's Mother of God** (727 5th Street, NW), a downsized copy of Germany's Ulm Cathedral, ministering to German immigrants, now drawing nostalgic Catholics to its Tridentine Latin masses. **St Patrick's Catholic Church** (619 10th Street, NW) was established in 1794 to serve the Irish immigrants who came to build the White House; the present building rose a century later. **Holy Rosary Church** (595 3rd Street, NW) has masses in Italian, plus cultural events at its Casa Italiana next door. In 2004 a cluster of Jewish congregations bought back the historic synagogue at 6th and I Streets from the black Baptist congregation that had long occupied – then outgrown – it. In 2005, the revived congregation of Adolf Cluss's **Calvary Baptist Church** (8th & I Streets) regained its innovative steeple (see p66 **Adolf Cluss's Capital**).

The District's long-frustrated goal of a 'living downtown' is finally real, as recent urban deserts bloomed with costly condos. The hottest coming property is north-east of Mount Vernon Square, in an area known as NoMa, named (after Manhattan's SoHo) for NOrth of MAssachusetts Avenue).

★ Smithsonian American Art Museum/ National Portrait Gallery (S)
Reynolds Center, Eighth & F Street, NW (1-202 633 1000, http://americanart.si.edu, www.npg.si.edu). Gallery Place-Chinatown Metro. **Open** 11.30am-7pm daily. **Admission** free. **Map** p285 J6.
See p68 **Profile**.

Ford's Theatre & Lincoln Museum
511 10th Street, NW, between E & F Streets (box office 1-202 347 4833, Park Service 1-202 426 6924, www.fordstheatre.org, www.nps.gov/foth). Metro Center or Gallery Place-Chinatown Metro. **Open** 9am-5pm daily. **Admission** free. **Map** p252 J6.
On Good Friday 1865, President Lincoln was enjoying a comedy in Ford's Theatre when actor John Wilkes Booth entered the presidential box and shot him. Wounded in his dramatic leap to the stage,

---

INSIDE TRACK
CATALYST OF CHANGE

The first time business magnate Abe Pollin visited the site where he would later build the **Verizon Center** (see p72), the area was so infested with crime and drugs that he was warned not to get out of his car. But he and his wife, Irene, were determined to move their surburban arena to Downtown, in the hope of encouraging urban renewal. The Center opened in 1997, and kick-started a dramatic revival of the area.

Chinatown.

Booth escaped painfully on horseback, only to be killed by US troops 12 days later. Today's active theatre looks as it did that day, although rather less-punishing chairs offer a concession to tender modern derrières. Exhibits in the Lincoln Museum downstairs include Booth's Derringer pistol and Lincoln's bloodstained clothes. Across the road, Petersen House (516 10th Street, NW, 1-202 426 6924), where Lincoln expired at 7.22am the next morning, is closed for renovations until 2011.

Madame Tussauds
1001 F Street, NW, between 10th & 11th Streets (1-202 942-7300, www.madametussauds.com/washington). **Open** 10am-4pm Mon-Thur; 10am-6pm Fri-Sun. **Admission** $20; $15-$18 reductions. **Credit** AmEx, MC, V. **Map** p252 H6.

Whoopi Goldberg waits to greet you outside Washington's version of Madame Tussauds. And isn't that Penelope Cruz over there by the counter? Inside you'll find all kinds of distinguished personages, beginning with historical figures such as King George III (this is where the labels come in handy) and the authors of the Declaration of Independence. You can sit next to Rosa Parks in the civil rights room and meet the likes of Martin Luther King and Malcolm X. There are little nuggets of information throughout, too, such as the fact that the FBI began wiretapping King in 1961, using information gained to try and blackmail him. This being DC, it's not surprising that the nation's presidents are immortalised here – among them President Obama in the Oval Office. A new presidents' gallery is due to open in early 2011; it will feature all 44 presidents. You have to wait until the end to find the celebrities: Beyoncé, George Clooney and Oprah among them.

Martin Luther King Jr Memorial Library
901 G Street, NW, between 9th & 10th Streets (general information 1-202 727 1111, www.dc library.org/mlk). Gallery Place-Chinatown Metro. **Open** noon-9pm Mon, Tue; 9.30am-5.30pm Wed-Sat; 1-5pm Sun. **Map** p253 J6.

The main premises of DC's public library system contains the third-floor Washingtoniana Room, where extraordinary reference librarians help sort through books, historical directories, maps and more than 13 million newspaper clippings concerning the District of Columbia and vicinity, fragile materials stored without climate control. Designed by Mies van der Rohe in steel, brick and glass, and built in 1972, the library is one of DC's few modernist buildings. It was listed on the National Register of Historic Places in 2007.

National Museum of Women in the Arts
1250 New York Avenue, NW, at 13th Street (1-202 783 5000, www.nmwa.org). Metro Center Metro. **Open** 10am-5pm Mon-Sat; noon-5pm Sun. **Admission** $10; $8 reductions; free members. **Credit** AmEx, MC, V. **Map** p252 H5.

Though it was founded in 1981 by Wallace and Wilhelmina Holladay to showcase important art by women, the museum didn't occupy its current 70,000sq ft Renaissance Revival building (by Waddy Butler Wood) until six years later. The museum provides a survey of art by women from the 1700s to the present. Highlights include Renaissance artist Lavinia Fontana's dynamic *Holy Family with St John* and Frida Kahlo's defiant 1937 self-portrait *Between the Curtains*. The museum offers sophisticated fare in its special exhibitions.

SIGHTS

SIGHTS

National Geographic Museum

1145 17th Street, NW, at M Street (1-202 857 7588, www.nationalgeographic.com). Farragut North Metro. **Open** 9am-5pm daily. **Admission** free. **Map** p252 H5.

Founded in 1890 by local patricians, the Geographic has funded nearly 6,000 exploration and research projects to destinations from China to Peru and pole to pole. The National Geographic Museum hosts changing exhibitions on subjects as diverse as Geckos: Tails to Toepads and the President's Photographers: 50 Years Inside the Oval Office. The adjacent Grosvenor Auditorium hosts traditional illustrated lectures by explorers, but also presents international concerts and videos, and even beer tastings.

National Museum of Crime & Punishment

575 7th Street, NW, between E & F Streets (1-202 393 1099, www.crimemuseum.org). Gallery Place-Chinatown Metro. **Open** *Sept-late May* 10am-7pm Mon-Thur, Sun; 10am-8pm Fri, Sat. *Late May-Aug* 9am-9pm Mon-Sat; 10am-7pm Sun. **Admission** $19.95; $14.95-$16.95 reductions; free under-5s. **Credit** AmEx, Disc, MC, V. **Map** p253 J6.

This rather grandly named attraction/museum has crime – real and fictional – covered. Reality bites in the lobby, where serial killer Ted Bundy's VW Bug (Beetle) that he used to pick up women who he killed is on display. Visitors head up a black stairwell to the first gallery, a romp through gruesome medieval tortures, gunslingers of the old Wild West, and so on, along with props from some of the big moments of Hollywood crime (Bonnie and Clyde's 1934 Ford, a machine gun used in *Scarface*). Elsewhere, there's lots of interactive stuff: you can take part in a line-up or try and beat a lie detector in the Consequences of Crime section, which also has a line-up of judicial killing machines – a lethal injection machine, gas chamber and Tennessee's electric chair, Old Smokey. The sections on crime fighting allow you to have a go on an FBI firing range, and take part in a simulated police motorcycle chase. The exploration of the work of CSIs and forensic scientists includes a 'body' on a slab showing different injuries and how to interpret them. There's also a section on *America's Most Wanted*.

Verizon Center

601 F Street, NW, at 7th Street (1-202 628 3200, www.verizoncenter.com). Gallery Place-Chinatown Metro. **Open** events only. **Map** p253 J6.

This huge arena hosts some 200 public events every year, including concerts, family entertainment, horse shows and college athletics, as well as professional games by the Washington Capitals NHL hockey team and the Washington Wizards NBA basketball team, along with college basketball. It involves all the economic excesses now de rigueur in American professional sport: startling admission prices, 110 exorbitant sky-boxes for corporate entertaining, restaurants restricting admission to top-end ticketholders, and so on. Still, it's well designed and conveniently stiuated on top of a Metro station.

PENN QUARTER

North of Federal Triangle, this developer-dubbed area is known simply as 'Downtown' to residents, who remember it as the main shopping district. In recent years, it has blossomed with a host of new restaurants, developments, displays and theaters.

Nineteenth-century District residents shopped along Pennsylvania Avenue and 7th Street. But then the success of the fixed-price Woodward & Lothrop department store after 1882 made F Street the principal shopping mecca, while business on the Avenue declined. Distressed by the tawdriness of Pennsylvania Avenue as he rode in his 1961 inaugural procession, President Kennedy charged a commission to revamp 'America's Main Street'. The Pennsylvania Avenue Development Corporation rose to the occasion.

The sinuous water crane perched on the quirky Temperance Fountain at 7th Street and Pennsylvania Avenue punctuates the 7th Street arts corridor of galleries and studios blooming behind Victorian storefronts. The former Lansburgh's department store now houses posh apartments above the **Shakespeare Theatre** (450 7th Street, NW; *see p204*). The **US Navy Memorial** plaza nicely frames the 8th Street axis between the **National Portrait Gallery/Smithsonian American Art Museum** (*see p70*) and the **National Archives** (*see p60*). The **International Spy Museum** at 9th and F has been a smash hit, despite its decidedly un-Washingtonian admission fees. Nearby, the **Marian Koshland Science Museum** beckons more soberly.

In the vicinity of the White House, hotels like the **W** (*see p95*), with its famous rooftop »bar, and the lavish and historic **Willard Inter-Continental** (*see p97*) prove that the area has recovered all its luster. JFK would have been pleased.

The **J Edgar Hoover FBI Building** (935 Pennsylvania Avenue, NW, between 9th & 10th Streets) presents a sterile streetscape because Hoover vetoed planned street-level shops and restaurants as potential security threats.

A locally popular pastime is the day-long Wednesday auction conducted at **Weschler's** (909 E Street, NW, 1-202 628 1281, www.weschlers.com) for over a century. Treasures, trash and grab bags keep the bidders lively.

US Navy Memorial.

★ International Spy Museum

800 F Street, NW, between 8th & 9th Streets (1-202 393 7798, www.spymuseum.org). Gallery Place-Chinatown Metro. **Open** *Mid Mar-Apr* 9am-8pm daily. *May-early Sept* 9am-7pm daily. *Early Sept-mid Mar* 10am-6pm daily. Hours can vary; check website for details. *Last admission* 2hrs before closing. **Admission** $18; $15 5-11s; free under-5s. **Credit** AmEx, Disc, MC, V. **Map** p253 J6.

If your idea of a fun museum experience includes adopting a cover and memorizing your alias's vitals – age, provenance, travel plans and itinerary (you'll be asked questions later) – you've come to the right spot. Testing your sleuthing abilities, along with gawking at an array of funky spy gadgets, including KGB-issued poison pellet shooting umbrellas and Germany's Steineck ABC wristwatch camera, adds up to fun for some folks – many of them under 20. Be aware that this is an 'event' museum: expect to be herded in groups and subjected to overhead public addresses at the beginning of your tour. Despite the racket, James Bond junkies will be in heaven – the groovy silver Aston Martin from 1964's *Goldfinger* assumes a central spot on the circuit. There's interesting stuff, too, about the part played by codes and codebreaking in World War II, about the spying heyday of the Cold War, and the modern world of cyber attacks and cyber forensics. Not surprisingly, the museum has proved a huge hit since it opened in 2002; consider booking tickets in advance.

Marian Koshland Science Museum of the National Academy of Sciences

6th Street & E Street, NW (1-202 334 1201, www.koshland-science-museum.org). Gallery Place-Chinatown Metro. **Open** 10am-5pm, Wed-Sun. **Admission** $5; $3 reductions. **Credit** MC, V. **Map** p253 J6.

Though modestly sized and featuring only four exhibitions at a time, this museum, named after immunologist and molecular biologist Marian Koshland, proves something of an eye-opener. State-of-the-art, interactive displays teach visitors by doing, not just showing. At the time of writing, exhibitions covered global warming, images of earth at night and infectious diseases. In addition, Wonders of Science examines recent research aiming to unravel some of the greatest mysteries of the universe.

US Navy Memorial & Heritage Center

701 Pennsylvania Avenue, NW, between 7th & 9th Streets (1-202 737 2300, www.navy memorial.org). Archives-Navy Memorial Metro. **Open** *Mar-Oct* 9.30am-5pm Mon-Sat. *Nov-Feb* 9.30am-5pm Tue-Sat. **Admission** free. **Map** p253 J6.

Dedicated on the Navy's 212th birthday in 1987, this memorial features the world's biggest map of itself – a flat granite circular map 100ft across, with this very spot at its center – compassed by an apron with 22 bas-reliefs depicting naval highlights like Teddy Roosevelt's globe-circling Great White Fleet of 1907, Commodore Perry's 1854 expedition to Japan and the 'Silent Service' of submarines. Off-center stands a statue of the Lone Sailor, stolid in his pea jacket. The subterranean visitor center contains a cinema with a 52ft screen, showing authentically noisy depictions of navy life.

JUDICIARY SQUARE

Judiciary Square is the hub of the city's courts. The **National Building Museum** occupies the 1883 Pension Building, a Renaissance palace sporting an extraordinary frieze of Civil War troops perpetually patroling the premises. Its atrium is spectacular and its gift shop imaginative. Across F Street, bronze lions flank the **National Law Enforcement Officers Memorial** to the nearly 19,000 cops killed in the line of duty since 1792 with an explanatory visitors' center (605 E Street, NW, 1-202 737 3213).

The Court of Appeals building (5th & D Streets) was once Washington's city hall, a chaste 1820 Greek Revival design by British architect George Hadfield. Lincoln's statue at the front is significant as the first public memorial to the murdered president, sculpted by his acquaintance, Lot Flannery, who knew how he looked while orating, and dedicated in 1868 on the third anniversary of his death.

Profile Newseum

All the news about the news.

The line of stands by the Pennsylvania Avenue entrance, filled with copies of today's front pages from newspapers around the world, draws passers-by to this museum dedicated to journalism and free speech, which opened in 2008. The museum's mission is further clarified by a huge marble tablet stretching most of the height of the striking, blue-grey rectilinear building, engraved with the words of the First Amendment, guaranteeing free speech.

Visitors first take an escalator down to **concourse level**, where they are drawn to eight large, graffitied sections of the Berlin Wall, displayed along with an East German watchtower. Photos and words tell the story of the Wall, while screens focus on the media: news reporting from East and West Germany, and, in particular, coverage of the Wall and its fall.

One of the world's largest glass hydraulic lifts speeds visitors straight to the **Level 6**, and one of the city's most magnificent panoramas (there's a clear view of the Capitol from the terrace), as well as a display of more than 80 more front pages from around the world. The Covering Katrina exhibit, running until 5 September 2011, explores local and national coverage of the disaster, highlighting the bravery of journalists who risked their lives to report in emergency conditions, and also dealing with moral issues: the issue of taking photographs of people in extremis, for examle, and the dangers of sensationalism.

Level 5 contains a theater with a 90ft screen, showing multiple images of unforgettable news moments. It is also home to the News History exhibition, built around the museum's collection of over 30,000 newspapers, and tracing more than 500 years of news and covering any number of issues – slavery, the Scopes trial

and women's suffrage among them. Also explored here are issues of media bias and credibility, modern phenomena of blogging and 'citizen journalists' and the environment of 24-hour rolling news. The Great Books gallery, meanwhile, features books and documents influential to ideas of press freedom. Touch screens allow visitors to see digital images of pages.

The First Amendment is explored on **Level 4**, through current issues such as prayer in schools as well as historic milestones. Also on this level, the 9/11 Gallery has as its centerpiece the upper section of the antenna mast from the World Trade Center's North Tower. There are 9/12 front pages from all 50 states and many other countries, along with first-person accounts from journalists who covered the story. Also included are pictures by photojournalist William Biggart, taken moments before he was killed when the second tower collapsed.

News in an electronic age is the theme of the Internet, TV & Radio Timeline exhibit on **Level 3**. The timeline traces media milestones, with examples of technology and

photographs from the different eras. Touch screens allow visitors to view and listen to important media moments, such as the 1960 Nixon Kennedy presidential debates and the election of Obama. Coming up to the present, the exhibition looks at the decline of print publications and the role of new media.

The World News Gallery, meanwhile, covers press freedom around the world and highlights hazards faced by journalists. One startling photo depicts photojournalists in the midst of a battle, lying prone on the ground shooting pictures of gunmen, who are shooting their weapons, also lying prone. The Journalists Memorial is a two-story glass structure that includes the names of thousands of journalists who have died reporting the news. More are added every year. Also on this level are two TV control rooms, sometimes used for broadcasts by major networks, when visitors may have the opportuniity to join the audience. At other times there are guided tours.

Things get interactive on **Level Two**, a popular spot for younger visitors. Here you can try reading the news or weather in front of a live camera, and watch your TV performance later (videos can be downloaded at www. newsmuseum.org). Be A Reporter is an animated game

that puts the player in the role of a reporter trying to file a story before deadline. Touch screens in the Ethics Center deal with real ethical questions faced by real journalists, and asks viewers to decide what they would do in similar circumstances.

On **Level 1**, the Pulitzer Prize Photographs Gallery includes every prize-winning entry from 1942 onwards. Over 1,000 images can be viewed through interactive screens. The 535-seat Walter and Leonore Annenberg Theater is the museum's largest, currently showing *I-Witness*, a 4D interactive film that gives viewers an in-the-thick-of-it experience of news events: Isiah Thomas reporting on the Battle of Lexington, Nellie Bly going undercover at an asylum in 1887 and Edward R Murrow broadcasting from London during World War II. Viewers wear 3D glasses; the extra dimension comes from the movement of seats to create motion effects.

At the museum's core is the **Great Hall of News**, a 90-foot atrium that houses some of the biggest artifacts, including the first satellite to send and receive signals simultaneously, thus allowing the first global TV broadcast, as well as a giant media screen, playing reports of historic events, documentaries and breaking news.

TAKE A BREAK
Tucked under the Newseum, Wolfgang Puck's **Source** has a ground-floor lounge (*see p135*) that's ideal for an upscale post-museum drink.

Down the stairs that constitute 4th Street, beside the statue of Chief Justice John Marshall that once graced the Capitol grounds, the **Canadian Embassy** (501 Pennsylvania Avenue, NW) – awarded its prominent site in honor of close bi-national relations – houses a gallery spotlighting Canadian artists. The distinctive and strikingly rectangular **Newseum** rises adjacent on its west side.

Protected by statues of General Meade, victor at Gettysburg, and legal commentator Sir William Blackstone, the US Court House opposite the embassy has gradually lost its 'Watergate Courthouse' identity over the years, as subsequent scandals unfold before interminable grand juries. A new wing to the east has enlivened its appearance.

The **Japanese-American Memorial** at Louisiana and D, NW, honors Americans of Japanese descent interned during World War II, and the Nisei regiments of their sons who fought for the US. An eloquent sculpture depicts traditional Japanese cranes trapped in barbed wire.

Dating from 1876, Washington's first synagogue now houses the **Jewish Historical Society** and its museum.

Jewish Historical Society of Greater Washington

701 Third Street, NW, at G Street (1-202 789 0900, www.jhsgw.org). Judiciary Square Metro. **Open** 1-4pm Mon, Tue, Thur; for admission, call or ring bell at office, 701 4th Street, Suite 200. **Admission** suggested donation $5. **Credit** MC, V. **Map** p253 K6.

Exhibits of local Jewish history organized by the Jewish Historical Society occupy the ground floor of this now-landmarked former synagogue – the oldest in Washington. Built in 1876 of red brick, the structure was adopted by the society in 1960; its sanctuary was restored in the 1970s, preserving the original ark, pine benches, and slender columns that support the women's balcony.

National Building Museum

401 F Street, NW, between 4th & 5th Streets (1-202 272 2448, www.nbm.org). Judiciary Square Metro. **Open** 10am-5pm Mon-Sat; 11am-5pm Sun. **Admission** suggested donation $5; *LEGO Exhibition* (until 15 Sept 2011) $5. **Credit** AmEx, MC, V. **Map** p253 J6.

A privately run collection, the National Building Museum produces smart, noteworthy exhibits focusing on architects and the built environment, both contemporary and historical. However, the main attraction is without doubt the building's Italian Renaissance-style Great Hall, with its central fountain and eight colossal 75ft-high Corinthian columns: visitors crane their necks for a vertiginous look at the ceiling 15 storys above. The red-brick building,

designed as the US Pension Building, was completed in 1887. Cityscapes Revealed, an ongoing exhibition, uses items from the museum's permanent collection to highlight architectural styles and materials that defined urban America from the end of the 19th through the first half of the 20th centuries. Washington: Symbol and City examines how residents experience the city and the tension between DC's roles as working seat of government, national symbol and residential city. The museum shop offers the quirkiest museum buys in town, with all manner of gadgets and gizmos up for grabs.

★ Newseum

555 Pennsylvania Avenue, at 6th Street, NW (1-888 639 7386, www.newseum.org). Archives-Navy Memorial Metro. **Open** 9am-5pm daily. **Admission** $19.95; $12.95-$17.95 reductions; free under-6s. **Map** p253 J6. *See p74* **Profile**.

DUPONT CIRCLE

Dupont Circle is perhaps one of the most cosmopolitan DC neighborhoods, its bars and restaurants drawing a diverse public. The circle itself is a popular green space, with a collection of chess tables in constant use. A central marble fountain sprays into the air in honor of Civil War admiral Samuel Francis Dupont. In the late 19th century, mansions began sprouting in what had been a backwater to accommodate arriviste millionaires, in time morphing into Embassy Row. The area was a countercultural hotbed in the 1960s, when anti-Vietnam War and Black Power activists claimed the circle for demonstrations.

Today, though, the neighborhood has hit the mainstream. Chain stores have infiltrated Connecticut Avenue, but enough idiosyncratic bookstores and bistros and galleries (sporting open-house receptions every first Friday evening) survive to reward a wander.

Large hotels and apartment buildings start to dominate the landscape about four blocks north, heading towards Adams Morgan (*see p78*). The pavement outside the Washington Hilton on the corner of Connecticut Avenue and T Street was the site of John Hinckley's attempted assassination of President Reagan in 1981.

Off Connecticut Avenue, the blocks north of the circle consist largely of well-kept Edwardian rowhouses, art galleries and gorgeous mansions now occupied by embassies or non-profit associations. If the weather is fine, amble northwards through the blocks west of Connecticut Avenue – known as Kalorama – to check out the impressive architecture and exhibitions. The galleries display contemporary, experimental and traditional art, from painting to sculpture to photography. At the heart of them all is the **Phillips Collection**, opened in 1921 as the first permanent museum of modern art in America. For more information on other galleries, *see p178*.

Massachusetts Avenue, from Scott Circle, east of Dupont Circle, through to Upper Northwest (*see p80*) is known as 'Embassy Row'. For a cheap tour, catch any westbound 'N' Metrobus at Dupont Circle and cruise past the mosque established for diplomats in the 1950s (No.2551, at Belmont Road, Kalorama), the embassies of Turkey, the Netherlands, Brazil, the Vatican, and others. Further on, into Upper Northwest, the British Embassy (No.3100) sports a statue of Churchill, with one foot on British soil (all embassies are deemed their nations' territory) and the other on American, reflecting his ancestry. The US confiscated the former Iranian Embassy across the way following the seizure of the American Embassy in Tehran and the holding of its staff hostage in 1979, only to rent it out for extremely expensive parties and wedding receptions. Lots of embassies open their doors for concerts, art displays and charity events (see www.embassyseries.org).

Foreign heroes patrol this strand: there's a statue of Gandhi at 21st Street, near the Indian Embassy; Czechoslovakian leader Masaryk adorns 22nd Street; and, further north, political martyr Robert Emmet gazes toward the Irish Embassy from the 2200 block. At the Norwegian Embassy (2720 34th Street, NW), in 2005, King Harald V dedicated a statue of his mother, Crown Princess Märtha, who stayed at the White House with the Roosevelts after the Nazis overran her country in 1940.

★ Phillips Collection

1600 21st Street, NW, at Q Street (1-202 387 2151, www.phillipscollection.org). Dupont Circle Metro. **Open** 10am-5pm Tue, Wed, Fri, Sat; 10am-8.30pm Thur; 11am-6pm Sun. **Admission** *Sat, Sun & special exhibitions* $12; $10 reductions; free under-18s. If no special exhibitions in progress $10; $8 reductions. **Mon-Fri** (permanent collection only) free; donations encouraged. **Credit** AmEx, MC, V. **Map** p282 G4.

This mansion was opened as a gallery in the 1920s by Marjorie and Duncan Phillips as a memorial to his father. The building was remodeled in the 1960s and underwent further renovation in the '80s, when an extension increased its space by almost 20,000sq ft. In 2006, the museum unveiled its Sant Building, another expansion project that added airy galleries for modern art, an outdoor sculpture terrace and café, an art and technology laboratory and an auditorium. The museum's signature painting, Renoir's *Luncheon of the Boating Party*, enjoys pride of place in the permanent collection galleries. There, significant Van Gogh oils rub shoulders with Steiglitz prints and a solid selection of lesser-known works by Picasso,

Bacon, Vuillard and Rothko – that is, if a travelling show hasn't deposed them temporarily. The historical surveys and one-person shows held here tend to be crowd-pleasers – Impressionists and 20th-century photography, say – or scholarly efforts examining the likes of Hiroshige and Paul Klee.

Society of the Cincinnati, Anderson House Museum

2118 Massachusetts Avenue, NW, at 21st Street (1-202 785 2040, www.societyofthecincinnati.org). Dupont Circle Metro. **Open** *Guided tours* 1.15pm, 2.15pm, 3.15pm Tue-Sat. **Admission** free. **Map** p282 G4.

Practically unknown to most Washingtonians, this museum, the former residence of American diplomat Larz Anderson III and his wife Isabel, contains works acquired on the couple's many trips to Asia and Europe. Anderson, a direct descendant of a founding member of the Society of the Cincinnati, bequeathed his house to that organization, which was formed just after the American Revolution with the aim of sharing wealth among bereft army veterans who had fought for independence (the group included Founding Father George Washington). In 1902, the Andersons hired Boston architectural firm Arthur Little and Herbert Browne to construct the limestone Beaux Arts mansion, and imported Italian artisans to carve and inlay wood and gilt floors and ceilings. Downstairs, one room is devoted to an exhibition about the American Revolution; another is devoted to the history of the Cincinnati Society. Rooms on the first and second floors house the Anderson Collection, whose treasures include numerous bejewelled Chinese semi-precious stone and jade trees and Flemish Renaissance tapestries dating from the late 16th and early 17th centuries.

▶ *Tapestries depicting the biblical battle of David and Goliath that once hung in the ballroom at the Anderson House were donated to Washington National Cathedral (see p82). They can be seen today in St Mary's Chapel.*

Textile Museum

2320 S Street, NW, between 23rd & 24th Streets (1-202 667 0441, www.textilemuseum.org). Dupont Circle Metro. **Open** 10am-5pm Mon-Sat; 1-5pm Sun. **Admission** suggested donation $5. **Credit** AmEx, MC, V. **Map** p282 F4.

SIGHTS

A modest collection nestled amid regal townhouses, the Textile Museum has two permanent exhibitions: the Textile Learning Center describes the history and procedures of textile production, while the Collections Gallery rotates selections of historic rugs and textiles. The recent exhibition, Colors of the Oasis: Central Asian Ikats, featured colorful yet harmonious work, in stunning patterns, from Central Asian weavers. On Saturdays the museum hosts textile and rug appreciation mornings.

ADAMS MORGAN

To the east of Dupont Circle, 18th Street becomes the main strip of lively Adams Morgan some nine walkable blocks north, known for its ethnic restaurants and diversity. Streetlife started out as leisurely Latino, with Africans and others livening the mix today. The pace picks up at night, when 18th Street (up to and including the spots along Columbia Road, which intersects 18th Street at the top of the hill) morphs into a big bar and dining scene. The bars range from flat-out frat-boy hangouts to salsa and reggae clubs, and on warm summer evenings outdoor cafés pack in customers while the streets pack automobiles in futile late-night quests for parking spaces.

Adams Morgan got its name in the 1950s, when progressive-minded residents opted to integrate the white Adams school with the black Morgan school. One place in Adams Morgan that is always lively during the day is **Malcolm X Park** – officially Meridian Hill Park (bordered by 16th, Euclid, 15th and W Streets, NW).

SHAW

Bounded by North Capitol Street and 16th Street on the east and west, and by Irving Street and M Street to the north and south, Shaw embraces historic neighborhoods, including Howard University, the U Street Corridor and Logan Circle. All were bastions of African American DC, fostering black businesses, churches and scholarship during the decades of racial segregation. Today Shaw has bounced back from long decline, exacerbated by the disastrous 1968 riots (see p25).

U Street/14th Street Corridor

Once known as America's 'Black Broadway', U Street has been reborn as a centre of commerce, restaurants and nightlife, surrounded by rowhouses that have become magnets for the city's hipsters. The neighborhood is bisected by 14th Street, and the area around where the two intersect is perhaps the hottest spot or all.

Anchored by **Howard University**, the neighborhood became the hub of African

American culture. Poet Langston Hughes and jazz great Duke Ellington matured here. Along with Ella Fitzgerald, Nat King Cole and Redd Fo, they made 'You' Street world-famous. During the 1930s, 'Black Broadway' was a cultural powerhouse.

Restaurant, café and art space **Busboys & Poets** (1390 V Street, NW, see p128) represents the new U Street; its old-school neighbor is **Ben's Chili Bowl** (see p128), on U Street between 12th and 13th Streets, a restaurant frequented by celebs such as Bill Cosby and ex-mayor Marion Barry, famous for its chili dogs and energy. The **Lincoln Theatre** (see p70), next door, was once a grand stage for black performances in the age of segregation. At the U Street-Cardozo Metro station is an **African-American Civil War Memorial**. Nearby, on 14th Street, aside from a couple of swanky lounges, the main attraction is music space the **Black Cat** (see p186). For more on U Street's attractions, see right U **Street Highlights**.

Howard University

2400 6th Street, NW, at Howard Place (1-202 806 6100, www.howard.edu). Shaw-Howard University Metro then 70, 71 bus. **Map** p283 J2. With a hall of fame that includes former mayors and Supreme Court justices, Howard University has a legacy to brag about. It was chartered in 1867 as a theological seminary to train black ministers to teach slaves emancipated by the Civil War. By 1940, half of African Americans in college studied here, including much of the leadership that planned the legal assault on Jim Crow segregation. Howard holds some of the best collections on African history and art in the country at the Howard University Museum on the first floor of the Founders Library.

MOUNT PLEASANT/ COLUMBIA HEIGHTS

Columbia Heights has become a hot neighborhood in recent years. It's home to the **GALA Hispanic Theatre** (see p208), which moved into what had been the old Tivoli Theatre in 2005, along with bars, restaurants and a young population of gentrifiers who have made their mark on an area that has traditionally had a large Latino population.

GEORGETOWN

George, Maryland, was laid out in 1751 and variously tried to unite with Washington City (1857) and secede from the District (often). Losing its separate government in 1871, Georgetown drew the line at its proposed designation as 'West Washington'. Today's Georgetown is unlike the rest of the city, with tranquil residential streets lined with historic homes, and haughty boutiques.

U Street Highlights

This street is back where it belongs, as a center of eating and entertainment.

Known during the Jazz Age of the 1930s as DC's Black Broadway, U Street hosted Duke Ellington, Ella Fitzgerald, and other greats. The neighborhood bustled with nightclubs, restaurants, and black-owned businesses until the 1968 riots, which began at the corner of 14th and U Street after the news reached Washington that Martin Luther King Jr had been shot.

The riots hastened the decline of the old U Street, and the area languished for many years, with empty storefronts and high crime. Thankfully, it has since come back to life as a nightlife corridor for a diverse group of diners, drinkers and partyers.These days, it seems a new business opens along the stretch between 9th Street and 16th Street nearly every week.

Along with the nearby Logan Circle neighborhood, U Street is the best part of the city for music. The **9:30 Club** (*see p186*) is Washington's top rock venue, with concerts that sell out nearly every night. But smaller clubs like **Twins Jazz** (*see p189*), **Velvet Lounge** (*see p189*), and the new **U Street Music Hall** (*see p196*) bring in good performers, too. And it's not unusual to find a jazz trio playing at one of the low-key bars along this stretch.

The other establishments are an interesting mix. At the high end, there are places like the **Gibson** (*see p141*),

a speakeasy-style bar with dark wood paneling, flickering candlelight, and $17 cocktails; and **Tabaq Bistro** (*see p129*), a restaurant/bar in a glassed-in roof terrace with phenomenal views. At the lower end, places like **Oohhs & Aahhs (**1005 U Street, NW, 1-202 667 7142, www.oohhsn aahhs.com), a no-frills soul-food joint that serves crispy fried chicken and creamy macaroni and cheese joins the legendary **Ben's Chili Bowl** (*see p128*), a 50-year-old landmark beloved for late-night chili cheese fries and its trademark half-smoke sausages.

U Street is fun during the daytime, too. For shoppers, there are funky furniture stores and chic boutiques. **Millennium Decorative Arts** (1528 U Street, NW, 202-483-1218, www.millenniumdecorative arts.com) sells unusual antiques, and **Rckcndy** (1515 U Street, NW, 1-202 332 5639, www.rckndy.com) has stylish modern decorations. **Caramel** (1603 U Street, NW, 1-202 265-1930, http://caramelfashion. com . **Lettie Gooch Boutique** (1517 U Street, NW, 1-202 332 4242, www.lettie gooch.com) are good bets for stylish women's clothes. For an afternoon break, stop in at **Love Café** (1501 U Street, NW, 1-202 265-9800, http://lovecafe. cakelove.com) for a cupcake, or at the always buzzing **Busboys and Poets** (*see p128*) for coffee and a snack.

Its physical division from the rest of the District by Rock Creek – and lack of Metro coverage – enhances its insularity.

At the upriver limit of navigation for ocean vessels, the town started life as a colonial tobacco port. Oxen pulled huge cylinders of 'sot weed' down its 'rolling road', now Wisconsin Avenue. Construction on the **C&O Canal**, running 185 miles from the Potomac to Cumberland, Maryland, began in 1828. The towpath makes a pleasant walk. From the mid 1800s, black Georgetown thrived south of P Street between Rock Creek and 31st Street. Some 1,000 African-American families slept here at night, working by day as cooks, domestics and stable boys. Although it's hard to fathom now, Georgetown was dwindling into slumishness by the 1930s. Then, a 'colonial revival' made old homes fashionable again. Many of FDR's New Dealers moved in amid the multi-generation 'cave dwellers', turning Georgetown into a chic address; JFK's 'New Frontiersmen' finished the transformation. **Georgetown University** is an academically rigorous institution; its students populate the nightlife throngs.

The intersecting shopping strips are M Street and Wisconsin Avenue. The sidewalks are crowded at weekends with people throwing money around at the chic clothing stores. Built by cabinet-maker Christopher Layman in 1765, the **Old Stone House** (3051 M Street, NW, 1-202 426 6851, www.nps.gov/olst/index.htm, usually open noon-5pm daily) is the oldest home in DC, its garden offering repose to the weary consumer. The garden is open during daylight hours and is accessible through the gate on M Street.

Stately **Tudor Place** (1644 31st Street, NW) rests serenely isolated on extensive grounds, while **Dumbarton Oaks** is home to a first-class collection of Byzantine and pre-Columbian art. Landscape architect Beatrix Farrand designed its celebrated formal gardens.

At night Georgetown jumps with dozens of bars and restaurants filled with suburban twentysomethings and international glitterati. In the summer, garish **Washington Harbour**, at the southern end of Wisconsin Avenue on the Potomac River, is overrun with people looking to eat, drink and flirt. The restaurants are forgettable and the drinks overpriced, but breezes off the Potomac make the promenade a nice stroll. Just west of here, Jack's Boathouse (*see p197*) still rents out canoes to enable aquatic sightseeing.

Georgetown University

37th & O Streets, NW (1-202 687 0100, www.georgetown.edu). Dupont Circle Metro then G2 bus, Foggy Bottom-GWU Metro then 30, 32, 34, 35, 36, 38B bus or Circulator bus. **Map** p281 D4.

A Jesuit institution founded in 1789 by John Carroll, first Catholic bishop in the United States. Alumni fought on both sides in the Civil War, inspiring the school colors, blue and gray. Equally polarising alumni of more recent vintage include Bill Clinton and pundit Pat Buchanan. Georgetown Law School across town is highly ranked; the School of Foreign Service draws top geopolitical junkies.

Upper Northwest

The affluent sector north of Georgetown is often referred to as 'West of the Park', the park being the extensive, leafy landscape of **Rock Creek Park**. It is home to some of the city's wealthiest residents. Massive homes and posh boutiques stack up, one after another, on streets such as Foxhall Road and upper Wisconsin Avenue.

Washington National Cathedral is the second-largest place of worship in the US. On the cathedral grounds are two selective prep schools favored by the children of the elite: St Alban's and National Cathedral School. Beyond lies another, Sidwell Friends. Nearby are the **Khalil Gibran Peace Garden** and the **US Naval Observatory** (3450 Massachusetts Avenue, NW, 1-202 762 1467), housing the official residence of the vice-president. Its first occupant, multimillionaire Nelson Rockefeller, reportedly found the mansion too small.

Dumbarton Oaks Research Library & Collections

1703 32nd Street, NW, between R & S Streets, Georgetown (1-202 339 6401, www.doaks.org). Bus 30, 32, 34, 36. **Open** *Museum* 2-5pm Tue-Sun. *Gardens* mid Mar-Oct 2-6pm Tue-Sun. Nov-mid Mar 2-5pm Tue-Sun. **Admission** *Museum* free. *Gardens* $8; $5 reductions. **No credit cards**. **Map** p249 E4.

Wealthy art connoisseurs Mildred and Robert Woods Bliss purchased the 19th-century Federal-style brick mansion Dumbarton Oaks in 1920. In 1940, they commissioned architects McKim, Mead and White to build an extension, which they filled with their modest-sized collection of Byzantine art. The array of portable, sumptuous Byzantine objects, including rare sixth-century ecclesiastical silver, is one of the world's finest. That same year the Blisses gave the property, collections and a newly endowed research library to Harvard University.

In 1963, the octagonal Philip Johnson-designed wing was completed; today it houses the pre-Columbian collection in galleries encircling a central fountain. Unmissable exhibits here include a miraculously preserved Peruvian burial mantle from 400 BC and the grotesque 'Head of a Maize God', originally crafted in AD 775 for a Honduran

Walk Georgetown

Affluent and distinctive, Georgetown is a different Washington.

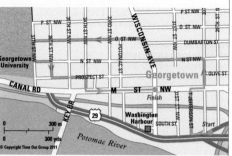

Starting the walk where Rock Creek flows into the Potomac, note the new House of Sweden, a unique embassy/trade office/condo at 2900 K Street, NW. A detour north on 30th Street leads to the C&O Canal visitor centre, embarkation point for leisurely mule-drawn barge-rides evoking early trade. An inviting towpath parallels the Potomac, although beware how far you go: it runs 186 miles west to Cumberland, Maryland.

Back on K Street, a turn north on Thomas Jefferson Street leads to the **Old Stone House** (*see left*), Georgetown's earliest, a modest home that dates from 1768. A right turn down M Street leads past historically plaqued buildings to the Thomas Sim Lee corner, which was Georgetown's original boundary.

A block north is the 3000 block of N Street, NW. Jacqueline Kennedy lived in the 1794 mansion at 3017 for a year after her husband's assassination.

Crossing Georgetown's shopping and bar-hopping throughfare, Wisconsin Avenue, at N Street, one finds Martin's Tavern thriving as it did when Jack Kennedy (by some accounts) proposed to Jackie in Booth #3. They lived down the street at 3307 when he was elected president. (JFK junkies can obtain a self-guided tour called 'The Kennedys' Georgetown' at www.georgetowndc.com.)

Ascending to O Street in search of other glam couples, one encounters antiquated cobblestones and streetcar tracks as well as the **Bodisco House** (3322 O Street, NW), home of the fiftysomething Russian ambassador who in 1840 married a local 16-year-old, the lovebirds being dubbed Beauty and the Beast. Now it is the home of sometime Democratic presidential candidate John Kerry, the wealthiest member of the US Senate through his ketchup-heiress spouse, Teresa Heinz Kerry.

Straight ahead looms **Georgetown University**, dominated by the distinctive neo-Gothic Healy Hall (1877). Founded in 1789, Georgetown is the nation's oldest Catholic and Jesuit college and one of America's hottest universities. If the

gatehouse information booth isn't open, any student can point you to Loyola Hall, where Bill Clinton '68 once bunked.

A turn down 37th Street passes **Holy Trinity Church**, where JFK last attended mass before his assassination. A left turn down N Street passes the renowned Georgetown School of Foreign Service, its building betraying its origins as the original university hospital. Nearby you'll find Georgetown's most iconic image: a turn down 36th Street dead-ends at Prospect Street, where a turn to the left in the 3500 block leads past the homes and the steep stairs immortalised on film in *The Exorcist*. Descend them if you dare. Note that the houses are considerably further from the steps than Hollywood magic placed them.

Passing the massive car-barn building, cross M Street at 34th Street to Francis Scott Key Park, flying a fifteen-star flag to honour the author of America's national anthem, 'The Star-Spangled Banner' (1814). Plaques here display Key's history, and that of the neighborhood. Key's home was torn down to build the western access loop to the bridge named for him, which at least affords splendid views of the river.

A stroll east down M Street – Georgetown's other commercial corridor – approaches the area's heart, the intersection of Wisconsin and M Streets, NW. Dean & Deluca gourmet grocery (3276 M Street, NW) occupies the old **Georgetown Market House** (1865), which spanned the Canal until raised 15 feet to its present site by mule-power in 1871. Nearby, Georgetown Park has imaginatively transformed a sprawling transit facility into an inviting shopping mall.

temple. The House Collection, principally in the Music Room, has tapestries, sculpture and paintings dating from the 15th to 19th centuries, with highlights including El Greco's *Visitation*. The 16 acres of flora-filled formal gardens skirting the mansion, the creation of Beatrix Farrand, are also open to the public and worth a wander.

Katzen Arts Center at American University

4400 Massachusetts Avenue, NW, at Nebraska Avenue (1-202 885 1300, www.american.edu/museum). Tenleytown-AU Metro then N2, M4 bus or Friendship Heights Metro then N3, N4, N6, N8 bus. **Open** *Museum* 11am-4pm Tue-Thur; 11am-7pm Fri, Sat; noon-4pm Sun. **Admission** free.

This 36,000sq ft public museum and sculpture garden is devoted to special exhibitions of contemporary art and student shows from the University's art department. Check the museum website for up-to-date listings.

▶ *For more on the museum, see p180.*

Kreeger Museum

2401 Foxhall Road, NW, between Dexter & W Streets (1-202 337 3050, reservations 1-202 338 3552, www.kreegermuseum.org). D6 bus. **Open** 10am-4pm Sat. *Guided tours* 10.30am, noon, 2pm. Open for guided tours only (must be booked in advance) 10.30am, 1.30pm Tue-Fri. **Admission** $10; $7 reductions. **Credit** AmEx, MC, V. **Map** p248 C3.

This intimate museum, housed in a spectacular 1967 Philip Johnson-designed travertine home nestled in woods, is best visited on one of its small, 90-minute guided tours. Alternatively, visitors may stop in during the day on Saturday. Either way, it's worth it: The late insurance magnate David Lloyd Kreeger and his wife Carmen amassed a small but striking collection of 180 works by 19th- and 20th-century heavyweights. The museum's scale allows visitors to savor the details of works by Kandinsky, Chagall, Stella and Braque; two rooms showcase Monet's cliffside landscapes. The Kreegers also collected African ceremonial art, and their outdoor sculpture terrace overlooking verdant woodland has bronzes by Henry Moore, Jean Arp and Aristide Maillol. An annual special exhibition augments permanent collection gems. Public transport doesn't take you very close to the museum; it's probably easier to take a cab. See the website for details of Open House events.

National Museum of Health & Medicine

6900 Georgia Avenue, NW, at Elder Street (1-202 782 2200, http://nmhm.washingtondc.museum). Silver Spring Metro then 70, 71 bus, Takoma Park Metro then 52, 53, 54, K2 bus. **Open** 10am-5.30pm daily. **Admission** free.

There's an emphasis on military medicine at this museum at the Walter Reed Army Medical Center.

The memorable exhibit on medicine during the Civil War includes the bullet that killed Abraham Lincoln, as well as a detailed account of Major General Daniel Sickles' annual visits to his formaldehyde-preserved amputated leg (lost during the Battle of Gettysburg). Elsewhere there is a section on battlefield surgery from the Civil War to Vietnam, while recent exhibit Trauma Bay II, Balad, Iraq offers a view inside a former Air Force tent hospital. More general exhibits focus on the evolution of the microscope, along with a presentation of various anatomical and pathological specimens, assembled from museum collections dating back more than 100 years. Although a visit will prove more informative than stomach-churning, it's probably best not to head out for dinner immediately afterwards.

Rock Creek Park

1-202 895 6070, www.nps.gov/rocr. **Open** *Park* dawn-dusk daily. *Nature Center & Planetarium* 9am-5pm Wed-Sun. **Map** p249 F3.

Nestled between sprawling condo corridors and busy commercial strips lie 1,750 acres of forest called Rock Creek Park, following that stream all the way to the city line to join an extension into Maryland. One of the largest such preserves in the nation, its 29 miles of hiking trails and ten miles of bridle paths intersect a net of bicycle paths. At weekends, several park roads close to motor vehicles. Its central thoroughfare, Beach Drive, a major commuter cut during weekday rush hour, is a quiet route to picnic groves (some with barbecue facilities) and playing fields at other times.

The park is a magnet for wildlife, its deer population swollen to nuisance levels. The Nature Center just off Military Road details its history and ecology, offering daily nature walks and similar events. The planetarium offers free star-gazing sessions from April to November. Staff also provide directions to the attractions concealed in the foliage, including a golf course, walking and biking trails, even the remains of Civil War fortifications. Birders flock to Picnic Groves 17 and 18 just south, prime perches from which to observe the warblers migrating during the spring and autumn, DC being fortuitously situated on the 'Eastern Flyway' migration route. The District's only public riding stable, sharing the Nature Center parking lot, offers guided trail rides through the hilly terrain. East lies Carter Barron Amphitheatre, which stages low-cost summertime shows, from free Shakespeare in the Park productions to R&B and gospel concerts. Nearby FitzGerald centre hosts major tennis competitions.

▶ *For more on Rock Creek's sporting facilities, see p199.*

Washington National Cathedral

Massachusetts & Wisconsin Avenues, NW (1-202 537 6200, www.cathedral.org/cathedral). Bus 30, 32, 34, 35, 36, 90, 92, 93, N2, N3, N4, N6 bus.

Open *Sept-May* 10am-5.30pm Mon-Fri; 10am-4.30pm Sat; 8am-6.30pm Sun. *June-Aug* 10am-8pm Mon-Fri; 10am-4.30pm Sat; 8am-6.30pm Sun. **Admission** free; suggested donation $3. **Credit** AmEx, Disc, MC, V. **Map** p249 E2.

Washington National Cathedral was built in 14th-century Gothic style, stone upon stone, without structural steel, an exercise that took most of the 20th century and was only finished in 1990. Its medievalism has been somewhat updated: there's a gargoyle of Darth Vader in the north-west corner, while the much-admired stained-glass Space Window contains a piece of lunar rock. The top of the tower is the highest point in DC; there are great views from the observation gallery.

The cathedral offers self-paced CD-based audio tours ($5); alternatively, join one of various guided tours, which are held at regular intervals. Special events can often mean that certain parts of the cathedral are closed at short notice, so it's best to phone first to check (the same applies if you have a specific tour in mind).

The Episcopalian cathedral holds some 1,200 services a year, yet has no congregation of its own. It is meant to be a church for all. Every president since Theodore Roosevelt has visited, as have Martin Luther King Jr and the Dalai Lama. Funeral services of various distinguished national figures have been held here. Medieval gardens appropriately adorn the cathedral's spacious grounds, supporting a popular herb shop.

WOODLEY PARK

East towards Connecticut Avenue before Rock Creek Park, Woodley Park is a small but bustling neighborhood featuring upscale homes, varied restaurants and the **National Zoo**.

★ National Zoo

3001 block of Connecticut Avenue, NW, at Rock Creek Park (1-202 673 4800, www.natzoo.si.edu). Woodley Park-Zoo/Adams Morgan Metro. **Open** *Apr-Oct* 10am-6pm daily. *Nov-Mar* 10am-4.30pm daily. **Admission** free. **Map** p249 F2.

The free-admission National Zoo offers a diverting escape. Particularly during the off-season, when the paths are not cluttered by pushchairs, the zoo offers a perfect (albeit hilly) stroll, away from the bustle of Connecticut Avenue. Tree-shaded paths wind

through the margins past the various animals. The stars are two pandas, Mei Xiang and Tian Tian, brought on ten-year loan from China in 2001; their cub Tai Shan was returned to China in 2010. The panda habitat is part of the Asia Trail, which links the habitats of sloth bears, fishing cats, red pandas, clouded leopards, Asian small-clawed otters and a Japanese giant salamander. The zoo is in the process of building a new environment for Asian elephants as part of its effort to preserve these endangered animals. The first phase of Elephant Trails is now open; the new home includes two acres of outdoor space and the Elephant Exercise Trek, which takes the elephants uphill along a wooded track.

CLEVELAND PARK

Further north is Cleveland Park, an affluent enclave sited on the farm where in 1886 President Cleveland and his gorgeous 21-year-old bride preferred to live rather than the White House. It boasts a mix of restaurants and the AMC Loews Uptown (*see p173*), a premier venue with a gigantic screen and comfy seats.

North of Cleveland Park is **Hillwood Museum & Gardens**, with late socialite Marjorie Merriweather Post's remarkable collection of Russian objets d'art and serene Japanese landscaping.

Hillwood Museum & Gardens

4155 Linnean Avenue, NW, between Tilden & Upton Streets (1-202 686 8500, reservations 1-202 686 5807, www.hillwoodmuseum.org). Van Ness-UDC Metro. **Open** 10am-5pm Tue-Sat (reservations required). Also occasional Sun, check website for details. Closed Jan. *Guided tours* 11.30am, 1.30pm Tue-Sat. **Admission** suggested donation $12; $7-$10 reductions; $5 under-18s. **Credit** AmEx, MC, V.

It's not for nothing that it's known as a museum and a garden: the grounds are as much a reason as the collection of Russian art for making the trek from Downtown to this quiet, residential neighborhood. The house and garden were purchased by cereal heiress Marjorie Merriweather Post in 1955 to house her collection of French and Russian decorative art. Seduced by Russian culture after living there for 18 months in the 1930s, Post amassed the largest collection of imperial Russian art objects outside that country. Portraits of tsars and tsarinas, palace furnishings and a porcelain service commissioned by Catherine the Great are displayed in Hillwood's gilt and wood-paneled rooms. The French collection includes Sèvres porcelain, 18th-century furniture and Beauvais tapestries.

Visitors can also roam the 12-acre manicured grounds, including a Japanese-style garden with plunging waterfall. Guided evening tours, when offered, are not to be missed: the waning light makes for romantic strolls in the gardens.

Northeast

Washington was never known for industry. Today, its minimal manufacturing and warehouse area, mostly along New York Avenue, NE, is sprouting high-tech businesses.

A couple of blocks east of the Supreme Court is the **Frederick Douglass Museum** (316 A Street, NE, 1-202 547 4273), early residence of the famous abolitionist, now housing the Caring Foundation, celebrating worthy philanthropists but maintaining one room as it was in Douglass's time. It is open for guided tours by arrangement. Constantino Brumidi, the artist who painted the frescos in the Capitol, lived nearby, at 326 A Street.

To the north, the **Catholic University of America** (620 Michigan Avenue, NE) is a pontifical institution known for its drama

A Taste of H Street

Eastern promise.

Until recently, Washington's H Street, NE, corridor was a rundown stretch of road still scarred by the 1968 riots, in which many of the storefronts here burned down. It remains rough around the edges, but H Street is gentrifying rapidly and the area towards the intersection with Florida and Maryland Avenues now vies for the title of DC's most vibrant nightlife strip. Revelers here tend to be more casual than those on U Street, and they're generally older than the early-twentysomethings who flock to 18th Street in Adams Morgan.

Among the businesses that have opened in recent years are a slew of fun bars, each with its own personality. The **Rock & Roll Hotel** (*see p188*) – which is a bar/music venue, not an actual hotel – has live bands and DJs. Next door **Biergarten Haus** (No.1355, 1-202 388-4053,

http://biergartenhaus.com) is a Bavarian-style beer hall with one-liter pours. A couple of blocks west, **Little Miss Whiskey's Golden Dollar** (No.1104, 1-202 555 1212, www.littlemisswhiskeys.com) is popular for its dance parties. The **H Street Country Club** (No.1335, 1-202 399 4722, www.thehstreetcountryclub.com), meanwhile, is a bar with a difference: it has an indoor miniature-golf course where drinkers can putt around tiny versions of Washington landmarks.

Probably the zaniest act on the strip, the vaudevillian Palace of Wonders, has recently joined forces (and buildings) with the Red & the Black to emerge as **Red Palace** (pictured, *see p188*). You'll still find burlesque, but the focus is on music too.

Some good restaurants have settled into the street, too, including **Granville Moore's**

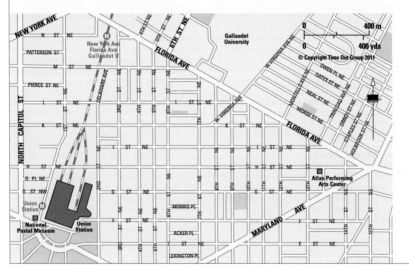

department (its members perform at the university's **Hartke Theatre**). Adjoining the university is the **National Shrine of the Immaculate Conception** (400 Michigan Avenue, NE, 1-202 526 8300). Begun in 1914 in a Byzantine style rarely seen in US Catholic churches, it was only completed in 1959.

Across Harewood Road at No.4250 gleam the traditional golden domes of the **Ukrainian Catholic National Shrine of the Holy**

(No.1238, 1-202 399 2546, www. granvillemoores.com), a snug Belgain place known for its mussels and frites; and **Sticky Rice** (No.1224, 1-202 397 7655, www.stickyricedc.com), a hip Asian bar and restaurant. Mention should also be given to **Ethiopic** (No.401, 1-202 675 2066, www.ethiopicrestaurant.com), slightly off the main drag at the Union Station end of H Street, between 4th and 5th Streets, thought by many to be DC's best Ethiopian restaurant.

For dessert, there's **Dangerously Delicious Pies** (No.1339, 1-202 398 7437, www.dangerouspiesdc.com). The owner used to play in a rock band, and along with tasty pies (there are savory ones too), the place has that little touch of edge that defines this neighborhood.

Plans are under way for a streetcar line that will connect H Street to downtown DC. In the meantime, it's accessible by bus from the Union Station or New York Avenue Metro stations.

Family (1-202 526 3737). Downhill is the ambitious **Pope John Paul II Cultural Center** (3900 Harewood Road, NE, 1-202 635 5400), displaying mementos of the late pontiff and interactive exhibits about his spiritual and worldly concerns.

Across North Capitol Street is the leafy campus of the **Armed Forces Retirement Home**, founded as the Soldiers' Home with Mexican War tribute. On its grounds, **President Lincoln's Cottage**, the 34-room Gothic Revival house that Lincoln used as his retreat, is to open to the public for guided tours (1-202 829 0436, www.lincolncottage.org, Visitor Center open 9.30am-4.30pm Mon-Sat, 11.30am-5.30pm Sun, tours on the hour, 10am-3pm Mon-Sat, noon-4pm Sun). Access to the house is from the Eagle Gate entrance on the corner of Rock Creek Church Road, NW, and Upshur Street, NW.

The **Franciscan Monastery** (1400 Quincy Street, NE, 1-202 526 6800, www.myfranciscan. org) has a glorious mixture of influences: the church is modeled on Hagia Sophia in Istanbul, while beneath is a replica of the catacombs of Rome; the splendid garden's meandering paths connect replicas of religious sites.

Along the west bank of the Anacostia, DC's previously neglected river now enjoying ecological restoration, is the **United States National Arboretum**, a 440-acre enclave containing both local and exotic foliage. Near the arboretum is **Mount Olivet Cemetery** (1300 Bladensburg Road, NE, between Montana Avenue & Mount Olivet Road, 1-202 399 3000), final resting place of White House architect James Hoban and of Mary Suratt, who was hanged for her alleged role in Lincoln's assassination. On the New York Avenue side of the arboretum, one brick kiln stands as a reminder of the brickyards that constituted Northeast's first major industry. Anacostia Park follows the river's east bank and contains **Kenilworth Aquatic Gardens**. Although located near a highway that shares its name, the gardens are a quiet retreat full of aquatic plants, including lilies and lotuses. Now that the Anacostia is getting cleaner, this area attracts all sorts of reptiles, amphibians and water-loving mammals.

In the south of the area, bordering on Capitol Hill, **H Street, NE**, has undergone a radical revival following decades of decline in the wake of destruction in the 1968 riots that followed the assassination of Martin Luther King. H Street and Florida Avenue near its intersection with H Street are now home to bars, art galleries and performance spaces, including the **Atlas Performing Arts Center** (*see p192*) and the **H Street Playhouse** (*see p208*). For more on H Street's attractions, *see left* **A Taste of H Street**.

SIGHTS

Kenilworth Aquatic Gardens

Anacostia Avenue & Douglas Street, NE, at Quarles Street (1-202 426 6905, www.nps.gov/ keaq/index.htm). Deanwood Metro. **Open** 7am-4pm daily. **Admission** free.

Kenilworth Aquatic Gardens is a 12-acre garden with a network of ponds displaying a variety of aquatic plants. A one-armed Civil War veteran started water gardening here as a hobby in 1880; then, in the 1920s, the public – and President Coolidge – began to visit for a stroll. On the northern boundary, a path leads to the Anacostia River. On the southern boundary, a boardwalk leads to vistas of the reviving wetlands. During the week you may have the place to yourself. It's off the beaten track, and shunned by some who assume the low-income neighborhood at the approach is dangerous.

United States National Arboretum

3501 New York Avenue, NE, entrance at Bladensburg Road & R Street (1-202 245 2726, www.usna.usda.gov). Stadium-Armory Metro then B2 bus. **Open** *Grounds* 8am-5pm daily. *National Bonsai & Penjing Collection* 10am-4pm daily. **Admission** free.

Technically a research division of the Agriculture Department, this 446-acre haven always has many more trees than people, even on its busiest days during the spring azalea season. Highlights include a boxwood collection, dwarf conifers, an Asian collection, a herb garden and 'herbarium' of dried plants, as well as the National Bonsai Collection, which contains more than 200 trees donated by Japan and is said to be worth something in the order of $5 million. Also on display, somewhat incongruously, are 22 columns removed from the Capitol's East Front during its 1958 expansion. See the website for details of tram tours, talks and other events such as garden fairs.

Southeast

There's Southeast and then there's 'Southeast'. The latter usually refers not to the whole quadrant but to some of the city's rougher neighborhoods, across the Anacostia River and far from the center of town.

CAPITOL HILL

Bounded to the west by the Capitol building and South and North Capitol Streets, to the south by the Southeast Freeway, to the north by H Street, NE, and to the east by 11th Street, this genteel neighborhood overlays two quadrants – Southeast and Northeast. Since more of it falls into the former, most of it is dealt with here.

East of the Capitol building, a working-class town developed around the Navy Yard, separated from the rest of the city by a 'desert', as a Swiss visitor noted in 1825. Today, its

parochial small-town origins afford it a distinctively strollable ambience, although million-dollar home sales are no longer news. Businesses along Pennsylvania Avenue, SE, include bars and restaurants luring a youthful, politics-obsessed crowd. There are still vintage hangouts like the fabled Tune Inn (331 Pennsylvania Avenue, SE, *see p135*), little changed since VJ Day. The neighborhood's heart is **Eastern Market**, recently restored after being damaged by fire, now complemented by the revived Barracks Row on 8th Street between Pennsylvania Avenue and M Street, SE. Its growing restaurant roster dishes out a wide variety of cuisines – available without the congestion of Adams Morgan.

Aside from Pennsylvania Avenue itself, the Hill's principal shopping streets are the 7th-8th Street dogleg from Eastern Market, featuring food stores, galleries and craft shops, supplemented by the market's weekend flea and craft marts.

The **US Marine Barracks** (8th and I Streets, SE) has been on this site since 1801 and its commandant's house is the second oldest federal residence after the White House. On Friday nights from May to September, an impressive Marine parade drill is held (reservations required; call 1-202 433 6060).

Capitol Hill's largest open space is **Lincoln Park**, which interrupts East Capitol Street between 11th and 13th Streets. Grateful freedmen chipped in for its Emancipation Monument (1876), depicting Abraham Lincoln and a newly freed slave, though the monument was criticized when it was unveiled because the bondsman seemed to be kneeling before the president. Nearby is a sculpture of African-American educator Mary McLeod Bethune, flanked by festive children.

Congressional Cemetery (1801 E Street, SE) is the resting place of such eminent Washingtonians as photographer Matthew Brady, Choctaw chief Pushmataha and 'March King' John Philip Sousa. Look for free guide pamphlets at the gatehouse. Plots are available if you care to stay permanently.

Eastern Market

225 7th Street, SE, between C Street & North Carolina Avenue (1-202 544 0083, www.eastern market.net). Eastern Market Metro. **Open** dawn-late afternoon Sat, Sun. *Permanent inside stalls* 7am-6pm Tue-Sat; 9am-4pm Sat. **Map** p253 L7.

Built in 1873 on plans by Adolf Cluss, Washington's last remaining public food market has become the heart of the Capitol Hill community; its weekend flea and craft markets are a popular draw. The market building was badly damaged by fire in 2007. It reopened in 2009 after painstaking reconstruction work, including restoration of the roof, allowing the

Congressional Cemetery.

Frederick Douglass National Historic Site (Cedar Hill)

1411 W Street, SE, at 14th Street (1-877 444 6777, www.nps.gov/frdo). Anacostia Metro then B2 bus. **Open** *Tours* Mid Oct-mid Apr 9am-4.30pm daily. Mid Apr-mid Oct 9am-5pm daily. Tour times vary, phone or check website for details. **Admission** $1.50. **Credit** MC, V.

Built in 1854, this Victorian country house was the home of black leader Frederick Douglass from 1877 until his death in 1895. Born a slave in Maryland, Douglass escaped to found an abolitionist newspaper, eventually advising Lincoln and other presidents. The museum's visitor center shows *Fighter For Freedom*, a 17-minute film on Douglass's life. There's a sweeping view of downtown Washington from the grounds.

Southwest

There's not much of Southwest DC, the reason being that Virginia took back its quadrangle in 1846. The sliver of territory east of the Potomac that remained was not helped by a massive 1950s 'urban renewal' project that obliterated neighborhoods in favor of office space. Its primary draws are the museums and federal buildings to the south of the Mall, and the Tidal Basin, which are covered – down to the Eisenhower Freeway – in the Monumental Center chapter (*see pp42-63*).

Fishing boats have hawked their catch near the Tidal Basin inlet since 1790, before there was a city. You can still get seafood at the **Fish & Seafood Market** on Maine Avenue, just south of the Case Memorial Bridge; some vendors will even cook it up for you. The ponderous waterfront development, largely comprising oversized tour-bus restaurants, is due to be redeveloped, though the lively houseboat colony should stay anchored. The promenade climaxes at the willowy memorial to the gentlemen who gave ladies their seats on the *Titanic*'s lifeboats. Beyond, Fort McNair – the Army's oldest post – is off-limits for security reasons.

Inland, **Wheat Row** (1315-21 4th Street, SW) is a curiosity of the 1950s urban renewal program. Built in 1794, these distinguished residences were incorporated into a modern apartment complex. The area's theoretical juxtaposition of rich and poor populations did not uniformly foster the envisioned social harmony. Law House (1252 6th Street), dubbed 'Honeymoon House' in 1796 when its prominent owners moved in, kept the tag, despite their messy celebrity divorce a while later. Nearby, the pioneering theater company **Arena Stage** (1101 6th Street, SW) continues its vital dramatic presence in a gleaming new landmark building (*see p206* **Crystal Palaces**).

previously hidden historic skylight to be reintroduced as a prominent architectural feature of the South Hall.

SOUTHEAST

South of Capitol Hill, the once-dodgy tract by the Washington Navy Yard is the site of DC's new ballpark, **Nationals Park**, constructed after Washington regained a major league baseball team after three dark decades (*see p201* **Hitting in the Major League**). The new ballpark has brought some revival to the surrounding area – it still has a way to go, though.

Anacostia

Anacostia Community Museum (S)

1901 Fort Place, SE, at Martin Luther King Jr Avenue (1-202 287 3306, www.si.edu/anacostia). Anacostia Metro then W2, W3 bus. **Open** 10am-5pm daily. **Admission** free.

Housed in an unprepossessing red-brick building at the top of a hill in the District's historically black Anacostia neighborhood, this modest museum hosts changing thematic exhibitions spotlighting history, culture and creative expression from an African-American perspective. Exhibits include the 19th-century diary of one-time slave Adam Francis Plummer, who wrote of his foiled plan to escape on the Underground Railroad, and a section on black baseball in segregated DC.

SIGHTS

Arlington & Alexandria

Virginia highlights.

Northern Virginia is a comparatively liberal pocket of a famously conservative state. As well as being a dormitory suburb for DC, Northern Virginia (or NOVA to some) is home to some of the capital's important institutions, among them the Pentagon, the CIA's headquarters at Langley and Arlington Cemetery.

Arlington and part of Alexandria were part of the original District of Columbia diamond from 1800 to 1846, when they retroceded to Virginia, claiming federal neglect but covertly fearing that Congress might ban slavery in the capital.

Map p90, p246   **Restaurants** p133
Hotels p109

Map p90, p246   **Restaurants** p133
Hotels p109

Beyond its military precinct along the river – with Arlington Cemetery and the Pentagon – Arlington is a lively suburb, popular with young professionals, with a restaurant and entertainment strip sprouting above Metro stations along Wilson Boulevard. Its Fashion Center mall at Pentagon City draws throngs of visitors. Self-consciously quaint but vigorous 'Old Town' Alexandria, a restored riverport with a history that pre-dates the capital by half a century, can make a welcome break from all that federal seriousness.

ALEXANDRIA

Downstream on the Potomac river, the town of Alexandria was established in 1749 by Scottish traders and laid out by a young surveyor named George Washington. Old Town's 18th-century charm started drawing crowds of sightseers and shoppers back in the 1960s. The cobbled streets, which had survived more from lethargy than historical sensibility, were re-stoned at vast expense, and once-neglected houses meticulously restored; the vacant warehouses along King Street sprouted bars, boutiques and antiques shops. Commerce now extends 19 blocks

from the river to King Street Metro station, with an atmosphere that is vibrant yet leisurely.

Old Town rewards random wanderings. For background and orientation arm yourself with some maps and pamphlets from the visitors' center in historic **Ramsay House** (221 King Street, 1-703 838 4200) before setting out to discover the flounder houses, dwellings with half-gable roofs descending asymmetrically, that are characteristic of 18th- and early 19th-century Alexandria dwellings. Forty originals survive, with dozens of neo-flounders marking recent developments.

The Civil War indelibly marked the town; some reminders include the Confederate Statue (1888), glowering in the middle of the intersection of South Washington and Prince Streets, its back defiantly turned on the nation's capital. A free map of significant local war sites is available at the nearby **Lyceum, Alexandria's History Museum**.

A few blocks east, at 121 N Fairfax Street, is the 18th-century **Carlyle House**. Next door, the old Bank of Virginia has been restored for use – as a bank, surprise, surprise. Across the street is **Gadsby's Tavern Museum**.

George Washington prayed as well as played in Alexandria, attending **Christ Church**. He was also a patron of the voluntary fire company that built the original **Friendship Fire House**, west on King Street.

From 1792 until 1933, Quaker druggist Edward Stabler's family made medicines for patrons including Washington and Lee. Today the **Stabler-Leadbeater Apothecary Shop** on Fairfax Street appears just as it did for generations. Further north is the **Alexandria Black History Museum**.

Alexandria is not only a heritage town; at the **Torpedo Factory Art Center** local artists create new sculpture and painting, although the past can't be escaped even here: the site is a renovated factory that produced munitions for World War I.

Back towards King Street Metro station, Dulany Street is the home of the **National Inventors Hall of Fame & Museum**. To the west, on Callahan Drive you'll find the **George Washington Masonic National Memorial**.

Alexandria Black History Museum

902 Wythe Street, at Alford Street (1-703 746 4356, http://oha.alexandriava.gov/bhrc). Braddock Road Metro. **Open** 10am-4pm Tue-Sat. **Admission** $2.

Paintings, photographs, books and other artifacts document the African-American experience in Alexandria and Virginia from 1749 to the present. The museum occupies a former Jim Crow library built in 1940 to escape racially integrating the Alexandria Public Library.

Carlyle House Historic Park

121 N Fairfax Street, between King & Cameron Streets (1-703 549 2997, www.nvrpa.org/park/carlyle_house_historic_park). King Street Metro then 15min walk. **Open** 10am-4pm Tue-Sat; noon-4pm Sun. Guided tours every 30mins. **Admission** $5; $3 reductions; free under-11s.

John Carlyle built his Scottish-Palladian stone palace here in 1753 and it was then used as the meeting place for British colonial governors to plan their campaign against the French forces squeezing the Crown's claims to the Ohio river valley. General Edward Braddock then marched down the eponymous road west, towards Pennsylvania – and disaster.

Christ Church

Cameron & N Washington Streets (1-703 549 1450, www.historicchristchurch.org). King Street Metro then 15min walk. **Open** 10am-4pm Mon-Sat; 8.45am-1pm Sun. **Admission** free.

Dubbed 'the Church in the Woods' in 1773, this Episcopal house of worship has been in continuous service since. Designed by James Wren in the colonial Georgian style, George Washington and Robert E Lee were regular worshippers here. The pew assigned to Washington, No.15, is preserved in its original high-backed eminence.

Friendship Fire House

107 S Alfred Street, between King & Prince Streets (1-703 746 3891, http://oha.alexandriava.gov/friendship/). King Street Metro then 15min walk. **Open** 1-4pm Sat, Sun. **Admission** $2.

The volunteer fire brigade, formed in 1774, built this snug station in 1855. The museum has a display of antique firefighting apparatus.

Gadsby's Tavern Museum

134 N Royal Street, between King & Cameron Streets (1-703 746 4242, http://oha.alexandriava.gov/gadsby/). King Street Metro then 29K bus or Dash bus AT2, AT3, AT5, AT7. **Open** Nov-Mar 11am-4pm Wed-Sat; 1-4pm Sun. Apr-Oct 10am-5pm Tue-Sat; 1-5pm Mon, Sun. Guided tours every 30mins. **Admission** $5; $3 reductions; free under-11s. **Credit** MC, V.

These buildings comprise a tavern dating from 1785 and a hotel built in 1792. Towards the end of the 18th century they were joined together by Englishman John Gadsby and quickly became a local meeting place for many significant 18th-century figures. In 1798, George Washington graced a ball here, the first of two occasions on which he attended the celebrations in honor of his birthday. The 18th-century hostelry is well preserved in the older building. The tavern next door serves colonial-style food and drink.

George Washington Masonic National Memorial

101 Callahan Drive, between King & Duke Streets (1-703 683 2007, www.gwmemorial.org). King Street Metro. **Open** Oct-Mar 10am-4pm Mon-Sat; noon-4pm Sun. Apr-Sept 9am-4pm Mon-Sat; noon-4pm Sun. Guided tours 10am, 11.30am, 1.30pm, 3pm Mon-Sat; noon, 1.30pm, 3pm Sun. **Admission** 1st & 2nd floor free; tower exhibits & observation desk $5.

Sitting on a hill dominating low-lying Alexandria, in the imagined style of the ancient Pharos of Alexandria, the George Washington Masonic National Memorial is in striking contrast to the general's more famous tower across the river in DC. Masonic memorabilia related to US presidents who were Freemasons includes a reconstruction of the lodge hall Washington attended. The view from the top of the monument (only accessible as part of a guided tour) is impressive.

Lyceum, Alexandria's History Museum

201 S Washington Street, at Prince Street (1-703 746 4994, http://oha.alexandriava.gov/lyceum/). King Street Metro then 15min walk. **Open** 10am-5pm Mon-Sat; 1-5pm Sun. **Admission** $2.

In 1839, local notables with intellectual interests built a Greek Revival library-auditorium for debates, concerts and literary soirées. Today, the building celebrates Alexandria's unique heritage

SIGHTS

with changing displays on local history – from the town's founding and growth as a port, through its role as a Civil War railroad center, to its contemporary place as part of the DC metropolitan area.

Stabler-Leadbeater Apothecary Shop

105-107 Fairfax Street, at King Street (1-703 746-3852, http://oha.alexandriava.gov/ apothecary/). King Street Metro then 29K bus or Dash bus AT2, AT3, AT5, AT7. **Open** 10am-4pm Mon-Sat; 1-5pm Sun. **Admission** phone for details. **Credit** AmEx, Disc, MC, V.

When the original apothecary on this premises was forced to close during the Depression, in 1933, the doors were locked but the contents in the Gothic Revival interior were left intact: over 8,000 objects, including pill rollers, mortars and pestles and hand-blown medicine bottles with gold-leaf labels, remained. It reopened as a museum in 1939. There is also a collection of archive materials, with journals, letters, and prescription and formula books.

Torpedo Factory Art Center

105 N Union Street, at King Street (1-703 838 4565, www.torpedofactory.org). King Street Metro then 15min walk. **Open** *Building hours* (individual galleries vary) 10am-6pm Mon-Wed, Fri-Sun; 10am-9pm Thur. *Archaelogy Museum* 10am-3pm Tue-Fri; 10am-5pm Sat; 1-5pm Sun. **Admission** free.

Originally a World War I munitions plant, the Torpedo Factory now spawns arts rather than arms, with three storys containing 82 studios, six galleries – among them spaces dedicated to enameling, ceramics and photography – and two workshops, one devoted to fiberwork, the other to printmaking. Also on site is the Alexandria Archaeology Museum.

National Inventors Hall of Fame & Museum

400 Dulany Street (1-571 272 0095, www.uspto. gov/web/offices/ac/ahrpa/opa/museum/welcome.ht ml). King Street Metro. **Open** 9am-5pm Mon-Fri; noon-5pm Sat. **Admission** free.

In 2009, the National Inventors Hall of Fame moved from Akron, Ohio, to become part of the United States Patent & Trademark Museum. The new museum features interactive exhibits and a portrait gallery, along with a video theater, to tell tales of inventors and their inventions.

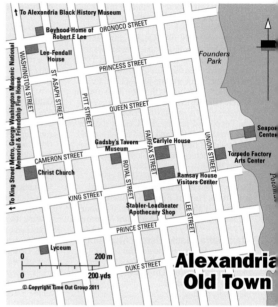

ARLINGTON

Stately **Memorial Bridge** (1932) formally connects Lincoln's memorial to the home of his Civil War nemesis, Robert E Lee, symbolically linking North and South. The bridge makes landfall at Lady Bird Johnson Park, which includes the discreet **Lyndon B Johnson Memorial Grove** (www.nps.gov/lyba). At the adjacent **Pentagon** is the **Pentagon Memorial**, opened in September 2008. The open-air memorial features a 1.93-acre maple grove (it's going to take a few years for the trees to grow), sheltering 184 cantilevered benches in marble, one for each person killed on 9/11 when terrorists flew a hijacked jet into the building. The days of public tours around the Pentagon, the world's largest public building, are long gone, but the memorial is open to all. The monument is on the Pentagon's west side. To reach it, travel to the Pentagon Metro station and follow the signs for the Memorial Gateway.

Another feature in this martial terrain is the **Air Force Memorial** (1-703 247 5808, www.airforcememorial.org), three stainless steel spikes soaring 270 feet from a promontory south of **Arlington National Cemetery**.

Arlington National Cemetery

1-703 607 8000, Tourmobile info 1-202 554 5100, www.arlingtoncemetery.org. Arlington

Cemetery Metro. **Open** *Apr-Sept* 8am-7pm daily.
Oct-Mar 8am-5pm daily. **Admission** free.
It is the right of anyone killed in action in any branch of military service, or who served for 20 years, to be buried at Arlington, along with their spouse. It's ironic, then, that the cemetery started almost as an act of Civil War vengeance: in 1861 Union forces seized the estate of Confederate General Robert E Lee and in 1864 they began burying soldiers close enough to Arlington House to make sure that Mr and Mrs Lee could never take up residence again. However, time has worked its healing magic and transformed Arlington into a place of honor and memory.

Built in 1802-16, Arlington House is now a museum (open 9.30am-4.30pm daily) and appears as it did in Lee's time. Entranced by the commanding view, President Kennedy was said to have murmured, 'I could stay here forever.' And shortly afterwards he took up residence in the cemetery, to be joined later by Robert F Kennedy and Jacqueline Kennedy Onassis.

Iwo Jima Memorial.

By an imposing marble amphitheater is the Tomb of the Unknowns, including unidentified casualties of US conflicts up to Vietnam. Today, the Pentagon keeps DNA samples of all military personnel, making it unlikely that future remains will be unidentifiable. The changing of the guard on the hour (every hour between October and March, every half an hour from April to September) remains moving in its reverent precision. Horse-drawn caissons still bear the remains of troops qualified for burial, from the dwindling veterans of World War II to those killed in Iraq and Afghanistan.

Tombs range from unadorned white headstones, such as that of actor Lee Marvin, to sculpted personal memorials, like the one to the former world heavyweight boxing champion Joe Louis (both men were veterans of World War II), that sits next to it. The Tourmobile route naturally features celebrity sites, but strollers can discover more obscure, but often just as interesting, memorials and tombs. Memorials include the mast of the battleship *Maine* (whose explosion in Havana harbour sparked the Spanish-American War), the monument to the Navajo Code Talkers (whose language baffled Japanese codebreakers during World War II), and commemorations of the Space Shuttle *Columbia* casualties.

At the north end is the Netherlands Carillon, a Dutch thank you for their liberation from the Nazis. Beyond is the US Marines' **Iwo Jima Memorial**, a giant re-creation of the celebrated photo of the raising of the flag during the 1942 battle.

The Women in Military Service to America Memorial is inset behind the original Main Gate wall to create a light-flooded arch with 16 display niches. Three permanent photo displays survey women at war from the earliest days to the present. Late in 2005, a special exhibit of Women in the Global War on Terror opened.

Arlington Cemetery's visitors' center is just past the entrance on Memorial Avenue, close to the Metro station. Here you can locate particular graves or pick up maps to wander the cemetery on foot (note that some significant graves are a mile or more uphill). Alternatively, buy tickets for the Tourmobile coach circuit ($7.50; tickets also available from Ticketmaster). The coach makes brief stops at each major point of interest, but to avoid that cattle-drive feeling, take your time and reboard the subsequent service (tickets are valid).
► *The Iwo Jima Memorial is slightly closer to Rosslyn Metro station.*

Drug Enforcement Agency Museum
700 Army Navy Drive, across from Pentagon City Mall (1-202 307 3463, www.deamuseum.org).
Pentagon City Metro. **Open** 10am-4pm Tue-Fri.
Admission free.
The exhibits here trace the history of drugs and the law in America, primarily through the relics of 20th-century drug culture that have been collected by DEA agents.

World Class

Perfect places to stay, eat and explore.

Consume

Comet Ping-Pong. *See p131*.

Hotels	**94**
The Best Historic Hotels	96
Small Treats	99
The Best Style Hotels	103
Break a Sweat	105

Restaurants	**111**
The Best For Fun	116
Power Points	119
The Best DC Institutions	121
Meals on Wheels	123
The Best Hot Hangouts	131
Ethiopian Eats	132

Bars	**134**
Hotel Havens	138
The Best Back to Basics Bars	141
The Best Bars with a View	142

Shopping & Services	**143**
Where to Shop	145
Biagio Fine Chocolate	154
Museum Pieces	160

Hotels

Luscious lodgings.

Change has been the buzzword in Washington for the last few years, but it's more than a political mantra. It's indicative of what's been happening throughout the city. That's not to say you won't find those dark, wood-paneled spots with power players wheeling and dealing that DC is known for. Those lavish, expense-account places still exist, but even some of these have received a makeover.

The historic **Hay-Adams**, which opened in 1928, underwent a technological upgrade to enable the landmark hotel to offer all the modern amenities while holding on to that old-fashioned feel. The **Jefferson**, another grand old hotel, reopened after a two-year renovation that blends the contemporary with historic nods to the third president.

Change has also ushered in several new, more contemporary, hotels. The **Donovan House** (*see p103*) is decked out with hanging egg-shaped chairs, cylindrical-shaped showers and a rooftop pool that's got quite a party scene. And, on Capitol Hill, the **Liaison** (*see p97*) transformed an old Holiday Inn with a new bold, pop-art feel.

RATES & SERVICES

Except in the smallest hotels, there is no such thing as a fixed rate in Washington, or in Viriginia or Maryland for that matter. Because many visitors swoop into town on business and leave by the weekend, rooms cost much more from Monday to Friday. All in all, rates vary according to the time of year, the day of the week and what discounts you can wangle. The prices we quote are the standard rates for a double room, from the cheapest in low season to the most expensive in high season, but they should only be taken as a guide; rates change often and, in addition, it is often possible to find deals and special offers, especially at weekends.

When booking your room, ask about a corporate rate even if your company has no formal arrangement with the hotel. If relevant, inquire about senior rates too: some hotels offer 10 to 15 per cent off for guests over 65. Or just ask if there are any discounts, special offers or packages available.

Rates decrease during summer – when locals flee the humidity and visitors decide not to brave the conditions in large numbers – and are rock-bottom around Christmas. They are at their highest in spring, when DC sees an influx of school groups and cherry-blossom gazers; early autumn is another busy time. Bear in mind that taxes are added to prices quoted. In DC this is sales tax of six per cent, plus hotel tax of 14.5 per cent. This adds quite a chunk to any hotel bill.

You can find lower rates at just about any DC hotel through websites such as www.expedia.com, www.travelocity.com and www.orbitz.com. Internet wholesalers such as www.priceline.com offer hotel rooms at short notice or to the highest bidder. You can also reserve during office hours through Capitol Reservations (1-202 452 1270) or Washington, DC Accommodations (1-202 289 2220), which can sometimes get discounts and find a room even when the city's bursting with conferences.

In a town where the term 'presidential suite' might mean just that, there are only a handful of really low-budget options. DC has no campsites or RV/caravan sites. And there is only one official youth hostel in town (**Hostelling International Washington, DC,** *see p103*), but thankfully it's a very good one.

> **❶** Red numbers given in this chapter correspond to the location of each hotel as marked on the street maps. See pp248-53.

CONSUME

THE WHITE HOUSE & AROUND
Deluxe

Hay-Adams Hotel
*1 Lafayette Square, NW, at 16th & H Streets, DC
20006 (1-202 638 6600, www.hayadams.com).
Farragut North or McPherson Square Metro.*
Rates $249-$900. **Rooms** 145. **Credit** AmEx,
Disc, MC, V. **Map** p250/p252 H5 ❶

This grande dame across from Lafayette Square
recently received a subtle makeover to add more
contemporary touches to its early 20th century
core. Guest rooms now include in-room safes
large enough for laptops, as well as high-definition
televisions and Bose Wave systems with iPod capa-
bility. The renovations, which also include a mod-
ernized business center and new fitness room,
manage to update the hotel without taking away
from its elegant, old-fashioned feel. To really drink
in that clubby Washington feel, stop into the hotel's
basement bar.

*Bar. Business center. Concierge. Disabled-adapted
rooms. Gym. Internet (Wi-Fi, free). Parking
($42 per night). Restaurant. Room service. TV
(pay movies, DVD players on request).*

★ W
*515 15th Street, NW, at F Street, 20004 (1-202
661 2400, www.starwoodhotels.com/whotels).
Metro Center or McPherson Square Metro.* **Rates**
from $299. **Rooms** 317. **Credit** AmEx, Disc, MC,
V. **Map** p252 H6 ❷

The venerable old Hotel Washington has had the
W treatment, and it's every bit as fabulous as you
might imagine. Key historical fittings remain in the

lobby, like the old check-in/cash desk, original
stucco and chandeliers, incorporated into a reborn
and slightly fantastical 'living room'. There's a
touch of *Alice in Wonderland* in the check-in desks
that are upside- down tables and the big chairs on
small rugs. There's a riff on buttoned-down DC
masculine power going on, too, with clubby pin-
striped chairs meeting their match in hot-red vinyl
couches, while big black lamps drip with crystal
drops. Upstairs, rooms and suites have all the style
and comfort you would expect. For something truly
spectacular, the Extreme Wow Suite channels the
Oval Office with curved walls and strong, masculine colors, while the Marvelous Suite has an ethe-
real palette of pales. All rooms have waterfall
showers, and iPod docks are among the amenities.
The Bliss spa is, well, blissful, and Jean-Georges
Vongerichten's J&G Steakhouse, with chef Philippe
Reininger at the helm, delivers a melding of classic
steak and fish and clean, modish flavors in surroundings of simple elegance. (Michelle Obama has
eaten here with friends.)

*Bars (2). Business center. Concierge. Gym.
Disabled-adapted rooms. Internet (WiFi,*

Sofitel Lafayette Square.

$14.95 per day). Parking ($50 per night).
Restaurant. Room service. Spa. TV (pay movies).
▶ *For a review of POV, the W's rooftop bar,
see p134.*

Moderate

JW Marriott
*1331 Pennsylvania Avenue NW at 14th street, DC
20004 (reservations 1-800 393 250, hotel direct
1-202 393 2000, www.marriott.com). Metro
Center Metro.* **Rates** $129-$429. **Rooms** 737.
Credit AmEx, Disc, MC, V. **Map** p252 H6 ❸
Located on Pennsylvania Avenue near the White
House, National Mall and the theaters, the JW
Marriott sits on a prime location. For a view of the

THE BEST HISTORIC HOTELS

Hay-Adams
A landmark 1927 Italian-Renaissance
style building. *See p95.*

Willard Intercontinental
Early 20th-century opulence reflects the
optimism of the era. *See p97.*

Jefferson
An imposing 1923 Beaux Arts building.
See p101.

Washington Monument ask for a room facing
Pennsylvania Avenue between the third and 15th
floors. Those on the seventh and 12th floors have
balconies as well. Beyond the fantastic real estate,
the hotel recently underwent a $40 million renova-
tion that provided several technological upgrades
including a plug-in panel that lets guests split the
TV screen so they can check email and watch TV.
*Bars (2). Business center. Concierge. Disabled-
adapted rooms. Gym. Internet (wired, Wi-Fi,
$12.95 per day). Parking ($43.68 per night).
Restaurants (2). Room service. TV (pay movies,
DVD players on request). Spa. Swimming
pool (indoor).*

★ Sofitel Lafayette Square
*806 15th Street, NW, at 16th & H Streets,
DC 20005 (1-202 730 8800, www.sofitel.com).
McPherson Square Metro.* **Rates** $175-$320.
Rooms 237. **Credit** AmEx, Disc, MC, V.
Map p250/p252 H5 ❹
From the outside, the Sofitel looks like a typical big-
city American hotel, but there's a clue to some subtle differences: a French flag flying alongside the
Stars and Stripes. Inside, contemporary artworks
lift the traditional look of the wood-paneled lobby.
Rooms also have good, vibrant pictures livening
up neutral, comfortable, upscale decor and furnishings. European-style duvets are a welcome continental touch. TVs are high-definition, and marble
bathrooms have separate bathtubs and glass-
enclosed showers. There's more French influence

CONSUME

in the iCi Urban Bistro, where morning coffee comes in a French press (cafetière), and breakfast orders come with a croissant and a pain au chocolat as well as bread. Both the sophisticated Le Bar and the bistro have outside space, which is at a premium in this area. Many of the staff are French too. Vive la différence!

Bar. Business center. Concierge. Gym. Disabled-adapted rooms. Internet (Wi-Fi, $10 per day). Parking ($40 per night). Restaurant. Room service. TV (pay movies).

THE CAPITOL & AROUND
Moderate

Hyatt Regency Washington on Capitol Hill
400 New Jersey Avenue, between D & E Streets, DC 20001 (1-202 737 1234, http://washington regency.hyatt.com). **Rates** $109-$499. **Rooms** 834. **Credit** AmEx, Disc, MC, V. **Map** p253 K6 ❺
A hotel on a grand scale, guests take an escalator down to the lower-level entrance lobby, which is actually more like a small village, with enough check-in desks for an airline, a comfortable lounge and bar, and a restaurant space behind a low barrier. Off this expansive open-plan area are facilities including shops, a shoeshine area and a FedEx office. The Hyatt Capitol Hill is the sister hotel of the more styled and expensive Park Hyatt (*see p99*). This one can't be beaten for location, however – it's right beside the Capitol – and its rooms are comfortable, done out in neutral colors and equipped with iPod docking stations. The club floor allows access to a lounge with complimentary continental breakfast and snacks through much of the day.
Bar. Business center. Concierge. Disabled-adapted rooms. Gym. Internet (Wi-Fi, $9.99 per day). Parking ($41 per night). Restaurant. Room service. TV (pay movies).

★ Liaison Affinia Hotel
415 New Jersey Avenue, NW, between D & E Streets, DC 20001 (reservations 1-800 638 1116, hotel direct 1-202 638 1616, www.hionthehill dc.com). Union Station Metro. **Rates** $119-$400. **Credit** AmEx, Disc, MC, V. **Rooms** 343. **Map** p253 K6 ❻
Just blocks from the Capitol and Union Station, this former Holiday Inn was transformed into an Affinia hotel, complete with contemporary rooms and the chain's pillow menu. During the summer the rooftop swimming pool and sundeck offer up sweeping views of the city's skyline. Downstairs is Art and Soul, a Southern-food restaurant by Oprah favorite Art Smith.
Bar. Business center. Concierge, Disabled-adapted rooms. Gym. Internet, Wi-Fi ($9.95 per day). TV (pay movies, DVD player on request).

UNION STATION & AROUND
Expensive

Hotel George
15 E Street, NW, between New Jersey Avenue & North Capitol Street, DC 20001 (reservations 1-800 546 7866, hotel direct 1-202 347 4200, www.hotelgeorge.com). Union Station Metro. **Rates** $169-$499. **Rooms** 139. **Credit** AmEx, DC, Disc, MC, V. **Map** p253 K6 ❼
The first Kimpton Group property in DC, the George sets the bar high. From the sleek and airy lobby in light sandstone with grand piano to the hip, buzzy bar and excellent restaurant-bistro Bis, it succeeds in creating an urban brand of style. Rooms are generously sized and decorated with refreshing restraint and style – not a floral in sight, and the only flourish is a Warhol-like print of a dollar bill. The gym features high-tech equipment and steam rooms.
Bar. Business center. Disabled: adapted rooms. Gym. Internet (Wi-Fi, free to Kimpton In Touch members – can sign up when a guest). Parking ($26 per night). Restaurant. Room service. TV (pay movies).

Moderate

Phoenix Park Hotel
520 North Capitol Street, NW, at Massachusetts Avenue, DC 20001 (reservations 1-800 824 5419, hotel direct 1-202 638 6900, www.phoenixpark hotel.com). Union Station Metro. **Rates** $89-$459. **Credit** AmEx, Disc, MC, V. **Rooms** 149. **Map** p253 K6 ❽
Despite its location just blocks from the Capitol, this hotel is more green than red, white and blue. Named after a park in Dublin, the Phoenix features standard-sized rooms decorated with Irish artwork and linens. The ground-floor Irish pub, the Dubliner, provides nightly entertainment, an outdoor patio and a welcoming atmosphere.
Bar. Business center. Disabled-adapted rooms. Concierge.Gym. Internet (Wi-Fi, wired, $9.95 per day). Parking ($40 per night). Restaurant. Room service. TV (pay movies).

FEDERAL TRIANGLE
Deluxe

Willard InterContinental
1401 Pennsylvania Avenue, NW, at 14th Street, DC 20004 (reservations 1-800 327 0200, hotel direct 1-202 628 9100, http://washington continental.com). Metro Center Metro. **Rates** $259-$799. **Rooms** 375. **Credit** AmEx, Disc, MC, V. **Map** p252 H6 ❾
There is no DC hotel with more history than the Willard. The current building, completed in 1901, replaced the hotel's first incarnation; together they

CONSUME

have hosted every president, either as a resident guest or at a social function, since Zachary Taylor in 1850. The old Willard played a particularly strong role as a hub of political activity during the Civil War years. The current building closed during the mid 20th-century years of decline, reopening in 1986. The original, restored lobby is a real fin de siècle spectacle, with marble pillars, palms, and gilt-painted stucco on cornices and ceiling. Off the lobby is the iconic and aptly named Round Robin Bar (it's round), a real gentlemen's hangout. Follow the grand hallway called Peacock Alley, where tea is served, to learn more about the hotel's past in its History Gallery. Rooms are as comfortable, with furnishings as traditional, as one would expect. The Jenny Lind suite has a round window beside the big tub in its bathroom; it catches the Washington Monument directly in its center. The Café du Parc serves bistro-style cooking in an informal space.

The hotel has its own small museum, the History Gallery, with over 100 artifacts and photos tracing the fortunes of the hotel and its many famous guests. Among the collection are the menu from Lincoln's inaugural lunch – corned beef and cabbage, mock turtle soup, parsley potatoes and blackberry pie – and the bill for his stay at the hotel; he and his family lived at the Willard for a month before moving into the White House. The stay cost $773.

Bar. Business center. Concierge. Disabled-adapted rooms. Gym. Internet (wired & Wi-Fi $?? per day). Parking ($40 per night). Restaurants (2). Room service. Spa. TV (pay movies).
▶ *For the Round Robin Bar, see p135.*

SOUTH OF THE MALL
Deluxe

L'Enfant Plaza Hotel
480 L'Enfant Plaza, SW, between D Street & Dwight Eisenhower Freeway, DC 20024 (reservations 1-800 635 5065, hotel direct 1-202 484 1000, www.lenfantplazahotel.com). L'Enfant Plaza Metro. **Rates** $259-$399. **Rooms** 372. **Credit** AmEx, Disc, MC, V. **Map** p252 J7 ⑩
A large opulent hotel in an unusual south of the Mall location that is close to the Capitol. There are great views from the balconies but the business-heavy area largely shuts down at night. That said, the hotel goes out of its way to welcome families: children under 18 stay in parents' rooms for free, and pets are allowed in deluxe rooms only for a fee of $25. Business travellers are also very well catered for, and the seasonal, heated rooftop swimming pool is perfect for downtime.
Bar. Business center. Concierge. Disabled-adapted rooms (8). Gym. Internet (Wi-Fi, free). Parking ($42 per night). Restaurant. Room service. Swimming pool (outdoor). TV (pay movies).

INSIDE TRACK LOBBYING

President Ulysses S Grant liked to get away from the White House for a break with a brandy and cigar in the lobby of the **Willard** (*see p97*) in the evenings. But before too long it became public knowledge that he could be found here and those with causes to promote started to seek him out. President Grant began calling these unsolicited visitors 'lobbyists'.

Mandarin Oriental
1330 Maryland Avenue, SW, at 12th Street, DC 20004 (reservations 1-888 888 1778, hotel direct 1-202 554 8588, www.mandarinoriental.com/washington). Smithsonian or L'Enfant Plaza Metro. **Rates** $235-$545. **Credit** AmEx, Disc, MC, V. **Rooms** 415. **Map** p252 H7 ⑪
Many Washingtonians raised an eyebrow when the Mandarin chose a spot surrounded by government office buildings and a seafood market for its 400-room hotel. But the international chain saw potential in the site – which, in fairness, is only a few blocks from the Mall and two Metro stations – and went about proving that location isn't everything. The hotel is sumptuous in every detail, from the gorgeous spa, indoor pool and top-notch restaurant to the bed linens and bathroom toiletries. Some rooms have views of monuments and the Tidal Basin.
Bar (lobby). Business center. Concierge. Disabled-adapted rooms. Gym ($15 per day). Internet (Wi-Fi $14.95 per day, free for Fairmont Gold members). Parking ($40 per night). Restaurant. Room service (24hrs). Spa. Swimming pool (indoor). TV (pay movies, DVD players on request).

Expensive

Residence Inn by Marriott Capitol
333 E Street, SW, between 3rd & 4th Streets, DC 20024 (reservations 1-800 228 9290, hotel direct 1-202 484 8280, www.capitolmarriott.com). Federal Center SW Metro. **Rates** (incl breakfast) $159-$359 suites. **Rooms** 233. **Credit** AmEx, Disc, MC, V. **Map** p253 K7 ⑫
Opened in January 2005, the first Native American-owned Marriott is located four blocks south of the new National Museum of the American Indian and was built with the same limestone exterior. Inside, you'll find large suites with full kitchens (but uninspired decor) and good service. The hotel is especially family friendly; staff can configure four-bedroom suites and there are books and games available in the lobby. Ask for a room on one of the upper floors to escape the noise from nearby train tracks and construction. The surrounding area has few restaurants, so unless you plan to cook, you'll want to eat before returning to the hotel.

CONSUME

Business center (small). Disabled-adapted rooms. Gym. Internet (free Wi-Fi in lobby and wired in rooms, $9.95 per day). Parking ($30 per night). Swimming pool (indoor). TV (pay movies, DVD players on request).

FOGGY BOTTOM/WEST END

Deluxe

Park Hyatt
1201 24th Street, NW, at M Street, DC 20037 (reservations 1-800 233 1234, hotel direct 1-202 789 1234, www.parkwashington.hyatt.com). Foggy Bottom-GWU Metro. **Rates** $280-$695. **Rooms** 216. **Credit** AmEx, Disc, MC, V. **Map** p250/p252 F5 ⑬
This luxurious hotel features spacious rooms with thick down duvets, Americana accents like Shaker wooden boxes and coffee-table books on American culture, and all the most modern amenities. In the deluxe rooms and suites, a panel separating the bedroom and living area features a flat-screen TV on one side and a hand-carved checkerboard on the other, as well as spa-inspired bathrooms with large, sunken tubs. On the ground floor is the popular Blue Duck Tavern, which serves contemporary American fare. Bar. Business center. Concierge. Disabled-adapted rooms. Gym. Internet (Wi-Fi, $10 per day). Parking ($35 per night). Restaurant. Room service. Spa. Swimming pool (indoor). TV (pay movies).

★ **Ritz-Carlton, Washington, DC**
1150 22nd Street, NW, at M Street, DC 20037 (1-202 835 0500, www.ritzcarlton.com/hotels/washington_dc). Foggy Bottom-GWU Metro. **Rates** $279-$969. **Rooms** 300. **Credit** AmEx, Disc, MC, V. **Map** p250/p252 G5 ⑭

Both reassuringly traditional and warmly welcoming, the Ritz Carlton is definitely a hotel for off-duty enjoyment as well as business stays. Mellow wood paneling greets guests in the public areas, along with careful attention to detail: apples on a platter just so, glorious flowers, and well-placed art and ceramics. Not to mention little touches to make you feel special, like hot apple cider and lemon cookies in the lobby on an autumn Sunday afternoon. Guest rooms are the supremely comfortable affairs that one would expect. Marble bathrooms have separate tubs and shower cubicles; there are iPod docks and HD TVs; furnishings have deco-esque touches. A stay on the club floor allows access to a lounge where complimentary drinks and snacks are served all day. The West End Bistro by Eric Ripert is a lively, modern restaurant with a menu that mixes bistro classics with a robust, contemporary approach to local food and flavors in dishes such as short ribs with truffled potato puré e, roast veg and peppercorn sauce, or own-made Linguisa sausage with tomatoes, garlic and broccoli rabe. Bar. Business center. Concierge. Disabled-adapted rooms. Gym. Internet (Wi-Fi $?). Parking ($45 per night). Restaurant. Room service. Spa. Swimming pool (indoor). TV (pay movies, DVD players & game systems available for rent).

Expensive

Embassy Suites Hotel
1250 22nd Street, NW, at N Street, DC 20037 (reservations 1-800 362 2779, hotel direct 1-202 857 3388, www.embassysuites.com). Dupont Circle or Foggy Bottom Metro. **Rates** (incl breakfast) $129-$399 suite. **Credit** AmEx, Disc, MC, V. **Rooms** 318. **Map** p250/p252 G4 ⑮

Small Treats

Some vital snacks to fill the gap.

Whether you've spent the day trekking around the National Mall or locked in meetings, sometimes you just need a little pick-me-up. Several of Washington's hotels offer snacks to tide you over until dinner or satisfy you when you're still actually full from that power lunch but just need a little something.

The **Renaissance Mayflower** (see p101) teamed up with Eric and Bruce Bromberg, the brothers behind New York's Blue Ribbon Restaurants group, to offer a lounge menu that lets guests snack on miniature versions of Blue Ribbon favorites like smoked salmon toasts, grilled chicken burgers, pulled pork and the famed fried chicken.

Tucked into the minibar at the **W** (see p95) is a W Munchie Box. This box of treats is packed with healthy snacks like multi-grain tortilla chips, Popchips, energy bars and raw almonds as well as more decadent treats like cheese curls, Oreos and chocolate bars.

For those looking to satisfy their sweet tooth, the bar at the **St Regis** (923 16th Street, at K Street, NW, 1-202 638-2626, www.StRegis.com), just two blocks from the White House, dishes up a Sweet Bites & Sips menu. It pairs desserts from the award-winning Adour restaurant with wines – just perfect for those who are looking for a sweet end to their day.

CONSUME

Yes, it's a generic chain hotel with identical twins in other cities. But the large, reasonably priced suites make this a good choice for families and business travelers who need room to spread out. The complimentary breakfast is cooked to order, and there's a daily cocktail reception. Plasma-screen TVs and the swimming pool and sauna will help you relax after a day of sightseeing or board meetings.
Bar. Business center. Concierge. Disabled-adapted rooms. Gym. Internet (Wi-Fi, $12.95 per day). Parking ($28 per night). Restaurant. Room service. Swimming pool (indoor). TV (pay movies).

Fairmont

2401 M Street, NW, at 24th Street, DC 20037 (reservations 1-866 540 4508, hotel direct 1-202 429 2400, www.fairmont.com/washington). Foggy Bottom-GWU Metro. **Rates** (incl breakfast) $159-$499. **Rooms** 415. **Credit** AmEx, Disc, MC, V. **Map** p250/p252 F5 ⑯

The Fairmont's sunny, marble-floored lobby, so full of plants it looks like a greenhouse, instantly lifts the spirits. The pool, garden patio and 415 vast, bright rooms do the rest. The renovated fitness center offers up-to-date machines, a lap pool, squash and racquetball courts, aerobics classes and massages. Everyone, staff and guests alike, seems happy to find themselves here. Pets are also welcome, and owners can get advice on pet-friendly places to take them in DC. The Fairmont Gold, a 'hotel within a hotel', is a club floor with separate check-in, and free continental breakfast, afternoon tea and evening cocktails in the private lounge.
Bar (lobby). Business center. Concierge. Disabled-adapted rooms. Gym ($15 per 24hrs). Internet (Wi-Fi $14.95 per day, free for Fairmont Gold members). Parking ($40 per night). Restaurant. Room service (24hrs). Spa. Swimming pool (indoor). TV (pay movies, DVD player on request).

River Inn

924 25th Street, NW, between I & K Streets, DC 20037 (reservations 1-888 874 0100, hotel direct 1-202 337 7600, www.theriverinn.com). Foggy Bottom-GWU Metro. **Rates** $169-$225. **Credit** AmEx, Disc, MC, V. **Rooms** 125. **Map** p250/p252 F5 ⑰

Once a family-friendly lodging that drew primarily government and university types, the River Inn was reinvented as a boutique hotel a few years ago. It now exudes modern elegance, with dark wood and clean lines. The hotel pampers guests with plush robes, a video/CD library and in-room coffee makers; its restaurant, Dish, serves up nostalgic American food.
Bar. Business center (small). Disabled-adapted rooms. Gym. Internet (free Wi-Fi first floor, free wired high-speed other floors). Parking ($33 per night). Restaurant. Room service. TV (pay movies, DVD players in some rooms).

Moderate

Hotel Lombardy

2019 Pennsylvania Avenue, NW, at I Street, DC 20006 (reservations 1-800 424 5486, hotel direct 1-202 828 2600, www.hotellombardy.com). Foggy Bottom-GWU or Farragut West Metro. **Rates** $110-$359. **Credit** AmEx, Disc, MC, V. **Rooms** 140. **Map** p250/p252 G5 ⑱

Formerly a grand apartment building, this 134-unit boutique hotel retains some of that charm, with old-fashioned touches such as brass fixtures and crystal doorknobs, and a Middle Eastern-style bar. The views over Pennsylvania Avenue are good, but try not to get stuck in a room at the back of the building. There's also an attendant-operated elevator – when was the last time you saw that in a hotel? Access to the pool at the nearby Washington Plaza Hotel is included.
Bar. Concierge. Gym. Internet (wired, free). Parking ($36 per night). Restaurant. Room service. TV.

St Gregory Luxury Hotel & Suites

2033 M Street, NW, at 21st Street, DC 20036 (reservations 1-800 829 5034, hotel direct 1-202 530 3600, www.stgregoryhotelwdc.com). Dupont Circle or Foggy Bottom-GWU Metro. **Rates** $99-$350. **Rooms** 154. **Credit** AmEx, Disc, MC, V. **Map** p250/p252 G5 ⑲

A whimsically stylish hotel – there's a life-sized statue of Marilyn in the lobby, skirt up – where each of the 154 rooms and suites look as if they were decorated by a pro. No expense has been spared with the floral displays and high-quality furniture. Many rooms also have full kitchens and some have balconies. The staff more than match the decor, treating everyone like VIPs. Stop by the hotel bar for a mojito during happy hour.
Bar. Business center. Disabled-adapted rooms. Gym. Internet (wired high-speed, $11 per day). Parking ($29 per night). Room service. TV (pay movies, DVD players on request).

DOWNTOWN
Expensive

Madison

1177 15th Street, NW, at M Street, DC 20005 (reservations 1-800 424 8577, hotel direct 1-202 862 1600, www.loewshotels.com). McPherson Square Metro. **Rates** $140-$450 double. **Rooms** 363. **Credit** AmEx, Disc, MC, V. **Map** p250/ p252 H5 ⑳

A downtown hotel whose luxurious and very traditional feel – just as Founding Father James Madison would have wanted – make it popular with visiting foreign dignitaries. One of its two restaurants, Palette, is sleek and modern – a departure from the rest of the hotel. The surrounding area is dominated

Jefferson.

free). Parking ($40 per night). Restaurants (2). Room service. Spa. TV (pay movies, DVD players on request).

★ Hotel Monaco

700 F Street, NW, at 7th Street, DC 20004 (reservations 1-800 649 1202, hotel direct 1-202 628 7177, www.monaco-dc.com). Gallery Place-Chinatown Metro. **Rates** $219-$499 **Rooms** 183. **Credit** AmEx, Disc, MC, V. **Map** p253 J6 ㉒

The Monaco makes the most of its its grand setting – an imposing neo-classical building that was once the main Post Office sorting office. The unusual premises mean irregular shapes, high ceilings and features such as cornicing add an extra touch of originality to the guestrooms, where dramatic furnishings like black and white print headboards and drapes, with circles and stripes, add further individuality. It's not at the expense of comfort, however: furnishings are top of the range, bathrooms well appointed and rooms come with CD players and HD TVs. The large lobby/lounge is a stunner: painted a vivid kelly green and furnished with statement pieces, some modern classics, other one-off whimsical designs, that come together to create a gracious whole. There's a complimentary wine hour in the evening. The Monaco is the flagship property of the Kimpton group, which has several hotels in DC and Northern Virginia. Its conversion into a hotel was one step in the process of the regeneration of Downtown.

Bar. Business center. Concierge. Disabled-adapted rooms. Gym. Internet (Wi-fi, free to Kimpton In Touch members – can sign up when a guest). Parking ($38 per night). Restaurant. Room service. TV (pay movies).

► *For a review of bar/restaurant Poste, see p137. For more on the regeneration of Downtown, see p69.*

Renaissance Mayflower Hotel

1127 Connecticut Avenue, NW, between L & M Streets, DC 20036 (reservations 1-800 228 9290, hotel direct 1-202 347 3000, www.renaissance hotels.com). Farragut North or West Metro. **Rates** $149-$400. **Credit** AmEx, Disc, MC, V. **Map** p250/p252 G5 ㉓

Near the Washington Convention Center and Verizon Center, this large hotel features 64,000sq ft of flexible function space, a 6,000sq ft fitness center and a 4,000sq ft spa that offers a variety of therapeutic treatments. For a more intimate vibe, the newly renovated lobby offers several cozy spots where guests can hold small meetings or meet friends. Each of the unique seating areas offers free Wi-Fi and food and beverage.

Bars (2). Business center. Concierge. Disabled-adapted rooms. Gym. Internet (wired, Wi-Fi, $15 per day; free in suites). Parking ($25 per day/$42 overnight). Restaurants (2). Room service. TV (pay movies).

by office buildings and is a little dull after dark, but you can easily walk to the livelier Dupont and Logan Circle neighbourhoods.

Bars (2). Business center. Concierge. Disabled-adapted rooms. Gym (with steam room). Internet (Wi-Fi, wired high-speed, $12.95 per day). Parking ($40 per night). Restaurants (2). Room service. TV (pay movies, Sony PlayStations).

Jefferson

1200 16th Street, NW, at M Street, DC 20036 (1-202 448 2300/www.jeffersondc.com). Farragut North or Farragut West Metro. **Rates** $320-$500. **Rooms** 99. **Credit** AmEx, Disc, MC. V. **Map** p250/p252 H5 ㉑

Just blocks from the White House, this Beaux Arts building has reopened after a two-year renovation that blends the modern – complimentary Wi-Fi – and the historic, with elegant nods to Thomas Jefferson. Four-poster beds have linens that feature the third president's Monticello home and grounds. Downstairs is a clubby bar, snug library and Plume, an upscale French restaurant nestled under the lobby's barrel-vaulted skylight.

Bars (2). Business center. Concierge. Disabled adapted rooms. Gym (24hr). Internet (Wi-Fi,

CONSUME

Donovan House.

CONSUME

Moderate

Comfort Inn Downtown/Convention Center

1201 13th Street, NW, at M Street, DC 20005 (reservations 1-877 424 6423, hotel direct 1-202 682 5300, www.choicehotels.com). Mt Vernon Square/7th Street-Convention Center or McPherson Square Metro. **Rates** (incl breakfast) $159-$309. **Rooms** 100. **Credit** AmEx, Disc, MC, V. **Map** p250/p252 H5 ㉔

A well-appointed hotel, Comfort Inn Downtown provides 100 surprisingly decent and, of course, comfortable rooms in an up-and-coming neighbourhood three blocks from the convention center. The cheerful staff serve a free continental breakfast every morning.

Business center. Concierge. Disabled-adapted rooms. Gym. Internet (Wi-Fi, wired, free). Parking ($27 per night). TV.

★ Donovan House

1155 14th Street, NW, at Thomas Circle, DC 20005 (reservations 1-800 383 6900, hotel direct 1-202 737 1200, www.thompsonhotels.com/hotels/dc/donovan-house). Mc Pherson Square Metro. **Rates** $99-$350. **Rooms** 193. **Credit** AmEx, Disc, MC, V. **Map** p250/p252 H5 ㉕

This contemporary hotel features guest rooms in purples and browns with hanging egg chairs, cylindrical-shaped showers and iPod docking stations. Floor-to-ceiling windows overlook Thomas Circle. The best views, however, are found people-watching on the ground-floor Asian fusion restaurant, Zentan, or at the seasonal rooftop pool.

Bars (2). Business center. Disabled-adapted rooms. Gym. Internet (Wi-Fi, $11 per day). Restaurant. Room service. Swimming pool (outdoor). TV (pay movies).

Hamilton Crowne Plaza

1001 14th Street, NW, at K Street, DC 20005 (reservations 1-800 227 6963, hotel direct 1-202 682 0111, www.hamiltonhoteldc.com).

THE BEST STYLE HOTELS

Monaco
A contemporary interior in a neo-classical structure. *See p101.*

Donovan House
Hanging pod chairs and cylindrical showers. *See above.*

Palomar
Sleek, seductive browns dominate in these retro-stylish premises. *See p105.*

McPherson Square Metro. **Rates** $99-$459. **Rooms** 318. **Credit** AmEx, Disc, MC, V. **Map** p250/p252 H5 ㉖

The gorgeous Beaux Arts architecture of the Hamilton dates from the 1920s, the elegant exterior on Franklin Square complementing the 318 small but elegantly appointed rooms and suites inside. Some of the rooms have skyline views. Club Level guests get the use of a private elevator, plus free breakfast and use of the club lounge, and there's a women's floor for female business travelers; the 14K restaurant also has a 'captain's table' for women travelling alone.

Bar. Business center. Concierge. Disabled-adapted rooms. Gym. Internet (Wi-Fi, $12.95 per day). Parking ($37 per night). Restaurant. Room service. TV (pay movies).

Hampton Inn Washington, DC-Convention Center

901 6th Street, NW, at Massachusetts Avenue, DC 20001 (hotel direct 1-202 842 2500, www.hamptoninn.com). Gallery Place-Chinatown Metro. **Rates** (incl breakfast) $129-$269. **Rooms** 228. **Credit** AmEx, Disc, MC, V. **Map** p251/p253 J5 ㉗

Affordable, convenient and sparklingly clean, this chain hotel, opened in 2005, has earned praise from visitors. Just two blocks from the Metro, it's convenient for sightseeing. For business guests there are meeting rooms available. You won't need the Metro to get to great dining and shopping, though; the immediate area is packed with restaurants and shops. The guestrooms are unremarkable, but why spend time in your room?

Business center. Disabled-adapted rooms. Gym. Internet (wired, free; free Wi-Fi in lobby). Parking ($34 per night). Swimming pool & hot tub (indoor). TV (pay movies).

Budget

Hostelling International Washington, DC

1009 11th Street, NW, at K Street, DC 20001 (1-202 737 2333, www.hiwashingtondc.org). Metro Center Metro. **Rates** (incl breakfast) $29-$45 dorm style; $89.95-$109 per person private room. **Rooms** 250. **Credit** MC, V. **Map** p250/p252 J5 ㉘

A top-notch, dirt-cheap hostel close to the Metro and Downtown Washington, Hostelling International offers 250 beds divided between singles and doubles and larger dorm-style single-sex rooms or 'family' rooms of four-, six-, eight- and ten-bed configurations. Private rooms sleep two hostellers in twin beds. Most have shared bathrooms, but there are a limited number with en suite bathrooms. You can reserve online for a $5 discount – you'll have to forgo the breakfast, but you won't miss it. Kitchens, lockers, a new games room and a laundry (self-service) are all at your

disposal during your stay, and the staff arrange group walking tours and theatre outings. Most importantly, there is no lock-out time. We recommend booking well in advance, because large groups often take up most of the beds. Rates include linen. Non-members of Hostelling International are subject to a temporary membership fee of $3 per person.
Disabled-adapted rooms. Internet (pay terminal). TV (in games room).

PENN QUARTER
Moderate

Hotel Harrington
436 11th Street, NW, at E Street, DC 20004 (reservations 1-800 424 8532, hotel direct 1-202 628 8140, www.hotel-harrington.com). Metro Center Metro. **Rates** $109-$155. **Rooms** 242. **Credit** AmEx, Disc, MC, V. **Map** p252 J6 ❷
The Hotel Harrington is a family-owned budget hotel, plain and simple. The lobby and rooms are clean but outdated, the staff welcoming and helpful. People choose to stay here for two reasons: price and location. The hotel is surrounded by a neighborhood where you'll never get bored, and the Smithsonian museums and the Mall are also within easy reach. Family rooms sleep up to six people, and the hotel has a self-service laundry.

Bars (2). Disabled-adapted rooms. Internet (Wi-Fi, free). Parking ($15 per night). Restaurants (2). Room service. TV.

DUPONT CIRCLE
Deluxe

Mansion on O Street
2020 O Street, NW, between 20th & 21st Streets, DC 20036 (1-202 496 2000, www.omansion.com). Dupont Circle Metro. **Rates** rooms and suites, incl full English breakfast) $350-$2,000. **Rooms** 23. **Credit** AmEx, Disc, MC, V. **Map** p250 G4 ❸
Discretion exemplified, the 27-room B&B Mansion is hidden away on a quiet residential side street, with no sign to announce its presence. Each room in the three interconnected townhouses has a different theme: the Log Cabin suite, for example, has huge log beams, cow-hide rugs and three Frederic Remington sculptures; prices vary dramatically. The complex also serves as a private club and non-profit museum, and much of what you see, from the furniture to the wall hangings, is for sale. Some visitors love staying in a private mansion with 30 secret doors; others miss the better (and more accessible) service offered at conventional hotels. There are no 'standard' rooms here; rooms and suites are individually priced.

Palomar.

Break a Sweat

Hotels that help you stay healthy.

There's no excuse for being a slouch when you're staying in most Washington hotels. Gyms are pretty standard these days, but some hotels do a lot more to see that their guests keep fit. The **Fairmont** (*see p100*), for instance, has a 17,000-square-foot gym that includes a lap pool, and also offers classes ranging from Pilates to kickboxing. Guests who forget their gear can borrow complimentary athletic clothes, so there are no excuses for missing a workout.

At the **W** (*see p95*), guests can work out on one of the cardio machines, use the free weights or strap on boxing gloves and go a few rounds on the heavy bag. But it's the hotel's Beach Bums and Bellinis fitness sessions that can't be missed. Throughout the summer, the hotel offers an hour-long yoga class on the roof deck, followed by a buffet brunch complete with bottomless bellinis.

Throughout the warmer months the **Liaison** (*see p9*) also offers free daily vinyasa-based yoga classes on its expansive rooftop. Yoga mats, bottled water and towels are provided.

Kimpton group hotels, which include the **Palomar** (*see p105*), **George** (*see p97*) and **Monaco** (*see p101*), along with several others, offer in-room on-demand video workouts. Yoga, Pilates, core-strengthening and meditation are all complimentary and guests can request an exercise tote that includes a yoga mat, strap and block for use during their stay. For relaxation afterwards, the hotels offer in-room spa treatments.

The **Park Hyatt** (*see p99*) has a fitness center with an indoor pool. And guests who want to get out and explore the city and its miles of park and bike trails can take advantage of the Bicycle Valet, which offers a free hybrid bike rental for adults and children. The rental includes a helmet, bike lock, bottled water and map of the area's trails.

The **Mandarin Oriental** (*see p98*) has some of the most extensive fitness facilities to be found in DC hotels, with a 1,400-square-foot gym that includes a heated indoor lap pool and sun deck. Personal training and private yoga classes in the garden are also available. The fitness center also offers several unique sessions including a facial fitness program that works to tighten the muscles in your face and neck, a pool-based workout and Cardio-Core-Combo, which incorporates hand-eye coordination, strength and flexibility through cardio drills.

Bar (2, self-service). Business center. Concierge. Internet (Wi-Fi, wired, free). Parking ($25 per night). Room service. TV.

Expensive

Palomar

2121 P Street, NW, between 21st & 22nd Streets, DC 20037 (reservations 1-877 866 3070, hotel direct 1-202 448 1800, www.hotelpalomar-dc.com). Dupont Circle Metro. **Rates** $169-$379. **Credit** AmEx, Disc, MC, V. **Map** p250 G4 ⓷

The old Radisson that was on this site bequeathed large-sized rooms, an asset for the sleek, retro-styled Palomar. The spacious guestrooms use a soft palette of taupes, browns and mushroom, with a hint of leopardskin in the taupe jacquard carpet,

plus odd flashes of color. Headboards come in beige leather, and rooms are also equipped with capacious armchairs with footstools. Some, 'Spa Kings', come with Fuji soaking tubs (in serene bathrooms of white marble and dove grey). Eight 'Motion Rooms' have exercise equipment, such as a yoga mat and ball, as well as soaking tubs. All have DVD/CD players and iPod docks. The lobby has a touch of the exotic, with chocolate browns, dark woods and 60s-style chandeliers. On one white wall is a large mural of three faces.

Bar. Business center. Concierge. Disabled-adapted rooms. Gym. Internet (Wi-Fi, free to Kimpton In Touch members – can sign up when a guest). Restaurant. Room service. Parking ($36 per night). Swimming pool (outdoor). TV (pay movies).

CONSUME

Moderate

Beacon Hotel

1615 Rhode Island Avenue, NW, at 17th Street, DC 20036 (reservations 1-800 821 4367, hotel direct 1-202 296 2100, www.beaconhotelwdc.com). Dupont Circle or Farragut North Metro. **Rates** $99-$285. **Rooms** 97. **Credit** AmEx, Disc, MC, V. **Map** p250 G/H4 ⓷⓶

Once the stodgy Governor's House Hotel, the Beacon has been completely remade into a boutique-style lodging befitting the trendy Logan Circle neighborhood. Four nights a week, you can head to the rooftop for great views, designer martinis and appetizers (weather permitting). The Beacon is convenient for Connecticut Avenue shopping and a short stroll to the White House. Passes to the YMCA are available on request. Some suites resemble small apartments, complete with kitchens.

Bar. Business center. Concierge. Disabled-adapted rooms. Parking ($29 per night). Room service. Internet (Wi-Fi, $12.50 per day). TV (pay movies, DVD players in some rooms).

Dupont at the Circle

1604 19th Street, NW, between Q & Corcoran Streets, DC 20009 (reservations 1-888 412 0100, hotel direct 1-202 332 5251, 1-202 332 3244, www.dupontatthecircle.com). Dupont Circle Metro. **Rates** (incl breakfast) $165-$225. **Rooms** 11. **Credit** AmEx, Disc, MC, V. **Map** p250 G4 ⓷⓷

Just off bustling Dupont Circle, this elegant B&B is housed in two connected townhouses dating from 1883. Thickly blanketed beds, a luxurious parlor and a charming family-style dining room make the place feel ritzy but comfy. The owner is friendly and helpful, and guests receive free passes to a nearby fitness center.

Internet (Wi-Fi, free). Parking ($20 per night; reserve in advance). TV (certain rooms, some have DVD players).

Hotel Madera

1310 New Hampshire Avenue, NW, between N & 20th Streets, DC 20036 (reservations 1-800 430 1202, hotel direct 1-202 296 7600, www.hotelmadera.com). Dupont Circle Metro. **Rates** $119-$459. **Rooms** 82. **Credit** AmEx, DC, Disc, MC, V. **Map** p250 G4 ⓷⓸

More muted than the other Kimpton properties – for example, the flamboyant Hotel Rouge (*see p108*) or whimsical Hotel Monaco (*see p101*) – Madera plays with natural hues and materials so as to create a warm, soothing and sophisticated ambience. Guest rooms here are less dramatic-looking than those in many of the group's other properties. The location is hard to beat, and we like the wood and country look of the Firefly bar and restaurant. Speciality rooms include extras such as exercise equipment and kitchenette. There's a wine hour in the evening.

Bar. Business center. Disabled-adapted rooms. Internet (Wi-Fi, free to Kimpton In Touch members – can sign up when a guest). Parking ($36 per night). Restaurant. Room service. TV (pay movies).

▶ *for a review of Firefly, see p138.*

Swann House

1808 New Hampshire Avenue, NW, at 18th Street, DC 20009 (1-202 265 4414, www.swannhouse.com). Dupont Circle Metro. **Rates** (incl breakfast) $169-$329; $35 per additional person. **Rooms** 12. **Credit** AmEx, Disc, MC, V. **Map** p250 G4 ⓷⓹

Unlike Washington's townhouse B&Bs, the Swann House, built in 1883, is a freestanding mansion, which means the hallways aren't cramped and the lighting is good throughout. The pleasant rooms, which vary in their color schemes, are romantic without being twee, and some have working fireplaces and jacuzzis. A small swimming pool nestles in a brick courtyard at the back. Although it's a four-block walk to the nearest Metro station, you are rewarded with a beautiful tree-lined neighborhood within an easy stroll of the trendy bars on U Street and the hip strip of 17th Street. Room prices include breakfast, afternoon nibbles and an evening sherry. Note: children under 12 are not allowed. A two-night stay is usually required at weekends.

Internet (Wi-Fi, free). Parking ($14 per night; reserve in advance). Swimming pool (outdoor). TV (DVD player on request).

★ Tabard Inn

1739 N Street, NW, between Connecticut Avenue & 17th Street, DC 20036 (1-202 785 1277, www.tabardinn.com). Dupont Circle Metro. **Rates** (incl breakfast) for single occupancy with a $15 supplement for 2nd occupant $120-$145 (shared bath); $165-$230 double (private bath). **Rooms** 40. **Credit** AmEx, Disc, MC, V. **Map** p250/p252 G4 ⓷⓺

Each of the Tabard's 40 rooms is decorated in brilliant colours with a hotchpotch of slightly chipped antiques. Unique and classy, the hotel draws locals, who come to enjoy its excellent restaurant, the garden courtyard in summer and a roaring fire in winter. It's made up of three 19th-century townhouses and is the oldest continuously operated hotel in DC – the floors and doors squeak and there's no lift. Guests can use the nearby YMCA.

Bar. Internet (Wi-Fi, free). Parking ($35 per night). Restaurant. TV (on request).

Topaz Hotel

1733 N Street, NW, between Connecticut Avenue & 17th Street, DC 20036 (reservations 1-800 775 1202, hotel direct 1-202 393 3000, www.topazhotel.com). Dupont Circle Metro. **Rates** $119-$459 double. **Rooms** 99. **Credit** AmEx, DC, Disc, MC, V. **Map** p250/p252 G4 ⓷⓻

Helix. *See p108.*

Bold stripes meet bright patterns in the gue-strooms of the Topaz, a Kimpton group hotel that focuses on mind, body and spirit. Some rooms are done out as 'energy rooms' with exercise and yoga facilities. There's also a morning 'power hour', when healthy energy drinks are served. The Topaz bar contains a hidden nook called the Zen Den. It's not just for health nuts, though: in the evening, the small Topaz Bar comes to life with a complimentary wine hour, exotic cocktails, Asian-influenced fare and dance music.

Bar (with food service). Business center. Disabled-adapted rooms. Parking ($35 per night). Internet (Wi-Fi, free to Kimpton In Touch members – can sign up when a guest). Room service. TV (pay movies).

ADAMS MORGAN/ WOODLEY PARK

Expensive

Marriott Wardman Park
2660 Woodley Road, NW, at Connecticut Avenue, DC 20008 (reservations 1-800 228 9290, hotel direct 1-202 328 2000, www.marriott.com). Woodley Park Zoo/Adams Morgan Metro. **Rates** $159-$479. **Rooms** 1,314. **Credit** AmEx, Disc, MC, V. **Map** p249 F2 ⓷⓼
A huge and labyrinthine hotel perched on a hill near the Woodley Park-Zoo/Adams Morgan Metro stop. If you get lost (as you inevitably will), ask the friendly staff, who seem to be everywhere. Although the 1918 building is gorgeous and surrounded by luscious greenery, the larger wing of the complex is monolithic and lacks character. Expect to see weddings or conferences here; the hotel has extensive facilities for the latter.

Bar (1). Business center. Coffee shop. Disabled-adapted rooms. Gym. Parking ($32-$37 per night). Restaurants (2). Swimming pool (outdoor). Internet (wired $12.95 per day; free Wi-Fi in public areas). TV (pay movies).

Normandy Hotel
2118 Wyoming Avenue, NW, at Connecticut Avenue, DC 20008 (reservations 1-800 423 6953, hotel direct 1-202 483 1350, www.doylecollection. com/normandy). Dupont Circle Metro then L1 bus. **Rates** $99-$450 standard double. **Rooms** 26. **Credit** AmEx, Disc, MC, V. **Map** p250 G3 ⓷⓽
Tucked along a quiet street amid some of Washington's most expensive homes, what used to be Jury's Normandy has been transformed into a comfortable boutique hotel. The look is disceetly elegant, rooted in tradition but with some lively modern touches. Rooms have duck-down duvets, entertainment systems and in-room Nespresso machines. There are complimentary wine and cheese evenings on Tuesdays.

Disabled-adapted rooms. Internet (Wi-Fi, wired, free). Parking ($25 per night). TV (DVD players).

Omni Shoreham
2500 Calvert Street, NW, at Connecticut Avenue, DC 20008 (reservations 1-800 545 8700, hotel direct 1-202 234 0700, www.omnishoreham hotel.com). Woodley Park-Zoo/Adams Morgan Metro. **Rates** $99-$459. **Credit** AmEx, Disc, MC, V. **Map** p250 F2 ⓸⓪
One of Washington's largest and grandest hotels, the Omni Shoreham is located on 11 acres in the pleasant Woodley Park neighborhood, thus allowing the space for beautiful, formal gardens. The National Zoo, Rock Creek Park, Adams Morgan and the Metro are all within easy walking distance.

CONSUME

All this outdoors space makes it a good choice for families with children and the hotel has a program for child guests. The lobby and restaurant are quite posh, though the hotel is showing its age (75 years) in some places. Many of the bedrooms are former apartments, which means they're among the largest in town.

Bar. Business center. Concierge. Disabled-adapted rooms. Gym. Internet (wired $9.95 per day). Parking ($28 per night). Restaurant. Room service (24hrs). Spa. Swimming pool (outdoor). TV (pay movies, DVD player on request).

Moderate

Adam's Inn

1746 Lanier Place, NW, at 18th Street, DC 20009 (reservations 1-800 578 6807, hotel direct 1-202 745 3600, www.adamsinn.com). Woodley Park-Zoo/Adams Morgan Metro then 90, 92, 93, bus. **Rates** (incl breakfast) $89-$169 single with shared bath; $99-$179 single with private bath; $10 per extra person. **Rooms** 26. **Credit** AmEx, Disc, MC, V. **Map** p250 G2 ❹

Clean, sunny rooms fill the inn's three 100-year-old townhouses on a quiet and pretty street in Adams Morgan. The welcoming staff and old-fashioned furnishings and fireplaces make for a cozy stay. While the rooms don't have phones or TVs (invaluable for those seeking peace and quiet), there is a common lounge, kitchen and garden patio if you crave company, and nearby 18th Street offers enough bars and restaurants for a week. There's a minimum two-night stay for Saturday reservations.

Internet (Wi-Fi, free). Parking ($20 per night; reserve in advance). Payphone.

LOGAN CIRCLE
Moderate

Hotel Helix

1430 Rhode Island Avenue, NW, between 14th & 15th Streets, DC 20005 (reservations 1-800 706 1202, hotel direct 1-202 462 9001, www.hotel helix.com). Dupont Circle or McPherson Square Metro. **Rates** $119-$459. **Rooms** 178. **Credit** AmEx, DC, Disc, MC, V. **Map** p250 H4 ❷

The lobby may be channelling the Starship Enterprise, with flashing light squares and blue plastic check-in stands, and you may enter it through a purple curtain that sweeps open as you approach, but this does nothing to diminish the well-thought-out style and comfort of the guestrooms. Here, daring color matches (blue-green velour couch meets brownish-red footstool in a suite, for example) work, and there's attention to detail with Formica-look walls in the bathroom, and contemporary art on the walls. Curtains come in colorful retro prints and a whole-wall black and white surfing mural is the backdop to beds. The whole is actually pretty

relaxing, in a pop culture kind of way. This is perhaps the Kimpton group's most far-out property (speaking metaphorically, not geographically). You'll recognize it by the large Magritte-style painting on the outside. There's a complimentary champagne hour in the evening. *Photo p107.*

Bar (with food service). Business center. Disabled-adapted rooms. Gym. Parking ($33 per night). Room service. Internet (Wi-Fi, free to Kimpton In Touch members – can sign up when a guest). TV (pay movies).

Hotel Rouge

1315 16th Street, NW, at Massachusetts Avenue & Scott Circle, DC 20036 (reservations 1-800 738 1202, hotel direct 1-202 232 8000, www.rouge hotel.com). Dupont Circle or McPherson Square Metro. **Rates** $119-$459 double. **Rooms** 137. **Credit** AmEx, DC, Disc, MC, V. **Map** p250 H4 ❸

When the theme of your hotel is red, and your material of choice is leather, you're going to end up with something louche and loungey, and the Rouge has those qualities. Just down the road from the Helix (*see above*), this is another distinctive Kimpton hotel. A studded oriental-look doorway leads into a stylish retro lobby. The adjoining Rouge Bar is a dark, red-accented and stylish space that looks built for intrigue. Spacious rooms are a decadent combo of padded red leather ceiling-height headboards, huge lamps and armchairs, some in white leather. They're equipped with HD TVs, PlayStations, Wii and CD players. There's a complimentary wine hour in the evening.

Bar (with food service). Business center. Disabled-adapted rooms. Gym. Parking ($33 per night). Room service. Internet (Wi-Fi, free to Kimpton In Touch members – can sign up when a guest). TV (pay movies).

GEORGETOWN
Deluxe

Four Seasons

2800 Pennsylvania Avenue, NW, between 28th & 29th Streets, DC 20007 (reservations 1-800 819 5053, hotel direct 1-202 342 0444, www.four seasons.com/washington). Foggy Bottom-GWU Metro then 30, 32, 34, 35, 36 bus or Circulator bus. **Rates** $495-$675. **Rooms** 222. **Credit** AmEx, Disc, MC, V. **Map** p249 F5 ❹

One of DC's most comfortable hotels, the Four Seasons has long attracted VIP guests. The health spa is both serious and sybaritic, and good art is displayed throughout. Even if you're not lucky enough to be staying here, you can at least treat yourself to afternoon tea on the Garden Terrace. If you can stump up the money for a reservation, ask to stay in the east wing, where a $40 million renovation a few years ago enlarged the rooms and updated the decor.

Bar. Business center. Concierge. Disabled-adapted rooms. Gym. Internet (Wi-Fi, wired, $10 per day). Parking ($42 per night). Spa. Swimming pool (indoor). Restaurants (2). Room service. Satellite TV (pay movies, DVD players).

Ritz-Carlton, Georgetown

3100 South Street, NW, at 31st Street, DC 20007 (reservations 1-800 241 3333, hotel direct 1-202 912 4100, www.ritzcarlton.com/hotels/georgetown). Foggy Bottom-GWU Metro then 30, 32, 34, 35, 36 bus or Circulator bus. **Rates** *$349-$599.* **Rooms** 86. **Credit** AmEx, Disc, MC, V. **Map** p249 E5 ㊺

With just 86 guest rooms – about a third of which are executive suites – the Ritz's Georgetown property is more intimate than its Foggy Bottom sister hotel (*see p99*). Located near the Potomac River waterfront, the hotel is housed in a renovated red-brick building with a 130ft smokestack. The industrial architecture makes a striking backdrop for the chic modern furnishings. Some rooms have views of Downtown and the river. The building also houses a cinema, spa and coffee shop, as well as a restaurant (Fahrenheit) and martini lounge (Degrees). The upmarket neighborhood is not near the Metro, but there's plenty going on in the area to keep you entertained.

Bar. Business center. Concierge. Disabled-adapted rooms. Gym. Internet (wired, $9.95 per day). Parking ($39 per night). Restaurant. Room service. Spa. TV (pay movies, DVD players).

Moderate

Georgetown Suites

1111 30th Street, NW, between K & M Streets, & 1000 29th Street, NW, at K Street, DC 20007 (reservations 1-800 348 7203, hotel direct 1-202 298 7800, www.georgetownsuites.com). Foggy Bottom-GWU Metro then 30, 32, 34, 35, 36 bus, or Circulator bus. **Rates** *(incl breakfast) $125-$255 standard suite.* **Rooms** 222. **Credit** AmEx, Disc, MC, V. **Map** p249 F5 ㊻

This all-suites hotel, divided into two buildings, is on a quiet street off the main drag of M Street. Formerly condominiums, each suite is well equipped with full kitchens and some units have patios. It's well situated for forays into Georgetown and along the Potomac river. The rooms are bright and spacious – some are absolutely huge.

Business center. Concierge. Disabled-adapted rooms (1). Gym. Internet (Wi-Fi, free). Parking ($20 per night). TV (DVD player on request).

Hotel Monticello

1075 Thomas Jefferson Street, NW, between M & K Streets, DC 20007 (reservations 1-800 388 2410, hotel direct 1-202 337 0900, www.monticellohotel.com). Foggy Bottom-GWU Metro then 30, 32, 34, 35, 36 bus or Circulator bus.

Rates *(incl breakfast) $109-$359.* **Credit** AmEx, Disc, MC, V. **Map** p249 F5 ㊼

The charming Hotel Monticello, named after Thomas Jefferson's country estate (the man himself once lived on this street), offers quiet rooms amid the hubbub of Georgetown. All 47 suites have roomy living areas, complete with microwave and mini-fridge, and big, modern bathrooms with upmarket toiletries and fluffy robes. Get a room with a view of M Street and indulge in some people-watching from your window.

Business center. Concierge. Disabled-adapted rooms. Internet (Wi-Fi, free). Parking ($30 per night). TV. Rooms (47).

SOUTHWEST
Moderate

Capitol Skyline

10 I Street, SW, between South Capitol Street & Half Street, DC 20024 (1-202 488 7500, www.capitolskyline.com). Metro Navy Yard. **Rates** *$90-$349.* **Rooms** 203. **Credit** AmEx, Disc, MC, V. **Map** p253 K7 ㊽

This space-age looking hotel with a honeycomb exterior sits in the shadow of the Capitol and the Nationals ballpark in the up-and-coming Navy Yard neighborhood. The rooms are pretty standard; it's the pool that draws a crowd. Surrounded by neon pink and orange Adirondack chairs, the large pool attracts families during summer mornings and adults looking for a Miami vibe in the afternoon and evenings.

Bar (2). Business center. Concierge. Disabled adapted rooms. Gym. Internet (Wi-Fi, free). Parking ($25 per night). Restaurant. Swimming pool (outdoor). TV (pay movies). Room service.

ALEXANDRIA, VA
Expensive

★ Monaco Alexandria

480 King Street, Alexandria, VA 22314 (reservations 1-800 368 5047, hotel direct 1-703 549 6080, www.monaco-alexandria.com). King Street Metro then 10min walk. **Rates** *$149-$299.* **Rooms** 241. **Credit** AmEx, Disc, MC, V.

Unlike its sister hotel, Morrison House (*see p110*) down the road, Monaco Alexandria makes a bold design statement with its lobby/lounge. Walls and pillars are a glowing, striking blue, and there's just a touch of Old Shanghai in the gold on black patterned walls behind the red padded-leather reception desk. Furnishings here are eclectic: lots of shades and patterns are thrown together to great effect, with hints of whimsy in a leopardskin-painted fire surround. Bedrooms continue the bold theme. They're luxurious, many with brown-khaki walls, and lots of black and white in comfortable

CONSUME

Monaco Alexandria. *See p109.*

the fireplace. We like the quiet sitting room with polished parquet floor and wood panelling. In the guestrooms, discreet contemporary artwork mediates the yellows and peaches and Colonial-style furniture. Beds in some rooms are four-posters (with steps to help you climb in). There's a complimentary wine hour in the evening.

Bar. Business center. Disabled-adapted rooms. Internet (Wi-Fi, free to Kimpton In Touch members – can sign up when checked in). Parking ($24 per night). Room service. TV (pay movies).

ARLINGTON, VA
Moderate

Key Bridge Marriott
1401 Lee Highway, at Wilson Street, VA 22209 (reservations 1-800 228 9290, hotel direct 1-703 524 6400, www.marriott.com). Rosslyn Metro.
Rates $119-$369. **Rooms** 582. **Credit** AmEx, Disc, MC, V.
You won't find a better view of the Washington skyline at night than from the top of the Key Bridge Marriott. A large and luxurious hotel built for conventions (it has 17 meeting rooms), it's about a mile from Arlington National Cemetery and a quick walk across the bridge to Georgetown. The Metro, too, is nearby. A $13 million renovation a few years ago included an expanded 24-hour gym and improved business center and new lobby. Be sure to request a room with a city view.
Bar. Business center. Gym. Concierge. Disabled-adapted rooms. Parking ($17 per night). Restaurant. Swimming pools (indoor/outdoor). Room service. Internet (wired in rooms, $12.95 per day; free Wi-Fi in lobby). TV (pay movies).

BETHESDA, MD
Moderate

Hyatt Regency Bethesda
1 Bethesda Metro Center, 7400 Wisconsin Avenue at Old Georgetown Road, MD 20814 (1-301 657 1234, www.bethesda.hyatt.com). Bethesda Metro.
Rates $99-$369 double. **Rooms** 390. **Credit** AmEx, Disc, MC, V.
Children will adore this luxurious hotel for its rooftop pool (there's also a whirlpool and sauna), thrilling 11-story atrium lobby and three speedy glass elevators. Each of the 390 rooms has huge desks and black and white photographs of the city's monuments. Another perk: the Metro station is directly underneath the hotel.
Bar. Business center. Concierge. Disabled-adapted rooms. Gym. Internet (Wi-Fi, $9.95 per day). Parking ($20 per night). Restaurants (2). Room service. Swimming pool (indoor). TV (pay movies, DVD players on request).

armchairs and chaises longues. Some feature bathrooms with two-person soaking baths. There's an indoor swimming pool in the third-floor fitness center. The Monaco's well-known restaurant, Jackson 20, has a distinctive approach to local food traditions, with its own take on the likes of pot roast and pork and sweet potato pie.
Bar. Business center. Disabled-adapted rooms. Gym. Internet (Wi-Fi, free to Kimpton In Touch members – can sign up when a guest). Parking ($24 per night). Pool (indoor). Restaurant. Room service. TV (pay movies).

Morrison House
116 S Alfred Street, Alexandria, VA 22314 (reservations 1-866 834 6628, hotel direct 1-703 838-8000, www.morrisonhouse.com).
Rates $159-$309. **Rooms** 45. **Credit** AmEx, Disc, MC, V.
A graciously appointed, intimate hotel in Old Town Alexandria, Morrison House is actually part of the Kimpton group, representing its take on traditional, Colonial style. In this it goes more or less all the way. Colours are subtle in the gleaming public rooms, their furnishings revealing just tiny hints of a different design ethos, in the raw silk pastel-striped drapes in the lounge, perhaps, or the modern candleabra in

CONSUME

Restaurants

From power dining to ethnic enclaves.

As the DC dining scene finally shakes off its inferiority complex with relation to the country's other dining powerhouses, the options for eating out have never been more diverse. From ethnic enclaves of Ethiopian and Vietnamese fare to modern hotspots with month-long waiting lists, the culinary landscape in the nation's capital is rapidly maturing.

One noteworthy trend is that celebrity chefs are flocking to DC to capitalize on a savvy dining public. Ask a local and they may bristle at the notion of absentee chefs, but their presence has raised the bar around town.

EATING IN WASHINGTON

Jean-Georges Vongerichten (**J&G Steakhouse**, *see p95*), Wolfgang Puck (**The Source**, *see p121*) and Eric Ripert (**Westend Bistro**, *see p99*) have opened restaurants recently and more are on the way. Meanwhile, several of DC's top chef talents, such as Jose Andres (*see p118*), have garnered national fame and are expanding their own restaurant empires beyond the city.

Another fun prevailing force on the culinary scene: the new wave of food trucks rolling around town serving portable fare ranging from lobster rolls to cupcakes (*see p123* **Meals on Wheels**).

Intimate wine bars serving cheese, charcuterie and dozens of choices by the glass have helped fill what used to be a void in neighborhood restaurants. And as in many big cities, DC diners are becoming more relaxed about eating out. Restaurants are responding by ditching the white tablecloths, relaxing dress codes and crafting menus made for sharing. Fine dining chefs are branching out with more casual options, like Michel Richard's bustling bistro **Central** (*see p118*) and Robert Wiedmaier's **Brasserie Beck** (1101 K Street, NW, 1-202 408 1717, http://76.12.24.170/beck_home.html) and **Mussel Bar** (7262 Woodmont Avenue, Bethesda, MD, 1-301 215 7817, www.musselbar.com).

❶ Blue numbers given in this chapter correspond to the location of each restaurant and café as marked on the street maps. *See pp248-53.*

TIPPING

Whatever your preference and budget, keep in mind that Washington is an expensive city and servers essentially earn their living from gratuities. Natives tend to tip 20 per cent or even higher; 15 per cent on the pre-tax bill is expected, even at the most humble of restaurants.

MONUMENTAL CENTER
White House & around

$ Breadline

1751 Pennsylvania Avenue, NW, between 17th & 18th Streets (1-202 822 8900, www.breadline dc.com). Farragut West Metro. **Open** 7.30am-3.30pm Mon-Fri. **Main courses** $5.50-$11. **Credit** AmEx, MC, V. **Map** p252 G5 ❶
Sandwich bar
On a downtown block with plenty of other quick breakfast and lunch options available in the area, Breadline is always packed. This counter-order eaterie has earned cult status among Washingtonians for its soups, salads and gargantuan sandwiches, made with artisanal loaves, which are baked on the premises, and quality fillings. The food isn't cheap, but the portions are large enough to keep the average person going all day. The turkey sandwich, for example, comes with so much meat that it is physically impossible to keep more than half between the slabs of fresh bread. If you've got room, add some boutique soda and Route 11 chips – Virginia-made potato crisps that come in a variety of novelty flavors.

INSIDE TRACK QUICK TIPS

A quick way to figure the standard 20 per cent tip: simply double the sales tax on your bill.

Capitol & around

Johnny's Half Shell
400 North Capitol Street, NW, at Louisiana Avenue.(1-202 737 0400, www.johnnyshalf shell.net). Union Station Metro. **Open** 7.30-9.30am (breakfast), 11.30am-2.30pm, 5-10pm Mon-Fri; 5-10pm Sat. **Main courses** $18.25-$32.50. **Credit** AmEx, MC, V. **Map** p253 K6 ❷ Fish
Owned and run by renowned culinary pair Ann Cashion (chef) and John Fulchino, Johnny's relocated to North Capitol Street a few years ago. The restaurant has stayed the same, though: it's famous for its super high-grade seafood ingredients, from oysters on the half shell to grilled sea scallops, prepared to simple perfection. Jazz and blues – and strong drinks – create a vibrant atmosphere and the restaurant hums with its own success.

DC NEIGHBORHOODS
Foggy Bottom

Café Asia
1721 I Street, NW, between 17th & 18th Streets (1-202 659 2696, www.cafeasia.com). Farragut West Metro. **Open** 11.30am-10pm Mon-Wed; 11.30am-midnight Thur, Fri; noon-midnight Sat. **Main courses** $10-$29. **Credit** AmEx, MC, V. **Map** p252 G5 ❹ Asian
If you like your sushi loud and upfront, then you'll thoroughly enjoy Café Asia. It's pretty hard to ignore the blaring music coming from the bar/lounge area, which always seems to be hopping with excited singles. The pan-Asian menu is far from inspiring, but its survey coverage of the region is above average and everything is well done. The new downtown location has two floors, each with a bar, and offers communal tables for larger groups.
Other locations 1550 Wilson Boulevard, at Pierce Street, Rosslyn (1-703 741 0870).

★ Equinox
818 Connecticut Avenue, NW, between H & I Streets (1-202 331 8118, www.equinoxrestaurant. com). Farragut West Metro. **Open** 11.30am-2pm, 5.30-10pm Mon-Thur; 11.30am-2pm, 5.30-10.30pm Fri; 5.30-10.30pm Sat; 5.30-9pm Sun. **Main courses** $28- $35. **Credit** AmEx, MC, V. **Map** p252 H5 ❺ Contemporary American
Chef Todd Gray is known for his emphasis on the seasonal and regional; Equinox's three- to six-course tasting menu generally includes such delicacies as

Chesapeake Bay crab, Carolina grouper and locally grown organic vegetables. The suited power brokers who frequent the place – conveniently located halfway between the White House and K Street – may or may not appreciate Gray's efforts to acquire sustainably farmed fish and humanely raised meat, but they surely appreciate the deceptively simple preparations in which such ingredients shine. Service in the understated dining room, presided over by Ellen Kassoff-Gray, is deft and friendly. Call well in advance for reservations.

Kaz Sushi Bistro
1915 I Street, NW, between 19th & 20th Streets (1-202 530 5500, www.kazsushibistro.com). Farragut West Metro. **Open** 11.30am-2pm, 6-10pm Mon-Fri; 6-10pm Sat. **Main courses** $10-$16 lunch; $12-$25 dinner; $14-$15 bento boxes. **Credit** AmEx, MC, V. **Map** p252 G5 5 ❻ Japanese
Sushi king Kazuhiro Okochi made his mark at Sushi-Ko (*see p133*), successfully melding Asian and Western ingredients, before bringing the winning formula here. The sushi itself is top-notch, featuring fish that is gorgeous and glistening, while the rice has a touch of sweetness unlike any you'll find elsewhere. But should your tastes not include raw fish, there's also a bounty of wonderfully cooked items on offer, including grilled baby octopus, coriander-crusted calamari and Asian-style short ribs.

Kinkead's
2000 Pennsylvania Avenue, NW, between 20th & 21st Streets (1-202 296 7700, www.kinkead.com). Foggy Bottom-GWU Metro. **Open** 11.30am-2.30pm, 5.30-10pm Mon-Thur, Sun; 11.30am-2.30pm, 5.30-10.30pm Fri; 5.30-10.30pm Sat. **Main courses** $15-$21 lunch; $25-$32 dinner. **Credit** AmEx, Disc, MC, V. **Map** p252 G5 ❼ Fish
This upscale brasserie features some of the finest fish in the region and one of Washington's best wine lists. The bar area is lively, with nightly jazz piano/bass, and roomy enough to accommodate bar-side nibbling. Although seafood is the menu's focus, the meaty items carry their weight. Oyster-lovers, take note: the raw bar gets top marks.

★ Marcel's
2401 Pennsylvania Avenue, NW, between 24th & 25th Streets (1-202 296 1166, www.marcels dc.com). Foggy Bottom-GWU Metro. **Open** 5.30-10pm Mon-Thur; 5.30-11pm Fri, Sat; 5.30-9.30pm Sun. **Set meals** (3-5 courses) $65-$130. **Credit** AmEx, MC, V. **Map** p252 F5 ❽ French
Marcel's is the kind of restaurant that you'd expect to find on Pennsylvania Avenue: exquisite food, beautifully served in a sumptuous dining room by adept professionals. Chef Robert Wiedmaier's Flemish-inflected French fare manages the classical balance of taste and textures: subtle versus sharp-flavored, savory versus sweet, generous versus leaving you wanting more. Boudin blanc and duck

CONSUME

Bibiana. *See p115.*

Whatever your carbon footprint, we can reduce it

For over a decade we've been leading the way in carbon offsetting and carbon management.

In that time we've purchased carbon credits from over 200 projects spread across 6 continents. We work with over 300 major commercial clients and thousands of small and medium sized businesses, which rely upon our market-leading quality assurance programme, our experience and absolute commitment to deliver the right solution for each client.

Why not give us a call?

T: London (020) 7833 6000

www.CarbonNeutral.com

breast with apple butter and honey crisp apples is exemplary, and a gratin of mussels is an essay on the varieties of sensation contained within the words salty, rich and intense. The servers get extra points for friendliness: even if you're not one of the place's traditional, old-money clients, they'll still treat you as if you were.

★ Ris

2275 L Street, NW, at 23rd Street (1-202 730 2500, www.risdc.com). Foggy Bottom-GWU Metro. **Open** 11.30am-11pm Mon-Fri; 5.30-11pm Sat; 10am-3pm (brunch), 3-9pm Sun. **Main courses** $22-$36. **Map** p252 F5 ❾ Contemporary American
Ris Lacoste, who earned her stellar reputation as former executive chef of Georgetown's classic 1789 (*see p129*), struck out on her own with this comfortable West End restaurant. (Pronunciation hint: Ris is short for Doris.) Neighbors, power players and the chef's devotees fill the 200-some seats, spread over a bar, café, patio and segmented dining areas with plush banquettes. The American menu taps into international influences, with dishes like monkfish osso bucco, braised lamb shank with chickpeas and yogurt, and sesame crusted salmon with red curry broth. Regular daily specials include meatloaf on Mondays.

Vidalia

1990 M Street, NW, between 19th & 20th Streets (1-202 659 1990, www.vidaliadc.com). Dupont Circle Metro. **Open** 11.30am-2.30pm, 5.30-9.30pm Mon-Thur; 11.30am-2.30pm, 5.30-10pm Fri; 5.30-10pm Sat; 5-9pm Sun. **Main courses** $16-$26 lunch; $30-$36 dinner. **Credit** AmEx, Disc, MC, V. **Map** p250 G5 ❿ Southern
Onions are much in evidence in the hushed, golden dining room of Vidalia, which itself is named after the Southern sweet variety. You'll find them in a spread for the complimentary bread, in a rich hot soup made with duck broth and in the discreet artwork adorning the walls. But the restaurant's raison d'être is neither single-ingredient schtick nor even strictly Southern cooking; it proudly proclaims its cuisine to be 'American regional'. There are many dishes in which pork is the star player – a cassoulet comes in several varieties – and grits and oysters are likely suspects on winter menus.

Downtown

Austin Grill

750 E Street, NW, at 8th Street (1-202 393 3776, www.austingrill.com). Gallery Place-Chinatown or Archives Navy-Memorial Metro. **Open** 11am-11pm Mon-Thur; 11am-1pm Fri, Sat; 11am-10pm Sun. **Main courses** $9-$18.50. **Credit** AmEx, Disc, MC, V. **Map** p253 J6 ⓫ Tex-Mex
The Tex-Mex cousin of Jaleo (*see p118*), located next door, Austin Grill fills the gap between upscale dining and fast-food munching. It's popular with a variety of diners – families who don't want to deal with high-maintenance restaurants and singles who are looking for chow that doesn't interrupt meeting potential suitors. It also offers a gluten-free menu. There are plenty of tequilas to sample and everything comes with chips and salsa.
Other locations throughout the city.

★ Bibiana

1100 New York Avenue, NW, between 11th & 12th Streets (1-202 216 9550, http://bibiana dc.com). Metro Center Metro. **Open** 11.30am-10.30pm Mon-Wed; 11.30am-11pm Thur, Fri; 5.30-11pm Sat. **Main courses** $7-$29. **Credit** AmEx, MC, V. **Map** p250 J5 ⓬ Italian
A sleek and sophisticated downtown spot, Bibiana is the newest member of restaurateur Ashok Bajaj's empire, which also includes the Oval Room, Rasika (*see p118*), Bombay Club (*see below*), 701 and Ardeo+Bardeo. Chef Nick Stefanelli's well-executed Italian menu features exceptional pastas such as black spaghetti with Maryland lump crab as well as fish and meat entrées. The dining room, often packed with a diverse mix of stylish Washingtonians, is done up with dark wood, warm orange tones and sculptural silver pendant lights hanging overhead. A seat at the bar, with its black and white photos of Italian scooters and a small window that looks in on the kitchen action, is a great perch for cocktails, such as the signature Bibiana (Prosecco and fresh peach purée) or one of the housemade liqueurs. *Photos p113.*

Bombay Club

815 Connecticut Avenue, NW, between H & I Streets (1-202 659 3727, www.bombayclub dc.com). Farragut West or Farragut North Metro. **Open** 11.30am-2.30pm, 5.30-10.30pm Mon-Thur; 11.30am-2.30pm, 5.30-11pm Fri; 5.30-11pm Sat; 11.30am-2.30pm, 5.30-9pm Sun. **Main courses** $16-$32. **Set brunch** $18.50. **Credit** AmEx, MC, V. **Map** p252 H5 ❸ Indian
Bombay Club evokes not the multihued Mumbai of today but India in the time of the Raj, when English gentlemen could sit in restrained, masculine dining rooms and, presumably, cherry-pick the best of the subcontinent's cuisine. Decorous waiters in penguin suits warn against the supposed heat of a non-threatening lamb vindaloo (thali platters, tandoori meats and Goan curries are also on offer); the menu offers discreet explanations of the various regional styles.

Capital Q

707 H Street, NW, at 7th Street (1-202 347 8396, www.capitalqbbq.com). Gallery Place-Chinatown Metro. **Open** 11am-9pm Mon-Wed; 11am-midnight Thur-Sat. **Main courses** $8.50-$26. **Credit** ($15 minimum) AmEx, MC, V. **Map** p253 J5 ⓭ Southern
The down-home vibe of this Texas-style barbecue joint – with rustic walls, classic rock and the side dishes served out of big vats, like at a church picnic

CONSUME

– makes it an appealing alternative in a neighborhood clotted with chain restaurants. You decide on your meat – brisket or short ribs, sausage, pulled pork or chicken – pick sandwich or platter, and load up on sides. The Texas caviar (a black-eyed pea salad) is a nice counterpoint to all the heat and meat.

Ceiba

701 14th Street, NW, at G Street (1-202 393 3983, www.ceibarestaurant.com). Metro Center Metro. **Open** 11.30am-2.30pm, 5.30-10.30pm Mon-Fri; 5.30-11pm Sat. **Main courses** $16-$27. **Credit** AmEx, Disc, MC, V. **Map** p252 H5 ❷ Latin/Caribbean

Brightly colored murals, discreetly placed, are about the only whimsical touches in Ceiba's majestic space, much frequented by expense-account diners. Otherwise, the look is sleek, modern neutrals, with furniture from Brazil and stone and tiles from Yucatan. The cuisine, though, is an abundance of invention, with Latin American and Caribbean food as inspiration. There's a lot of seafood – conch chowder, crab fritters, several variants on ceviche – as well as Cuban pork sandwiches and black bean soup. It's hearty rather than homey food, as studied as its slick presentation.

DC Coast

Tower Building, 1401 K Street, NW, at 14th Street (1-202 216 5988, www.dccoast.com). McPherson Square Metro. **Open** 11.30am-2.30pm, 5.30-10.30pm Mon-Thur; 11.30am-2.30pm, 5.30-11pm Fri; 5.30-11pm Sat; 5.30-9.30pm Sun. **Main courses** $13-$28 lunch; $23-$29 dinner. **Credit** AmEx, MC, V. **Map** p252 H5 ❶ Contemporary American

The 'coast' of the name refers not just to the Atlantic but also the West and Gulf Coasts. It's a pretty wide net to cast, but the brains behind DC Coast – and they are brains, the creators of several of Washington's hottest dining spots – have found a way to integrate Southern, Southwestern and even Pacific Rim influences on the menu in their cavernous, well-appointed dining room. Soy sauce and tabasco share space in the kitchen; bok choy and bacon both

---

THE BEST FOR FUN

With burgers
Good Stuff Eatery. *See p121.*

With wine
Cork Wine Bar. *See p127.*

With sushi
Sushi Taro. *See p124.*

With table tennis
Comet Ping Pong. *See p131.*

---

grace the tables. The busy, businessy crowd eats it all up with gusto. Reservations recommended.

Georgia Brown's

950 15th Street, NW, between I & K Streets (1-202 393 4499, www.gbrowns.com). McPherson Square Metro. **Open** 11.30am-10pm Mon-Thur; 11.30am-11pm Fri; noon-11pm Sat; 10am-2.30pm, 5.30-10pm Sun. **Set brunch** $41, $21.95 under-12s, drinks not included. **Credit** AmEx, Disc, MC, V. **Map** p252 H5 ❶ Southern

One of DC's earliest and best attempts to upscale Low Country cooking, Georgia Brown's makes the case for saying that Washington is, in fact, a Southern city. Soul music plays softly in the warm-wood dining room; cornbread and dense, creamy biscuits, served with sweet butter, accompany the entrées. Fried green tomatoes, a showpiece of the restaurant, involve thin slices of the vegetable layered with herbed cream cheese, breaded, and laced with a spicy remoulade. In another twist on tradition, there are even a few decent vegetarian options. Beloved of local politicos, the restaurant serves power lunches, dinners, and a Sunday jazz brunch.

Matchbox

713 H Street, NW, at 7th Street (1-202 289 4441, www.matchboxdc.com). Gallery Place-Chinatown Metro. **Open** 11am-midnight Mon-Fri; 10am-midnight Sat, Sun. **Main courses** $14-$28. **Credit** AmEx, Disc, MC, V. **Map** p253 J5 ❶ Pizza/American

Aptly named, this narrow, three-storey restaurant is always packed. Why? Three reasons: the thin-crust pizzas that come out of Matchbox's brick oven; the platters of mini-hamburgers, and the casual, fun atmosphere. In the mood for something a little fancier? Matchbox also serves traditional bistro dishes like pork tenderloin and rockfish. **Other locations** 521, 8th Street, Capitol Hill (1-202 548 0369).

Oceanaire Seafood Room

1201 F Street, NW, at 12th Street (1-202 347 2277, www.oceanaireseafoodroom.com). Metro Center Metro. **Open** 11.30am-10pm Mon-Thur; 11.30am-11pm Fri, Sat; 5-9pm Sun. **Main courses** $14-$43 lunch; $23-$52 dinner. **Credit** AmEx, Disc, MC, V. **Map** p252 H6 ❶ Fish

Don't be surprised if you spot senators and lobbyists making back-room deals at this see-and-be-seen spot for Washington's power set. Seafood is given steakhouse treatment – in other words, served in huge portions – in this art deco-styled dining room that feels like an ocean liner. The menu, of sustainably caught seafood, changes daily, reflecting availability and seasonality of the goods. Ever tried Arctic char? Now's your chance. Or sample oysters, clams, crab and lobster at the raw bar. And for dessert? Go for the baked Alaska.

The Source. *See p121.*

Potenza

1430 H Street, NW, at 15th Street (1-202 638 4444, http://potenzadc.com). McPherson Square Metro. **Open** 11.30am-10pm Mon-Thur; 11.30am-11pm Fri; 10am-3pm (brunch), 5-10pm Sun.
Main courses $17-$29. **Credit** AmEx, MC, V.
Map p252 H5 ⑲ Italian

Executive chef Bryan Moscatello traveled around Italy for menu inspiration for Potenza, a sprawling downtown restaurant that offers several speeds of dining. There's the Italian bakery, where you can pick up a cappuccino and cherry pistachio sticky bun to start the day, then meatball subs and cannoli in the afternoon. The main restaurant, with velvety red booths and a rustic Italian menu, features a salumi counter, raw bar, 6,000lb pizza oven and a roomy bar. In summers, an outdoor grill on the patio turns out Italian sausages for diners on the go, and a boutique wine shop sells Italian vintages.

★ Proof

775 G Street, NW, between 7th & 8th Streets (1-202 737 7663, www.proofdc.com). Gallery Place-Chinatown Metro. **Open** 11.30am-2pm, 5.30-10pm Tue-Thur; 11.30am-2pm, 5.30-11pm Fri; 5.30-11pm Sat; 5-9.30pm Sun. *Bar* 5.30pm-1am Mon; 11.30am-2pm, 5.30pm-1am Tue-Thur; 11.30am-2pm, 5.30pm-2am Fri; 5.30pm-2am Sat; 5pm-midnight Sun. **Main courses** $24-$29.
Credit AmEx, MC, V. **Map** p253 J6 ⑳
Fusion/wine bar

Former tax attorney Mark Kuller turned his passion for great food and wine (his home cellar boasts some 7,000 bottles) into his first foray into the restaurant business: the wine-focused Proof. (He followed up with Estadio, *see 127,* in July 2010.) The hotspot is a tough table to snag at the last minute, so plan ahead to get a taste of chef Haidar Karoum's excellent cooking. His ahi tuna tartare with wasabi soy emulsion makes the cliché dish fresh again, and his veal sweetbreads are some of the best around. The hip young staff, including the irreverent and punky wine director Sebastian Zutant, make the bustling dining room all the more welcoming. A seat at the bar in front of the shiny Enomatic wine dispenser comes with a side of culture – the flat screens overhead display a mesmerizing rotation of artwork from the neighboring National Portrait Gallery.

Zaytinya

Pepco Building, 701 9th Street, NW, at G Street (1-202 638 0800, www.zaytinya.com). Gallery Place-Chinatown Metro. **Open** 11.30am-10pm Mon, Sun; 11.30am-11.30pm Tue-Thur; 11.30am-midnight Fri, Sat. **Main courses** $6-$14.50.
Credit AmEx, Disc, MC, V. **Map** p253 J5 ㉑
Mediterranean

With a stunning white and blue interior, this place finds inspiration in Greece, Turkey and Lebanon. Trendy Zaytinya is one of Washington's most popular restaurants. Once parties are seated, cones of piping hot bread arrive, and the fun begins. The menu of 60-plus meze dishes is kind to both vegetarians and carnivores. Our tips? grape leaves dolmades or piyuz (warm giant beans with oven roasted tomato, garlic and kale) to start, followed by braised lamb shank with eggplant purée.

Penn Quarter

Café Atlántico

405 8th Street, NW, at D Street (1-202 393 0812, www.cafeatlantico.com). Archives-Navy Memorial or Gallery Place-Chinatown Metro. **Open** 11.30am-2.30pm, 5-10pm Tue-Thur, Sun; 11am-2.30pm, 5-11pm Fri, Sat. **Main courses** $13-$16 lunch; $26-$28 dinner. **Credit** AmEx, Disc, MC, V. **Map** p253 J6 ❷ Latin

José Andrés' nuevo latino cuisine goes beyond the predictable upscaling of tacos, introducing innovative ingredients – *huitlacoche*, or corn fungus, and corn nut powder – and combinations thereof on a menu as whimsical as the decor of his three-level restaurant. The most well-known and recognizably Latino of Café Atlántico's dishes is the popular guacamole, made to order tableside; toward the other end of the spectrum is shrimp with candied pumpkin seeds and 'lime air'. At the six-seat restaurant-within-a-restaurant Minibar – reservations well in advance are essential – diners are presented, sometimes spoon-fed, 30-odd courses of food essences, spritzes and foams. A slightly more down-to-earth experience is available at weekends, when the restaurant serves 'Latino dim sum'. Gluten free and vegan options available.

Central

1001 Pennsylvania Avenue, NW, between 10th & 11th Streets (1-202 625 0015, www.centralmichel richard.com). Federal Triangle Metro. **Open** 11.45am-2.30pm, 5-10.30pm Mon-Thur; 11.45am-2.30pm, 5-11pm Fri; 5-11pm Sat; 5-9.30pm Sun. **Main courses** $18-$32. **Credit** AmEx, MC, V. **Map** p252 J6 ❷ French/American

Central is the energetic and effusive little brother of celebrated chef Michel Richard's upscale and sophisticated Citronelle (*see p132*). The newcomer snagged the prestigious James Beard award for best new restaurant in the country in 2008, so yes, a reservation can be hard to come by. But once you get in, you can see why the Pennsylvania Avenue brasserie wins raves. The playful menu fuses American and French classics with Richard's signature whimsy. There's 'faux' gras (made from chicken liver not foie gras), a towering lobster burger, a spin on fried chicken, and a monstrous banana split sure to attract any nearby spoon.

Jaleo

480 7th Street, NW, at E Street (1-202 628 7949, www.jaleo.com). Gallery Place-Chinatown or Archives Navy-Memorial Metro. **Open** 11.30am-10pm Mon, Sun; 11.30am-11.30pm Tue-Thur; 11.30am-midnight Fri, Sat. **Tapas** $5-$22. **Main courses** $32-$48. **Credit** AmEx, Disc, MC, V. **Map** p253 J6 ❷ Spanish

With Jose Andres (Café Atlántico, *see p118*; Zaytinya, *see p117*) at the helm, Jaleo focuses on tapas: garlic shrimp, chorizo with garlic mash, salads of apple and manchego cheese and marinated mushrooms – to name just a few. Don't miss the date and bacon fritters or the patatas bravas, a steaming hot bowl of potatoes with a spicy sauce.

Other locations 7271 Woodmont Avenue, Bethesda, MD (1-301 913 0003); 2250A Crystal Drive, Arlington, VA (1-703 413 8181).

★ Rasika

633 D Street, NW, between 6th & 7th Streets (1-202 637 1222, www.rasikarestaurant.com). Archives-Navy Memorial Metro. **Open** 11.30am-2.30pm, 5.30-10.30pm Mon-Thur; 11.30am-2.30pm, 5.30-11pm Fri; 5-11pm Sat. **Main courses** $12-$28. **Credit** AmEx, Disc, MC, V. **Map** p253 J6 ❷ Indian

Rasika brings the delicacy of upmarket Indian cooking to Washington. One of restaurateur Ashok Bajaj's empire, which also includes the Oval Room, Bombay Club (*see p115*), 701, Ardeo+Bardeo and Bibiaba (*see p115*), Rasika is under the creative eye of Vikram Sunderam, who ran the kitchen at London's Bombay Brasserie for 14 years. Grouped into categories including 'chaat', 'tawa' and 'tandoor', the menu covers much ground, with ample choices for both vegetarians and carnivores. Whatever you do, try the palak chaat, a signature dish of crispy baby spinach leaves dressed with yoghurt that melts on the tongue.

Judiciary Square area

Bistro Bis

Hotel George, 15 E Street, NW, between North Capitol Street & New Jersey Avenue (1-202 661 2700, www.bistrobis.com). Union Station or Judiciary Square Metro. **Open** 7-10am, 11.30am-2.30pm, 5.30-10.30pm daily. **Main courses** $14.50-$21 brunch; $15.75-$23.50 lunch; $26-$33 dinner. **Credit** AmEx, Disc, MC, V. **Map** p253 K6 ❷ French

A soigné hotel restaurant within walking distance of the Capitol and Union Station, Bistro Bis serves the gamut of French food, from mussels and pommes frites to complicated preparations and composed plates. Tourists rub elbows with the occasional celebrity, onion soup with sea scallops Provençale. Of-the-moment design firm Adamstein & Demetriou created the decor, a riff on the classic brasserie: the dining room features warm woods, tile floors and frosted glass; and the front room, which opens on to a patio with more tables, has a zinc-topped bar. Weekend brunch, which adds egg dishes and beef-based bloody Marys to the mix, is justly popular.

Full Kee

509 H Street, NW, between 5th & 6th Streets (1-202 371 2233, www.fullkeedc.com). Gallery Place-Chinatown Metro. **Open** 11am-2am daily. **Main courses** $8-$22. **Credit** MC, V. **Map** p253 J5 ❷ Asian

Power Points

Meals, deals and presidential favorites.

Ben's Chili Bowl.

Washington is the kind of place where the person at the next table may be discussing state secrets and the president himself could very well walk into the neighborhood burger joint. (Of course, the massive motorcade would probably tip you off.)

While it's possible to visit the DC and opt out of the well-trodden political sights, it's hard to ignore that the city is crawling with the world's most powerful people. People who get hungry just like the rest of us.

Unlike the Bushes, who went to bed early and rarely dined out, the Obamas moved into the White House and made it very clear they were savvy diners and passionate foodies. Date nights for the president and first lady have taken them to the tiny foodie mecca **Komi** (*see p122*), where Johnny Monis's multi-course tasting menu is a revelation, the stylish **Blue Duck Tavern** in the Park Hyatt (*see p99*) and, just a few blocks from the White House, **Equinox** (*see p112*), where chef Todd Gray celebrates the food of the mid-Atlantic – and Michelle Obama celebrated her birthday.

The couple nearly sparked a burger war when Michelle pledged allegiance to Capitol Hill's **Good Stuff Eatery** (*see p121*), where a free-range turkey burger is now named for her, while her husband chose to hit Arlington's **Ray's Hell Burger** (1725 Wilson Boulevard, Arlington, VA, 1-703 841 0001), with Vice-President Joe Biden for the massive prime beef patties. The pair have found common ground with an affinity for **Five Guys**, the locally based burger chain.

Visiting dignitaries know whose lead to follow when they come to town. French president Nicolas Sarkozy took supermodel wife Carla Bruni to one of Barack Obama's favorites, the legendary **Ben's Chili Bowl** (*see p128*), for the famous half smokes.

Of course, the current power players certainly weren't the first to hit the town for a meal. The historic **Martin's Tavern** (1264 Wisconsin Avenue, NW, 1-202 333 7370, www.martins-tavern.com) in Georgetown claims to have hosted every president from Harry Truman to George W Bush. You can request a seat in the proposal booth (that's booth #3) where John F Kennedy supposedly popped the question to Jackie. Despite questions of historical accuracy, it's a story the family that has owned the restaurant for 75 years stands by.

A great spot for oysters and late-night wings, the **Old Ebbitt Grill** (*see p134*) was reportedly favored by Teddy Roosevelt and is still frequented by political big-wigs.

These days, thanks to the young Obama administration, the power center has moved away from stuffy steakhouses to more urbane locales. The hip 14th Street corridor, including **Cork Wine Bar** (*see p127*), **Marvin** (*see p129*) and **Estadio** (*see p127*), has been a favorite of the president's team.

And if you're not rubbing elbows with Barack over burgers, you can get a bird's eye view of his backyard from **POV** (*see p134*), the uber chic rooftop lounge at the W hotel. That is, if you can get past the velvet rope. See, it's all about access in this town.

Good Stuff Eatery.

One of several old-school joints still hanging on in gentrified Chinatown, Full Kee meets all the criteria for a Chinese-food snob: poultry hanging in the window, menu additions posted on the walls on brightly colored paper, a largely Asian clientele. Short on luxury, the place is long on food options. DC foodies rave about Full Kee's noodle soups. The place now serves beer and wine by the glass.

Kushi

465 K Street, NW, between 4th & 5th Streets (1-202 682 3123, http://eatkushi.tumblr.com). Mount Vernon Square/7th Street Convention Center Metro. **Open** 11.30am-2.30pm Mon; 11.30am-2.30pm, 5.30-11pm Tue-Thur; 11.30am-2.30pm, 5.30pm-1am Fri; noon-2.30pm, 5.30-11pm Sat, Sun. **Main courses** $12-$28. **Credit** AmEx, MC, V. **Map** p251 J5 ㉘ Japanese

In the up-and-coming neighborhood just north of Penn Quarter, this Japanese Izakaya-style restaurant draws a young and hip crowd with its pristine sushi and excellent small plates. The spare space centers around a lively robata grill, where diners at the bar can watch as the flames lick skewers loaded with pork belly, cubes of beef and whole fish. Across the restaurant is the sushi bar, another prime seat, where the chefs masterfully slice fish. The huge menu can be daunting, but if you're looking for a little bit of what the restaurant does best, go for the omakase tasting menu, available Wednesday through Saturday.

★ The Source

575 Pennsylvania Avenue, between 6th Street & Constitution Avenue (1-202 637 6100, www. wolfgangpuck.com/restaurants/fine-dining/3941). Archives-Navy Memorial or Penn Quarter Metro. **Open** 11.30am-2pm, 5.30-10pm Mon-Thur; 11.30am-2pm, 5.30-11pm Fri; 11.30am-3pm (brunch), 5.30-11pm Sat. **Main courses** $30-$45. **Credit** AmEx, MC, V. **Map** p253 K6 ㉙ Modern Asian

Plenty of celebrity chefs have staked a claim in Washington recently but few have done it as well as Wolfgang Puck. The Source, located adjacent to the Newseum, feels less like an absentee-chef outpost and more like a vibrant part of the city thanks to executive chef Scott Drewno and an eclectic mix of diners, from city-dwelling twentysomethings to tourists to famous TV talking heads. If fine dining is on the agenda, book a table in the elegant and sleek upstairs dining room for Drewno's well-executed menu of modern Asian fare. Or stick to the more casual downstairs bar and lounge for delicious dumplings, udon noodles and mini banh mi. *Photo p117.*

Capitol Hill

$ ★ DC-3

423 8th Street, between D & E Streets (1-202 546 1935, www.eatdc3.com). Eastern Market Metro. **Open** 11am-10.30pm daily. **Main courses** $3.99-$6.99. **Credit** MC, V. **Map** p253 M7 ㉚ American

The team behind Matchbox (*see p116*) and Ted's Bulletin have another crowd-pleaser in DC-3, their hot dog joint on Capitol Hill. Named for the Douglas DC-3 air plane from the 1930s – which explains the giant vintage propeller on one wall – the counter-service restaurant dishes up a roster of regional hot dogs from around the US, from the famous DC half smoke to the New Jersey bacon-wrapped ripper, the Chicago 7 with pickles and tomatoes, and even a version of the standard New York dirty water dog. And then there's the not so classic. The Bay Bridge pretzel dog nods to the mid-Atlantic with crab dip heaped on the hot dog. Fried pickles, cotton candy and soft-serve ice-cream round out the playful menu.

$ ★ Good Stuff Eatery

303 Pennsylvania Avenue, between 3rd & 4th Streets (1-202 543 8222, www.goodstuff eatery.com). Capitol South Metro. **Open** 11.30am-11pm Mon-Sat. **Main courses** $5.50-$10. **Map** p253 L7 ㉛ American

DC claims several stars from the popular *Top Chef* reality cooking competition, and one of the most recognizable is the often-fedora-wearing Spike Mendelsohn. His fun, laid-back burger joint on Capitol Hill (right next to his We, The Pizza restaurant) is a favorite of Hill staffers and First Lady Michelle Obama. The Michelle Melt, a free-range turkey burger with Swiss cheese and a wholewheat bun, is named after her. Grab your order at the counter and don't miss the dipping bar where you can doctor up your handcut fries with flavored mayonnaises and sauces. The delicious toasted marshmallow milkshake is the stuff of legend.

$ Market Lunch

Eastern Market, 225 7th Street, between Pennsylvania & North Carolina Avenues (1-202 547 8444, www.easternmarket.net). Eastern Market Metro. **Open** 7.30am-2.30pm Tue-Fri; 8am-3pm Sat; 11am-3pm Sun. **Main courses** $3-$5. **No credit cards. Map** p253 L7 ㉜ American

On weekends, the crab-cake sandwiches at this counter-service-only restaurant vie with outdoor craft vendors as Eastern Market's main draw. But Market Lunch is perhaps best visited on weekdays: the line is shorter then and you're more likely to get

---

THE BEST DC INSTITUTIONS

For chili and half smokes
Ben's Chili Bowl. See p128.

For old-school powerbroking
Old Ebbitt Grill. See p134.

For seafood
Johnny's Half Shell. See p112.

CONSUME

a seat at the communal table in the center aisle of the historic food hall. It's also a popular spot for breakfast, with locals waiting in line for the famous 'blue bucks' (blueberry buckwheat pancakes).

Montmartre

327 7th Street, between C Street & Pennsylvania Avenue (1-202 544 1244, www.montmartre dc.com). Eastern Market Metro. **Open** *Brunch* 10.30am-3pm; Sat, Sun. *Lunch* 11.30am-2.30pm Tue-Fri. *Dinner* 5.30-10pm Tue-Thur; 5.30-10.30pm Fri, Sat; 5.30-9pm Sun. **Main courses** $16-$22. **Credit** AmEx, Disc, MC, V. **Map** p253 L7 ⑤ French

Its dining room bustling even when it's not full, its patio seats constantly occupied, Montmartre is much beloved of Capitol Hill residents, who stop by for weekend brunch and people-watching (Eastern Market is just steps away) as well as reliable daily dinners. The walls bear the inevitable Moulin Rouge poster, but the vibe is sophisticated, and the elegantly presented food is more than just café fare: in addition to hanger steak and duck confit, the menu includes such dishes as braised rabbit leg, or lighter fare such as a crispy brie salad with pecans and apricots or the home-made country pâté.

$ Ugly Mug

723 8th Street, at G Street (1-202 547 8459, www.uglymugdc.com). Eastern Market Metro. **Open** 11.30am-1.30am Mon-Thur; 11.30am-2.30am Fri; 11am-2.30am Sat; 11am-1.30am Sun. **Main courses** $8-$14. **No credit cards**. **Map** p253 M8 ④ American

At first glance, the Ugly Mug is a neighborhood pub with plenty of beer (20-plus on tap) and sports TV (five flat screens). Attracting both old timers and new college grads, the Mug is undoubtedly a popular local watering hole, but it's not the beer alone that's roping them in – it's the food. Offering brunch, pizza and sandwiches it departs from standard bar grub, offering a twist on some of the old classics: an elegant eggs benedict and egg Chesapeake – poached egg, crab meat and hollandaise sauce. For a really healthy option the *huevos rancheros* have diced tomatoes, green pepper, onions and so on, and are followed with fresh fruit.

Dupont Circle

Afterwords Café

1517 Connecticut Avenue, NW, at Q Street (1-202 387 3825, www.kramers.com). Dupont Circle Metro. **Open** 7.30am-1am Mon-Thur; 7.30am Fri-1am Mon continuously. **Main courses** $9-$15. **Credit** AmEx, Disc, MC, V. **Map** p250 G4 ⑤ Contemporary American

The best place in DC for a first date – you meet in the adjoining Kramerbooks and rejoice or despair at your new friend's taste in literature – Afterwords Café tries to be all things to all people. Bustling and

capacious, the glass-enclosed dining room serves food from morning until late night, including 'sharezies' – make-your-own appetizer platters, ambitious New American dinners with suggested wine or beer pairings, and decadent desserts. You and your date are sure to find common ground somewhere on the menu. And when you've got to know each other better, you can return for Afterwords' hearty weekend brunch.

Hank's Oyster Bar

1624 Q Street, NW, between Church and 16th Streets (1-202 462 4265, www.hanksdc.com). Dupont Circle Metro. **Open** 5.30-10pm Mon, Tue; 5.30-11pm Wed, Thur; 5.30pm-midnight Fri; 11am-3pm (brunch), 5.30pm-midnight Sat; 11am-3pm (brunch), 5.30-10pm Sun. **Main courses** $15-$23. **Credit** AmEx, Disc, MC, V. **Map** p250 H4 ③ Fish Offering a daily rotation of oysters on the half shell, Hank's has become a serious contender among Washington raw bar destinations. For this reason alone, a visit is worthwhile. But there are lots of other reasons to hit this popular neighborhood spot with a café feel. Here, you can make a meal of small plates (garlic steamed mussels, popcorn shrimp and calamari, peel 'n' eat shrimp) or dive right into a larger plate of lobster roll with fries. There are also daily 'Meat and Two' specials, where the 'two' means side dishes (including seasonal veg, macaroni and cheese and buttermilk onion rings). The only thing that's missing is dessert, the reason for the parting gift of dark chocolate chunks delivered with the bill.

Heritage India

1337 Connecticut Avenue, NW, between N Street & Dupont Circle (1-202 331 1414, www.heritage indiausa.biz). Dupont Circle Metro. **Open** 11.30am-2.30pm, 5.30-10.30pm daily. **Main courses** $12-$25. **Credit** AmEx, Disc, MC, V. **Map** p250 G4 ③ Indian

Top-quality, complex-flavored Indian food (the chef once plied his trade at Bombay Club, *see p115*) and an interesting wine list, without the worry of getting overly dressed up. Vegetarians love this place, where meatless dishes make up about a third of the menu – including the fabulous begumi khazana, a feast served on a silver platter.

Other locations 2400 Wisconsin Avenue, NW, at Calvert Street, Glover Park (1-202 333 3120).

★ Komi

1509 17th Street, NW, between P & Q Streets (1-202 332 9200, www.komirestaurant.com). Dupont Circle Metro. **Open** 5.30pm-late Tue-Sat. **Set menu** $135. **Credit** AmEx, MC, V. **Map** p250 H4 ③ Contemporary American

Johnny Monis is gathering quite a following for himself in his tiny Dupont Circle restaurant. Komi's low-key dining room, a straight shot from front window to kitchen window, is home to some of the most adventurous eating in the city; the youthful chef is

Meals on Wheels

Food that gets around town.

Once upon a time, thanks to a moratorium on food truck licenses, DC's street food landscape was limited to mediocre half-smoke hot dogs and stale pretzels. You'd be lucky to find a burrito cart or anything that broke the monotonous mold.

But no longer. The moratorium was lifted a few years ago, ushering in a new age of creativity for the city's street food scene. It seems like a new truck gets rolling each week, and no visit to Washington would be complete without stopping by one for a meal on the go.

Short of happening on to a truck on a corner, Twitter is the best way to track their movements. At lunchtime, many congregate in office-heavy Downtown, including Franklin Park. A few trawl around nightlife spots such as Adams Morgan to feed hungry bargoers. And many spend time running from parking meter attendants.

Some of the longest lines form at the **Red Hook Lobster Pound** (@LobsterTruckDC), which serves amazing lobster rolls and shrimp rolls with buttery buns. Then there's the irreverent culinary carnival that is the **Fojol Bros of Merlindia** (@fojolbros), where chicken masala, curry and mango lassi pops are dished up by a bunch of guys in fake mustaches and turbans. They make lunch feel like a party, with loud music blaring from the bright truck. They often throw colorful patchwork quilts out for customers to sit on on the lawns in the city's squares.

TaKorean (@takorean) peddles an Asian spin on tacos, like bulgogi steak with spicy kimchi slaw, while **Eat Wonky** (@eatwonky) sells versions of Canadian *poutine*, fries topped with cheese curds and gravy. Try the Wonky dog, an all-beef jumbo hot dog piled with fries, gravy and cheese. Pasta-lovers will want to hunt down **CapMac DC** (@capmacdc), which serves an incredible macaroni and cheese as well as chicken parm meatballs and 20-layer lasagne.

Dessert is well represented curbside, too. Find a slice of apple, blueberry or pecan pie at **Dangerously Delicious Pies'** truck (@dcpietruck), or popsicles made with local fruits from **Pleasant Pops** (@pleasantpops). Cupcake shops have popped up all over the city, so naturally there are cupcake trucks: **Curbside Cupcakes** (@curbsidecupcake) and **Sweetbites** (@sweetbitestruck). And local salad chain Sweetgreen serves delicious organic frozen yoghurt with toppings like agave syrup, coconut and berries from the **Sweetflow Mobile** (@sweetflowmobile).

Northern Virginia is also in on the action. **Rebel Heroes** (@rebelheroes) serves modern versions of Vietnamese banh mi; **BBQ Bandidos** (@bbqbandidos) has pulled pork and brisket, and **Solar Crepes** (@solarcrepes) has a cart outfitted with solar panels.

CONSUME

Sweetbites.

essaying New American cuisine with nods to his Mediterranean heritage and whatever else strikes his fancy. But neither he nor his staff of personable, fashionable servers is lacking in discipline; just as his talent is for showcasing unusual ingredients without showboating, theirs is for putting guests at ease with the ever-changing menu. Foodies will be talking about Monis's suckling pig for years. *See also p119* **Power Points**.

$ Lauriol Plaza

1835 18th Street, NW, at T Street (1-202 387 0035, www.lauriolplaza.com). Dupont Circle Metro. **Open** 11.30am-11pm Mon-Thur; 11.30am-midnight Fri, Sat; 11am-11pm (11am-3pm brunch) Sun. **Main courses** $7.50-$19. **Credit** AmEx, Disc, MC, V. **Map** p250 G3 ❸ Tex-Mex

This has to be DC's most popular restaurant: even with a capacity for up to 350 diners in its two tiered dining area (plus rooftop), the line for a table often spills over on to the sidewalk. Food is reasonably priced Tex-Mex fare. From margaritas and salsa, to Mexican staples such as enchiladas and fajitas, to specialties from Peru, Cuba and elsewhere, there's a little of everything for the Latin food fan, and the scene is always jumping.

Obelisk

2029 P Street, NW, between 20th & 21st Streets (1-202 872 1180). Dupont Circle Metro. **Open** 6-10pm Tue-Sat. **Set dinner** $75 5 courses. **Credit** MC, V. **Map** p250 G4 ❸ Italian

The menu changes constantly at Peter Pastan's prix-fixe-only, reservations-required townhouse, depending on what's fresh and what catches the chef's fancy. But you can always count on an array of antipasti; pasta, meat, cheese and dessert courses; and exemplary service. Squab makes regular appearances – it's worth the awkwardness of dealing with the tiny bones – as do seasonal vegetables and fish. Nominally Italian, the cooking is both catholic and classical. The wine list is extensive, the breads baked in-house, the atmosphere unpretentious.

$ Pizzeria Paradiso

2003 P Street, NW, between 20th & 21st Streets (1-202 223 1245, www.eatyourpizza.com). Dupont Circle Metro. **Open** 11.30am-11pm Mon-Thur; 11.30am-midnight Fri, Sat; noon-10pm Sun. **Main courses** $6-$19. **Credit** MC, V. **Map** p250 G4 ❹ Pizza/Italian

Good quality, wood-oven pizza that keeps locals coming back for more. Expect to wait for a table, even at the larger Georgetown location. The salad of white beans and tuna, plus the antipasti plate of salami and Italian cheeses, are worth considering if pizza is not your thing. But do try the effervescent lemonade. All in all, a fun excursion.

Other locations 3282 M Street, NW, between Potomac & 33rd Streets, Georgetown (1-202 337 1245).

Raku

1900 Q Street, NW, at 19th Street (1-202 265 7258, www.rakuasiandining.com). Dupont Circle Metro. **Open** 11.30am-10pm Mon-Thur; 11.30am-11pm Fri; noon-11pm Sat; noon-10pm Sun. **Main courses** $15.50-$24.50. **Credit** AmEx, MC, V. **Map** p250 G4 ❹ Asian

Choosing between Thai, Japanese, Korean or Chinese restaurants can be a bit difficult. But at Raku, you don't have to. The menu includes staples from all four national cuisines, including fried egg rolls, sushi (try the tuna tartare sushi roll with peanuts, lemon and basil) and pad Thai. If you feel like trying something new, go for the sea urchin or eel. Raku bills itself as an 'Asian diner'. The atmosphere inside is appropriately frenetic, while the food is simple and satisfying.

Other locations 7240 Woodmont Avenue, at Elm Street, Bethesda, MD (1-301 718 8680).

Regent

1910 18th Street, NW, between Florida Avenue & T Street (1-202 232 1781, www.regentthai.com). Dupont Circle Metro. **Open** 11.30am-3pm, 5-10pm Mon-Thur; 11.30am-3pm, 5-11pm Fri; noon-3pm, 5-11pm Sat; 5-10pm Sun. **Main courses** $9-$20. **Credit** AmEx, Disc, MC, V. **Map** p250 G3 ❹ Thai

This newcomer is slightly dressier and more refined (and also somewhat more expensive) than most of DC's other Thai restaurants. The flavors – lots of coconut milk, green and red curry, lemongrass and chilli paste – are perfectly balanced, and the setting is serene, with large wood carvings and quiet fountains. Try the panang chicken, green curry and pad eggplant, which comes in a spicy black bean sauce. For dessert, the mango sticky rice is unbeatable.

Sette Osteria

1666 Connecticut Avenue, NW, at R Street (1-202 483 3070, www.setteosteria.com). Dupont Circle Metro. **Open** 11.30am-1am Mon-Thur, Sun; 11.30am-1am Fri; 11am-1am Sat. **Main courses** $9-$19. **Credit** AmEx, Disc, MC, V. **Map** p250 G4 ❹ Italian

From wood-fired pizzas to veal scaloppine with lemon and caper sauce, this stylish Dupont Circle restaurant serves excellent (and affordable) Neapolitan fare. The pastas are especially good; try gnocchi alla Sorrentina (with tomato, mozzarella and basil) or baked lasagne. In warm weather, Sette's large outdoor seating area comes into its own as an arena for people-watching, while in winter, the indoors is cosy.

Sushi Taro

1503 17th Street, NW, at P Street (1-202 462 8999, www.sushitaro.com). Dupont Circle Metro. **Open** 11.30am-2pm, 5.30-10pm Mon-Thur; 11.30am-2pm, 5.30-10.30pm Fri; 5.30-10.30pm Sat. **Main courses** $15-$40. **Credit** AmEx, Disc, MC, V. **Map** p250 H4 ❹ Japanese

Located above a drugstore on the strip of 17th Street, NW, that is the centre of gay life in DC, Sushi Taro is large, informal and fun. There are low tables for traditional Japanese dining, but only a few; most of the diners seem to come for big platters of sushi and sashimi, delivered from the long bar by servers in Hawaiian shirts. There are relatively few exotic fish on offer – though, of course, the daily sampler changes according to what's available – but there are also refreshingly few novelty rolls. Tables are close together, and the restaurant can get loud when it's crowded – which is often; the place is popular.

Tabard Inn

1739 N Street, NW, between 17th & 18th Streets (1-202 833 2668, www.tabardinn.com). Dupont Circle Metro. **Open** 7-10am, 11.30am-2.30pm, 6-9.30pm Mon-Thur; 7-10am, 11.30am-2.30pm, 6-10pm Fri; 8-9.45am, 11am-2.30pm, 6-10pm Sat; 8-9.15am, 10.30am-2.30pm Sun. **Main courses** $11-$17 lunch; $23-$33 dinner. **Credit** AmEx, MC, V. **Map** p250 G4 ⑮ Contemporary American
Tucked at the back of a 19th-century brownstone, home to a family-run hotel, the Tabard is an eclectic and shamelessly romantic destination. Dine in the lounge in front of the fireplace, in the garden under the shade of a silk parachute, or in the private dining room. The menu favors crisp and local ingredients: fried oysters top a salad of corn and baby spinach. Salmon and trout, both house-smoked, are an excellent standby. Sunday's crowds (seriously, make reservations far in advance) brunch on just-made donuts and eggs benedict.
▶ *For a review of the hotel, see p106.*

$ Teaism

2009 R Street, NW, at Connecticut Avenue (1-202 667 3827, www.teaism.com). Dupont Circle Metro. **Open** 8am-10pm Mon-Thur; 8am-11pm Fri; 9am-11pm Sat; 9am-10pm Sun. **Main courses** $7.75-$12. **Credit** AmEx, MC, V. **Map** p250 G4 ⑯ Café/Asian
Freshly baked naan and Thai chicken curry are on offer at this café-style oasis from the bustle of urban living. Whether you stop off for a cup of chai or a bento box, you'll feel ready to pound the pavement once again. Afternoon tea with ginger scones and lime curd tartlets can be quite reviving in winter, or in warm weather, try the iced Moroccan mint tea; there's nothing more refreshing. The spacious 8th Street branch, with its downstairs hideout, has a calmer vibe.
Other locations 800 Connecticut Avenue, NW, at H Street, Downtown (1-202 835 2233); 400 Eighth Street, NW, at D Street, Penn Quarter (1-202 638 6010).

$ Thaiphoon

2011 S Street, NW, between 20th Street & Connecticut Avenue (1-202 667 3505, www. thaiphoon.com). Dupont Circle Metro. **Open**

11.30am-10.30pm Mon-Thur, Sun; 11.30am-11pm Fri, Sat. **Main courses** $8-$14. **Credit** MC, V. **Map** p250 G4 ⑰ Thai
Shiny stainless steel and a striking front window invite you to be part of the buzz at this bright, bustling place. The menu is lengthy, covering many Thai classics, from papaya salad to lemongrass chicken; the presentation is pretty and the flavors freshly assertive. Try the crispy bananas with berry sauce. Vegetarians are well fed here.

Adams Morgan

$ Amsterdam Falafelshop

2425 18th Street, NW, at Belmont Road (1-202 234 1969, http://falafelshop.com). Dupont Circle Metro then 42 bus or Woodley Park-Zoo/Adams Morgan Metro. **Open** 11am-midnight Mon, Sun; 11am-2.30am Tue, Wed; 11am-3am Thur; 11am-4am Fri, Sat. **Main courses** $5.50-$9.50. **No credit cards. Map** p250 G3 ⑱ Middle Eastern
This is the perfect place for a quick bite, whether it's two in the afternoon or two in the morning (although beware the long, hungry lines that form in the early hours). The choices at the counter are simplicity itself: small or large? Wholewheat pitta or white? Fries with that? (Say yes – they're the best in town.) You'll face tougher decisions at the extensive toppings bar, which includes houmous, grilled eggplant, marinated cucumber, and more – much more, sadly, than can fit in one pitta. This might be the best deal in town.

$ Diner

2453 18th Street, NW, between Kalorama & Columbia Roads (1-202 232 8800, www.trystdc. com/diner). Dupont Circle Metro then 42 bus or Woodley Park-Zoo/Adams Morgan Metro. **Open** 24hrs daily. **Main courses** $9-$18. **Credit** MC, V. **Map** p250 G3 ⑲ American
One of DC's few 24-hour joints, the Diner is brought to you by the same folks who own coffee lounge Tryst (*see p127*) just two doors away. True to its name, there's home-style chow such as home-made meatloaf with gravy and mash for lunch and buttermilk pancakes for 4am. The Diner is constantly packed with neighborhood hipsters and night owls, but we don't think it's the food that keeps people going back for more. It's those long

---

**INSIDE TRACK
KITCHEN ON SHOW**

Julia Childs, the subject of 2009 film *Julie and Julia* and perhaps America's best-known chef, donated the kitchen from her Massachusetts home, complete with equipment, to the Smithsonian. It's on display at the **National Museum of American History** (*see p49*).

CONSUME

CONSUME

Estadio.

counters, great for flirting, sipping coffee and playing with your food behind the Sunday paper.

Perry's

1811 Columbia Road, NW, at Biltmore Street (1-202 234 6218, www.perrysadamsmorgan.com). Dupont Circle Metro then 42 bus or Woodley Park-Zoo/Adams Morgan Metro then 90, 92, 93, L2 bus. **Open** 5.30-10.30pm Mon-Thur; 5.30-11.30pm Fri; 11am-3pm, 5.30-11.30pm Sat; 10am-2.30pm (brunch), 5.30-10.30pm Sun. **Main courses** $14-$26. **Credit** AmEx, Disc, MC, V. **Map** p250 G2/3 ⑤⓪ Fusion

Stand smack in the middle of Adams Morgan Party Central, the intersection of 18th Street and Columbia Road, NW (the traffic is so gridlocked on weekend nights that you can often do so without any significant risk to either life or limb), and you'll see the illuminated rooftop of Perry's, hangout of beautiful people and their attendant wannabes. The largely twentysomething crowd is attracted not just to the lights – and the lively scene under them – but to the array of well-executed sushi prepared downstairs, where a classic wood-panelled dining room offers a more sedate setting for unwinding. Along with sushi, the menu features a short list of New American starters and entrées, with such favorites as seasonal heirloom tomato salad, grilled swordfish steak with lemon chutney and the chef's veg platter. Perry's drag queen brunch is offered every Sunday. The fixed price includes all you can eat and dancers to entertain you. Arrive early for the show.

$ Tryst

2459 18th Street, NW, between Belmont & Columbia Roads (1-202 232 5500, www.tryst dc.com). Dupont Circle Metro then 42 bus or Woodley Park-Zoo/Adams Morgan Metro. **Open** 6.30am-midnight Mon-Wed; 6.30am-2am Thur; 6.30am-3am Fri, Sat; 7am-midnight Sun. **Credit** AmEx, Disc, MC, V. **Map** p250 G2/3 ⑤① Café

Not quite a club, a bar, or even a coffeehouse for that matter, Tryst makes a great community living room. Overstuffed chairs, comfy sofas and country-style kitchen tables – not to mention the free Wi-Fi access – create a hip, relaxed vibe without feeling collegiate. If you want to drink alcohol, fine. If not, the coffee, served in enormous mugs, is very good. There is also a range of 13 sandwiches from $5 (half of which are vegetarian). We recommend the Alisha, a houmous-and-veggie combo on thick farm bread, or the wasabi, cream cheese and smoked salmon for $9.50. Alternatively, you could create your own salad for $9 or order several small plates for nibbling.

Logan Circle

★ Birch & Barley

1337 14th Street, NW, between N Street & Rhode Island Avenue (1-202 567 2576, http://birchandbarley.com). Dupont Circle,

Mount Vernon Square or Shaw-Howard University Metro. **Open** 5.30-10pm Tue-Thur; 5.30-11pm Fri, Sat; 11am-8pm Sun (all-day brunch). **Main courses** $14-$29. **Credit** AmEx, MC, V. **Map** p250 H4 ⑥② Contemporary Mediterranean

Look for the line on the sidewalk in front of the glass garage door and you've found Birch and Barley and its raucous upstairs beer bar Churchkey (*see p140*). (The line is for the latter, though you'll need a reservation for the dining room many nights.) Inside, a massive copper beer 'organ' funnels some 500 choices, all served at the proper temperature and in the correct glassware, to thirsty patrons. The kitchen here turns out rustic yet elegant dishes such as risotto dotted with chorizo and shrimp and flatbreads topped with figs and prosciutto. Do not skip dessert – you'll find clever renditions of all-American sweets like peanut butter cheesecake and an updated hostess cupcake. Then head upstairs to the casual Churchkey, with low lighting and its own beer-friendly menu (think grilled cheese, wings and poutine).

★ Cork Wine Bar

1720 14th Street, NW, between R & S Streets (1-202 265 2675, http://corkdc.com). U Street/African-American Civil War Memorial/Cardozo Metro. **Open** 5pm-midnight Tue, Wed, Sun; 5pm-1am Thur-Sat. **Main courses** plates to share $8-$15. **Credit** AmEx, MC, V. **Map** p250 H4 ⑥③ Wine bar

One of the best of the new wave of convivial neighborhood wine bars that have popped up in the city, Cork offers about 160 wines by the bottle, 50 wines by the glass and thoughtful wine tasting flights. The bar area of the historic 14th Street building is regularly packed, so come early for the best chance of scoring a seat. Dark wood floors, exposed brick walls and bare bulbs that give off a soft glow make the wine bar feel older than its actual age. Chef Ron Tanaka oversees the menu, which includes shareable plates, such as a pan-crisped brioche sandwich of prosciutto, fontina and a soft-cooked egg, rosemary chicken liver bruschetta and braised pork cheeks with creamy polenta. Husband and wife owners Khalid Pitts and Diane Gross also have a terrific wine shop and gourmet market just up the street.

▶ *For more venues on U Street, see p79* **U Street Highlights**.

★ Estadio

1520 14th Street, NW, at Church Street (1-202 319 1404, www.estadio-dc.com). U Street/African-American Civil War Memorial/Cardozo Metro. **Open** 5-10pm Mon-Thur; 11am-2pm, 5-11pm Sat; 11am-2pm, 5-9pm Sun. *Bar* 5pm-midnight Mon-Wed; 5pm-12.30am Thur; 5pm-1am Fri, Sat; 5-11pm Sun. **Main courses** tapas $4-$14. **Credit** AmEx, V. **Map** p250 H4 ⑥④ Tapas

This 14th Street tapas joint is regularly packed to the brim and for good reason. The menu reads like a

CONSUME

grazer's dream with a host of traditional Spanish snacks perfect for sharing – cheeses and meats, toothpicks called pintxos stacked with anchovies, olives and chorizo, fresh figs stuffed with cheese and wrapped in jamon, and croquetas in mushroom or jamon. Vintage World Cup soccer games play on TVs over the bar. Don't miss the 'slushitos', boozy frozen slushies that change flavors to suit the season. Feeling daring? Order wine out of a glass porron. The traditional Spanish wine spouts will have you dribble wine down your shirt at least once, depending on your learning curve, but they make for great fun. *Photos p127*.

Rice

1608 14th Street, NW, between Q & Corcoran Streets (1-202 234 2400, www.ricerestaurant.com). Dupont Circle or U Street/African-American Civil War Memorial/Cardozo Metro. **Open** 11am-2.30pm, 5-10.30pm Mon-Thur; 11am-11pm Fri, Sat; 11am-10.30pm Sun. **Main courses** $14-$18. **Credit** Disc, MC, V. **Map** p250 H4 🔢 Thai
The chicest of urban-chic Thai places, Rice takes minimalism to the max. The expanse of its cool and neutral-toned walls contrasted with exposed brick is interrupted only by a small fountain; its coconut-milk-scented rice arrives artistically mounded in the center of the plate. Appetizers and entrées are divided into categories of authentic Thai food, healthy options and house specialties; stick with the latter two for originality and assurance of execution. Vegetarians have plenty of choice here.There's no reason not to order a saké Martini or other fancy drink from your young, black-clad server.

U Street/14th Street Corridor

★ Ben's Chili Bowl

1213 U Street, NW, between 12th & 13th Streets (1-202 667 0909, www.benschilibowl.com). U Street/African-American Civil War Memorial/Cardozo Metro. **Open** 6am-2am Mon-Thur; 6am-4am Fri, 7am-4am Sat; 11am-11pm (no breakfast) Sun. **Main courses** $4-$9. **No credit cards.** **Map** p250 H3 🔢 American
Looking like a museum piece on the yuppified, buppified stretch of U Street once known as Black Broadway, Ben's Chili Bowl, opened in 1958, is in no danger of moldering away, thankfully. In fact, its claim to be a 100% wind-powered business makes it very contemporary. This family-owned institution's appeal rests on three legs: nostalgia (past

INSIDE TRACK HALF-SMOKES

So what exactly is a half-smoke? Not even natives can definitively define it. DC's signature specialty is a plump sausage, sometimes smoked, sometimes split, and usually a treat.

customers include Duke Ellington, Miles Davis, Bill Cosby and, more recently, Barack Obama), the insatiable late-night hunger of young partiers, and, of course, the great bang for the buck afforded by burgers, fries and chilli. In-the-know customers order chilli on a dog or half smoke (arguably Washington's signature specialty) and cheesefries, but you can also get a turkey sub or a veggie burger. These days, in fact, you can even order Ben's over the internet. *See also p119* **Power Points.**
▶ *For more venues on U Street, see p79* **U Street Highlights.**

Busboys & Poets

2021 14th Street, NW, between U & V Streets (1-202 387 7638, www.busboysandpoets.com). U Street/African-American Civil War Memorial/Cardozo Metro. **Open** 8am-midnight Mon-Thur; 8am-2am Fri; 9am-2am Sat; 9am-midnight Sun. **Main courses** $8.50-$22. **Credit** MC, V. **Map** p250 H3 🔢 Café
It may not have the most exciting food (burgers, salads, sandwiches, pizza), but no matter. Busboys & Poets is an exciting space in and of itself. Located at the corner of 14th and U Streets, NW, it was established by Andy Shallal an Iraqi American artist, restauranteur and activist in 2005 in an area with a history of 1960s civil rights activism. With its communal tables, sofas and cushy chairs, Busboys is the ultimate urban living room, where people meet for coffee or drinks or a snack in between meals. Open-mike poetry readings, live music and book discussions are also on the menu.
Other locations 1025 5th Street, NW, (1-202 789 2227); 4251 South Campbell Avenue, Arlington, (1-202 379 9757).

Coppi's Organic

1414 U Street, NW, between 14th & 15th Streets (1-202 319 7773, www.coppisorganic.com). U Street/African-American Civil War Memorial/Cardozo Metro. **Open** 6-11pm Mon-Thur; 5pm-midnight Fri, Sat; 5-10pm Sun. **Main courses** $26-$27. **Credit** AmEx, Disc, MC, V. **Map** p250 H3 🔢 Pizza
Crispy crusted pizzas and chewy calzones come dressed in the finest mozzarella and fresh basil, with gourmet toppings like pancetta and portobellos – and it's all organic. For pudding, treat yourself to a Nutella dessert calzone. It's pure heaven. The space is dimly lit and cosy.

$ Love Café

1501 U Street, NW, at 15th Street (1-202 265 9800, www.cakelove.com). U Street/African-American Civil War Memorial/Cardozo Metro. **Open** 11am-9pm Mon, Tue; 9am-9pm Wed, Thur, Sun; 9am-10.30pm Fri, Sat. **Credit** AmEx, MC, V. **Map** p250 H3 🔢 Café
Run by the folks behind Cake Love, a high-end bakery just across the street, this little spot offers a place

Ben's Chili Bowl.

to sample the bakery's wares – including a wide array of cupcakes and, weight watchers beware, what have to be the largest slices of cake in town. Not in the mood for sweets? Sip a latte while browsing the internet (there's free Wi-Fi), or snack on a sandwich. It really would be a shame to leave without at least one little treat, though – so why not try the 'bed rolls' (walnut cake rolled in cream cheese) or chocolate covered strawberries?

★ Marvin
2007 14th Street, NW, between U & V Streets (1-202 797 7171, www.marvindc.com). U Street/ African-American Civil War Memorial/Cardozo Metro. **Open** 5.30pm-2am Mon-Thur; 5.30pm-3am Fri, Sat; 10.30pm-2am Sun. **Main courses** $14-$27. **Credit** AmEx, MC, V. Map p250 H3 ⑳
Belgian/soul food
From the owners of the ever-hip Eighteenth Street Lounge (*see p195*), Marvin turned a former Subway fast-food shop into one of the 14th and U Street neighborhood's coolest hangouts. The name is a nod to Marvin Gaye, one of owner (and half of DC's music duo Thievery Corporation) Eric Hilton's musical role models. The dimly lit space is two floors – a bistro on the ground level serves a hipster crowd a clever mix of Belgian dishes and soul food, like moules frites, shrimp and grits, and fried chicken with waffles. A lounge with a regular line-up of talented DJs resides on the second floor. Also up top: a spacious outdoor deck complete with heaters for chilly nights.

Tabaq Bistro
1336 U Street, NW, at 13th Street (1-202 265 0965, www.tabaqdc.com). U Street/Cardozo Metro. **Open** 5-11pm Mon-Thur; 5pm-midnight Fri; 10am-4pm (brunch), 5pm-midnight Sat; 11am-4pm (brunch), 5-11pm Sun. **Main courses** $14-$23. **Credit** AmEx, Disc, MC, V. **Map** p250 H3 ⑳
Mediterranean
The attraction here lies more in the setting than in the menu. Diners enjoy a dramatic rooftop view year-round in the glass-enclosed terrace, which opens up in summer for fresh air. (Be prepared to climb several flights of stairs to reach it, though.) Not that the food – kebabs, roast chicken and lamb, plus small plates from Turkey, Morocco and elsewhere – is poor. Far from it. It's hard to live up to the spectacular location, though. But what a view to aspire to.

Georgetown

1789
1226 36th Street, NW, at Prospect Street (1-202 965 1789, www.1789restaurant.com). Foggy Bottom-GWU Metro then 30, 32, 34, 35, 36, 38B, Circulator. **Open** 6-10pm Mon-Thur, Sun; 6-11pm Fri; 5.30-11pm Sat. **Main courses** $18-$35. **Credit** AmEx, Disc, MC, V. **Map** p249 E5 ⑳
American
Georgetown's 1789, site of countless graduation fêtes and anniversary dinners, is evocative of a Washington of old, when men wore ties and women smiled and nodded. These things still happen, of course, and the main dining room, with its antique-style china and gold-framed historical prints, is an appropriate setting for them. The menu stresses local provenance – rockfish from Kent Island, Maryland, say, with celery root purée, braised escarole with citrus and black trumpet mushrooms, or Shenandoah Valley lamb with arugula, potatoes and roast garlic. The food is exceptional; the service, as might be expected, impeccable.

Bangkok Joe's
3000 K Street, NW, at Thomas Jefferson Street (1-202 333 4422, www.bangkokjoes.com). Foggy Bottom-GWU Metro then 30, 32, 34, 35, 36, 38B, Georgetown Metro Connection bus. **Open** 1.30am-10.30pm Mon-Thur; 11.30am-11.30pm Fri; noon-11.30pm Sat; noon-10.30pm Sun. **Main courses** $10-$18. **Credit** AmEx, Disc, MC, V. **Map** p249 F5 ⑳ Thai
Vibrant colors and sleek design set the tone at this stylish Thai establishment, definitely the best bet for food among the restaurants in Washington Harbor, along the Georgetown waterfront. While the cooking lacks some of the complex flavors you'll find at somewhere like the Regent (*see p124*), Bangkok Joe's features a dumpling bar (try the mushroom and ginger dumplings), plus lots of delicious noodle dishes.

CONSUME

CONSUME

Bourbon Steak

Four Seasons, 2800 Pennsylvania Avenue, NW, at 28th Street (1-202 944 2026, www.bourbon steakdc.com). Foggy Bottom-GWU Metro. **Open** 11.30am-2.30pm Mon; 11.30am-2.30pm, 6-10pm Tue-Thur; 11.30am-2.30pm, 5.30-10.30pm Fri; 5.30-10.30pm Sat.* **Main courses** $9-$65. **Credit** AmEx, MC, V. **Map** p250 F5 ㉞ American

If you're looking for a decadent splurge and a high probability of a celebrity sighting, head to this modern restaurant inside Georgetown's Four Seasons hotel, where steaks are poached in butter and movie stars and power players rub shoulders. California-based chef Michael Mina opened a branch of his contemporary steakhouse as part of a very posh makeover of the Four Seasons. On executive chef David Varley's menu, steakhouse classics such as an aged porterhouse, creamed spinach and shrimp cocktail are joined by locally sourced fare such as Virginia striped bass and bison. The complimentary fries that land on the table are crisped in duck fat and very addictive. The swank bar is a regular hangout for VIP guests and, true to its name, offers a nice selection of rare bourbons and Scotches.

Café Milano

3251 Prospect Street, NW, at Wisconsin Avenue (1-202 333 6183, www.cafemilanodc.com). Foggy Bottom-GWU Metro then 30, 32, 34, 35, 36, 38B, Georgetown Metro Connection bus. **Open** 11.30am-11pm Mon, Tue, Sun; 11.30am-2am Wed-Sat; 11.30am-midnight Sun.* **Main courses** $29-$44. **Credit** AmEx, MC, V. **Map** p249 E5 ㉟ Italian

The crowd here is as much of an attraction as the food; you might spot Michael Jordan or a visiting movie star in this multi-room complex. Even the non-famous clientele are for the most part young, rich and glamorous. The menu – and the atmosphere – ranges from casual to chic; you can choose from a selection of pizzas and pastas, or opt for duck breast in Marsala wine or spaghetti with fresh clams.

Café La Ruche

1039 31st Street, NW, between K & M Streets (1-202 965 2684, www.cafelaruche.com). Foggy Bottom-GWU Metro then 30, 32, 34, 35, 36, 38B, Georgetown Metro Connection bus. **Open** 11am-10.30pm Mon-Thur; 10am-12.30pm Fri, Sat; 10am-11pm Sun.* **Main courses** $8.55-$22. **Credit** AmEx, MC, V. **Map** p249 E5 ㊱ French

Quaint from the outside, a little more hip on the inside, La Ruche (which means 'beehive') is a comfort zone for Francophiles who don't want to drop a big wad of cash on their cuisine of choice. They gather here in swarms, making a buzz of conversation while waiting for chef Jean-Claude Cauderlier's cooking. The food comes café-style, with a wide range of choices in the quiche/sandwich/salad range, plus a smattering of daily entrée specials such as mussels and duck à l'orange. Desserts, which include a range of traditional tarts, are made in-house. Brunch (10am-3pm weekends) is popular, especially in the garden when the weather's good.

Clyde's of Georgetown

3236 M Street, NW, between Wisconsin Avenue & Potomac Street (1-202 333 9180, www.clydes.com). Foggy Bottom-GWU Metro then 30, 32, 34, 35, 36, 38B, Georgetown Metro Connection bus. **Open** 11.30am-midnight Mon-Thur; 11.30am-1am Fri; 10am-1am Sat; 9am-midnight Sun.* **Main courses** $14-$24. **Credit** AmEx, Disc, MC, V. **Map** p249 E5 ㊲ American

No visit to Georgetown's see-and-be-scene M Street promenade is complete without a stop at one of the neighborhood's many watering holes, and Clyde's of Georgetown is first among the local equals. High-volume in both senses of the phrase, the place easily absorbs busfuls of tourists yet somehow still manages to attract regulars to its brass-railed bar. Perhaps it's the food. In addition to serving tavern staples – herb-roasted half chicken, for example – Clyde's showcases seasonal, local ingredients in such dishes as porterhouse pork chop with sweet potatoes au gratin and collard greens. Well-chosen wines and craft-brewed beers complete your meal, served by efficient, preternaturally cheery youngsters.

Mendocino Grill & Wine Bar

2917 M Street, NW, between 29th & 30th Streets (1-202 333 2912, www.mendocinodc.com). Foggy Bottom-GWU Metro then 30, 32, 34, 35, 36, 38B, Georgetown Metro Connection bus. **Open** 5.30-10pm Mon-Thur; 5.30-11pm Fri, Sat; 5.30-9pm Sun.* **Main courses** $24-$30. **Credit** AmEx, MC, V. **Map** p249 F5 ㊳ Fusion

The cuisine is West Coast, the ingredients East Coast – Mendocino has a commitment to local producers and seasonal produce. In the wine bar, and in the intimate, mirror-decked dining room, patrons are treated to simple, well-executed plates along with interesting wines, mostly from California, of course. The young servers are well informed about not only the wine but the excellent variety of artisanal cheeses.

Michel Richard Citronelle

Latham Hotel, 3000 M Street, NW, at 30th Street (1-202 625 2150, www.citronelledc.com). Foggy Bottom-GWU Metro then 30, 32, 34, 35, 36, 38B, Georgetown Metro Connection bus. *Restaurant* **Open** 6-10pm Tue-Thur; 6.30-10.30pm Fri, Sat.* **Set meals** $85 3 courses, $105 4 courses, $125 5 courses. *Lounge/bar* **Open** 5-10pm Mon-Thur; 5-10.30pm Fri, Sat.* **Main courses** $30-$36. *Both* **Credit** AmEx, Disc, MC, V. **Map** p249 F5 ㊴ French

This is the sort of place where diners have an 'experience' rather than just a meal. Hailed as one of the country's best chefs, Michel Richard has built a reputation for innovative combinations, with a presentation that introduces a touch of whimsy. While Richard's creations might encompass the likes of foie gras and venison, dishes are light and imaginative, never heavy. The 8,000 or so bottles of wine, sitting comfortably in their state-of-the-art cellar, get equal billing. Be prepared to shell out in a big way.

$ Moby Dick House of Kabob

1070 31st Street, NW, at M Street (1-202 333 4400, www.mobysonline.com). Foggy Bottom-GWU Metro then 30, 32, 34, 35, 36, 38B, Georgetown Metro Connection bus. **Open** 11am-10pm Mon-Thur; 11am-11pm Fri, Sat; noon-11pm Sun. **Main courses** $7-$15. **No credit cards.** **Map** p249 E5 ⑳ Middle Eastern

This tiny establishment, like its many cousins throughout the metro area, serves simple, traditional Middle Eastern dishes – felafel, houmous, kebabs of chicken or lamb – with little fanfare and to many fans. You order at the counter, get a number, and then take your place at one of only two small communal tables – sit even if you're getting takeout, because this fast food isn't necessarily fast. The houmous is exceptionally creamy; the pitta bread, made fresh throughout the day, manages to be simultaneously lighter and more substantial than the ordinary.

Pâtisserie Poupon

1645 Wisconsin Avenue, NW, between Q Street & Reservoir Road (1-202 342 3248, www.patisseriepoupon.net). Foggy Bottom-GWU Metro then 30, 32, 34, 35, 36, Georgetown Metro Connection bus. **Open** 8.30am-6pm Tue-Fri; 8-5.30pm Sat; 8am-4pm Sun. **Credit** AmEx, MC, V. **Map** p249 E4 ⑪ Café

Light and airy in a modern European sort of way, Pâtisserie Poupon gets points for presentation and attitude. The tarts and cakes are just like you'd find in Paris, and the menu is short but oh-so-French: salade niçoise, crudités, quiches,baguettes and brioche sandwiches. All coffee drinks are made in the back at the espresso bar and delivered by the barista himself.

Upper Northwest

$ Comet Ping Pong

5037 Connecticut Avenue, NW, at Nebraska Avenue (1-202 364 0404, www.cometping pong.com). Bus L1, L2, L4. **Open** 5-9pm Mon; 5-9.30pm Tue-Thur; 5-10.30pm Fri; 11.30am-10.30pm Sat; 11.30am-9pm Sun. **Credit** AmEx, MC, V. Pizza

A little off the beaten path for downtown visitors, Comet's blistery thin-crust pizzas and warehouse chic vibe are worth the trip to upper Connecticut Avenue. A rousing game of table tennis is also a

THE BEST HOT HANGOUTS

For Belgian moules and soul food **Marvin's**. *See p129.*

With a focus on wine **Proof**. *See p117.*

For tapas **Estadio**. *See p127.*

draw – the restaurant's back room is home to several tables for ping pong. A kid-heavy crowd (watch out for flying ping pong balls) early in the evenings gives way to hipsters, artists and musicians (your server is probably at least one of those) as the night progresses. They all come for the wood-fired pies, with toppings like soft shell crab, smoked mozzarella and tangy sauce made from locally farmed tomatoes.

Lebanese Taverna

2641 Connecticut Avenue, NW, at Woodley Road, Woodley Park (1-202 265 8681, www.lebanese taverna.com). Woodley Park-Zoo/Adams Morgan Metro. **Open** 11.30am-2.30pm, 5-9pm Mon; 11.30am-2.30pm, 5-11pm Tue-Fri; noon-11pm Sat; noon-9pm Sun. **Credit** AmEx, Disc, MC, V. **Map** p249 F2 ⑫ Lebanese

This popular family-owned operation, part of a local mini-chain, starts filling up early for dinner. The friendly crowd is a mix of families, couples and more formal business groups. Make a meal of appetizers, which are quite substantial, fun to share and a bit more of a bargain. There's the familiar tabouleh and falafel as well as more interesting variations, such as houmous bel shawarma (houmous with pieces of lamb), shankleesh (herbed and spiced feta with a tomato salad) and manakish b'sabanigh, a special bread topped with a spinach, pine nut and cheese mixture. Save room for baklava, and round things off with an Arabic coffee scented with cardamom. **Other locations** 5900 Washington Boulevard, between McKinley Road & Nicholas Street, Arlington, VA (1-703 241 8681); Pentagon Row, 1101 S Joyce Street, Arlington, VA (1-703 415 8681).

Palena

3529 Connecticut Avenue, NW, between Ordway & Porter Streets (1-202 537 9250, www.palena restaurant.com). Cleveland Park Metro. **Open** 5.30-10pm Tue-Sat. **Set menus** $50-$68. **Credit** AmEx, Disc, MC, V. **Map** p249 F1 ⑬ Italian/pizza

A terracotta Minerva presides over the elegant formal dining room at the back, where chef Frank Ruta's tasting menu offers seasonal and fashionable delicacies; a bar menu of American favorites is served in the casual and equally elegant café at the front. The former might feature monkfish Milanese

CONSUME

Ethiopian Eats

East Africa in the heart of DC.

Washington is home to the US's largest population of Ethiopians and Eritreans, and one result of this influx has been a blossoming of Ethiopian restaurants in the city. Ethiopian food is a mainstay in the diet of many young Washingtonians. Diners sit around a communal platter of *injera* – a spongy, pleasantly sour giant pancake of bread. Stews are served on the top – and diners scoop up bites of food with more *injera*, torn into bite-sized pieces. Meat tends to come in conveniently sized chunks; vegetables, in properly textured piles. It's great fun, it's economical, and it's a good base for a night on the town.

For many years, Adams Morgan was the epicentre of Ethiopian cuisine, with senior statesman **Meskerem** (2434 18th Street, NW, between Columbia & Belmont Roads, 1-202 462 4100, www.meskeremethiopian restaurantdc.com) holding its own over competitors with its decor: authentic low tables and a pleasant, rustic look. The vegetarian sampler here is a great way to go; the spicy red-lentil purée is a favorite. A block south is **Awash** (No. 2218, 1-202 588 8181), less of a looker but easily Meskerem's match for cuisine; the tables outdoors are a draw in the warmer months.

These days, however, the locus of Ethiopian activity has shifted down on to U Street, NW, and 9th Street, a strip now informally dubbed Little Ethiopia. Some are large venues with bars and established nightlife, others mere townhouses with tables. **Dukem**, an old timer at the corner of 11th and U (1114-1118 U Street, 1-202 667 8735, www.dukemrestaurant.com), is one of the former, beloved for its outdoor seating and its multiple versions of *kitfo*, spiced raw minced beef. At **Axum** (1934 Ninth Street, 1-202 387 0765, www. axumethiopianrestaurant.com), a pleasant, sociable dining room serves not only such dishes as crispy, pleasantly chewy derek *tibs* – lamb cubes cooked with onions and jalapeños, accompanied by a pool of fiery sauce – but also Italian-style *cotoletta* sandwiches. **Etete** (1942 9th Street, 1-202 232 7600, www.eteterestaurant. com), another small wonder, is a critics' darling – especially for its spicy beef and lamb dishes.

Meanwhile, over on T Street, the very modest **Zenebech Injera** (No.608, 1-202 667 4700) has made a great name for itself for superb food, with dishes like a finely but strongly spiced *kitfo* and big, comforting stews. Much of its business is takeaway – it's a grocery too and there are just two tables – and it is also a major supplier of *injera* bread to the city's bigger restaurants.

For expert guidance around the U Street Ethiopian hub, **Washington DC Food Tours** (www.dcmetrofoodtours.com) runs a Little Ethiopia tour, stopping off at different spots for a full range of culinary highlights.

Zenebech Injera.

CONSUME

with Seville orange-scented tomato sauce and clams; the latter, an impossibly upscale cheeseburger with seasonal pickles, hot-dog and fries (including not only potatoes but also onions and, yes, those are lemon slices). You can order from the tasting menu in the café; whatever your choice, consider leaving room for Ann Amernick's much-loved caramels, cookies or pastries.

Sushi-Ko

2309 Wisconsin Avenue, NW, at Observatory Lane, Glover Park (1-202 333 4187, www. sushiko.us). Foggy Bottom-GWU Metro then 30, 32, 34, 35, 36 bus. **Open** 6-10.30pm Mon; noon-2.30pm, 6-10.30pm Tue-Thur; noon-2.30pm, 6-11pm Fri; 5.30-11pm Sat; 5.30-10pm Sun. **Main courses** $16-$27. **Credit** AmEx, MC, V. **Map** p249 D3 🅰 Asian

Behind a mock-industrial façade is a sleek little dining room containing one of the city's best sushi bars. The decor is simple – design within reach, as the furniture store name would have it – the menu compact, venturing beyond sushi and sashimi but not detracting from their star power. Tuna Six Ways, a frequent special, accentuates variations of texture and flavor; simple preparations showcase unusual fish nightly. The vibe here is casual: neighbors stop by for carryout, club kids come in to start their nights, and solo diners make friends at the sushi bar.

Mount Pleasant & north

Tonic Restaurant

3155 Mount Pleasant Street, NW, between 16th & 17th Streets (1-202 986 7661, www.tonic restaurant.com). Columbia Heights Metro. **Open** 5-10.30pm Mon-Thur; 5-11pm Fri; 10am-3pm (brunch), 5-10.30pm Sat, Sun. **Main courses** $10-$17. **Credit** AmEx, Disc, MC, V. **Map** p250 H2 🅰 American

The funky, still-in-transition neighborhood of Mount Pleasant has been graced with a few tasty new arrivals, including Tonic, a homey two-storey bar/restaurant on the main drag. Depending on your mood, you've got a choice of dining experiences: upstairs is for a quieter, sit-down, tablecloth vibe; downstairs is a cavernous bar, with dark wood, television and plenty of beer on tap. No matter where you choose, the menu is the same, a shout-out to comfort food with regional American touches. Think macaroni and cheese, meatloaf sandwiches, pulled pork, a lox plate for brunch or roasted tomato salad with goat's cheese.

ALEXANDRIA

Majestic Café

911 King Street, between North Patrick & Alfred Streets (1-703 837 9117, www.majesticcafe.com). King Street Metro then 10min walk. **Open** 11.30am-2.30pm, 5.30-10pm Mon-Thur; 11.30am-2.30pm, 5.30-10.30pm Fri, Sat; 1-9pm Sun. **Main courses** $20-$27. **Credit** AmEx, Disc, MC, V. Southern

The menu at the Majestic Café is Southern, the mood sweetly nostalgic. This deco establishment was saved from closure in 2007 and is now under new management. Framed black and white photos from the 1930s and '40s line the walls, heels click on the terrazzo floor, and period touches abound. There's nothing old-fashioned about the food presentation, though. Fried green tomatoes arrive in a 'napoleon'; an appetizer invokes a fried chicken picnic. There is a vegetarian option too, but only one or two. The dining room is frequently full, particularly during Sunday brunch, but there are often seats at the bar. Dessert is worth saving room for.

Restaurant Eve

110 S Pitt Street, at King Street (1-703 706 0450, www.restauranteve.com). King Street Metro then Dash bus 2, 5. **Open** 11.30am-2.30pm, 5.30-10pm Mon-Fri; 5.30-10pm Sat. **Main courses** (Bistro) $34-$40. **Set meals** (Tasting Room) $110 7 courses, $125 8 courses, $150 9 courses. **Credit** AmEx, Disc, MC, V. Modern European

There are two ways to eat at Eve: in the Bistro, a bar/lounge area, and in the Tasting Room, where only seven, eight or nine-course prix-fixe menus are offered. Either way is pretty special, as you'll get to taste the culinary work of Dublin native Cathal Armstrong, whose creative menu is chock-full of local and seasonal ingredients. Armstrong is whipping up stuff like confit of house-cured pork belly, roasted darne of king salmon with sunflower purée, and Maine mussels in saffron broth. Emphasis is on using the best and freshest of local ingredients. The Bistro is decidedly more casual; locals drop in for a quick bite and one of the bartender's signature cocktails.

ARLINGTON, VA

Ray's the Steaks

2300 Wilson Boulevard (entrance on Clarendon Boulevard) (1-703 841 7297). Court House Metro. **Open** 5-10pm Mon-Thur; 5-11pm Fri, Sat; 4.30-10pm Sun. **Main courses** $17-$34. **Credit** AmEx, MC, V. Steakhouse

Ray's positions itself as the anti-steakhouse steakhouse, substituting happy clamor for cigar-bar murmur, hipsters and young parents for besuited fat cats. Prices are notably lower than at downtown steakhouses, and quality is as high, and locals appreciate this: it can get rammed on weekend nights. There are seafood options, too, and even a mushroom entrée, but big, hand-cut, well-cooked meat is the order of the day.

Other locations 3509 Dix Street, NE (1-202 396 7297); 8606 Colesville Road, Silver Spring, MD (1-303 588 7297).

Bars

Romance and glamor, or beer and pool.

Washington might be all about politics, but that's all the more reason why bars do such a roaring trade in the nation's capital. Where else can you rub shoulders with some of the world's most powerful law makers while you're nursing a martini (or three)? While Washington's stuffy reputation allows for plenty of Scotch 'n' schmoozing joints, the city's bar scene is surprisingly diverse, especially in the Logan Circle and U Street areas and along the newly thriving H Street, NE, Corridor. Look out for a particular resurgence in speakeasies and craft cocktails.

INFORMATION

The Metro runs until 3am on Friday and Saturday nights, although the last train from your station may be earlier. If you're planning to party late into the night, it's probably easier hto get a cab home.

Be aware that the drinking age is strictly enforced in Washington. *See p137* **Inside track**. Smoking is banned in bars.

For gay-oriented bars and clubs, *see pp181-85*.

THE WHITE HOUSE & AROUND

Old Ebbitt Grill

675 15th Street, NW, between F & G Streets (1-202 347 4800, www.ebbitt.com). Metro Center Metro. **Open** 7.30am-2am Mon-Thur; 7.30am-3am Fri; 8.30am-3am Sat; 8.30am-2am Sun. **Credit** AmEx, Disc, MC, V. **Map** p252 H6 ❶

The Old Ebbitt first opened in 1856 as a boarding house, and over the years its more illustrious guests have included Presidents Grant, Johnson, Cleveland and Teddy Roosevelt. Just a block from the White House, it's a popular place for the power lunch (in the main dining room, that is, not in the atrium). The two bars – one at the back, one at the front – are always packed, usually with men who ensure that no nubile young thing has to pay for her own drinks.

---

❶ Green numbers given in this chapter correspond to the location of each bar on the street maps. *See pp248-253.*

★ POV

W Hotel, 515 15th Street, NW, at F Street (1-202 661 2400/starwoodhotels.com). Metro Center Metro. **Open** 5pm-2am Mon-Thur, Sun; 5pm-3am Fri, Sat. *Rooftop terrace* 11am-2am Mon-Fri; noon-2am Sun. **Credit** AmEx, Disc, MC, V. **Map** p252 H6 ❷

See p138 **Hotel Havens**.

CAPITOL HILL & AROUND

Hawk & Dove

329 Pennsylvania Avenue, SE, between 3rd & 4th Streets (1-202 543 3300, www.hawk anddoveonline.com). Capitol South or Eastern Market Metro. **Open** 10am-2am Mon-Thur, Sun; 10am-3am Fri, Sat. **Credit** AmEx, DC, Disc, MC, V. **Map** p253 L7 ❸

Claiming to be DC's 'most historic Irish bar', the Hawk & Dove is classic Capitol Hill, attracting partisan staffers who enjoy the political atmosphere as much as the pool games. It's a hunting lodge-esque relic from the Vietnam War era (hence the name, which recalls the heated debates from those days). To go with the hunting theme, the political memorabilia has to compete for attention with game trophies (aka dead animals). It's also a sports bar. Today, it attracts a slightly older and wealthier Hill crowd than the Tune Inn (*see p135*) next door – in other words, plenty of thirtysomething types in suits – though the free food at happy hour is a big draw for the young and the hungry.

Sonoma

223 Pennsylvania Avenue, SE, between 2nd & 3rd Streets (1-202 544 8088, www.sonomadc.com). Capitol South or Eastern Market Metro. **Open**

CONSUME

11.30am-2.30pm, 5-10pm Mon-Thur; 11.30am-2.30pm, 5-11pm Fri; 5-11pm Sat; 5-9pm Sun.
Credit TK. **Map** p253 L7 ④
Sonoma offers a welcome grown-up respite from all the other dives and sports bars stretching down Pennsylvania Avenue. The long granite bar, exposed brick and extensive wine list make for a stylish, urban feel, and the upstairs lounge has plenty of comfortable alcoves to settle in to (although it's often closed for political functions and events). Sonoma's proximity to the House office buildings also allows for great eavesdropping while you're savoring that Russian River Valley pinot gris – as long as you're not put off by the ping of a thousand BlackBerrys.

Tune Inn
331 Pennsylvania Avenue, SE, at 4th Street (1-202 543 2725). Capitol South Metro. **Open** 8am-2am Mon-Thur, Sun; 8am-3am Fri, Sat.
Credit AmEx, MC, V. **Map** p253 L7 ⑤
The Tune Inn is one of the few places in DC that starts serving beer at 10am – and you'll probably need a pint to deal with the rowdy blue-collar crowd and the sometimes surly staff. There are no fancy artisan brewed beers on offer here – this place regularly wins awards for being Washington's best dive bar, with prices to match.

THE FEDERAL TRIANGLE

★ Round Robin Bar
Willard Inter-Continental Hotel, 1401 Pennsylvania Avenue, NW, at 14th Street (1-202 637 7348, www.washington.intercontinental.com/washa). Metro Center Metro. **Open** noon-1am Mon-Thur; 3pm-1am Fri; noon-1am Sat; noon-midnight Sun.

INSIDE TRACK MINT JULEPS

That quintessential Southern drink, the mint julep, is said to have been introduced to DC by Kentucky senator Henry Clay in the early 19th century, at the old Willard Hotel, on the site where the Willard Intercontinental now stands. A fabulous version is now the signature drink at the Willard's **Round Robin Bar** (*see below*).

Credit AmEx, Disc, MC, V. **Map** p252 H6 ⑥
See p138 **Hotel Havens**.

★ The Source
575 Pennsylvania Avenue, NW, at Sixth Street. (1-202 637 6100, www.wolfgangpuck.com/restaurants/fine-dining/3941). Archives or Judiciary Square Metro. **Open** 11.30am-2pm, 5.30-10pm Mon-Thur; 11.30am-2pm, 5.30-11pm Fri; 11.30am-3pm (brunch), 5.30-11pm Sat.
Credit AmEx, MC, V. **Map** p253 J6 ⑦
Wolfgang Puck's dramatic Asian-Fusion restaurant tucked under the Newseum also has a ground-floor lounge ideally located for an upscale post-museum fortifier. The minimalist/contemporary scene attracts a diverse crowd, with power players watching sports on the three flatscreen TVs joining the tourists. Try the extensive (and inventive) cocktail list (sample: Asian Pear Drop with saké and pear puree); or one of the hundreds of bottles of wine lining the walls. And if you're in the area between 4pm and 6pm, stop by for happy hour and sample some of the city's best small plates for a fraction of the usual price.
► *For the neighboring Newseum, see p76.*

Bar Rouge. *See p138.*

CONSUME

1000s of
things to do…

UNION STATION & AROUND

Union Pub

*201 Massachusetts Avenue, NE, at 2nd Street
(1-202 546 7200, www.unionpubdc.com). Union
Station Metro.* **Open** 11.30am-2am Mon; 11.30am-
3am, Tue-Fri; noon-3am Sat; noon-midnight Sun.
Credit AmEx, MC, V. **Map** p253 L6 ⑧

Not all outdoor patios are created equal. At Union Pub
a giant awning covering the 80 or so seats elevates
the al fresco concept to greatness. Happy hour is also
bumped up a few notches, with an extraordinary
array of cut-price drinks available seven nights a
week. Wednesday happy hour offers $2 bottled beers
until 10pm, while on Tuesday night women can drink
for free (domestic beer and rail drinks, ie the cheaper
brands of spirits) from 5pm to 7pm.

DOWNTOWN

★ The Passenger/Columbia Room

*1021 Seventh Street, NW, between L Street
& New York Avenue (1-202 393 0220, www.
passengerdc.com). Mount Vernon Square Metro.*
Open 5pm-1.30am Mon-Thur; 5pm-2.30am Fri,
Sat; 2pm-midnight Sun. **Credit** AmEx, MC, V.
Map p251/p253 J5 ⑨

GQ recently declared that mixologist Derek Brown
makes the best martini in America. Judge for yourself
at the Passenger, the former Gibson bartender's
newest venture in the gentrifying Vernon Square area.
The bar is named after the Iggy Pop song; inside
you'll find an informal drinking den with bespoke
cocktails (there's no list, but tell the bartender what
drinks you like and he'll cater one to your preferences)
and gourmet bar snacks. Behind an unmarked door
at the back of the bar lies the Columbia Room, a 12-
seat, reservations-only speakeasy with some of the
most inventive cocktails in the city. For a flat rate
(around $50), Brown will mix you three craft cocktails
with some nibbles on the side, and lecture you at
length on the art of drinking.

Gordon Biersch

*900 F Street, NW, at 9th Street (1-202 783 5454/
www.gordonbiersch.com). Gallery Place-Chinatown
Metro.* **Open** 11am-midnight Mon-Thur; 11am-
1am Fri, Sat; 11am-11pm Sun. **Credit** AmEx,
Disc, MC, V. **Map** p253 J6 ⑩

The California microbrew chain's first appearance
in the region is an impressive one. Inside a beautifully restored 1890s bank, four traditional German
lagers are brewed on site – no stouts or ales, though.

★ Poste

*Hotel Monaco, 555 8th Street, NW, between
E & F Streets (1-202 783 6060, www.poste
brasserie.com). Gallery Place-Chinatown Metro.*
Open 11.30am-1am daily. **Credit** AmEx, Disc,
MC, V. **Map** p253 J6 ⑪

See p138 **Hotel Havens**.

INSIDE TRACK
SHOW YOUR AGE

The drinking age in the US is 21, and it's
strictly enforced, especially in venues
popular with young people and areas like
Georgetown and Adams Morgan, which
get a lot of college-age traffic. So bring
a photo ID with you, even if you reckon
you look well over 30.

Rosa Mexicano

*575 7th Street, NW, at F Street (1-202 783 5522/
www.rosamexicano.com). Gallery Place-Chinatown
Metro.* **Open** 11.30am-4pm, 5-10.30pm Mon-Thur;
11.30am-4pm, 5-11.30pm Fri; noon-4pm, 5-11.30pm
Sat; noon-4pm, 5-11.30pm Sun. **Credit** AmEx, DC,
MC, V. **Map** p253 6J ⑫

Sip a pomegranate margarita and watch the beautiful people – made even more gorgeous by a backdrop of glittering blue tiles and rose petals
embedded in clear Lucite – eye each other's press
credentials under the pink-hued lights. Then order
some guacamole, which comes in strengths from
mild to medium to wowee. It's whipped up tableside
in a volcanic stone mortar and pestle. And remember, things really do look better through rose-
colored sangria glasses.

St Regis Bar

*St Regis Hotel, 923 16th Street, NW, at K Street
(1-202 638 2626, www.starwoodhotels.com).
McPherson Square, Farragut North or Farragut
West Metro.* **Open** 11.30am-midnight Mon-Thur,
Sun; 11.30am-1am Fri, Sat. *Lunch served* 11am-
2pm daily. **Credit** AmEx, Disc, MC, V. **Map**
p250/p252 H5 ⑬

See p138 **Hotel Havens**.

★ Donovan House Side Bar

*Donovan House Hotel, 1155 14th Street, NW, at
Thomas Circle (1-202 737 1200, www.thompson
hotels.com). McPherson Square Metro.* **Open**
5-11.30pm Mon-Thur; 5pm-midnight Sat; 5-10pm
Sun. **Credit** AmEx, Disc, MC, V. **Map** p250/
p252 H5 ⑭

See p138 **Hotel Havens**.

FOGGY BOTTOM

Science Club

*1136 19th Street, NW, between L & M Streets
(1-202 775 0747, www.scienceclubdc.com).
Farragut North Metro.* **Open** 4.30pm-2am Mon-
Thur; 4.30pm-3am Fri; 7pm-3am Sat. **Credit** MC,
V. **Map** p252 G5 ⑮

Rest assured, you don't need to know the difference
between the second law of thermodynamics and the
third law of motion to get in here. In fact, the name

CONSUME

comes from the decor: bar-goers in this four-level space sit on round metal stools salvaged from a high-school chemistry lab. Apart from that, Science Club sticks with tried and trusted new bar practice. The $5 bottles of Yuengling are mixed with DJs who spin dub and funk, plus there's a basement bar that looks like a Prohibition speakeasy.

DUPONT CIRCLE

Bar Rouge
Rouge Hotel, 1315 16th Street, NW, at Scott Circle (1-202 232 8000, www.rougehotel.com). Dupont Circle Metro. **Open** 11.30am-midnight Mon-Wed, Sun; 11.30am-2am Thur-Sat. **Credit** AmEx, Disc, MC, V. **Map** p250 H4 ⑯
See below **Hotel havens**. *Photo p135.*

★ Firefly
Hotel Madera, 1310 New Hampshire Avenue, NW, between N Street & Sunderland Place (1-202 861 1310, www.firefly-dc.com). Dupont Circle Metro. **Open** 5.30-10pm Mon-Thur, Sun; 5.30-10.30pm Fri, Sat. **Credit** AmEx, Disc, MC, V. **Map** p250 G4 ⑰
See below **Hotel Havens**.

Fly Lounge
1802 Jefferson Place, NW, intersection of 18th Street, Connecticut Avenue & Jefferson Place (1-202 828 4433, www.theflylounge.com/dc). Dupont Circle Metro. **Open** 10pm-2am Mon-Thur, Sun; 10pm-3am Fri, Sat. **Credit** AmEx, MC, V. **Map** p250 G5 ⑱
If your idea of bacchanalian bliss is downing your Snow Queen vodka on the inside of a 747, then Fly

---

Hotel Havens
Some of the city's most sophisticated and stylish bars are in hotels.

Come on, you're in Washington, spook central, surely you want to have a secret assignation in a hotel bar? The trouble is, it's much harder these days to find somewhere quiet where you and your personal Deep Throat can plot the downfall of governments and decide what to do after dinner: those pesky locals have commandeered all the best bars. Still, on the basis that if you can't beat them you might as well drink with them, we offer here some hotel bars suitable for meeting a generous lobbyist.

Where better to start than the bar where, it's said, the term 'lobbying' was first coined. Those wanting a quiet word in President Grant's ear used to hang around in the lobby of the Willard Inter-Continental Hotel hoping perhaps to stand the president or one of his advisors a drink in the **Round Robin Bar** (*see p135*). The lobbyists may have moved on but you'll find that the bar is still reminiscent of an old-fashioned gentlemen's club. Take a seat in the dark green, round space and see how many of the portraits of previous guests you can recognize: Walt Whitman, Mark Twain, Nathaniel Hawthorne and President Abraham Lincoln, who lived at the hotel for two weeks before his inauguration, are among the distinguished subjects.

If you're looking for proximity to the White House, the W Hotel's **POV** (*see p134*) is hard to beat: the rooftop terrace has such great views of 1600 Pennsylvania Avenue that you can see the snipers lurking on the roof. The bar gets packed in good

POV.

weather so reservations are recommended. Just a few blocks away the **St Regis** (*see p137*), the bar next to Alain Ducasse's Adour restaurant, makes for a stylish and discreet assignation. Former Obama chief of staff Rahm Emanuel was a regular before he moved back to Chicago.

A generous lobbyist would be an ideal drinking companion at **Degrees Bar & Lounge** (*see p143*) in the Ritz-Carlton Georgetown: if you have to buy your own classic-with-a-twist cocktails be prepared to hand over $10-$15 a go. Degrees aims to capture the clubby feel of a 1940s

CONSUME

Lounge's friendly sky (in this case, a dropped ceiling that resembles a fuselage) is just what you've been looking for. Your flight attendant/cocktail server (in a low-cut stewardess dress – complete with neckerchief) will land it gently in the built-in ice bucket in the middle of your table, which, in keeping with the aeronautical theme, is modelled on the afterburner of an F-15 fighter plane. At the center of Fly is the DJ booth, with one of the best sound systems in the city. With the seatbelt sign permanently off, late-night revelers dance, often on top of the padded banquettes, to everything from Madonna to deep house.

Russia House Restaurant & Lounge

1800 Connecticut Avenue, NW, at Florida Avenue (1-202 234 9433, www.russiahouselounge.com).
Dupont Circle Metro. **Open** 5pm-midnight Mon-Thur; 5pm-2am Fri; 6pm-2am Sat. **Credit** AmEx, MC, V. **Map** p250 G3 ⑲
Once a private restaurant and lounge, Russia House retains something of the mystery of the Kremlin, despite the fact that any Tom, Dick or Vladimir can now down vodka here. The walls are covered in bordello-red silk and serious Russian oils, with cushy sofas and low coffee tables adding to the room's intimacy. A selection of more than 160 vodkas – a mix of Russian favorites, Eastern European brands and American blends – further aids foreign affairs, as do the hordes of homesick hockey players (Washington Capital Alex Ovechkin is a regular). There's also a downstairs restaurant, serving the likes of chicken kiev and beef stroganoff. *Photo p140.*

supper club, and patrons can pose to their heart's content at the sleek 25-seat bar.

A different kind of chic dominates **Bar Rouge** (*see above*) at the Hotel Rouge. The bar is comfortable, with throne-like armchairs, long couches and white leather seats. Cocktails are pricey ($8-$14) and a little too syrupy, but strangely addictive, especially in combination with the hypnotic acid jazz oozing out of the sound system.

The Madera, meanwhile, goes for a 'contemporary rustic' aesthetic with its **Firefly** bar (*see above*), which features a lot of wood, including a huge tree trunk with miniscule copper lanterns hanging from its branches. Seating is comfy, with intimate nooks and low, expansive tables for cocktails and small plates.

East of Dupont Circle, the Donovan House Hotel has a snazzy rooftop pool complete with bar, **Donovan House Side Bar** (*see p137*), and glittering views of the city. The gay-friendly location has reasonably priced drinks, sun loungers, and even an outdoor fireplace, making for a relaxed vibe and an ideal spot after dinner at Susur Lee's Zentan restaurant downstairs.

Heading downtown, **Poste** (*see p137*), part of the Monaco Hotel, is set in the restored sorting office of the 1841 General Post Office, which explains the high ceilings and skylights: they made it easier for the letter sorters to read addresses. The courtyard – reached through a long arcade that was designed for horse-drawn mail wagons – is one of the loveliest outdoor spots in DC. Cocktails are full of fresh herbs and vegetables – like the Basil Lemontini, courtesy of the hotel's herb garden.

Finally, the **Tabard Inn** (*see p137*) makes for a most relaxing place to start, end or break a day of sightseeing. The bar is set in a shabby-chic, living-room-like front room, where patrons can relax on Victorian sofas in front of a log fireplace that might have come straight from the pages of *Wuthering Heights*, while sipping a fortifying glass of wine or brandy.

Poste

Russian House Restaurant & Lounge. See p139.

CONSUME

Tabard Inn

1739 N Street, NW, between 17th & 18th Streets (1-202 785 1277, www.tabardinn.com). Dupont Circle Metro. **Open** 11.30am-12.30am Mon-Fri; 11am-12.30am Sat; 10.30am-11pm Sun. **Credit** AmEx, DC, MC, V. **Map** p250 G4 ⑳
See p138 **Hotel Havens**.

Trio's Fox & Hounds

1533 17th Street, NW, between Church & Q Streets (1-202 232 6307). Dupont Circle Metro. **Open** 4pm-2am Mon-Thur, Sun; 11am-3am Fri; 10am-4am Sat. **Credit** AmEx, Disc, MC, V. **Map** p250 G4 ㉑
A local pub that's dim and cave-like, with hardcore drinkers hunched over the bar. It becomes a real biergarten in warm weather, when crowds pack the patio and swarm the jukebox. This is a place for lingering.

ADAMS MORGAN

Bedrock Billiards

1841 Columbia Road, NW, between 18th Street & Belmont Road (1-202 667 7665, www.bedrock billiards.com). Dupont Circle Metro then 42 bus or Woodley Park-Zoo/Adams Morgan Metro. **Open** 4pm-2am Mon-Thur; 4pm-3am Fri; 1pm-3am Sat; 1pm-2am Sun. **Credit** AmEx, MC, V. **Map** p250 G3 ㉒
An unpretentious pool hall and games room (with 30 pool tables, plus Scrabble, Connect Four and other childhood favorites) that aims for a quasi-prehistoric look, with caveman drawings on the green walls (although these often get covered with photos, murals and paintings from local artists). The place is popular with a young, beer-drinking crowd that is out for a good time and doesn't take itself too seriously.

Reef

2446 18th Street NW, between Belmont & Columbia Roads (1-202 518 3800, www.thereef dc.com). Woodley Park-Zoo/Adams Morgan Metro then 98 bus or Dupont Circle Metro then 42 bus. **Open** 5pm-2am Mon-Thur; 5pm-3am Fri, Sat; 5pm-2am Sun. **Credit** AmEx, MC, V. **Map** p250 G3 ㉓
Fish tanks as decorations, trippy fluorescent lighting, long lines to get in: all are hallmarks of the Reef. The second-storey floor-to-ceiling windows offer a good vantage point for watching the foot traffic on 18th Street. The bar showcases a wide selection of beers – nothing in bottles – and is spacious enough to facilitate the requisite hook-up mingling.

LOGAN CIRCLE

★ ChurchKey

1337 14th Street, NW, at Rhode Island Avenue (1-202 567-2576, www.churchkeydc.com). U Street/McPherson Square Metro. **Open** 4pm-12.15am Mon-Thur; 4pm-1am Fri; noon-1am Sat; noon-midnight Sun. **Credit** AmEx, Disc, MC, V. **Map** p250 H4 ㉔
The upstairs bar above sister restaurant Birch & Barley has one thing on its mind: beer. More than 500 varieties, to be precise. But this isn't your average brewhouse – the shiny wood floors, sculptural light fixtures, and bustling crowd should tell you that. ChurchKey opened in late 2009 and has barely had time to breathe since, drawing crowds nightly for its gourmet lagers and ales (housed in state-of-the-art, temperature-controlled vaults), upscale comfort food (tater tots and grilled cheese), and energetic scene. Wednesday through Saturday, expect long waits and don't bank on a table.
► *For downstairs restaurant Birth & Barley, see p124.*

U STREET/14TH STREET CORRIDOR

Another popular fixture in this, one of the city's most vibrant areas, is **Nellie's** (*see p182*), a gay-friendly sports bar that is also big on bingo and other games.

Bar Pilar

1833 14th Street, NW, between S & T Streets (1-202 265 1751, www.barpilar.com). U Street/African-American Civil War Memorial/Cardozo Metro. **Open** 5pm-2am Mon-Thur, Sun; 5pm-3am Sat; 5pm-2am Sun. **Credit** AmEx, MC, V. **Map** p250 H3 ㉕
The younger and less popular sister of Café Saint-Ex (*see p141*), Bar Pilar is affectionately referred to as a dive bar, dressed up. The vibe is intimate, with just 38 seats, and the low-key attractions include bacon bloody marys at brunch (sort of a liquefied BLT, hold the lettuce) and a kitschy photo booth.

Bohemian Caverns

2001 11th Street, NW, at U Street (1-202 299 0801, www.bohemiancaverns.com). U Street/ African-American Civil War Memorial/Cardozo Metro. **Open** 5.30-10pm Tue, Wed, Thur; 5.30-10.30pm Fri, Sat; 11am-3pm, 5-9pm Sun. **Credit** AmEx, MC, V. **Map** p250 J3 ㉖

Dance, dine, drink, it's all available at this throwback of a bar. The chandelier-hung main floor restaurant is total 1920s glamor. The lower-level Caverns Jazz Lounge – complete with cave-like walls – is a nightclub; upstairs, you'll find a bar and a dancefloor.
▶ *For a review of the Bohemian Caverns as a music venue, see p189.*

Café Saint-Ex

1847 14th Street, NW, at T Street (1-202 265 7839, www.saint-ex.com). U Street/African-American Civil War Memorial/Cardozo Metro. **Open** 5pm-1.30am Mon; 11am-1.30am Tue-Sun. **Credit** AmEx, MC, V. **Map** p250 H3 ㉗

Named for Antoine de Saint-Exupery, the French aviator and author of *The Little Prince*, this brasserie aims to evoke the watering holes of Paris's Latin Quarter and, in the basement-level lounge, the heroic days of aviation. And if pressed-tin ceilings, tobacco-stained walls and borderline service are your thing, then *voila*! DJs spin ironically hip new wave nightly.

★ The Gibson

2009 14th Street, NW, between U & V Streets (1-202 232-2156, www.thegibsondc.com). U Street/ African-American Civil War Memorial/Cardozo Metro. **Open** 6pm-late daily. **Credit** AmEx, MC, V. **Map** p250 H3 ㉘

THE BEST
BACK TO BASICS BARS

With beer served from 10am
Tune Inn. *See p135.*

For pool
Bedrock Billiards. *See p140.*

For a 'real' Irish feel
Nanny O'Brien's. *See p142.*

If you're in a bar in Washington drinking a cocktail, listening to dub bossa nova and watching hipsters at play, chances are that the bar is owned by Eric Hilton. Hilton, who makes up one half of DJ duo Thievery Corporation, has been slowly taking over DC's bar scene in his spare time (Eighteenth Street Lounge, Marvin, Dickson Wine Bar). The Gibson is Hilton's take on the New York speakeasy. First, you'll need to find the entrance, an unobtrusive doorbell next to Marvin. Once inside you'll find some of the best cocktails in the city, with drinks updated on a chalkboard daily, and ingredients from celery-infused Pisco to burnt cinnamon. Reservations recommended.
For Marvin, see p127; for Eighteenth Street Lounge, see p196.

Velvet Lounge

915 U Street, NW, between Vermont Avenue & 9th Street (1-202 462 3213, www.velvetlounge dc.com). U Street/African-American Civil War

Churchkey.

THE BEST BARS WITH A VIEW

Overlooking the White House
POV. *See p134.*

With sunloungers and an
outdoor fireplace
Donovan House Side Bar. *See p137.*

Looking out over to Potomac
Sequoia. *See p142.*

Memorial/Cardozo Metro. **Open** 8pm-2am Mon-
Thur, Sun; 8pm-3am Fri, Sat. **Credit** MC, V.
Map p251 J3 ㉙

Comfy, funky and groovy, the Velvet Lounge is a
popular, divey kind of place to stop off for a drink
when on the way out for the night, or on the way
back after a concert at the nearby 9:30 Club (*see
p186*). It's like a neighborhood bar that just happens to have live music: many come to enjoy martinis and beers with friends, while others are here
for the band.

▶ *For a review of Velvet Lounge as a music venue,
see p189.*

GEORGETOWN

Birreria Paradiso

*3282 M Street, NW, between Potomac Street &
Georgetown Park (1-202 337 1245, www.eatyour
pizza.com). Farragut West Metro then 35 bus or
Foggy Bottom-GWU Metro then 32 bus.* **Open**
11.30am-11pm Mon-Thur; 11.30am-midnight Fri,
Sat; noon-10pm Sun. **Credit** AmEx, MC, V.
Map p249 E5 ㉚

Pizza paradise above, beer heaven below, what
more could you want? Birreria Paradiso, one of
Georgetown's newest destinations, is in the basement of the hugely popular Pizzeria Paradiso (*see
p122*) and the English-style hand pumps behind
the bar serve up cask-conditioned ales that will
soon produce heavenly visions in imbibers. The
brews on offer include Britain's Old Speckled Hen,
Belgium's Chimay Cinq Cents and a blood-colored
Flemish beer named the Duchesse de Bourgogne.
There are three- and four-taste flights ($9 and $11),
so sensation seekers can sample a cross-section of
Birreria's extensive offerings – culled from a six-
page menu.

Degrees Bar & Lounge

*Ritz-Carlton Georgetown, 3100 South Street,
NW, at 31st Street (1-202 912 4100/www.ritz
carlton.com/hotels/georgetown). Foggy Bottom/
GWU Metro then 34 bus.* **Open** 2.30-10pm Mon-
Thur, Sun; 2.30pm-midnight Fri, Sat. **Credit**
AmEx, DC, MC, V. **Map** p249 E5 ㉛
See p138 **Hotel Havens**.

J Paul's

*3218 M Street, NW, at Wisconsin Avenue (1-202
333 3450, www.j-pauls.com). Foggy Bottom-GWU
Metro then 30, 32, 34, 35, 36, Georgetown Metro
Connection bus.* **Open** 11.30am-2am Mon-Thur;
11.30am-3am Fri, Sat; 10.30am-2am Sun. **Credit**
AmEx, Disc, MC, V. **Map** p249 E5 ㉜

In good weather, young DC professionals fight for
the seats of choice along the open windows facing
M Street. They're also drawn to the good raw shell-
fish and the 30 varieties of Scotch. Like almost every
other drinking hole in Georgetown, this bar gets its
fair share of student drinkers.

Sequoia

*3000 K Street, NW, at Wisconsin Avenue,
Washington Harbor (1-202 944 4200, www.ark
restaurants.com). Foggy Bottom-GWU Metro then
30, 32, 34, 35, 36, Georgetown Metro Connection
bus.* **Open** 11.30am-11pm Mon-Thur; 11.30am-
midnight Fri, Sat; 10.30am-3pm, 4-11pm Sun.
Credit AmEx, Disc, MC, V. **Map** p249 E5 ㉝

This enormous bar and restaurant is people-watching
central. The interiors are spacious, with high ceilings
and tall windows. The outside bar, which looks out
over the Potomac River and has views of Georgetown
University and the Kennedy Center, is a popular
nightspot-cum-pickup joint in the summer.

CLEVELAND PARK

Nanny O'Brien's

*3319 Connecticut Avenue, NW, between Macomb
& Newark Streets (1-202 686 9189, www.nanny
obriens.com). Cleveland Park Metro.* **Open** 4pm-
1.30am Mon-Thur; 4pm-2.30am Fri; noon-2.30am
Sat; noon-1.30am Sun. **Credit** AmEx, DC, Disc,
MC, V. **Map** p249 F1 ㉞

Much smaller (and more crowded) than the Four
Provinces across the street, Nanny's is closer to an
'authentic' Irish pub than most DC bars. The traditional music sessions, held on Monday nights at 9pm,
are legendary. Three dartboards in the back attract
many locals and some of the city's sharpest shooters.

H STREET CORRIDOR

Red Palace

*1210 H Street, NE, at 12th Street (1-202 399
3201, www.redandblackbar.com). Union Station
Metro.* **Open** 7pm-2am Mon-Thur, Sun; 7pm-3am
Fri, Sat. **Credit** DC, MC, V. **Map** p84.

When two of H Street's beloved institutions (the Red
and the Black and Palace of Wonders) announced
they'd merged, locals wondered what would become
of the indie music venue and the sideshow bar. The
result, Red Palace, combines the best of both venues
(burlesque, freakshow acts, live bands) with an
expanded, 200-capacity stage for shows. If you like
sword-swallowing and belly dancing on a Saturday
night, plenty of wonders remain inside.

Shops & Services

What to buy and where to buy it.

Washington has managed to survive the recession pretty much unscathed, and so have many of the city's retailers. It's just as well that most of DC's museums and tourist attractions are free, given the burgeoning number of shops ready to relieve you of your cash. And, as neighborhoods across town have redeveloped and gentrified, so the retail scene has followed. The 14th Street/U Street Corridor, for example, has become a new shopping hub in recent years. Of course, Washington has all the international brands and the city's malls (*see below*) are good places to find them. However, what any real shopper wants is the inside information on the stores and services that only a resident would know, and we aim to provide that here.

GENERAL

Department stores

Don't forget **Nordstrom** and **Bloomingdales** at **Tysons Corner Center** and **Macy's** at the **Fashion Centre at Pentagon City** (for both, *see p144*).

Lord & Taylor
5255 Western Avenue, NW, at Wisconsin Avenue, Chevy Chase, Upper Northwest (1-202 362 9600, www.lordandtaylor.com). Friendship Heights Metro. **Open** 10am-9.30pm Mon-Thur; 10am-10pm Fri; 10am-9.30pm Sat; 11am-7pm Sun. **Credit** AmEx, Disc, MC, V.
Grown-ups' and children's dresses and sportswear with broad, basic appeal by the likes of Calvin Klein and Perry Ellis, with the requisite cosmetics and jewelry departments. There are plus sizes for women, too.

Macy's
1201 G Street, NW, at 12th Street, Downtown (1-202 628 6661, www.macys.com). Metro Center Metro. **Open** 10am-8pm Mon-Sat; noon-6pm Sun. **Credit** AmEx, Disc, MC, V. **Map** p252 H6.
What was Hecht's now belongs to Macy, so you know what to expect: reasonably priced, mid-range fashions by famous makers, and an outstanding source of undies, socks, ties, shades and cologne. If you see a cool cake mixer at Williams-Sonoma, you can probably buy it slightly cheaper here.
Other locations: 5400 Wisconsin Avenue, at Western Avenue, Chevy Chase (1-301 654 7600).

Neiman Marcus
5300 Wisconsin Avenue, NW, at Western Avenue, Upper Northwest (1-202 966 9700, www.neiman marcus.com). Friendship Heights Metro. **Open** 10am-8pm Mon-Fri; 10am-7pm Sat; noon-6pm Sun. **Credit** AmEx, DC, Disc, MC, V.
With Corneliani men's suits, Ugg handbags, flirty Anna Sui dresses, Prada shoes, Wedgwood dinner services and Acqua di Parma beauty products, you can smell the money when you walk in.

Saks Fifth Avenue
5555 Wisconsin Avenue, NW, at South Park Avenue, Chevy Chase, MD (1-301 657 9000). Friendship Heights Metro. **Open** 10am-7pm Mon-Wed, Fri; 10am-8pm Thur; 10am-6pm Sat; noon-6pm Sun. **Credit** AmEx, DC, Disc, MC, V.
Luxury a go-go from casual to couture, with designers such as Marc Jacobs, Michael Kors and John Varvatos, and cosmetics by La Prairie, Chanel and Kiehl's. Guys would rue missing the Saks men's shop at 5300 Wisconsin Avenue.
Other locations Tysons Galleria, 2051 International Drive, McLean, VA (1-703 761 0700).

Malls

Chevy Chase Pavilion
5335 Wisconsin Avenue, NW, at Western Avenue, Friendship Heights, Upper Northwest (1-202 686 5335, www.ccpavilion.com). Friendship Heights Metro. **Open** 9am-9pm Mon-Sat; 11am-6pm Sun. **Credit** varies.

Feeding mainly off the better stores across the street at Mazza Gallerie (*see below*) this minor mall offers clothing and home stuff, plus a food court. Highlights include Pottery Barn and Alpaca for Peruvian hand-crafted woollen garments.

Collection at Chevy Chase

5471 Wisconsin Avenue, Chevy Chase, MD (www.thecollectionatchevychase.com). Friendship Heights Metro. **Open** 10am-9pm Mon-Sat; 11am-6pm Sun. Store opening times vary. **Credit** varies. Quite near Mazza Gallerie (*see below*), this shopping center combines a line-up of magnetic retail names under one roof, including Jimmy Choo, Louis Vuitton, Tiffany & Co, Ralph Lauren, Barney's New York, Christian Dior, Cartier and Gucci.

Fashion Centre at Pentagon City

1100 South Hayes Street, between Army Navy Drive & 15th Street, Arlington, VA (1-703 415 2400, www.simon.com). Pentagon City Metro. **Open** 10am-9.30pm Mon-Sat; 11am-6pm Sun. **Credit** varies.

Not bad for an old-school mall, with copious daylight and royal palms in its deep, plunging atria; its levels accessible by glass elevator. Anchored by department stores Macy's and Nordstrom, this mall offers better (but not the best) apparel, gifts and speciality goods from 160-odd national franchises such as Gap, Limited and Kenneth Cole, and is surrounded by big-box discount stores to its east and a flank of decent shops in a too-cute outdoor mall to its west.

Mazza Gallerie

5300 Wisconsin Avenue, NW, between Western Avenue & Jenifer Street, Friendship Heights, Upper Northwest (1-202 966 6114, www.mazza gallerie.net). Friendship Heights Metro. **Open** 10am-8pm Mon-Fri; noon-6pm Sun. **Credit** varies. Stores here run from snooty (Neiman Marcus) to congenially high-end (Saks Fifth Avenue's Men's Store) to over-a-barrel discount (Filene's Basement). Also houses a multi-screen cinema.

Shops at Georgetown Park

3222 M Street, NW, at Wisconsin Avenue, Georgetown (1-202 298 5577, www.shopsat georgetownpark.com). Foggy Bottom-GWU Metro then 30, 32, 34, 35, 36 bus. **Open** 10am-8pm Mon-Sat; noon-6pm Sun. **Credit** varies. **Map** p249 E5.
Tucked between M Street and the C&O Canal, this skylit, air-conditioned escape from Georgetown's hectic streets has major clothing chains such as J Crew and Sisley, jewelry craft at the Joy of Beading, and presents for pets at Phat Dog. But if you get peckish, skip the meager food court and pay a visit to Dean & Deluca (*see p153*) next door on M Street, NW.

Shops at Union Station

50 Massachusetts Avenue, NE, at North Capitol Street, Union Station & Around (1-202 371 9441, *1-202 289 1908/www.unionstationdc.com). Union Station Metro.* **Open** 10am-9pm Mon-Sat; noon-6pm Sun. **Credit** varies. **Map** p253 L6.
In the 1980s, before all the airports became malls, the refurbished Union Station assembled a lively range of boutiques and cafés beneath its soaring, coffered vaults. Thus the future of this magnificent building, under threat of demolition due to the long-term decline in the numbers of rail passengers, was ensured. Before traveling you can shop at several gift shops, bookshops and chocolatiers as well as an eclectic mix of stores such as Rosetta Stone for language learning packs or Appalachian Spring for handmade crafts and ceramics. You can also get your shoes polished, your eyebrows done or your jewelry and watches fixed.

Tysons Corner Center

1961 Chain Bridge Road, McLean, VA (1-888 289 7667, 1-703 893 9400/www.shoptysons.com). West Falls Church-VT/UVA Metro then 28A, 28B or 3T bus. By car: Route 66 west to Route 7 west to Tysons Corner. **Open** 10am-9.30pm Mon-Sat; 11am-7pm Sun. **Credit** varies.
You could spend an entire weekend inside TCC, grounded at one end by Bloomingdale's and at the other by Nordstrom, with over a hundred shops such as Benetton, Banana Republic and West Elm elsewhere on two levels. It also hosts higher-end retailers like Armani Exchange.

BOOKS & MAGAZINES

All the big national chain bookstores have stores in Washington. There are two branches of **Borders** downtown (1801 K Street, NW, 1-202 466 4999; and 5333 Wisconsin Avenue, 1-202 686 8270) plus a **Barnes & Noble** in Georgetown (3040 M Street, NW, 1-202 965 9880). What was once Washington's most well known local chain, Olsson's Books & Records, is now sadly closed. Listed below are DC's remaining independent and speciality booksellers.

General

Chapters Literary Art Center & Bookstore

445 11th Street, at E Street, NW, between Pennsylvania Avenue & E Street, Downtown (1-202 737 5553). Metro Center Metro. **Open** 10am-7pm Mon-Fri; noon-7pm Sat; 2-7pm Sun. **Credit** AmEx, Disc, MC, V. **Map** p252 J6.
This independent bookstore became a not-for-profit literary arts center in 2007, but has kept its inventory of literary titles. Luckily for DC residents this means more literary evenings with authors and other cultural events. New book releases are highlighted at the front of the store, and the staff's own reading picks are prominently displayed within. Check out the center's Facebook page for more information.

★ Kramerbooks

1517 Connecticut Avenue, NW, at Q Street, Dupont Circle (1-202 387 1400, www.kramers.com). Dupont Circle Metro. **Open** 7.30am-1am Mon-Thur, Sun; 24hrs Fri, Sat. **Credit** AmEx, Disc, MC, V. **Map** p250 G4.

Not just a bookshop, but an episode of *Blind Date*, Kramerbooks is an oft-used venue for a first assignation. First, meet in the bookshop, then repair to the attached café (Afterwords, *see p122*), which serves meals and snacks throughout the day. Possibilities of romance aside, the book selection is good.

★ Politics & Prose

5015 Connecticut Avenue, NW, between Fessenden Streets & Nebraska Avenue, Upper Northwest (1-800 722 0790, 1-202 364 1919, www.politics-prose.com). Van Ness-UDC Metro t hen northbound L1, L2, L4 bus. **Open** 9am-10pm Mon-Sat; 10am-8pm Sun. **Credit** AmEx, Disc, MC, V.

As you might guess, Politics & Prose carries a lot of both, plus a large section that is set aside for children and teenagers, and there's a coffee shop downstairs too. The store is much more than just a thriving independent bookshop, it's a much-loved institution and a must-stop for prominent authors who are on the reading-tour circuit. Carla Cohen, the shop's well-known founder and co-owner, died in late 2010.

Specialist

Big Planet Comics

3145 Dumbarton Street, NW, between 31st & 32nd Streets, Georgetown (1-202 342 1961, www.bigplanetcomics.com/stores). Foggy Bottom-GWU Metro then 30, 32, 34, 35, 36 bus. **Open** 11am-7pm Mon, Tue, Thur, Fri; 11am-8pm Wed; 11am-6pm Sat; noon-5pm Sun. **Credit** AmEx, MC, V. **Map** p249 E4.

Underground comics and graphic novels.

Where to shop

The city's top retail locations.

Georgetown
Assuming you're the owner of a well-endowed bank balance, this gracious district is a great place to shop, and to live. You'll find a positive portmanteau of fine antiques stores on upper Wisconsin Avenue, NW, and a veritable outdoor mall of global retail chains – from Armani Exchange to Zara – around lower Wisconsin Avenue and along M Street, NW.

Dupont Circle
You can walk from Georgetown to Dupont Circle, home to several of DC's favorite local merchants selling books, records, clothes, jewelry and household wares.

14th Street/U Street Corridor & Logan Circle
Dupont's retail energy has spread eastward, expanding with the march of new apartment blocks along the 14th Street, NW corridor, U Street, NW, and Logan Circle. To the continuing amazement of local folks, the once left-for-dead 14th Street has reawakened as a bona fide retail row.

Adams Morgan
Just north of Dupont Circle, the 18th Street strip in Adams Morgan has more food and beverage (especially beverage) purveyors than anything, but if you go there to eat,

you'll come across plenty of good finds in its clothing, music and home stores.

Connecticut Avenue, NW
South of Dupont, lower Connecticut Avenue, NW, on the way to the White House, has an array of excellent if businesslike clothiers (Brooks Brothers, Burberry, et al).

Chinatown
More or less everything authentically Chinese has disappeared from the area around the MCI Center, with popular brand stores moving in instead.

Capitol Hill
Away from everything else is Capitol Hill – perhaps you've heard of it – a hotbed of lobbying and, occasionally, legislation. But influence is not all that the place sells. There are fresh foods galore and, at weekends, arts and crafts at Eastern Market, a creditable remnant of a more agrarian age, and an expanding row of shops along 8th Street, SE.

Friendship Heights
For the fancy stuff, follow the money to upper Wisconsin Avenue, NW, at DC's border with Maryland, where you can stare into a firmament that includes Neiman Marcus, Saks Fifth Avenue, Louis Vuitton and Jimmy Choo.

CONSUME

Used & antiquarian

Capitol Hill Books
*657 C Street, SE, at 7th Street, Capitol Hill
(1-202 544 1621/www.capitolhillbooks-dc.com).
Eastern Market Metro.* **Open** 11.30am-6pm
Mon-Fri; 10am-6pm Sat, Sun. **Credit** AmEx,
MC, V. **Map** p253 L7.
Two floors of secondhand books – fiction, mysteries,
politics, cooking and more – plus rare and first editions. An excellent place for browsing.

Second Story Books
*2000 P Street, NW, at 20th Street, Dupont Circle
(1-202 659 8884, www.secondstorybooks.com).
Dupont Circle Metro.* **Open** 10am-10pm daily.
Credit AmEx, Disc, MC, V. **Map** p250 G4.
A venerated, musty space, chock-a-block with all
kinds of curious used titles, plus second-hand music
and prints. Check the sidewalk bins for bargains.
This shop, along with its counterpart in Rockland,
stocks over a million rare and used books.

CHILDREN

You can find clothes and shoes for youngsters
at **H&M** (*see p150*), **Macy's** (*see p143*) and
Lord & Taylor (*see p143*). There's a **Gap
Kids** in Georgetown (1267 Wisconsin Avenue,
NW, 1-202 333 2411) and in Chevy Chase. Any
CVS drug store has baby and child sundries
galore. And check the museum shops (*see p161*
Museum Pieces) for one-of-a-kind toys.

Dawn Price Baby
*3112 M Street, NW, between 31st Street &
Wisconsin Avenue, Georgetown (1-202 333 3939,
www.dawnpricebaby.com). Foggy Bottom, GWU
Metro then 30, 32, 34, 35, 36 bus.* **Open** 11am-
6pm Mon-Sat; noon-5pm Sun. **Credit** AmEx, MC,
V. **Map** p249 E5.
A handy place to pick up gifts for newborns or young
children. In keeping with the DC location, you can find
'Tiny Democrat' and 'Tiny Republican' emblazoned
T shirts. Also in stock are knitted animal backpacks
and personalized first plates and christening mugs.
Other locations 325 7th Street, SE, Capitol Hill
(1-202 543 2920).

Kid's Closet
*1226 Connecticut Avenue, NW, at N Street,
Dupont Circle (1-202 429 9247). Dupont Circle
Metro.* **Open** 10am-6pm Mon-Fri; 11am-5pm Sat.
Credit AmEx, Disc, MC, V. **Map** p250 G4.
Miniature fashions by OshKosh, Rare Editions,
Carter's and others. Cute and not so common toys too.

Monkey's Uncle
*321 & 323 7th Street, SE, between Pennsylvania
Avenue & C Street, Capitol Hill (1-202 543 6471,
www.monkeysuncleonthehill.com). Eastern Market*

INSIDE TRACK SALES TAX

In DC and Maryland, the sales tax is six per
cent, which is added to the ticket price. In
Virginia, sales tax is five per cent.

Metro. **Open** 10.30am-6pm Tue, Wed, Fri; 11am-
7pm Thur; 9am-6pm Sat; 11am-5pm Sun. **Credit**
AmEx, Disc, MC, V. **Map** p253 L7.
Clothes for babies up to preteens, with the usual
chances for sartorial serendipity and a high base-
line of quality. Discerning Hill mothers go to
Monkey's Uncle for on-the-cheap party clothes and
seasonal wear for their children and maternity
clothes for themselves. The owners have started a
useful and popular sideline business of renting
baby gear: there's travel equipment for local parents flying out, highchairs and play yards for local
grandparents hosting in.

Toys

Fairy Godmother
*319 7th Street, SE, between Pennsylvania Avenue
& C Street, Capitol Hill (1-202 547 5474). Eastern
Market Metro.* **Open** 10.30am-6pm Mon-Fri;
10am-5pm Sat; 10.30am-3.30pm Sun. **Credit**
AmEx, MC, V. **Map** p253 L7.
This tiny shop holds a remarkable range of children's books and toys. The emphasis is on parent
favorites: Haba and Plan wooden toys, Corolle and
Madame Alexander dolls. There is a good selection
of fiction for second-graders up to teens, plus French
and Spanish books for babies and toddlers. New picture books get prominent placement, and staff are
friendly and knowledgeable.

Sullivan's Toy Store
*3412 Wisconsin Avenue, NW, between Norton
Avenue & Newark Street, Cleveland Park (1-202
362 1343). Tenleytown-AU Metro then 30, 32,
34, 35, 36 bus.* **Open** 10am-6pm Mon, Tue, Sat;
10am-7pm Wed-Fri; noon-5pm Sun. **Credit**
AmEx, Disc, MC, V.
Before the onslaught of Toys 'R' Us, the world was
full of toy stores like this one, which stocks craft kits,
kites and puzzles, dolls and action figures and a separate section for proper art supplies.

ELECTRONICS & PHOTOGRAPHY

CVS drugstores, with branches all over the city,
offer a one-hour photo developing service. Radio
Shack has stores throughout the area.

Best Buy
*4500 Wisconsin Avenue, NW, at Albemarle Street,
Tenleytown, Upper Northwest (1-202 895 1580,*

CONSUME

www.bestbuy.com). Tenleytown-AU Metro.
Open 10am-9pm Mon-Sat; 11am-7pm Sun.
Credit AmEx, Disc, MC, V.
A carnival of mass-media gizmos that offers just about anything you want – if it's in stock.

Graffiti

4914 Wisconsin Avenue, NW, Upper Northwest (1-202 244 9643, www.graffitiaudio.com). Friendship Heights Metro. **Open** 10am-7pm Mon-Sat; noon-6pm Sun. **Credit** AmEx, Disc, MC, V. **Map** p250 G4.
TV and audio equipment of the better kind. Home cinemas and discreet audio systems.

Penn Camera

840 E Street, NW, between 8th & 9th Streets, Penn Quarter (1-202 347 5777, www.penn camera.com). Gallery Place-Chinatown Metro. **Open** 8.30am-6pm Mon-Fri; 10am-5pm Sat, Sun. **Credit** AmEx, Disc, MC, V. **Map** p253 J6.
All the equipment a pro could need, but the smart staff will help novices too. Camera equipment also available on rental basis too.
Other locations: throughout the city.

FASHION

Designer

The greatest concentration of designer clothing is to be found in Washington's better department stores, such as **Neiman Marcus** and **Saks Fifth Avenue** (for both, *see p143*). **Betsey Johnson** keeps her stylish pieces at 3029 N Street, NW (1-202 338 4090). If you're feeling especially thin, you can take a trip to visit the **Chanel** boutique in Tysons Galleria (2001 International Drive, McLean, VA, 1-703 874 0555). Women of a certain quiet sophistication have shopped at **Claire Dratch** for 63 years (7615 Wisconsin Avenue, Bethesda, MD, 1-301 656 8000). Or they visit **Rizik's** (1100 Connecticut Avenue, NW, Downtown, 1-202 223 4050), across the street from which is a convenient **Burberry** store (No.1155, 1-202 463 3000).

In addition to the boutiques listed below, **Tabandeh** (*see p151*) stocks lines from the likes of Rick Owens, Ann Demeulemeester, and KristenseN du Nord.

Betsy Fisher

1224 Connecticut Avenue, NW, between N Street & Jefferson Place, Dupont Circle (1-202 785 1975, www.betsyfisher.com). Dupont Circle Metro. **Open** 10am-7pm Mon-Wed; 10am-8pm Thur, Fri; 10am-6pm Sat; noon-4pm Sun. **Credit** AmEx, DC, Disc, MC, V. **Map** p250 G4.
Approachable chic, from the tailored to the saucy. Ensembles, dresses and the rest by the likes of Caractere, Gazebo and Three Dots.

Nana

1528 U Street, NW, between 15th & 16th Streets, U Street/14th Street Corridor (1-202 667 6955, www.nanadc.com). Dupont Circle Metro. **Open** *Winter* noon-7pm daily. *Summer* noon-7pm Tue-Sun. **Credit** MC, V. **Map** p250 H3.
Wearing escapism on its sleeveless little dress, Nana sells fun, funky dresses, blouses, skirts and more by designers such as Kelly Lane, Classic Girl and Dear Creatures, using eco-friendly materials and ethical practises. Then she tosses some wonderful accessories from the likes of Angela Adams (handbags) and Lilian Hartman (jewelry) into the mix. Fresh!

Relish

3312 Cady's Alley, NW, M Street between 33rd & 34th Streets, Georgetown (1-202 333 5343, www.cadysalley.com). Foggy Bottom Metro then 38B bus. **Open** 10am-6pm Mon-Wed, Fri, Sat; 10am-7.30pm Thur. **Credit** AmEx, MC, V. **Map** p249 E5.
Relish is in an airy loft on Georgetown's design-oriented Cady's Alley, and its designer lines are similarly rarefied: dresses by Marni, DVN or Missotten for women and shirts by Comme des Garçons, Dries van Noten and Junya Watanabe for men. Plus shoes by Collection Privée and Punkt.

Discount

Filene's Basement

1133 Connecticut Avenue, NW, Downtown (1-202 872 8430, www.filenesbasement.com). Farragut North Metro. **Open** 9.30am-8pm Mon-Sat; noon-5pm Sun. **Credit** AmEx, Disc, MC, V. **Map** p250 G5.
Massive markdowns on every category of clothing and accessories by familiar names.
Other locations: National Press Building, 529 14th Street, NW, Downtown (1-202 638 4110); Mazza Gallerie, 5300 Wisconsin Avenue, NW, Chevy Chase (1-202 966 0208).

General

Most of the mainstream clothiers make appearances in the District – American Apparel, Banana Republic, J Crew, Gap. Georgetown has one of nearly all of them, plus choicer chains like Club Monaco, French Connection, Diesel and Armani Exchange. You will also find them in most of the city's malls (*see p143*).

Commander Salamander

1420 Wisconsin Avenue, NW, between O & P Streets, Georgetown (1-202 337 2265). Foggy Bottom-GWU Metro then 30, 32, 34, 35, 36 bus. **Open** 10am-9pm Mon-Sat; 11am-6pm Sun. **Credit** AmEx, Disc, MC, V. **Map** p249 E4.

Tabandeh. *See p151.*

CONSUME

Urbanwear and accessories for men and women by Antik, Black Label, Taverniti and other hot favorites, are available at this underground headquarters for those who want to advertise their nonconformity in expensive clothes.

H&M

1025 F Street, NW, Downtown (1-202 347 3306, www.hm.com). Metro Center Metro. **Open** 10am-8pm Mon-Sat; noon-6pm Sun. **Credit** AmEx, DC, Disc, MC, V. **Map** p252 J6.
The Swedish retailer has taken DC by storm, selling sportswear and dresswear (including plus sizes) for men, women and children under its own label.
Other locations shops at Georgetown Park, 3222 M Street, NW (1-202 298 6792).

Urban Outfitters

3111 M Street, NW, between 31st & 32nd Streets, Georgetown (1-202 342 1012). Foggy Bottom-GWU Metro then 30, 32, 34, 35, 36 bus. **Open** 10am-10pm Mon-Thur; 10am-11pm Fri, Sat; 10am-9pm Sun. **Credit** AmEx, Disc, MC, V. **Map** p249 E5.
Young neo-bohemians trawl the creaky floors of this bazaar for geek fashions and groovy house wares with a folkloric theme.
Other locations: 737 7th Street, NW, between G & H Streets, Chinatown (1-202 737 0259).

Secondhand & vintage

Annie Creamcheese

3279 M Street, NW, between 32nd & 33rd Streets, Georgetown (1-202 298 5555, www.annie creamcheese.com). Foggy Bottom Metro then 38B bus. **Open** 11am-8pm Mon-Sat; noon-6pm Sun. **Credit** AmEx, Disc, MC, V. **Map** p249 E5.
Vintage designer clothes by Pucci, Missoni, Lanvin and the like, from the 1940s to the '90s. Annie also imports new items from minor designers in Miami and Los Angeles.

Junction

1510 U Street, NW, between 15th & 16th Streets, U Street/14th Street Corridor (1-202 483 0260). Dupont Circle or U Street, African-American Civil War Memorial/Cardozo Metro. **Open** 3-7pm Tue, Wed; noon-7pm Thur-Sat; noon-5pm Sun. **Credit** AmEx, MC, V. **Map** p250 H3.
A collectively run vintage and resale boutique selling original designs for men and women from the 1930s onwards, plus accessories, photography and handmade gifts.

Meep's & Aunt Neensie's

2104 18th Street, NW, between California Street & Wyoming Avenue, Adams Morgan (1-202 265 6546/www.meepsdc.com). Woodley Park-Zoo/Adams Morgan Metro, then 90, 92, 93 bus. **Open** noon-7pm Tue-Sat; noon-5pm Sun. **Credit** MC, V. **Map** p250 G3.

Remember that shirt you had when you were 16? The one that, when you put it on, you knew made you look the absolute business. Would you like to find it again? It's at Meep's, where DC's slackers and band kids flock to get that *Quadrophenia* look. It doesn't sell mopeds, but has all the other retro-chic essentials for both sexes.

FASHION ACCESSORIES & SERVICES
Cleaning, laundry & repairs

Imperial Valet

1331 Connecticut Avenue, NW, between Dupont Circle & N Street, Dupont Circle (1-202 785 1444, www.sterlingcleaner.com). Dupont Circle Metro. **Open** 7.30am-6.30pm Mon-Fri; 9am-3pm Sat. **Credit** AmEx, MC, V. **Map** p250 G4.
In an hour, you can have a hat dry-cleaned. In a day, laundry done. Imperial Valet also undertakes reasonably fast alterations and repairs and will also fix your shoes so you can walk comfortably back down Connecticut Avenue.

Clothing hire

Backstage

545 8th Street, SE, at G Street, Capitol Hill (1-202 544 5744). Eastern Market Metro. **Open** 11am-7pm Mon-Sat. **Credit** AmEx, MC, V. **Map** p253 M8.
While the masses might pile in here for Halloween, it's the troupers in Washington's enormous theater-community who constantly bang on the doors for costumes, masks, makeup, hair and nails.

Georgetown Formal Wear & Custom Tailor

1804 Wisconsin Avenue, NW, Georgetown (1-202 337 4800). Foggy Bottom-GWU Metro then 30, 32, 34, 35, 36 bus, or Circulator bus. **Open** 10am-7pm Mon-Sat. **Credit** AmEx, Disc, MC, V. **Map** p249 E5.
Sudden invitation to a formal state dinner? Forgot to pack the black tie and tails in your luggage? Head here for a tux and all the trimmings.

Hats

Proper Topper

1350 Connecticut Avenue, NW, between Dupont Circle & N Street, Dupont Circle (1-202 842 3055, www.proppertopper.com). Dupont Circle Metro. **Open** 10am-8pm Mon-Fri; 10am-7pm Sat; noon-6pm Sun. **Credit** AmEx, Disc, MC, V. **Map** p250 G4.
The chic and very wearable hat selection includes elegant cloches by Louise Green for women and suave fedoras for men. Accessories for both men and women make good gifts and the jewelry selection for ladies is reasonably priced.

CONSUME

Jewelry

Jewelerswerk Galerie

*3319 Cady's Alley, Georgetown, (1-202 337
3319, www.jewelerswerk.com). Foggy Bottom-
GWU Metro.* **Open** 11am-6pm Mon-Sat; noon-
5pm Sun. **Credit** AmEx, Disc, MC, V. **Map**
p252 G5.

This cool little gallery, now relocated to Cady's
Alley, near the Francis Scott Key Bridge, sells
unique jewelry made by over 50 international artists
in a variety of media.

★ Tabandeh

*5300 Wisconsin Avenue, NW (Mazza Gallerie),
Friendship Heights (1-202 244 0777, www.
tabandehjewelry.com). Friendship Heights Metro.*
Open 10am-8pm Mon-Fri; 10am-6pm Sat; noon-
5pm Sun. **Credit** AmEx, MC, V.

The glittering window displays of Tabandeh stop
passers-by in the basement of the Mazza Gallerie in
their tracks. This jewelry and clothing boutique features offerings from high-end designers scarcely
available elsewhere in the city. Giant grey and white
Tahitian pearls from Samira 13, stunning chunky
gemstone convertable pieces from Iradj Moini, and
case after case of precious gems tempt the buyer of
means. More-affordable pieces include Swedish
reindeer-hide wristbands, wrap bracelets from Chan
Luu, and Hollywood-popular Gas Bijoux. Clothing
lines include slouchy-elegant Rick Owens, Ann
Demeulemeester, and KristenseN du Nord. There
are also small, well-curated collections of designer
shoes and evening bags. *Photo p149.*

Tiny Jewel Box

*1147 Connecticut Avenue, NW, between L & M
Streets, Downtown (1-202 393 2747, www.tiny
jewelbox.com). Farragut North or Farragut West
Metro.* **Open** 10am-5.30pm Mon-Sat. **Credit**
AmEx, MC, V. **Map** p252 G5.

A vast range of pieces, from classic to contemporary and from antique to modern one-off designer
pieces, are to be found in this long-established,
well-respected three-story downtown favourite.
Other products for sale here include scarves, bags,
gloves and gifts.

Menswear

BOSS Hugo Boss

*1517 Wisconsin Avenue, NW, between P & Q
Streets, Georgetown (1-202 625 2677, www.
hugoboss.com). Foggy Bottom-GWU Metro then
30, 32, 34, 35, 36 bus.* **Open** 11am-7.30pm Mon-
Sat; noon-6pm Sun. **Credit** AmEx, Disc, MC, V.
Map p249 E4.

A range of smart city clothing: suits, coats, shirts
and trousers. All are made in good-quality fabrics
and prices aren't unreasonable for this standard of
gentlemen's clothing. .

Brooks Brothers

*1201 Connecticut Avenue, NW, at M Street,
Dupont Circle (1-202 659 4650). Farragut North
or Dupont Circle Metro.* **Open** 9.30am-7pm Mon-
Fri; 9.30am-6pm Sat; 11am-6pm Sun. **Credit**
AmEx, Disc, MC, V. **Map** p250 G5.

Ever the classicists, Brooks Brothers has elegant and
sober men's and women's clothes ideal for politicking on Capitol Hill.

Other locations: 5504 Wisconsin Avenue, Chevy
Chase, MD (1-301 654 8202).

Everard's Clothing

*1802 Wisconsin Avenue, NW, at S Street,
Georgetown (1-202 298 7464/www.everards
clothing.com). Foggy Bottom-GWU Metro then
30, 32, 34, 35, 36 bus.* **Open** 10am-6pm Mon-Sat.
Credit AmEx, DC, Disc, MC, V. **Map** p249 E3.

The well-dressed Washington man knows Louis
Everard, and Mr Everard knows the well-dressed
Washington man – or at least his measurements.
This is the place to come for suits beautifully made
to customer specifications. An added bonus is that
you never know which of the rich and powerful
you might see within, or upstairs browsing
through the fine women's collections.

Other locations 1120 20th Street, NW
(1-202 457 0077).

Shoes

Georgetown has several good shoe stores, including **Steve Madden** (3109 M Street, NW, 1-202
342 6194) and the **Walking Company** (3101
M Street, NW, 1-202 625 9255).

Carbon

*2643 Connecticut Avenue, NW (1-202 232 6645,
www.carbondc.com). Woodley Park-Zoo/Adams
Morgan Metro.* **Open** noon-7.30pm Tue-Sat; noon-
5pm Sun. **Credit** MC, V. **Map** p250 H3.

Hard-to-find brands for men include Mark Nason,
Blackstone and Pikolinos; women can choose among
Biviel, Matiko and Shoola. Plus gorgeous hand-
crafted belts and jewelry.

Soulier

*1434 Wisconsin Avenue, NW, between O & P
Streets, Georgetown (1-202 342 7160). Foggy
Bottom-GWU Metro then 31 or DC Circulator bus.*
Open 10.30am-8pm Mon-Thur; 10.30am-8.30pm
Fri, Sat; 12.30-6.30pm Sun. **Credit** AmEx, Disc,
MC, V. **Map** p249 E4.

In a stretch of Wisconsin Avenue dominated by
stores for gentlemen, Soulier stands out for its
excellent selection of sleek European-style men's
shoes. Look for Bally, Bruno Magli and Magnanni,
as well as the more widely available Cole Haan.
Other makers include Cesare Paciotti, Moreschi and
Aldo Bruè. Pointy toes abound; there's nary a
clunker is in sight.

FOOD & DRINK

Bakeries

La Madeleine

3000 M Street, NW, at 30th Street, Georgetown (1-202 337 6975, www.lamadeleine.com). Foggy Bottom-GWU Metro then 30, 32, 34, 35, 36 bus. **Open** 7am-10pm Mon-Thur, Sun; 7am-11pm Fri, Sat. **Credit** AmEx, Disc, MC, V. **Map** p249 F5.

A decent chain French bakery with all the classics, such as chocolate almond croissants, crème brûlée and decadent mini parfaits. Baguettes and other breads are baked on the premises.

Marvelous Market

3217 P Street, NW, at Wisconsin Avenue, Georgetown (1-202 333 2591, www.marvelous market.com). Foggy Bottom-GWU Metro then 30, 32, 34, 35, 36 bus. **Open** 6.30am-9pm Mon-Sat; 7am-10pm Sun. **Credit** AmEx, MC, V. **Map** p249 E4.

Delicious breads, rolls, scones and pastries can be paired with ready supplies of cheeses, salami and olives. Home deliveries of deli fare also available. **Other locations** throughout the city.

★ Patisserie Poupon

1645 Wisconsin Avenue, NW, between Q & R Streets, Georgetown (1-202 342 3248). Foggy Bottom-GWU Metro then 30, 32, 34, 35, 36 bus. **Open** 8.30 am-6.30pm Tue-Fri; 8am-5.30pm Sat; 8am-4pm Sun. **Credit** AmEx, Disc, MC, V. **Map** p249 E4.

All the calorific authentic French pastries and breads are here. Opera cake is a favorite.
▶ *Poupon is also a café, see p131.*

Drink

Best Cellars

1643 Connecticut Avenue, NW, between Q & R Streets, Dupont Circle (1-202 387 3146, www.bestcellars.com). Dupont Circle Metro. **Open** 10am-9pm Mon-Thur; 10am-10pm Fri, Sat. **Credit** AmEx, MC, V. **Map** p250 G4.

With stores in several US cities, these wine realists take you beyond the freemasonry of wine snobs and their secret codes and boil it down to a simple glossary of 'luscious' (an Alsatian pinot gris, for example), 'big' (Californian zinfandel or syrah from France), 'smooth' (Chilean merlot), and so on. Also 'handcrafted' beers and some small-batch spirits.

Calvert Woodley

4339 Connecticut Avenue, NW, at Windom Place, Upper Northwest (1-202 966 4400/www.calvert woodley.com). Van Ness-UDC Metro. **Open** 10am-8.30pm Mon-Sat. **Credit** Disc, MC, V.

The old hands here have mounted a large yet well-focused selection of voluptuary treats. The extensive

De Vinos.

CONSUME

wine shop is especially strong in Burgundy and Bordeaux and always has affordable specials. At the deli, the prodigious selection includes prosciutto, Serrano and pâtés, and a world of cheeses from Cotswold to mimolette.

★ De Vinos

2001 18th Street, NW, at Florida Avenue, Adams Morgan (1-202 986 5002, www.de-vinos.com). Dupont Circle Metro. **Open** noon-10pm Mon-Fri; 10am-10pm Sat, Sun. **Credit** AmEx, Disc, MC, V. **Map** p250 G3.

The wines at this friendly shop are arranged by country and region. The store also stocks a selection of tasty beers, plus soft and hard cheeses and the gourmet crackers necessary to carry them. The wine selection is adventurous – bottles range in price from $6 to $500, and you'll find appellations you've never heard of. But then, you only learn by learning, right?

Rodman's

5100 Wisconsin Avenue, NW, at Garrison Street, Friendship Heights, Upper Northwest (1-202 363 3466, www.rodmans.com). Friendship Heights Metro. **Open** 9am-9.30pm Mon-Sat; 10am-7pm Sun. **Credit** AmEx, Disc, MC, V.

Open since 1955, this family-owned discount drugstore has expanded greatly and now offers one of the best selections of wine in Washington. Plus gourmet cheeses, exotic snacks, coffees and teas to round out the repast.

Markets

The growing season in the DC region is quite long, hence an ever-flowing bounty of fruits and vegetables, not to mention artisanal cheeses, baked goods and cut flowers. **Eastern Market** (between C Street & North Carolina Avenue, www.easternmarket-dc.org, open 7am-7pm Tue-Fri, 7am-6pm Sat, 9am-5pm Sun) is an indoor space with a vast array of fresh produce; it also hosts a weekend fleamarket.

Vendors at **Fresh FarmMarkets** (1-202 362 8889, www.freshfarmmarkets.org, open Apr-Dec 9am-1pm Sun, Jan-May 10am-1pm Sun) all sell food that has been grown, raised or made on their own premises. Markets take place at several locations around town, including the Riggs Bank parking lot, 20th & Q Streets, NW, Dupont Circle.

INSIDE TRACK
EASTERN MARKET

The historic 19th-century building that is home to **Eastern Market** (*see p153*) was gutted by fire in 2007. However, in June 2009, a beautifully restored market building reopened for business.

Personally produced, local food is also sold at **Takoma Park Farmers' Market** (Laurel Avenue, between Eastern & Carroll Avenues, Takoma Park, MD, www.takomapark market.com, open 10am-2pm Sun).

Specialist

Some of the shops listed under **Drink** (*see p152*) also stock delicatessen-style food.

★ Biagio Fine Chocolate

1904 18th Street, NW, between T Street and Florida Avenue, Dupont Circle (1-202 328 1506, www.biagiochocolate.com). Dupont Circle or U Street/African-American Civil War Memorial/ Cardozo Metro. **Open** noon-8pm Tue-Sat; noon-5pm Sun. **Credit** AmEx, Disc, MC, V. **Map** p250 G3.

See p154 **Biagio Fine Chocolate**

★ Cowgirl Creamery

919 F Street, NW, between 9th & 10th Streets, Downtown (1-202 393 6880, www.cowgirl creamery.com). Gallery Place-Chinatown or Metro Center Metro. **Open** 10am-8pm Tue-Fri; 9am-6pm Sat. **Credit** MC, V. **Map** p253 J6.

From their original creamery in Point Reyes, California, the owners, who are daughters of the Washington DC area, have flown back to offer their celebrated cheeses here. Among the choices are the triple-cream Mount Tam, earthy Alpine Shepherd, buttery Constant Bliss, as well as cottage cheese and crème fraiche.

Dean & Deluca

3276 M Street, NW, at Potomac Street, Georgetown (1-202 342 2500, www.deande luca.com). Foggy Bottom-GWU Metro, then 30, 32, 34, 35, 36 bus. **Open** *Shop* 9am-8pm daily. *Café* 7am-8pm daily. **Credit** AmEx, MC, V. **Map** p249 E5.

Fresh regional produce, salads, pastries, meats and more, all of exceptional quality and for prices higher than you ever thought you'd pay.

★ Vace

3315 Connecticut Avenue, NW, at Macomb Street, Cleveland Park (1-202 363 1999). Cleveland Park Metro. **Open** 9am-9pm Mon-Fri; 9am-8pm Sat; 10am-5pm Sun. **Credit** MC, V. **Map** p249 F1.

There's not that much fresh Italian produce in DC, but most of what there is can be found at Vace. The aroma of freshly rolled and baked pizzas (slices or pies) will draw you inside, where you'll find freezers of ready-to-heat pastas, and coolers of soft, delicious linguines plus awesome imported parmesan and other cheeses, all across from a deli case of carpaccio, salamis, hams and, last but certainly not least, olives. And don't overlook the wine selection.

CONSUME

Whole Foods

1440 P Street, NW, between 14th & 15th Streets, Logan Circle (1-202 332 4300, www.wholefoods market.com). Dupont Circle Metro. **Open** 8am-10.30pm daily. **Credit** AmEx, Disc, MC, V. **Map** p250 H4.

Besides its piles of organic produce, mountains of granola and organically raised meats, this wonderful store has an excellent stock of wines, cheeses, antipasti and other grown-up finger foods. Though the store as a whole can be expensive, the wines are available in all price ranges. And if you buy a case there's 10% off.

GIFTS, STATIONERY & SOUVENIRS

See also p160 **Museum Pieces**.

A Little Shop of Flowers

2421 18th Street, NW, between Belmont & Columbia Roads, Adams Morgan (1-202 387 7255, www.alittleshopofflowers-dc.com). Woodley Park-Zoo/Adams Morgan Metro then 90, 92, 93 bus. **Open** 9am-7pm Mon-Sat; noon-5pm Sun. Closed Aug. **Credit** AmEx, Disc, MC, V. **Map** p250 G3.

Biagio Fine Chocolate

Biagio Abbatiello's crusade to bring the best chocolate to Washington.

Biagio Abbatiello calls himself a 'curator of fine chocolate' and his below-ground shop, on the border between upmarket Dupont Circle and trendy Adams Morgan, has a bit of a museum-like feel: the chocolates that line the walls and fill the cases at Biagio Fine Chocolate represent 20 years of research, passion and art appreciation for Abbatiello, and a visit there is as much about learning as shopping.

Abbatiello, a flight attendant, was living in Paris in 1986 when he walked into a venerable shop in the affluent St-Germain neighborhood and first saw chocolate categorized by its percentage of cocoa content. The taste, rich and intense, was worlds away from what he was accustomed to, and he was smitten. It was the beginning of a long adventure for Abbatiello, who thereafter made a point of visiting chocolatiers wherever his travels took him. At every opportunity, he learned more about the manufacturing, history, and enjoyment of chocolate.

It was not until 2005, however, when a friend essentially dared him to do so, that Abbatiello considered opening his own establishment. He set about deciding on an ideal look and location – taking into account not only store siting and visibility but also ideal storage conditions for his product, which thrives best in a wine-cellar-like environment. Biagio opened in December 2006.

The store's shelves represent producers from around the world – among them, François Pralus and Valrhona from France, London's Artisan du Chocolat and Tuscany's Amedei – as well as up-and-coming Americans, including several Washington-area makers. There are plenty of fair-trade and indigenously made bars, as well. The emphasis is on single-source and 'bean-to-bar' producers, but Abbatiello is no snob (and no fool): in addition to purists' favorites, he also stocks novelty flavored 'lifestyle' bars. The filled chocolates, available by the piece, represent a range of makers and varieties.

Washington has always had a well-traveled, sophisticated population, so speciality shops have never been scarce here. And, of course, in the past 20 years Americans have become more knowledgeable about food in general and more appreciative of artisanal products in particular. Biagio's well-versed employees, every one a convert to the chocolate cause, are testament to the power of self-education. Along with their expertise, the shop offers tastings several times a month. Abbatiello's favorite interaction, he says, 'is when a skeptical person attends a tasting and you can literally watch the transformation of a Doubting Thomas… into an avid chocolate-lover within minutes'.

For all the enthusiasm it engenders, Abbatiello insists that chocolate is not an addiction. What it is, he says, is a product he can stand by, one that 'sells itself'. Producers now come to him and vie for space in the shop. Even his competition only helps his cause, he says, because it 'raises the chocolate conversation'. Running a business entails its share of risks and headaches, of course, but Abbatiello seems contented with his choices. 'The best part,' he says, 'is that everyone comes in happy and everyone is even happier when they leave'.

For listings, *see p153*.

CONSUME

Copenhaver.

Stop in for sunflowers or alstromeria to freshen your room, or order an arrangement of any size for a friend. A florist of the more traditional and formal kind.

A Mano
1677 Wisconsin Avenue, NW, at Reservoir Road, Georgetown (1-202 298 7200, www.amano.bz). Foggy Bottom-GWU Metro then 30, 32, 34, 35, 36 bus. **Open** 10am-6pm Mon-Sat; noon-5pm Sun. **Credit** AmEx, MC, V. **Map** p249 E4.
Welcome to a world of handmade (hence the name) quality gifts, especially tableware, and corporate gifts too. Sourced from all over the world but definitely not 'ethnic'.

Allan Woods Florist
2645 Connecticut Avenue, NW, at 26th Street, Woodley Park (1-202 332 3334, www.allan woods.com). Woodley Park-Zoo/Adams Morgan Metro. **Open** 9am-7pm Mon-Fri; 9am-6pm Sat. **Credit** AmEx, Disc, MC, V.
Fresh, seasonal favorites abound at this shop – hydrangeas, peonies, lilies and lilacs in spring and summer and a parade of poinsettias at Christmas – alongside a deluge of cut flowers.

Appalachian Spring
1415 Wisconsin Avenue, NW, at P Street, Georgetown (1-202 337 5780, www.appalachian spring.com). Foggy Bottom-GWU Metro then 30, 32, 34, 35, 36 bus. **Open** 10am-6pm Mon-Sat; noon-6pm Sun. **Credit** AmEx, MC, V. **Map** p249 E4.

Why buy household gifts at the national chains when you can find wonderful handmade ceramics, carved-wood items, blankets and jewelry at this North American crafts boutique? Lead-free pewter ware harks back to the Founding Fathers, while iridescent 'fire and light' glass bowls in exquisite colors are very contemporary. The master glass blowers whose work is found here have helped define the contemporary American art glass movement.
Other locations East Hall, Union Station, 50 Massachusetts Avenue, NE (1-202 682 0505).

★ Copenhaver
1301 Connecticut Avenue, NW, between Dupont Circle & N Street, Dupont Circle (1-202 232 1200). Dupont Circle Metro. **Open** 9.30am-5.30pm Mon-Fri; 10am-4pm Sat. **Credit** AmEx, Disc, MC, V. **Map** p250 G4.
The decorous wooden shelves of Copenhaver hold the city's finest selection of stationery: Crane paper of all descriptions, Vera Wang and Martha Stewart invitations, insanely expensive letterpress notecards. If you're looking for somber double-folds for condolence letters or suitable cotton paper for your dissertation, this is your place. Come December, there's a lovely selection of holiday cards, along with proper red-bordered foldovers with lined envelopes for your Christmas letters. Staff will engrave your wedding invitations, too. Service is personal and exceptional.

Georgetown Tobacco
3144 M Street, NW, at Wisconsin Avenue, Georgetown (1-202 338 5100, www.gttobacco.

The Phoenix.

com). *Foggy Bottom-GWU Metro, then 30, 32, 34, 35, 36 bus.* **Open** 10am-9pm Mon-Thur; 10am-10pm Fri, Sat; noon-8pm Sun. **Credit** AmEx, MC, V. **Map** p249 E5.

Tobacco in every form, along with everything you'd ever need for smoking it for those connoisseurs who still inhale. Unusually, you can find authentic Venetian Carnival masks stocked here, which add a festive touch.

Ginza

1721 Connecticut Avenue, NW, between R & S Streets, Dupont Circle (1-202 332 7000, www. ginzaonline.com). Dupont Circle Metro. **Open** 11am-7pm Mon-Sat; noon-6pm Sun. **Credit** AmEx, Disc, MC, V. **Map** p250 G4.

Did you leave your heart in Tokyo? This intimate but comprehensive shop sells Japanese household items such as elegant saké sets, dinnerware and ike-bana vases plus specialities such as origami paper, kimonos and Japanese snacks.

★ The Phoenix

1514 Wisconsin Avenue, NW, between P Street and Volta Place, Georgetown (1-202 338 4404, www.thephoenixdc.com). Foggy Bottom-GWU Metro then 31 bus, or DC Circulator bus. **Open** 10am-6pm Mon-Sat; 1-6pm Sun. **Credit** AmEx, Disc, MC, V. **Map** p249 E4.

This family-owned Georgetown institution offers affordable designer jewelry and comfortable clothes for women, as well as sought-after Mexican imports – Day of the Dead figurines, *alebrijes* (colorful, fanciful animals) and antique silver. There is a wide selection of separates from the likes of Eileen Fisher, Cut Loose and White + Warren. Semi-precious-bead necklaces and earrings dominate the

numerous trinket cases, culled from the collections of local and international jewelry artists. Latico, Ellington and Carla Mancini bags and versatile knit dresses round out the wardrobe offerings.

★ Pulp

1803 14th Street, NW, between S & Swann Streets, Shaw: U Street/14th Street Corridor (1-202 462 7857, www.pulpdc.com). U Street/ African American Civil War Memorial/ Cardozo Metro. **Open** 11am-7pm Mon-Sat; 11am-5pm Sun. **Credit** AmEx, Disc, MC, V. **Map** p250 H3.

People drop in to Pulp for an ironic-chic greeting card and find themselves picking up things they didn't know they needed: the place has candles, masks, toys, and all manner of gag gifts for the hipsters and sophisticates who frequent the store's lively neighborhood. The paper goods are excellent: not just occasion cards but boxes of fine-quality cotton notes, plus gorgeous wrapping paper by the sheet – and fancy ribbons to go with them. Friends having a baby? No problem. Need a present for more mature sensibilities? Pulp's got you covered. *Photos p159.*

HEALTH & BEAUTY
Spas & salons

Aveda

1325 Wisconsin Avenue, NW, between N & Dumbarton Streets, Georgetown (1-202 965 1325, www.avedageorgetown.com). Foggy Bottom-GWU Metro then 30, 32, 34, 35, 36 bus. **Open** 10am-7pm Mon, Sun; 9am-8pm Tue; 9am-9pm Wed, Thur; 8.30am-8pm Fri, Sat. **Credit** AmEx, MC, V. **Map** p249 E4.

CONSUME

Disappear into this well-regarded salon and spa to treat your scalp, wax your brows, have a massage (hot stones optional), or reward your tired feet. **Other locations** throughout the city.

Blue Mercury

3059 M Street, NW, between 30th & 31st Streets, Georgetown (1-202 965 1300, www.bluemercury. com). Foggy Bottom-GWU Metro then 30, 32, 34, 35, 36 bus. **Open** 10am-8pm Mon-Sat; noon-6pm Sun. **Credit** AmEx, Disc, MC, V. **Map** p249 E5.
Try the wide range of body treatments, then browse through the fine selection of cosmetics, fragrances and moisturizers, including Acqua di Parma and Bumble & Bumble, and take some nirvana home. **Other locations** (store only) 1619 Connecticut Avenue, NW (1-202 462 1300).

Celadon

1180 F Street, NW, between 11th & 12th Streets, Downtown (1-202 347 3333, http://shop.celadon spa.com/store). Metro Center Metro. **Open** 8.30am-6pm Mon-Wed, Fri; 8.30am-7pm Thur; 8.30am-4.30pm Sat. **Credit** AmEx, Disc, MC, V. **Map** p252 J6.
Downtown's workaholics defuse their tensions at this subdued salon and spa, and often leave with a bag of skin and beauty products for carrying on the good work at home.

Grooming Lounge

1745 L Street, NW, between Connecticut Avenue & 18th Street, Downtown (1-202 466 8900). Farragut North Metro. **Open** 9am-7pm Mon-Fri; 9am-6pm Sat; 10am-5pm Sun. **Credit** AmEx, MC, V. **Map** p252 G5.
Men finally have a place to call their own in DC. This modern retreat with an old barber shop mood offers haircuts, hot shaves, facials and nail care, plus product lines by Anthony, Dermalogica and Jack Black. **Other locations** Tysons Galleria, 1732 International Drive, McLean, VA (1-301 288 0355).

Ilo

1637 Wisconsin Avenue, NW, between Q Street & Reservoir Road, Georgetown (1-202 342 0350/ www.salonilo.com). Foggy Bottom-GWU Metro then 30, 32, 34, 35, 36 bus. **Open** 10am-6pm Mon, Tue, Wed, Fri; 10am-7pm Thur; 9-am-5pm Sat. **Credit** AmEx, MC, V. **Map** p249 E4.
In town to accept an award and – gasp! – not looking your best after the red-eye flight? This spa offers traditional services, plus laser hair removal, microderm abrasion and botox to prepare you for your close-up. And it works just as well if you need to make a presentation in front of important new clients.

Splash at the Sports Club/LA

Ritz Carlton Hotel, 1170 22nd Street, NW, at M Street, Foggy Bottom (1-202 974 6600, www.mpsportsclub.com/clubs/washington-dc).

Foggy Bottom-GWU or Dupont Circle Metro. **Open** 5.30am-10.30pm Mon-Thur; 5.30am-10pm Fri; 8am-8pm Sat, Sun. **Credit** AmEx, Disc, MC, V. **Map** p250 G5.
Athletes and actors have been spotted at this plush spa, checking in for facials, massages, body treatments, waxing and the like. No doubt their wallets are lighter upon leaving.

Hairdressers & barbers

Axis

1509 Connecticut Avenue, NW, between Dupont Circle & Q Street, Dupont Circle (1-202 234 1166, www.axissalon.com). Dupont Circle Metro. **Open** 9am-7.30pm Tue-Fri; 9am-5pm Sat; 11am-5pm Sun. **Credit** AmEx, MC, V. **Map** p250 G4.
Prices may rise, but those in need of a cut or a trim or eyebrow expertise keep coming, attracted in part by the cheeky window displays and funky storefront.

Christophe

1125 18th Street, NW, between L & M Streets, Foggy Bottom (1-202 785 2222, www.christophe. com). Farragut North Metro. **Open** 9am-7pm Tue, Wed; 9am-8pm Thur, Fri; 9am-5pm Sat. **Credit** AmEx, MC, V. **Map** p252 G5.
The Washington branch of the Beverly Hills salon. You know what to expect: good haircuts, at a price.

Evolve

2905 M Street, NW, between 29th & 30th Streets, Georgetown (1-202 333 9872). Foggy Bottom-GWU Metro then 30, 32, 34, 35, 36 bus. **Open** 10am-6pm Wed-Sat. **Credit** AmEx, Disc, MC, V. **Map** p249 F5.
Two decades of keeping DC's ladies beautiful attests to the excellent standards of this salon, which also offers hair treatments and facials.

Ipsa

1629 Wisconsin Avenue, NW, between Q & R Streets, Georgetown (1-202 338 4100, www. ipsaforhair.com). Foggy Bottom-GWU Metro then 30, 32, 34, 35, 36 bus. **Open** 8am-6pm Mon-Fri; 9am-5.30pm Sat. **Credit** Disc, MC, V. **Map** p249 E4.
A chilled atmosphere makes for a pleasant visit and a satisfying hair-do.

Roche

3000 K Street, NW, at Thomas Jefferson Street, Georgetown (1-202 775 0775, www. rochesalon.com). Foggy Bottom-GWU Metro then 30, 32, 34, 35, 36 bus. **Open** 10am-7pm Tue-Fri; 8.30am-5pm Sat. **Credit** AmEx, MC, V. **Map** p249 F5.
Fashionistas know Roche because they see it written up in the glossies. With its poppy interior and cool attitude, it will send you out a changed person – and for the better, at least in externals.

CONSUME

Pharmacies

CVS

*6-7 Dupont Circle, NW, between Massachusetts &
New Hampshire Avenues, Dupont Circle (1-202
833 5704, www.cvs.com). Dupont Circle Metro.*
Open 24hrs daily. **Credit** AmEx, Disc, MC, V.
Map p250 G4.
Locals have a love-hate affair with this chain drug-
store. It carries just about anything you'd need at
2am, but some of the staff can be a bit clueless.
Other locations throughout the city.

Shops

Sephora

*3065 M Street, NW, between 30th & 31st Streets,
Georgetown (1-202 338 5644, www.sephora.com).
Foggy Bottom-GWU Metro then 30, 32, 34, 35,
36 bus.* **Open** 10am-9pm Mon-Sat; noon-6pm Sun.
Credit AmEx, Disc, MC, V. **Map** p249 E5.
The celebrated French chain is a beauty junkie's par-
adise, with skincare, cosmetics and designer scents
for both men and women.

HOUSE & HOME

Antiques

Most of the fancier antiques stores are in
Georgetown; they're ideal for browsing, though
pieces are inevitably pricey.

Goodwood

*1428 U Street, NW, U Street Corridor (1-202 986
3640/www.goodwooddc.com.). U Street/African-
American Civil War Memorial/Cardozo Metro.*
Open 5-9pm Thur; 11am-7pm Fri, Sat; 11am-5pm
Sun. **Credit** AmEx, MC, V. **Map** p250 H3.
Scouting the best auctions in the mid-Atlantic,
Goodwood brings in amazing wood tables, armoires,
bookcases and mirrors, plus ornamental follies you
won't find elsewhere for the prices. Go Thursday
evening for the picks of the week.

Miss Pixie's

*1626 14th Street, NW, between Belmont &
Columbia Roads, Adams Morgan (1-202 232
8171, www.misspixies.com). Woodley Park-
Zoo/Adams Morgan Metro, then 90, 92, 93 bus.*
Open noon-7pm Mon -Fri, 11am-7pm Sat,Sun.
Credit AmEx, Disc, MC, V. **Map** p250 G3.
Miss Pixie's brings in country and vintage furnish-
ings at very reasonable prices. Take home a porch
rocker, a 1950s sofa or cool garden ornaments.

General

Contemporaria

*3303 Cady's Alley, NW, M Street, between 33rd
& 34th Streets, Georgetown (1-202 338 0193,*
*www.contemporaria.com). Foggy Bottom-GWU
Metro, then 38B bus.* **Open** 10am-6pm Mon-Fri;
11am-6pm Sat; noon-5pm Sun. **Credit** AmEx,
MC, V. **Map** p249 E5.
Cruise down the curved concrete ramp to a minimalist world of Kartell chairs, Cappellini wall systems
and Minotti sofas. The owner is a Peruvian architect
but most of the furniture design is Italian. Less is
more, particularly when you come to paying the bill.

Home Rule

*1807 14th Street, NW, at S Street, Shaw: U
Street/14th Street Corridor (1-202 797 5544,
www.homerule.com). U Street/African-American
Civil War Memorial/Cardozo Metro.* **Open** 11am-
7pm Mon-Sat; noon-5.30pm Sun. **Credit** AmEx,
Disc, MC, V. **Map** p250 H4.
In this arresting little shop the walls are lined with
the latest kitchen utensils, desk supplies, incredible
soaps and lotions, and tons of stocking fillers. It also
has a 'made in the USA' selection, doing its bit to
support the economy.

Homebody

*715 8th Street, SE, between G & I Streets,
Capitol Hill (1-202 544 8445/www.homebody
dc.com). Eastern Market Metro.* **Open** 11am-7pm
Tue-Sat; noon-6 Sun. **Credit** AmEx, Disc, MC, V.
Map p253 M8.
Housewares, barware and gifts, with an emphasis
on the modern and the green. Saloom and Bontempi
Casa furniture, Bodum and Bialetti coffee makers,
and Chilewich table and floor mats are among the
well-designed domestic pieces on offer. Recycled
materials are everywhere: a local artist's Calder-
like mobiles with found-glass pendants share
space with Italian regenerated-leather wallets
and bags. Smaller souvenirs include gag gifts,
house-brand scented candles and reasonably
priced jewelry. Need a set of absinthe spoons?
Homebody's your place.

Illuminations

*415 8th Street, NW, between D & E Streets,
Penn Quarter (1-202 783 4888, www.
illuminc.com) Archives-Navy Memorial Metro.*
Open 10am-6pm Mon-Fri; 11am-5pm Sat.
Credit AmEx, MC, V. **Map** p253 J6.
Two showrooms display lighting from Artemide,
Ingo Maurer, Flos and Neidhardt, among others.
Illumination of the cleverest kind, hence much of it
is concealed.
Other locations 3323 Cady's Alley, NW,
Georgetown (1-202 965 4888).

★ Millennium Decorative Arts

*1528 U Street, NW, between 15th & 16th Streets,
U Street/14th Street Corridor (1-202 483 1218).
U Street/African-American Civil War Memorial/
Cardozo Metro.* **Open** noon-6pm Mon-Thur, Sun.
Credit AmEx, MC, V. **Map** p250 H3.

CONSUME

Pulp. *See p156.*

Stylish 1940s- to 1960s-vintage modern European furniture is stocked at this two-level store, and you'll find graphic glassware, vases and coaster sets too.

Reincarnations
1401 14th Street, NW, at Rhode Island Avenue, U Street/14th Street Corridor (1-202 319 1606, www.reincarnationsfurnishings.com). Dupont Circle Metro. **Open** 11am-8pm Tue-Sun. **Credit** AmEx, MC, V. **Map** p250 H4.
Furniture and accessories with great wit, in styles ranging from the baroque to the contemporary. You'll find something that will fit into any setting, or, alternatively, pick a definitive piece that calls the shots.

Sur La Table
5211 Wisconsin Avenue, NW, between Ingomar & Harrison Streets, Chevy Chase, Upper Northwest (1-202 237 0375, www.surlatable.com). Friendship Heights Metro. **Open** 10am-6pm Mon-Wed, Sat; 10am-8pm Thur, Fri; noon-6pm Sun. **Credit** AmEx, Disc, MC, V.
Here one can find hand mixers in a rainbow of colours and all the kitchen gadgets you could possibly want – and some you had never dreamed of. Staff are knowledgeable and happy to help those uncertain of the utility of a rechargeable milk frother.

Tabletop
1608 20th Street, NW, between Q & R Streets, Dupont Circle (1-202 387 7117,

---

Museum Pieces

The city's museums have some exceptional shops.

DC is museum central for the US. People travel hundreds, if not thousands, of miles to visit the capital's collections and many of the visitors want to take something home with them. That's where the museum shops come in. Here are some of the best.

Most things to most people, the **National Museum of American History** (for listings, *see p51*) has a shop as eclectic as its collections: replicas of major American milestone documents – the Declaration of Independence, the Emancipation Proclamation – and day-of-event newspapers share space with reproduction jewelry and White House china, as well as the usual T-shirts and tchotches. The bookstore area boasts a respectable range of scholarly and popular history, along with impressive cultural studies, musicology, and food sections. Most remarkable of all is the music area, with its array of Smithsonian Folkways recordings, the best of the best authentic American art.

The **Arthur M Sackler Gallery & Freer Gallery of Art** (for listings, *see p43, p44*) has books, music and DVDs relevant to the museum's Asian focus, as well as teapots, crystal objects, kimono gift sets, Chinese and Japanese prints, and arty umbrellas.

The **National Building Museum** (for listings, *see p76*) is often rated the best museum store in DC, and withgood reason. Opening on to the museum's loggia, the store sells a lot of one-off, beautiful items such as toys and gizmos, bowls, pillows, vases, mobiles,

neckties, architect-designed watches and a library's worth of design books.

In the cool lower floors of both buildings of the **National Gallery** (for listings, *see p47*) are huge shops with fine collections of books, prints, posters, cards and calendars, while the **National Museum of the American Indian** (for listings, *see p50*) has books and CDs, calendars, cards along with blankets and crafts resonant of the many Indian tribes that once populated North America.

Over at the **Renwick Gallery of the Smithsonian American Art Museum** (for listings, *see p54*), the pieces in ceramic, wood and glass are nearly good as the stuff on display. There is also a wide selection of books on American crafts; jewellery is available too.

Textiles and the crafts involved in making them are the focus of the comprehensive selection of books at the **Textile Museum** (for listings, *see p77*). Also here, naturally, is the final product: ties, scarves, shawls and other goods. Some merchandise is related to current exhibitions: at the time of writing, Colors of the Oasis featured Central Asian *ikats*, with beautifully colored examples available in the shop.

The **Washington National Cathedral** (for listings, *see p82*), meanwhile, has stained-glass reproductions, liturgical material, gold and silver jewellery, books, cards and the like. Also visit the Greenhouse (for plants) and Herb Cottage (for herbs and other food products) in the grounds.

CONSUME

www.tabletopdc.com). Dupont Circle Metro. **Open** noon-8pm Mon-Sat; noon-6pm Sun. **Credit** AmEx, Disc, MC, V. **Map** p250 G4.

The owners favor lesser-known designers and makers of playful, clean accessories, such as Klein Reid for vases and Panek Tobin for ceramics. These are sold alongside contemporary lighting and modern jewelry.

Vastu

1829 14th Street, NW, between S & T Streets, U Street/14th Street Corridor (1-202 234 8344/ www.vastudc.com). U Street/African-American Civil War Memorial/Cardozo Metro. **Open** 11am-7pm Tue-Sat; noon-5pm Sun. **Credit** AmEx, DC, Disc, MC, V. **Map** p250 H3.

Unifying this store is the warm modernism of Steven Anthony upholstered furniture, tables and cabinets by escribaStudio of Brazil, and Babette Holland spun-metal lamps. Vastu also sells Knoll furniture. The cool minimalism of a living room can always be made more cosy with the mobile steel and perspex ecosmart fireplaces, which burn like an eternal flame.

MUSIC & ENTERTAINMENT

Melody Records

1623 Connecticut Avenue, NW, between Q & R Streets, Dupont Circle (1-202 232 4002, www.melodyrecords.com). Dupont Circle Metro. **Open** 10am-10pm Mon-Thur, Sun; 10am-11pm Fri, Sat. **Credit** AmEx, MC, V. **Map** p250 G4.

Tunes in every imaginable genre are stuffed into this small, owner-operated landmark, which has the city's biggest collection of world music. Knowledgeable staff make you wish digital music had never dawned, because there's no place like a great record store.

Sankofa Video

2714 Georgia Avenue, NW, between Girard & Fairmont Streets, Shaw (1-202 234 4755, www.sankofa.com). Shaw-Howard U Metro. **Open** 11am-8pm Mon-Sat; 11am-7pm Sun. **Credit** AmEx, DC, Disc, MC, V. **Map** p251 J2.

The Ethiopian-born filmmaker Haile Gerima owns this store and stocks it with a spectrum of African and African-American films from the global African diaspora as well as books. Located across the street from Howard University.

SPORT

City Bikes

2501 Champlain Street, NW, at Euclid Street, Adams Morgan (1-202 265 1564, www.citybikes.com). Woodley Park-Zoo/Adams Morgan Metro then 90, 92, 93 bus. **Open** 10am-7pm Mon-Wed, Fri, Sat; 10am-9pm Thur; 11am-6pm Sun. **Credit** MC, V. **Map** p250 G2.

Hardcore cyclists frequent City Bikes for its excellent bikes, parts and mechanics. More casual cyclists show up to rent bicycles for a short ride. This shop (and website) is also a hub for a range of cycling activities; visitors to DC may want to take part.

Fleet Feet

1841 Columbia Road, NW, between Biltmore Street & Mintwood Place, Adams Morgan (1-202 387 3888, www.fleetfeetdc.com). Woodley Park-Zoo/Adams Morgan Metro, then 90, 92, 93 bus. **Open** 10am-8pm Mon-Fri; 10am-7pm Sat; noon-4pm Sun. **Credit** AmEx, DC, Disc, MC, V. **Map** p250 G3.

Judging by the number of runners that hang around here at weekends, it would seem that athletes can't tear themselves away from the first-rate selection of well-priced shoes to actually go running. You'll find everything here from arch-supporting insoles and sports bras to mp3 players and of, course, the shoes.

Hudson Trail Outfitter

4530 Wisconsin Avenue, NW, at Brandywine Street, Tenleytown (1-202 363 9810/www.hudsontrail.com). Tenleytown-AU Metro. **Open** 10am-9pm Mon-Sat; 11am-6pm Sun. **Credit** AmEx, Disc, MC, V.

Hudson Trail offers an extensive array of hiking clothes, shoes and gear, plus bicycles and stuff for climbing, kayaking, snow sports and fly-fishing. In fact, everything you'll need for the great outdoors.

Sports Zone

3140 M Street, NW, at Wisconsin Avenue, Georgetown (1-202 337 9773, www.sprtzone.com). Foggy Bottom-GWU Metro, then 30, 32, 34, 35, 36 bus. **Open** 10am-10pm Mon-Sat; 11am-8pm Sun. **Credit** AmEx, MC, V. **Map** p249 E5.

'Lifestyle' footwear' to get you out running on track or field or road by Ecko, Adidas and Avirex. Sporty but fashionable clothing to go with the shoes.

TICKETS

Tickets for many concerts and other events can often be obtained from the venues, but are not always obtainable online. The main booking agency is **Ticketmaster** (www.ticketmaster.com).

TRAVELERS' NEEDS

For mobile phones, there are branches of **Radio Shack** throughout the city; check the internet for your nearest. For computer repair, try **Geeks In Minutes** (1-202 629 9804, www.computerrepair.washington.com). Luggage can be bought at most department stores and malls (*see p143*).

Bags packed, milk cancelled, house raised on stilts.

You've packed the suntan lotion, the snorkel set, the stay-pressed shirts. Just one more thing left to do – your bit for climate change. In some of the world's poorest countries, changing weather patterns are destroying lives.

You can help people to deal with the extreme effects of climate change. Raising houses in flood-prone regions is just one life-saving solution.

Climate change costs lives.
Give £5 and let's sort it *Here & Now*

www.oxfam.org.uk/climate-change

Oxfam is a registered charity in England and Wales (No.202918) and Scotland (SCO039042). Oxfam GB is a member of Oxfam International.

Be Humankind (Ω) Oxfam

Arts & Entertainment

Nellie's. *See p182.*

Calendar	164
Children	168
Film	172
Galleries	175
Art, Not Cars	179
Gay	181
Music	185
City Sounds Indie	188
City Sounds Go-go	191
Nightlife	194
Sport	197
Hitting in the Major League	201
Theater	202
Crystal Palaces	206

Calendar

A city for all seasons.

Washington offers all the state ceremonies you would expect of a capital, and the Mall, Capitol and White House provide the background to great national events such as presidential inaugurations. Happily, it also has a calendar bursting with less formal occasions, from events associated with the big cultural institutions to lively weekends of streetside fun celebrating the diverse neighbourhoods where the District's real people live – Anacostia, Adams Morgan, Chinatown, Dupont Circle, Mount Pleasant, and many more.

You can keep track of events with the *Washington Post*'s Friday 'Weekend' section (www.washingtonpost.com/weekend), the *Washington City Paper* (www.washingtoncitypaper.com), or the events database at the www.washington.org tourist site. Note that most events are free unless otherwise stated. For information on Washington's various film festivals, *see p174*. For a list of national holidays, *see p234*.

SPRING

St Patrick's Day Celebrations

Constitution Avenue, NW, from 7th to 17th Streets, The Mall & Tidal Basin (1-202 637 2474, www.dcstpatsparade.com). Smithsonian, Federal Triangle, L'Enfant Plaza or Archives-Navy Memorial Metro. **Date** 17 Mar. **Map** p253 J6.

Washington's St Patrick's Day revelries draw the crowds with a parade of dancers, bands, bagpipes and floats along Constitution Avenue. In true Irish style, the partying continues well into the night in pubs around the city. When 17 March doesn't fall on a Sunday, the festivities take place on the previous Sunday. St Patrick's Day celebrations are also held in Alexandria in Virginia, where they're organized by a charity called Ballyshaners (1-703 237 2199, www.ballyshaners.org).

Annual White House Easter Egg Roll

White House South Lawn, 1600 Pennsylvania Avenue, NW, between 15th & 17th Streets (information 1-456 2200/2322, www.whitehouse.gov/easter). McPherson Square Metro. **Date** 1st Mon after Easter. **Map** p252 H6.

Since 1878, when Congress kicked them off the Capitol lawn, kids aged three to six have been invited to hunt Easter eggs – the egg count is up to 24,000-plus these days – hidden on the South Lawn of the Executive Mansion. A festival on the Ellipse features storytelling, children's authors, even astronauts sometimes – and, crucially for cranky parents, food. In this most political city, even the Easter Bunny can become a focus for pol-iticking: in 2006, a group of gay families attended en masse, quietly making the point that they exist, even if United States law barely acknowledges it. The event kicks off at the Southeast Gate at the corner of East Executive Avenue and E Street; it gets very crowded, so arrive early. Make sure the kids are with you around 7-7.30am, when the tickets are handed out (though the actual festivities run from 10am to 2pm).

Smithsonian Annual Kite Festival

Washington Monument Grounds, The Mall & Tidal Basin (information 1-202 357 2700, www.kitefestival.org). Smithsonian Metro. **Date** Sun late Mar. **Map** p252 H7.

Kite-lovers of all ages proudly show off their hand-made contraptions (and the serious ones even take part in competitions). There are also demonstrations with novelty and sport kites by 'kite-making masters'. Usually held on the first day of the National Cherry Blossom Festival (*see below*).

Cherry Blossom Festival

Information 1-202 547 1500, www.nationalcherry blossomfestival.org. **Date** late Mar-mid Apr.

Cherry blossom time is a big deal in Washington. In 1912, 3,000 cherry trees were donated to the city by Mayor Yukio Ozaki of Tokyo as a symbol of friendship between Japan and the United States. These original trees were planted along the Tidal Basin; today, the path that rings the basin becomes clogged during bloom time with ogling tourists – and even normally blasé Washingtonians. Ironically enough, given the World War II fate of the 'friendship' between Japan and the US, the city has become famous for the immigrant blossoms, and celebrates them with near-pagan worship and a weekend of special events, including a National Cherry Blossom Festival Parade and the Sakuri Matsuri Street Festival, a celebration of Japanese art, food and culture held on 12th Street between Pennsylvania and Constitution Avenues. To witness this explosion of color, try to visit between late March and mid April; the atmosphere is congenial and the blossoms are truly glorious.

Memorial Day

Date Memorial Day weekend (last Mon in May). On the Sunday evening, the National Symphony Orchestra performs a free concert on the West Lawn of the US Capitol (there's another one on Labor Day in September; details on 1-800 444 1324 or www.kennedy-center.org/nso). On Monday, the presidential wreath-laying and memorial services take place at Arlington National Cemetery (1-703 607 8000, www.arlingtoncemetery.org), the Vietnam Veterans Memorial (1-202 426 6841) and the US Navy Memorial (1-202 737 2300 ext 768). Rolling Thunder's Ride for Freedom, a massive motorcycle parade on Sunday morning, remembers POWs/MIAs and honors those who died in wars while serving the United States.

Memorial Day Jazz Festival

Alexandria, VA (1-703 838 4844). King Street Metro. **Date** around Memorial Day (last Mon in May).
Quaint Old Town Alexandria is the location for this day-long affair, which features half a dozen or so jazz artists, plus food stalls.

Black Pride

Multiple venues (1-202 737 5767, www.dcblack pride.org). **Date** Memorial Day weekend (last Mon in May).
Exhibitions, workshops and concerts over four days, when around 10,000 African-American gays and lesbians hit the city for Black Pride.

Capital Pride

Multiple venues (1-202 797 3510, www.capitalpride.org). **Date** early June.
Washington's GLBT community marks Capital Pride Week with parties, pageants, political forums, a Pennsylvania Avenue street festival, the inevitable parade – and even a mini film festival.
▶ *For more on gay life in DC, see pp181-84.*

SUMMER

Also check out the two-week Shakespeare Free For All festival held at the Carter Barron Amphitheatre in Rock Creek Park.

Fort Reno Summer Concert Series

Fort Reno Park, NW, between Wisconsin & Nebraska Avenues, Upper Northwest (www.fort reno.com). Tenleytown-AU Metro. **Date** June-Aug.
Both up-and-coming and well-known bands take to the outdoor stage at Fort Reno Park, on a hill over-looking Washington. Concerts are free and bands play for nothing; not surprisingly, long-term funding is a concern. Bring a picnic and soak up the music. No booze or glass bottles allowed.

Marine Band's Summer Concert Series & Evening Parades

West Terrace of the US Capitol *Capitol Hill, The Capitol & Around. Capitol South or Smithsonian Metro.* **Date** Wed, June-Aug. **Map** p253 K7.
US Marine Corps War Memorial *Arlington, VA. Rosslyn Metro.* **Date** Tue in June-Aug. **Both** *1-202 433 4011, 6060, www.marineband.usmc.mil.*
'The President's Own' – once led by John Phillip Sousa – performs free, twice-weekly outdoor concerts at the Capitol and/or on the Mall; the repertoire ranges from classical music to brass-band favorites, and the action starts at 8pm. (See website for days

Memorial Day.

and locations.) On summer Fridays, the band is also a featured element of the showy Evening Parade, which includes impressive precision formation drills; it begins at 8.45pm on the manicured grounds of the Marine Barracks (8th & I Streets, SE), the corps' oldest post. Reservations are required, though unclaimed seats are sometimes available at the time: see www.mbw.usmc.mil/parades for details. The affiliated Commandant's Own drum and bugle corps performs a weekly Sunset Parade at the Iwo Jima memorial statue, adjacent to Arlington Cemetery; start time is 7pm and reservations are not required.

Capital Jazz Fest

Merriweather Post Pavilion, Columbia, MD (1-301 218 0404, www.capitaljazz.com). **Date** early June.
Billed as 'the Woodstock of jazz festivals', this outdoor extravaganza serves up food, crafts, and, of course, some of the best jazz musicians around. Dave Koz, Eric Benét, Walter Beasley, David Benoit, Incognito and India Arie are among past headliners.

Dupont-Kalorama Museum Walk Weekend

1-202 387 4062 ext 12, www.dkmuseums.com. **Date** early June.
Hidden-treasure museums and historically important houses in Dupont Circle and the neighboring Kalorama area take part in an 'off the Mall' museum day for the public. Free food, music, tours and crafts are added bonuses.

Komen Global Race for the Cure

Starts at Constitution Avenue, NW, at Ninth Street for runners and 12th Street for walkers, The Mall & Tidal Basin (1-703 416 7223, http://globalrace.info-komen.org). Federal Triangle Metro. **Date** early June. **Map** p252 H6.
It's said to be the biggest five-kilometre run/walk in the world and the Global Race for the Cure draws tens of thousands of participants to raise money for and awareness of breast cancer.

DanceAfrica DC: The Annual Festival

Dance Place, 3225 8th Street, NE, at Monroe Street, Northeast (1-202 269 1600, www.dance place.org). Brookland-CUA Metro. **Date** early June. **Map** p251 M2.
A week of masterclasses culminates in a weekend festival celebrating African and African-American dance, with free outdoor performances, crafts and food, plus ticketed main stage events indoors. Note that an admission price is charged for some events.

National Capital Barbecue Battle

Pennsylvania Avenue, NW, between 9th & 14th Streets, Federal Triangle (1-301 860 0630, www.bbqdc.com). Metro Archives-Navy Memorial. **Date** late June. **Map** p252/p253 J6.
For more than a decade, barbecue wizards have gathered to compete for titles that now, astonish-ingly, carry more than $40,000 in prize money. Tens of thousands throng the nation's Main Street to sample glorious ribs, chicken and every other form of barbecue imaginable. Celebs, music, children's activities and much more to go with the food.

Caribbean Festival

Georgia Avenue, NW, between Missouri Avenue & Banneker Park, Mount Pleasant & North (1-202 726 2204, www.dccaribbeancarnival.org). **Date** last weekend in June.
Hundreds of thousands of islanders and others line Georgia Avenue for the DC Caribbean Carnival's big parade, the climax of a week of festivities featuring soca, calypso, steel band music, African drumming, stilt dancers and a few thousand people dancing through the streets while wearing some spectacular carnival costumes. A Sunday festival caps off the madness at Banneker Park.

Smithsonian Folklife Festival

National Mall, between 10th & 15th Streets, The Mall & Tidal Basin (1-202 357 2700, recorded information 1-202 633 9884, www.folklife.si.edu). Smithsonian Metro. **Date** late June & early July. **Map** p252 H7.
This monster festival celebrates the arts, crafts and food of selected US states and other countries. The focus for 2011 is on the topics of Colombia, the Peace Corps and rhythm & blues. Food and demonstration booths stretch down the National Mall, and there are evening celebrations and music performances. The atmosphere is cheerful, the weather usually hot and sticky, and parking very limited, so use the Metro.

Independence Day

Various venues (information 1-202 789 7000, www.washington.org). **Date** 4 July.
Steer clear of this one if you hate crowds (nearly 700,000 people generally turn up), or if the now rather pervasive security makes you think of Mr Orwell (the legacy of 9/11 means that Fourth of July revellers now encounter a fenced-off National Mall, with checkpoints through which to enter). Official events begin at 10am at the National Archives, with a dramatic reading of the Declaration of Independence, demonstrations of colonial military maneuvers, and more. Just before noon, the Independence Day parade starts to wind its way down Constitution Avenue (from the National Archives to 17th Street), and later (5-9.15pm) the grounds of the Washington Monument host entertainment – folk music, jazz, marching bands, military singers – and hordes of revelers. The National Symphony Orchestra performs a concert on the West Lawn of the US Capitol building at 8pm, traditionally concluding with a battery of cannons assisting in the finale of Tchaikovsky's *1812 Overture*; then, at roughly 9pm, a stupendous array of fireworks is set off over the Washington Monument. Logistical hassles or no, it's a grand sight: the monuments are lovely in the summer dusk,

Independence Day.

and the barrages involve thousands of rounds of explosives. Walk to the festivities if you can: Fourth of July crowds eat up parking spots and test the limits of the public transport system. Check local listings for smaller celebrations.

AUTUMN

Kennedy Center Open House Arts Festival/Prelude Festival

2700 F Street, NW, at New Hampshire Avenue & Rock Creek Parkway, Foggy Bottom (1-202 416 8000, www.kennedy-center.org). Foggy Bottom-GWU Metro. **Date** early-mid Sept. **Map** p252 F6.

The Open House – centerpiece of the sprawling autumn Prelude Festival – is a day-long weekend extravaganza celebrating the Center's birthday and showcasing the diversity of the arts it plays host to. Local and national artists strut their stuff on the plazas, on the river terrace overlooking the Potomac, and on the Kennedy Center stages. Children are kept entertained, too, with a National Symphony Orchestra 'petting zoo' where they get to bow, blow, drum or strum their favorite instruments. In 2010, Open House was part of the Kennedy Center's Celebrate Mexico event, and featured artists from both the DC region and Mexico, including rock band El Gran Silencio and Ballet Folklórico de la Universidad Veracruzana.

The weeks-long Prelude Festival is the unofficial kick-off of the city's autumn performing arts season, including symphony performances, a jazz series, and the Page to Stage theater event over Labor Day weekend; the latter is a new-works mini festival, with readings and performances involving no fewer than 35 local troupes.

Adams Morgan Day

18th Street, NW, between Columbia Road & Florida Avenue, Adams Morgan (1-202 328 9451, www.adamsmorgandayfestival.com). Dupont Circle or Woodley Park Metro. **Date** 2nd Sun in Sept. **Map** p250 G2.

For over a quarter of a century, thousands of DC residents have come out to celebrate this community, home to large Latino, white, African and African-American populations. Musicians, crafts and ethnic foods are in ample supply.

Black Family Reunion

National Mall/Washington Monument (1-202 383 9130, www.ncnw.org/events/reunion.htm). Smithsonian Metro. **Date** early-mid Sept. **Map** p252 H7.

Tens, if not hundreds, of thousands descend on the National Mall each year to celebrate 'the enduring strengths and traditional values of the African-American family'. Among the offerings: R&B and gospel concerts, a prayer breakfast, and a festival with a food fair and myriad themed pavilions.

National Book Fair

National Mall, NW, between 7th & 14th Streets (1-202 888 714 4696, www.loc.gov/bookfest). Archives-Naval Memorial or Federal Triangle Metro. **Date** late Sept or early Oct. **Map** p252 H7.

Sponsored by the Library of Congress, the Book Fair features dozens of authors, illustrators, poets and storytellers, all reading, performing and signing in block after block of pavilions themed around 'Fiction and Imagination', 'History and Biography', 'Mysteries and Thrillers' and so on. Admission is free.

Annual High Heel Race

17th Street, NW, between S & P Streets, Dupont Circle (information from JR's bar 1-202 328 0090, www.jrswdc.com). Dupont Circle Metro. **Date** on or around 31 Oct. **Map** p250 H4.
Dupont Circle residents and gawkers from across the city swarm to 17th Street to catch this ultimate drag race, which features outrageously costumed contestants promenading up and down – then sprinting down a two-block stretch in the heart of the capital's gay ghetto. The event itself lasts only minutes, but the street-party atmosphere is festive and the scenery fabulous.

Marine Corps Marathon

1-800 786 8762, www.marinemarathon.com. **Date** late Oct.
The 'Marathon of Monuments' draws around 30,000 runners from around the world, and no wonder: the course winds along the banks of the Potomac, through Georgetown and Rock Creek Park, past the city's most famous sites and monuments, finishing at the Iwo Jima memorial in Arlington. Spectators and supporters turn the route into a 26-mile street party.

Veterans' Day ceremonies

Arlington National Cemetery, Memorial Drive, Arlington Drive, VA (1-703 607 8000, www.arlingtoncemetery.org). Arlington Cemetery Metro. **Date** 11am Veterans' Day (11 Nov).
A solemn ceremony with military bands, in honor of the country's war dead. Ceremonies are also held at the Vietnam Veterans Memorial (details on 1-202 426 6841), Mount Vernon (1-703 780 2000) and the US Navy Memorial (1-202 737 2300).

WINTER

National Christmas Tree Lighting

The Ellipse, The Mall & Tidal Basin (1-202 426 6841). Federal Triangle Metro. **Date** early Dec. **Map** p252 H6.
The president kicks off the holiday season by switching on the lights on the giant National Christmas Tree. (There's a National Menorah, too, which gets lit on the appropriate night.) For a seat in the enclosure, you'll need a ticket: apply at least six weeks in advance as they run out fast. The ticketless, though, can usually get a glimpse from the other side of the fence. The ceremony begins at 5pm; arrive early. From now until New Year's Day, the Ellipse hosts Christmas performances as part of the annual Pageant of Peace.

New Year's Eve celebrations

Events around town range from relatively inexpensive celebrations at the Kennedy Center (music and dancing in the Grand Foyer) to dinners at some of the area's more upscale dining establishments costing hundreds of dollars. Restaurants and clubs often offer jazz, dinner and a champagne toast for a fixed but generally substantial price (most start taking reservations early); check ads in the *Washington City Paper* and the *Washington Post*.

Martin Luther King Jr's Birthday Celebrations

1-202 727 1186, WPAS concert information 1-202 833 9800, www.wpas.org. **Date** 3rd wk in Jan.
A birthday celebration is held on the steps of the Lincoln Memorial, where Dr King gave his famous 'I have a dream' speech in 1963. That's just one of many, many commemorations in DC. Among others: the Washington Performing Arts Society (WPAS) hosts an annual children's concert with Sweet Honey in the Rock, who combine gospel, African rhythms and rap into a cappella combinations. A tremendous show.

Chinese New Year

Chinatown, H Street, NW, between 6th & 9th Streets, Downtown. Gallery Place-Chinatown Metro. **Date** 23 Jan 2012, 10 Feb 2012. **Map** p253 J5.
Celebrations kick off with a bang – dancers, dragons, firecrackers and parades – and continue, a bit more muted, for ten days. Look out for details near the time or contact the Chinese Consolidated Benevolent Association at 1-703 851 5685.

Black History Month

Date Feb.
The Smithsonian Institution holds special events, exhibitions and cultural programs throughout the month. For more information on the activities on offer, check newspaper listings or contact the Martin Luther King Library (*see p228*).

Famous birthdays

Information Lincoln 1-202 426 6841, Washington 1-703 780 2000, Douglass 1-202 426 5960. **Date** Feb.
A trio of famous men's birthdays. A celebration of Abe Lincoln's birthday (12 February) is held at the Lincoln Memorial; Lincoln's Gettysburg Address is read and a wreath is laid. For hard-core history buffs only. George Washington's birthday celebration, with a patriotic military program and a George Washington impersonator, is held (on the third Monday in February) at Mount Vernon, Virginia (*see p216* **Presidential Homes**). The Frederick Douglass birthday tribute is held on or near 14 February at the Frederick Douglass National Historic Site, 1411 W Street, SE, at 14th Street, Anacostia.

Children

Nation's capital, children's playground.

Walk along the National Mall, especially on a summer day or weekend, and you'll find children everywhere. It's the museums and monuments that are the attraction. They're some of the world's finest, and most – including the Smithsonian museums – are free. The museums don't neglect their younger visitors, either, with special exhibits or trails to hold their attention.

DC is an easy city to get around with babies and young children, too. It's pedestrian-friendly, and Metro stations all have lifts.

The scale of Washington DC – low-rise buildings, tourist attractions centered in a compact area and plenty of open space – is inviting, and children are welcome nearly everywhere. To get a taste of the major sights, consider taking one of the tours offered by a company such as the National Park Service-approved **Tourmobile** (1-202 554 5100, www.tourmobile.com), which offers the chance to travel by open air trams. Family walking tour such as those offered by **Washington Walks** (1-202 484 1565, www.washingtonwalks.com) can be very enjoyable for children. The tour of 'Washington's most Haunted Houses' may be right up their street. Since most tours last approximately two hours, they may be more suitable for older children.

BABYSITTING

Childcare in Washington is not cheap, but most large hotels and those with concierge services can provide it, using in-house services or local companies. Last-minute requests can usually be accommodated (with extra fees), but it's best to book ahead. The leading childcare agencies include **White House Nannies** (1-800 266 9024 Virginia and Maryland, 1-703 250 0700 Washington DC, www.whitehousenannies.com), a well-respected service that uses thoroughly screened, independent carers at a flat fee. **Mothers' Aides Inc** (1-800 526 2669, www.mothersaides.com) offers a similar service and charges a $70 agency fee per day plus the caregiver's hourly wage (normally $15-$20 per hour).

ENTERTAINMENT

The listings below focus on attractions in or near central DC. For places further afield and in the suburbs, including parks and outdoor recreational facilities, buy a copy of *Going Places with Children in Washington, DC* or *Around Washington, DC with Kids*, both excellent specialist guides available from most decent bookshops.

Eating out

Children are welcome at all but the fanciest restaurants – where you're unlikely to want to take them anyway. For quick budget meals, fast-food restaurants are plentiful and easy to find, but if your offspring aren't fussy eaters, you might want to try one of the many moderately priced ethnic restaurants such as the Ethiopian choices found along Adams Morgan's 18th Street. The food court in the Pavilion at the **Old Post Office** (1100 Pennsylvania Avenue, NW, between 11th & 12th Streets) is near the museums of Natural History and American History, while the **National Gallery of Art** (*see p47*) has a nice self-service café with plentiful seating. Famished families at **Union Station** on Capitol Hill can find sustenance at the food court in the station (50 Massachusetts Avenue, NE, 1-202 289 6969), where a branch of the 1950's-style burger joint Johnny Rockets is a favorite.

If a trip to the zoo develops their appetites, the **Lebanese Taverna** (2641 Connecticut Avenue, NW, 1-202 265-8681, www.lebanese taverna.com) introduces children to the taste of

Middle Eastern food in bite-sized nibbles, tiny kafta burgers or pita pizzas with mozzarella cheese and veggies.

In the Dupont Circle neighborhood, **Firefly** (*see p138*) takes a positively child-friendly approach. Chef Daniel Bortnick offers a kids' menu for different age groups, featuring the likes of hamburgers and BLTs. Each small child gets an unbaked cookie at the beginning of the meal that can be decorated and baked.

Museums

All Smithsonian museums offer at least a few exhibits geared towards children, though three are consistently highly rated: the **National Air & Space Museum** (*see p46*), the **National Museum of American History** (*see p49*) and the **National Museum of Natural History** (*see p51*). Others making a special effort for children are the **National Building Museum** (*see p79*), the **International Spy Museum** (*see p73*) and the **Museum of the American Indian** (*see p50*). And though it's not a museum per se, don't miss the **Bureau of Engraving & Printing** (*see p62*). Children are fascinated by its 35-minute tour, where they can look at currency being printed.

Three more child-friendly museums:

National Geographic Museum at Explorers Hall

17th & M Streets, NW, Downtown (1-202 857 7588, www.nationalgeographic.com/museum). *Farragut North Metro.* **Open** 9am-5pm Mon-Sat; 10am-5pm Sun. **Admission** free. **Credit** AmEx, Disc, MC, V. **Map** p252 H5.
Filled with hands-on, science-oriented exhibits for the younger visitor, this museum-from-the-magazine offers free family programs each Friday morning.

National Postal Museum

2 Massachusetts Avenue, NE, Capitol Hill (1-202 633 5533, www.postalmuseum.si.edu). *Union Station Metro.* **Open** 10am-5.30pm daily. **Admission** free. **Credit** AmEx, MC, V. **Map** p253 K6.
More than 35 interactive games and screens make the mail fascinating for even the most technology-addled youngsters. Myriad stamp collections and a 'personal postcard' machine complete the experience.

★ Newseum

555 Pennsylvania Avenue, NW, Judiciary Square Area (1-888 639 7386, www.newseum.org). *Archives-Navy Memorial-Penn Center Metro.* **Open** 9am-5pm daily. **Admission** $19.95; $12.95 7-18s; free under-7s. **Credit** AmEx, MC, V.
Thoughtful, interactive entertainment is a hallmark of this new museum dedicated to journalism and free

Spy Museum.

speech. In the Interactive Newsroom, junior reporters can step in front of the cameras and file reports from a variety of backdrops, while touch-screen Be A Reporter and Be A Photographer games send kids on a quest to break stories and meet deadlines.

Animals & the outdoors

Within the District, the best outdoor activity for children, bar none, is a trip to the **National Zoo** (*see p83*). Particularly popular are the zoo's two giant pandas, the prairie dog community and the 11.30am daily sea lion feeding and training. Survival tip: the zoo slopes steeply downhill to Rock Creek from the entrance on Connecticut Avenue, so to avoid a long, hot climb at the end of your visit, plan a circular route that gets you back to the entrance before you run out of energy.

★ Rock Creek Nature Center & Planetarium

5200 Glover Road, NW, at Military Road, Upper Northwest (1-202 895 6070, www.nps.gov/rocr/naturecenter). *Friendship Heights Metro then E2, E3 bus.* **Open** 9am-5pm Wed-Sun. **Admission** free.
Rock Creek is a great place for cycling, skating, horse riding and exploring the old mill and the site of the Civil War battle at Fort Stevens. As well as the Nature Center's guided hikes, there's the highly entertaining Creature Feature programme (4pm on Fridays), which takes a close look at the park's wildlife. Inside Peirce Barn, kids can try on period clothing and play with 19th-century toys. The planetarium (on the park's western edge) hosts several free shows: check the website for details.

Cycling

Washington is a fantastic city for bike riding, with miles of family-friendly trails. Try the picturesque **C&O Canal Towpath** (www.nps.gov/choh, *see p80*) – where mule-drawn barge rides are also available – or the beautiful **Mount Vernon Trail** river ride (www.nps.gov/gwmp/mvt.html). The latter ends at George Washington's estate, where a tour is offered that younger children enjoy hugely (*see p216*). Also great are the 11 miles of the **Capital Crescent Trail** (*see p198*) and the loop through East Potomac Park. For maps and details, contact the Washington Area Bicyclist Association (*see p198*). For bike rental, *see p198*.

Theater & the arts

The 'Going Out Guide' in the 'Weekend' section of Friday's *Washington Post* (www.washington post.com) has a kids' page that covers the current week's events and activities in and around DC that are either specifically for children or at least child-friendly. Other institutions that occasionally offer art and theater programmes include the **National Gallery of Art** (*see p47*), the **Corcoran Museum of Art** (*see p53*), the **Hirshhorn Museum & Sculpture Garden** (*see p44*) and the **National Building Museum** (*see p79*).

Arthur M Sackler Gallery/ Freer Gallery of Art

1050 Independence Avenue, SW, between 11th & 12th Streets, The Mall & Tidal Basin (1-202 633 4880, www.asia.si.edu). Smithsonian Metro. **Open** 10am-5.30pm daily. ImaginAsia times vary. **Admission** free. **Map** p252 J7.
The Sackler and Freer galleries offer ImaginAsia, a family program with a special guided tour for children aged six to 14, who must be accompanied by an adult. They are given an activity book before entering the exhibition and the tour ends with the opportunity to create arts and crafts inspired by what they have seen. There is also a children's activity on most weekends. Traditional Asian festivals are celebrated here, giving children the chance to participate.
▶ *For more on the galleries' collections, see p43 and p44.*

Glen Echo Park

7300 MacArthur Boulevard, at Goldsboro Road, Glen Echo, MD (1-301 492 6229, www.glenecho park.org). Friendship Heights Metro then Ride-On Bus 29. **Carousel** *May, June* 10am-2pm Wed, Thur. *July, Aug* 10am-2pm Wed-Fri; noon-6pm Sat, Sun. *Sept* noon-6pm Sat, Sun.
Until 1968, Glen Echo was a popular amusement park just a trolley ride from Downtown. Today, it is preserved by the National Park Service (2pm weekend tours) and run by a non-profit group as a site for theatre, art and dance. It also has a playground, picnic tables, plenty of places to explore and a charming 1921 carousel. The following are highlights of the activities on offer:

Adventure Theatre *(1-301 320 5331, www.adventuretheatre.org; 1.30pm, 3.30pm Sat, Sun; admission $7).*
One-hour plays for fours and over based on fables, fairy tales, musicals and children's classics, using puppets and actors.

Discovery Creek Children's Museum *(1-202 337 5111, www.discoverycreek.org; 10am-3pm Sat, Sun; admission $5; free under-2s).*
This small nature center offers interactive events designed to teach children about nature and geography, as well as wildlife treks through the park.

Puppet Company Playhouse *(1-301 634 5380, www.thepuppetco.org; 10am, 11.30am Wed-Fri; 11.30am, 1pm Sat, Sun; admission $6).*
Plays for all ages, most of them adaptations of classic stories for children such as *Cinderella* and *The Jungle Book*. Reservations recommended.

Kennedy Center

2700 F Street, NW, at New Hampshire Avenue & Rock Creek Parkway, Foggy Bottom (1-800 444 1324, 1-202 467 4600, www.kennedy-center.org). Foggy Bottom-GWU Metro. **Admission** varies. **Credit** AmEx, DC, Disc, MC, V. **Map** p252 F6.
The Kennedy Center offers an amazing variety of dance, music and theater for youngsters. With subjects as diverse as West African dance and the history of Mexico in song, there is truly something for every taste (although most events are best for fives and over). The National Symphony also presents occasional family concerts here.

Saturday Morning at the National

National Theatre, 1321 Pennsylvania Avenue, NW, between 13th & 14th Streets, Federal Triangle (1-202 783 3372, www.national theatre.org). Metro Center Metro. **Admission** free. **Map** p252 H6.
Free entertainment for both children and adults at 9.30am and 11am, September-April. The one-hour events include theater, music, dance and magic by accomplished and professional children's entertainers. From jugglers to ventriloquists and fabulous magic shows, it is a real treat for children.Tickets are distributed half an hour beforehand so arrive early.

**INSIDE TRACK
SCHOOL FOR SPIES**

The School for Spies Gallery at the **International Spy Museum** (*see p73*) has over 50 years of spy technology, some of it still in use by intelligence agencies today. Would-be spies can test their skills of observation, surveillance and analysis at vthe gallery's interactive stations. Children can also take part in workshops on disguise, gadgetry and tradecraft.

Film

More than just multiplexes.

The dominance of multiplexes in the US is mitigated in Washington DC by the existence of a few independents and other venues screening films from outside the mainstream. In 2010, the **Avalon**, an old movie house dating from the 1920s, was joined by the **West End**. Founded by film-lovers in a previously disused cinema, it aims to be a new outlet for independent, foreign and documentary films. There is also an extensive array of non-commercial repertory film programs in the city's museums, while the American Film Institute's **Silver Theatre & Cultural Center**, housed in a restored art deco cinema in Silver Spring, also shows the kind of films that you won't see elsewhere.

Most DC-area cinemas, however, show the same formulaic product that's seen from coast to coast (and around the world). Nevertheless, declining returns for Hollywood-made films have had some impact, encouraging the major chains to book more documentaries and independent films.

Local filmmakers often claim that DC has the country's third-largest film industry, after LA and New York, but few features are produced locally. Instead, the emphasis is on documentaries, many of them made for the DC-based Discovery and National Geographic cable channels. There are many local showcases for non-fiction films, including the Silverdocs festival every June at the AFI Silver.

Washington has long been a useful location for Hollywood movies, but the crews often spend just a few days in town, filming at conspicuous landmarks before heading back to LA or continuing the shoot in cheaper locales. The Metro doesn't allow violent acts to be staged on its property, so subway scenes in Washington-based action movies are often shot in Baltimore. Still, Hollywood filmmakers keep coming.

THE CINEMAS

The **AMC Loews** chain dominates DC's mainstream cinema landscape. **Landmark**, the leading US arthouse chain, operates the eight-screen **E Street Cinema**, while **Regal** owns the 14-screen **Gallery Place** megaplex. The city currently has two independently owned cinemas, the **Avalon** and the new **West End**.

The E Street and Gallery Place cinemas returned cinema to Downtown, which was once full of opulent movie palaces. But most of the city's cinemas are found along Connecticut or Wisconsin Avenues, the major commercial arteries of the city's affluent west side.

TICKETS AND INFORMATION

Most cinemas have two or three screenings a night (usually between 7pm and 7.45pm, and 9pm and 9.45pm) and often a late show at the weekend. All DC theaters feature weekday and weekend matinées. Landmark E Street and Bethesda Row sometimes do weekend cult-film midnight shows. Washington filmgoers usually don't book in advance, although it's advisable to do so for the opening of heavily promoted new movies. Advance tickets for AMC Loews

---

INSIDE TRACK
EXORCIST STAIRS

The Exorcist was filmed in Georgetown: the university features, and so do some now-notorious outdoor stairs – the 75 steep steps down which Father Damien Karras threw himself to his death after the demon left Regan's body and entered his. Now popularly known as the Exorcist Stairs, they link Prospect Street with M Street below.

---

theaters are available at www.moviewatcher.
com. Purchase tickets for Regal Gallery Place
at www.fandango.com.

MAINSTREAM FILMS

AMC Loews Georgetown
*3111 K Street, NW, between 31st Street &
Wisconsin Avenue, Georgetown (1-202 342 6033,
www.amctheatres.com). Bus 30, 32, 34, 35, 36, 38,
D2, D4, D6, G2, DC Circulator.* **Tickets** *$6.50-$14.*
Credit AmEx, Disc, MC, V. **Map** p249 E5.
This 14-screen cinema, part of a complex that incorporates the old Georgetown Incinerator, has a large,
dramatic lobby. The theaters themselves, the biggest
of which have 300 seats, are standard stadium-seating
houses, with large screens and clear views.

AMC Loews Mazza Gallerie
*5300 Wisconsin Avenue, NW, at Jenifer Street,
Upper Northwest (1-888 262 4386, www.amc
theatres.com). Friendship Heights Metro.* **Tickets**
$6-$10.75. **Credit** AmEx, Disc, MC, V.
When Massa Gallerie opened in 1999 the seven-
screen cinema was the city's first with stadium seating, boasting large screens and excellent sightlines.
Alcoholic beverages and an expanded snack menu
are available in the two 'club cinemas'. The latter
auditoriums are restricted to viewers over 21,
although that doesn't guarantee that the movie
shown will be suitable for adults.

AMC Loews Uptown
*3426 Connecticut Avenue, NW, between Porter &
Ordway Streets, Cleveland Park (1-202 966 5400,
www.amctheatres.com). Cleveland Park Metro.*
Tickets *$6-$10.75.* **Credit** AmEx, Disc, MC, V.
Map p249 F1.
With the destruction of the last of the downtown
movie palaces in the 1980s, what was once just an

Avalon.

average neighborhood theater became the city's premier cinema. The 1936 art deco movie palace – with
1,500 seats it's the city's largest – now shows blockbusters and would-be blockbusters. Not everyone
applauds the curved screen, originally installed in
the 1960s for Cinerama movies.

Regal Gallery Place
*701 Seventh Street, NW, at G Street, Downtown
(1-202 393 2121). Gallery Place-Chinatown Metro.*
Tickets *$9-$11.* **Credit** AmEx, Disc, MC, V.
Map p253 J5.
Across the plaza north of Verizon Center and up two
flights of escalators awaits a sparkling new but otherwise standard contemporary megaplex, with 14
auditoriums. The screens are big for the size of the
houses, which range from 100 seats to about 300.

FOREIGN & INDEPENDENT FILMS

★ Avalon
*5612 Connecticut Avenue, NW, at McKinley
Street, Chevy Chase (1-202 966 6000, www.the
avalon.org). Friendship Heights Metro or E2, E3,
E4, E6, L1, L2, L4 bus.* **Tickets** *$6.50-$9.50.*
Credit MC, V.
Abandoned by its corporate operator, the city's oldest surviving moviehouse was rescued and restored
by a neighborhood group. Both inside and out, the
1923 structure has more charm than any number of
the cookie-cutter megaplexes that have sprouted like
mushrooms in the suburbs. It now shows a mix of
foreign, independent, documentary and Hollywood
fare, as well as classic and children's films. The small
second screen upstairs is nothing special.

Landmark E Street Cinema
*555 11th Street, NW (entrance on E Street),
Downtown (1-202 452 7672, www.landmark
theatres.com). Metro Center or Gallery Place
Metro.* **Tickets** *$7.50-$10.50.* **Credit** AmEx,
Disc, MC, V. **Map** p252 J6.
The eight-screen Landmark is the city's leading arthouse. Screens are big, even in the smallest of the auditoriums, and all but one of the theaters have stadium
seating. This is one of only three DC cinemas with a
liquor license. Landmark also operates the roomier
Bethesda Row in suburban Maryland, but the down-
town theater's bookings tend to be more adventurous.
O ther locations 7235 Woodmont Avenue,
Bethesda, MD (1-301 652 7273).

★ West End Cinema
*2301 M Street, NW, at 23rd Street, Foggy Bottom
(1-202 966 6000, www.westendcinema.com).
Foggy Bottom-GWU Metro or 31, 32, 36, 38B,
Circulator bus.* **Tickets** *$8-$11.* **Credit** AmEx,
MC, V. **Map** p250/252 F5.
Opened in late 2010, the city's newest arthouse
reclaims a three-screen cinema abandoned by a

ARTS & ENTERTAINMENT

national chain in 2004. The theaters are small, but the equipment is state-of-the-art and the projection excellent. Early offerings have been heavy on documentaries, but also include films by Gaspar Noe, Jean-Luc Godard and Woody Allen. Upscale snacks and alcoholic beverages are available.

REPERTORY

Washington no longer has any commercial repertory cinemas. It does, however, possess one of the country's most extensive non-commercial rep film scenes. Keeping abreast of the programs at these venues is a major undertaking, but not an expensive one: most of the screenings are free.

Among the many other local institutions that frequently screen films are the **National Archives** (documentaries from its collection or that uses its footage, 1-202 501 5000); the **Goethe Institut** (films about Germany, 1-202 289 1200); the DC Jewish Community Center (Jewish-related films, tickets 1-800 494 8497, information 1-202 518 9400 ext 229); the **National Museum of Women in the Arts** (films by women or linked to current exhibits, 1-202 783 7370); and several foreign embassies. See www.reeldc.com or the *Washington Post* for listings.

AFI Silver Theatre & Cultural Center

8633 Colesville Road, at Georgia Avenue, Silver Spring (1-301 495 6720, www.afi.com/silver). Silver Spring Metro. **Tickets** $10. **Credit** AmEx, Disc, MC, V.

As part of a suburban redevelopment project, the American Film Institute opened this handsome, state-of-the-art complex in 2003. The largest of the three houses is a restored (and reduced) version of the Silver, a 1938 art deco cinema. After drawing few patrons in its first two years, it began to emphasise first-run foreign, indie and documentary films. But it still hosts retrospectives of directors and stars, overviews of national cinemas, and series devoted to African and Latin American cinema.

Freer Gallery of Art

Meyer Auditorium, Jefferson Drive, SW, at 12th Street, Mall & Tidal Basin (1-202 357 2700, www.asia.si.edu). Smithsonian Metro. **Tickets** free in person 1hr before screening, or through Ticketmaster (www.ticketmaster.com) for $2.75 per ticket and $1.25 per order. **Screenings** usually 7pm Fri; 2pm Sun. **Map** p252 J7.

The films shown here come from the countries represented in the gallery's collection, predominantly Asia and the Middle East. It is one of the best places in town to see movies from India and Iran, but arrive early – the theater soon fills up with émigrés from those countries. Annual events include anime movies to mark the Cherry Blossom Festival.

Hirshhorn Museum & Sculpture Garden

7th Street & Independence Avenue, SW, Mall & Tidal Basin (1-202 357 2700, www.hirshhorn. si.edu). L'Enfant Plaza Metro. **Tickets** free. **Screenings** usually 8pm Thur, Fri. **Map** p253 J7.

The Hirshhorn showcases work by upcoming and experimental directors, often fresh from their successes on the international film festival circuit. Highlights from several alternative festivals are shown annually and filmmakers sometimes show works in progress.

Letelier Theatre

3251 Prospect Street NW, upper courtyard, near Wisconsin Avenue, Georgetown (338 5835, http://leteliertheater.com). Bus 31, 32, 36, 38B, G2, Circulator. **Tickets** free-$20. **Map** p249 E5.

That this is not a mainstream cinema is evident from its name, a tribute to the Chilean exile assassinated by Pinochet's agents in Washington in 1976. The 85-seat theater has no in-house programmer, but is used regularly for film series and special events. The Alliance Française screens new and classic French films and Global Lens shows features from the developing world; documentaries (often with a political edge) are frequently scheduled.

National Gallery of Art

East Building Auditorium, 4th Street & Constitution Avenue, NW, Mall & Tidal Basin (1-202 842 6799, www.nga.gov). Judiciary Square or Archives-Navy Memorial Metro. **Tickets** free. **Screenings** afternoon Sat, Sun, some weekdays. **Map** p253 J6.

This auditorium has one of the biggest screens and some of the most interesting programing in the city, as well as the most leg room. Film series are sometimes linked to major exhibitions, but the museum also hosts major retrospectives. Documentaries about art and related topics are shown on weekdays.

FILM FESTIVALS

The largest local annual festival is **Filmfest DC** (www.filmfestdc.org), which shows about 75 films, most of them international, during a two-week period beginning in late April. Its organizers also sponsor an annual overview of Arab films, usually in October. In October and November, the American Film Institute (www.afi.com) presents the European Film Showcase, introducing new films that recently premiered at the continent's leading festivals.

Other festivals of note are the **Environmental Film Festival** (www.dc environmentalfilmfest.org) in March; **Reel Affirmations** (www.reelaffirmations.org), the gay and lesbian film fest, in April and May; and the **Jewish Film Festival** (www.wjff.org) in December. Check the *Washington Post* listings for details.

Galleries

A vibrant art scene that has found space to grow.

Tensions between the local and the national inform so much of Washington, and the city's art scene is no exception. The District's creative world runs on two parallel artistic paths, one traveled by local artists who cater to home-grown tastes, the other trekked by artists and gallery owners working to boost the city's national and international reputation.

In recent years, the savviest District gallery owners and real-estate developers – the latter population mushroomed in the early 2000s when a condominium boom gripped the city – have sought to raise the city's profile by breaking out of traditional domestic-scaled gallery spaces. Dupont Circle's elegant but cramped brownstones once ruled the art world here; now expansive, New York-style art venues abound. Though Logan Circle is the city's gallery epicenter, the still-young art area of the Atlas District, or H Street, NE, offers the kinds of flexible, large-scale spaces favored for the exhibition of contemporary art.

DC still retains its less-polished venues and art events; the city's DIY spirit, so often manifest in local music, bleeds into visual arts, too, as younger artists crowd into alternative spaces and create one-off art shows. Local artists are known for co-opting fallow spaces in downtown office buildings or yet-to-be-purchased condominiums. Legislation mandating an arts district in the area around Penn Quarter ensured that new commercial developments were required to incorporate arts components. This resulted in some lacklustre lobby galleries but, as in the case of **Gallery at Flashpoint**, has also managed to cultivate interesting gallery spaces. Elsewhere, furniture and design stores stage mini exhibitions on their walls – so you may run into a show when you least expect it.

Washington collectors can be a savvy bunch, but again the local-national divide is felt. Many travel to New York or Art Basel Miami to purchase favorite artists. Others consider themselves boosters of the local scene and form collections around area artists. While the city's commercial gallery scene is less avant-garde than New York's, Washington patrons can still find ambitious work made by local artists as well as national and international ones. In general, the gallery-going community here is casual and supportive (some might argue insular).

ART AREAS

Logan Circle, the heart of the scene, shows the most refreshing art the city has to offer and should be the first stop on any aficionado's tour. **H Street, NE**, sometimes known as the **Atlas District**, plays host to just a handful of galleries, but they're very good ones. **Dupont Circle** once boasted a dense gallery concentration – the townhouses lining R Street between Connecticut and Florida Avenues still house well-loved galleries – but the few galleries that remain tend toward local artists of middling repute. Like Dupont, the downtown 7th Street corridor in **Penn Quarter** was once home to both galleries and artists, but while the area's soaring property prices gained the galleries wider audiences, the area became prohibitively expensive for most resident artists. Still, several art spaces here should not be missed. **Georgetown**, meanwhile, serves up a hotchpotch of art: galleries varying from avant-garde to conservative cater to both the blue-haired and the blue bloods.

About the author
Jessica Dawson *is the Washington Post's galleries critic and a visiting professor at University of California, Los Angeles.*

ARTS & ENTERTAINMENT

ARTS & ENTERTAINMENT

INFORMATION
The website www.pinklineproject.com is the best place for gallery listings, including many one-off events that happen frequently. Note that many galleries are closed on Sunday and Monday.

DOWNTOWN/PENN QUARTER

Carroll Square
975 F Street, NW, between 9th & 10th Streets (1-202 624 8643, 1-202 638 3000, www.carroll square.com/gallery.html). Metro Center/Gallery Place-Chinatown Metro. **Open** 10am-5pm Sat, and by appointment. **Credit** MC, V. **Map** p253 J6.
Run by the staff of Logan Circle's Hemphill Fine Arts, Carroll Square sits off the shiny marble lobby of a downtown office building. The dedicated gallery space is one of the city's most professional 'lobby galleries'. The site changes exhibitions four-to-five times a year.

Civilian Art Projects
1019 7th Street, NW, between L Street & New York Avenue (1-202 607 3804, www.civilianart projects.com). Mount Vernon Square/7th Street-Convention Center Metro. **Open** 1-6pm Wed, Thur, Sat; 4-8pm Fri. **No credit cards.** **Map** p251/p253 J5.
Civilian is run by a young, smart curator with ties to the city's DIY music scene. Exhibits here won't ever bore, and they sometimes spotlight younger artists still finding their way.

Gallery at Flashpoint
916 G Street, NW, between 9th & 10th Streets (1-202 315 1305, www.flashpointdc.org). Gallery Place-Chinatown Metro. **Open** noon-6pm Tue-Sat, and by appointment. **Credit** MC, V. **Map** p253 J6.
Gallery at Flashpoint occupies a multi-arts complex sponsored by the city's Cultural Development Corporation. Though the exhibitions vary widely, the programming is getting better with age and can be relied upon to favor young up-and-comers. The complex also houses a blackbox theater and dance studio.

Goethe-Institut
812 7th Street, NW, at I Street (1-202 289 1200, www.goethe.de/ins/us/was). Gallery Place-Chinatown Metro. **Open** 9am-5pm Mon-Thur; 9am-3pm Fri. **No credit cards.** **Map** p251, p253 J5.
The Goethe-Institut's FotoGalerie offers up some of the best young German and EU artists. In recent years, it's become the go-to spot for photography.

Reyes+Davis
No.302, 923 F Street, NW, between 9th & 10th Streets. (1-202 255 5050, www.reyesdavis.com). Gallery Place-Chinatown Metro. **Open** 1-6pm Wed-Fri; 1-5pm Sat, and by appointment. **Credit** MC, V. **Map** p253 J6.

This small gallery shows work by local, mid-career artists who've made a name in Washington.

Touchstone Gallery
901 New York Avenue, NW, between 9th & 10th Streets (1-202 347 2787, www.touchstone gallery.com). Mount Vernon Square or Metro Center Metro. **Open** 11am-6pm Wed, Thur; 11am-8pm Fri; noon-5pm Sat, Sun. **Credit** AmEx, MC, V. **Map** p253 J6.
Touchstone, an artist-owned cooperative gallery, shows works by area artists and lesser-known internationals. Quality is always hit or miss.

LOGAN CIRCLE

Curator's Office
Suite 201, 1515 14th Street, NW, at Church Street (1-202 387 1008, www.curatorsoffice.com). Dupont Circle or Shaw-Howard University Metro. **Open** noon-6pm Wed-Sat, and by appointment. **No credit cards.** **Map** p250 H4.
This tiny gallery might only be the size of most people's closets but it has an impact many times its dimensions. The curator is Andrea Pollan and this is indeed her office. It's also where sharp Washington artists such as Jason Horowitz and Victoria Gaitan exhibit. In recent years Pollan has stepped up her roster of rising international artists.

★ David Adamson Gallery
Suite 202, 1515 14th Street, NW, at P Street (1-202 232 0707, http://adamsongallery.jimdo. com/gallery). Dupont Circle or Shaw-Howard University Metro. **Open** 11.30am-5pm Tue-Fri; noon-5pm Sat. **Credit** MC, V. **Map** p250 H4.
A long-time Downtown favorite, David Adamson decamped to Logan during the great gallery exodus of 2004. Now a stand-alone exhibition space that's separate from its internationally recognised printmaking studio, the gallery continues to exhibit the fruits of its printmaking collaborations with contemporary art heavyweights such as Renate Aller and Chuck Close. One of Washington's blue chip spaces.

Hamiltonian Gallery
1353 U Street, NW, at 14th Street (1-202 332 1116, www.hamiltoniangallery.com). U-Street/ African-American Civil War Memorial/Cardoza Metro. **Open** noon-6pm Tue-Sat, and by appointment. **No credit cards.** **Map** p250 H3.
A gallery that also acts as an arts incubator, Hamiltonian offers young artists mentoring and exhibition space as part of its fellowship program. Shows are hit or miss, but the space is professional and worth a visit.

Hemphill Fine Arts
1515 14th Street, NW, Suite 300, at Church Street (1-202 234 5601, www.hemphillfine arts.com). Dupont Circle or Shaw-Howard

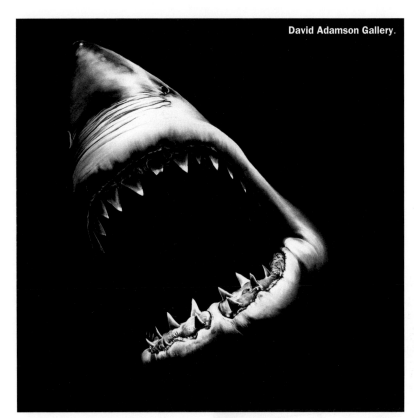

David Adamson Gallery.

University Metro. **Open** 10am-5pm Tue-Sat, and by appointment. **Credit** MC, V. **Map** p250 H4.

George Hemphill's contemporary art gallery plays host to many of Washington's strongest, and safest, artists. Occasional group shows add depth to the regular parade of solo exhibitions. The art tends mainly towards the decorative, but important works do still come through. *Photo p178.*

Irvine

1412 14th Street, NW, at Rhode Island Avenue (1-202 332 8767, www.irvinecontemporaryart.com). McPherson Square Metro. **Open** 11am-6pm Tue-Sat, and by appointment. **Credit** AmEx, MC, V. **Map** p250 H4.

Martin Irvine focuses on painting, drawing and photography but has recently begun a strong program of street art. Obama darling Shepard Fairey shows here alongside Washington area graffiti writers such as Gaia. When it comes to painting, though, Irvine's taste tends to veer toward the superficial and gaudy.

Plan b

1530 14th Street, NW, between Church & Q Streets (1-202 234 2711, www.galleryplanb.com). Dupont Circle Metro. **Open** noon-7pm Wed-Sat; 1-5pm Sun. **Credit** MC, V. **Map** p250 H4.

It may not be the most riveting art space in town, but it's worth stopping by if you're in the area. You might find something interesting among the paintings and prints, most by local artists.

Transformer

1404 P Street, NW, between 14th & 15th Streets (1-202 483 1102, www.transformergallery.org). Dupont Circle Metro. **Open** *during exhibitions* 1-7pm Wed-Sat, and by appointment. **No credit cards. Map** p250 H4.

Despite its size, this tiny, one-room non-profit space hosts some of the city's most daring shows. Some are duds, some gems, but each one makes a mark. And don't be alarmed by the gallery's downmarket digs; they're actually an asset: since no wall or window is sacred, artists can transform the place as they like.

Project 4

*3rd floor, 1353 U Street, NW, at 14th Street
(1-202 232 4340, www.project4gallery.com).
U-Street/African-American Civil War Memorial/
Cardozo Metro.* **Open** noon-6pm Wed-Sat and
by appointment. **No credit cards. Map** p251 J3.
Four friends, two of them architects, founded Project
4 when the U Street restaurant and shopping scene
was just taking hold. Their current, second-floor
location feels more like a shiny new condominium
than a gallery. Selections vary in quality but feature
young up-and-comers.

DUPONT CIRCLE

The few galleries left in this neighborhood
line R Street between Connecticut and Florida
Avenues; one is tucked in Hillyer Court, an
alley south of R Street between Florida
Avenue and 21st Street.

Fondo Del Sol

*2112 R Street, NW, between 21st Street &
Florida Avenue (1-202 483 2777, 265 9235,
www.fondodelsol.org). Dupont Circle Metro.*
Open 1-6pm Wed-Sat. **No credit cards.**
Map p250 G4.
Around the corner from the Phillips Collection, this
non-profit gallery dedicates exhibitions and sym-
posia to arts of the Americas; call for the performance and poetry reading schedule. The taste can be
bizarre and the space is more weird than worldly.

Hemphill Fine Arts. *See p176.*

Gallery 10 Ltd

*1519 Connecticut Avenue, NW, at Q Street (1-202
232 3326, www.gallery10dc.com). Dupont Circle
Metro.* **Open** 11am-5pm Wed-Sat. **Credit** MC, V.
Map p250 G4.
Many of the District's most respected artists jump-
started careers with shows at Gallery 10. Now the
place shows an older generation of District artists
whose exhibitions vary from undisciplined to cohe-
sive – you never know what you'll get.

Hillyer Art Space at International Art & Artists

*2nd floor, 9 Hillyer Court, NW, off 21st Street,
between Q & R Streets (1-202 338 0680,
www.artsandartists.org). Dupont Circle Metro.*
Open noon-6pm Tue-Fri; noon-5pm Sat and by
appointment. **No credit cards. Map** p250 G4.
A handsome gallery space inside the headquarters
of a company that organizes traveling art exhibitions. The program juxtaposes Washington-based
and international artists.

Marsha Mateyka Gallery

*2012 R Street, NW, between Connecticut Avenue
& 21st Street (1-202 328 0088, www.marsha
mateykagallery.com). Dupont Circle Metro.* **Open**
11am-5pm Wed-Sat, and by appointment. Closed
Aug. **Credit** MC, V. **Map** p250 G4.
Marsha Mateyka exhibits painting, sculpture and
works on paper by established contemporary
American and European artists. Past highlights have
included museum-quality paintings by Sam Gilliam
and Nathan Oliveira. The late 19th-century brownstone's interior features spectacular cherrywood fireplaces, wainscoting and carved wood transoms.

H STREET, NE, CORRIDOR

New to the gallery scene, the H Street area has
attracted several of the city's sharpest dealers.

★ Conner Contemporary Art

*1358 Florida Avenue, NE, between Orren &
Staples Streets (1-202 588 8750, www.conner
contemporary.com). McPherson Square or
Gallery Place/Chinatown Metro then X2 bus.*
Open 10am-5pm Tue-Sat. **Credit** AmEx, DC,
MC, V. **Map** p84.
Since Leigh Conner and Jamie Smith opened their
gallery in 1999, they have been showing prints,
photographs, paintings and sculptures by the kind
of cutting-edge artists Washingtonians usually
travel to New York to see. The pair's expansive
gallery on Florida Avenue, NE, is unrivaled in DC
– the massive, flexible space has played host to Leo
Villareal (whose LED-based light sculpture
Multiverse recently entered the National Gallery of
Art's collection) and video artist Federico Solmi.
Strong shows by DC's younger artists have been
well received.

Art, Not Cars

Former car showrooms and body shops make great gallery spaces.

As a purpose-built seat of government, Washington lacks the industrial core that provides other cities – New York, Philadelphia – with ideal real estate for studio and gallery conversions. That means that art spaces are created from what the city *does* have: lots of former car dealerships and body shops (most of which have moved to the suburbs).

On 14th Street in Logan Circle, developer Giorgio Furioso found elegant proportions, generous spaces and period details in a former auto dealership built in the 1920s; his team then refurbished the interior plasterwork and preserved exterior details, including the original rosettes and Greek motifs occupying the structure's cornice and lintels. Furioso, landlord to defunct alternative space Signal 66, solidified the Logan Circle gallery scene with the September 2004 opening of **1515 14th Street**, a building that collects some of the city's strongest dealers under a single roof.

Furioso and his gallery tenants were doing what gentrifiers usually do: they followed the pioneers. Erstwhile gallery Fusebox opened in late 2001 and launched the Logan Circle neighbourhood as an art destination; alternative space **Transformer** (*see p177*) followed soon afterwards. As chain stores and high-end furniture outlets moved in and condominiums mushroomed, Furioso and the galleries recognized an opportunity. Indeed, to some observers, the institutionalization of the Logan Circle

gallery neighborhood was more death knell than jubilee. One of the 1515 building's first tenants, **G Fine Art** (*see left*), has already decamped to the Atlas District in Northeast where cheaper rents beckon.

Though G's new space is small, Atlas district neighbor **Conner Contemporary Art** (*see left*) repurposed a former body shop to create a space that rivals those in Manhattan's Chelsea. The design-focused **Industry Gallery** (*see below*) rents space upstairs. Nowadays, a rear ramp once intended for cars shuttles art safely to and from the galleries.

G Fine Art

1250 Florida Avenue, NE, between Montello & Trinidad Avenues (1-202 462 1601, www.gfineartdc.com). Gallery Place-Chinatown Metro then X2 bus. **Open** noon-6pm Wed-Sat. **Credit** AmEx, MC, V. **Map** p84.

Annie Gawlak left her impressive Logan Circle space for a hole-in-the-wall space near power dealer Leigh Conner. G's program is international but also features Washington-based stars Dan Steinhilber and iona rozeal brown.

★ Industry Gallery

Suite 200, 2nd floor, 1358 Florida Avenue, NE, between Orren & Staples Streets (1-202 399 1730, www.industrygallerydc.com). Gallery Place-Chinatown Metro then X2 bus. **Open** noon-6pm Wed-Sat; by appointment Tue-Sun. **Credit** AmEx, MC, V. **Map** p84.

Industry is the city's only avant-garde design gallery. International artists creating functional art out of industrial materials are a speciality. Italian designer Antonio Pio Saracino and Dutch artists Tejo Remy and Rene Veenhuizen show here.

GEORGETOWN

There's no real gallery epicenter in Georgetown. Showrooms are located on or near M Street, the area's main east–west artery. Several galleries of middling quality occupy the Canal Square complex (1054 31st Street, NW), which hosts joint openings every third Friday of the month; in warmer weather, bands play music.

Addison/Ripley Fine Art

1670 Wisconsin Avenue, NW, at Reservoir Road (1-202 338 5180, www.addisonripleyfineart.com).

ARTS & ENTERTAINMENT

Foggy Bottom-GWU Metro then 30, 32, 34, 35, 36 bus, or Circulator bus. **Open** 11am-6pm Tue-Sat, and by appointment. **Credit** MC, V. **Map** p249 E4.
Addison/Ripley shows and sells high-calibre painting, photography and prints by contemporary American and European artists to an upscale and moneyed clientele. Gallerists Christopher Addison and Sylvia Ripley make an effort to look for nationally recognised names who might not otherwise be seen in Washington. Their selections, while always lovely, do tend towards the excruciatingly safe. Wolf Kahn shows regularly.

Cross/MacKenzie Ceramic Arts

1054 31st Steet, NW, at Blues Alley (1-202 337 7970, www.crossmackenzie.com). Foggy Bottom Metro then 30, 32, 34, 35, 36 bus, or Circulator bus. **Open** noon-6pm Tue-Sat, and by appointment. **Credit** AmEx, DC, MC, V. **Map** p249 E5.
A small space dedicated to ceramics both functional and artistic, the gallery sells and exhibits a wide array of craft pieces.

Maurine Littleton Gallery

1667 Wisconsin Avenue, NW, at Reservoir Road (1-202 333 9307, www.littletongallery.com). Foggy Bottom-GWU Metro then 30, 32, 34, 35, 36 bus. **Open** 11am-6pm Tue-Sat. **Credit** AmEx, MC, V. **Map** p249 E4.
The daughter of studio glass art pioneer Harvey Littleton founded her eponymous gallery to show glasswork that transcends the obvious goblet or bowl (although these are available as well) by incorporating photo images and collage.

Parish Gallery

1054 31st Street, NW, at M Street (1-202 944 2310, www.parishgallery.com). Foggy Bottom-GWU Metro then 30, 32, 34, 35, 36 bus. **Open** noon-6pm Tue-Sat, and by appointment. **Credit** AmEx, DC, MC, V. **Map** p249 E5.
Specializing in the art of the African diaspora, the Parish Gallery shows a mixed bag of abstraction and realism. The quality varies too.

ELSEWHERE

Arlington Arts Center

3550 Wilson Boulevard, at Monroe Street, Arlington, VA (1-703 248 6800, www.arlington artscenter.org/exhibitions). Virginia Square-GMU Metro. **Open** 1-7pm Tue-Fri; noon-5pm Sat, Sun.
After a lengthy renovation and expansion, this non-profit, non-collecting contemporary visual arts center now shows a regular roster of local names and ambitiously curated group shows.

Artisphere

1101 Wilson Boulevard, between N Kent & N Lynn Streets, Arlington, VA (1-703 875 1100, www.arlingtonarts.org). Rosslyn Metro. **Open** 11am-11pm Mon-Fri; 11am-2am Sat; 11am-9pm Sun. **Credit** AmEx, MC, V.
This Arlington County-sponsored space was inaugurated in October 2010. Its galleries show a wide variety of exhibitions; past events include a group show dedicated to skater culture. The complex includes multiple performance and film spaces.

District of Columbia Arts Center (DCAC)

2438 18th Street, NW, between Belmont & Columbia Roads, Adams Morgan (1-202 462 7833, www.dcartscenter.org). Woodley Park-Zoo/Adams Morgan Metro. **Open** 2-7pm Wed-Sun. **Credit** MC, V. **Map** p250 G3.
This independent company programs its small gallery and 50-seat theater in Adams Morgan with a selection of innovative avant-garde exhibitions.

Fraser Gallery Bethesda

Suite E, 7700 Wisconsin Avenue, at Middleton Lane, Bethesda, MD (1-301 718 9651, www. thefrasergallery.com). Bethesda Metro. **Open** 11.30am-6pm Tue-Sat, and by appointment. **Credit** AmEx, MC, V.
A bright, glass-walled gallery that exhibits realist painting and photography.

Katzen Arts Center at American University

4400 Massachusetts Avenue, NW, at Nebraska Avenue, Upper Northwest (1-202 885 1300, www. american.edu/museum). Tenleytown-AU Metro then N2, M4 bus or Friendship Heights Metro then N3, N4, N6, N8 bus. **Open** 11am-4pm Tue-Thur; 11am-7pm Fri, Sat; noon-4pm Sun. **Admission** free.
Three floors of this arts complex – a landmark of Upper Northwest – are dedicated to a revolving cast of exhibitions, many sponsored by Washington embassies. Critics point out that the space is ambitious but its program less so; the Katzen has yet to forge a national identity worthy of a university gallery its size.

McLean Project for the Arts

1234 Ingleside Avenue, McLean, VA, at McLean Community Center (1-703 790 1953, www.mclean art.org). Ballston Metro then 23A, 23C bus. **Open** 10am-4pm Tue-Fri; 1-5pm Sat, and by appointment. **Credit** MC, V.
Posh, suburban location; urban attitude.

Torpedo Factory Arts Center

105 N Union Street, at King Street, Alexandria, VA (1-703 838 4565 ext 4, www.torpedofactory .org). King Street Metro then 28A, 28B bus or Dash bus AT2, AT3, AT5, AT7. **Open** *Building (gallery hours vary)* 10am-6pm Mon-Wed, Fri; 10am-8pm Thur; noon-6pm Sat, Sun. **Credit** various.
The center woos tourists with three floors of studios and galleries. More homespun than sophisticated, its principal appeal is its warm atmosphere.

Gay & Lesbian

Where the boys – and girls – are.

Washington's gay and lesbian scene has been inching further east ever since it first staked its claim in Dupont Circle decades ago. Then it reached 14th Street, Logan Circle and Shaw, and it's still heading north- and eastwards, now making its presence felt in Columbia Heights, Petworth and over towards North Capitol Street and H Street.

The gay community's activists – who once received a great deal of attention by staging a 'nude-in' on the Mall – have found that they get even more respect with their clothes on. The AIDS crisis and its need for loud voices and charismatic leaders took the perennial outsiders off the city's streets and planted them inside the Capitol. Gays transformed themselves from a marginalized minority into a mainstream force to be reckoned with, complete with a smart downtown HQ for the lobbying organization, the Human Rights Campaign. The strength of the city's gay voice was demonstrated in March 2010, when DC became the sixth jurisdiction in the US to permit same-sex marriage.

After a hard day's lobbying, the District's gays and (to a lesser extent) lesbians can take advantage of a steady stream of bars, clubs and discos that keep them occupied after dark, and often right up until dawn. The second half of the millennium's first decade changed the rhythm of the night for Washington's gay crowd, as institutions went dark and some of the scene's biggest parties danced their last. None of this has come even close to derailing DC's queer community, though.

As one would expect in a town that has become increasingly partisan over the last decade, divisions abound in Washington's gay community as well. Bears and bikers and those who love them frequent **Blowoff** and the **DC Eagle**, while DC's D&G crowd are more likely to be found in the other dance venues. Race tends be another divider.

Finding places that separate the men from the boys might be easy enough but sadly the same can't be said for the District's lesbian bars; one would find it much easier to point to where the girls aren't, rather than are in this town. **Phase One** and **Lace** remain the only nightly options for women. Phase One has done much to move beyond its image of a place where gals shoot pool and watch the Redskins. Live performances

dot its calendar, and even if it's not the glitziest place in town, it is the city's longest running gay bar, making it worthy of a visit.

For news about the scene, try *Metro Weekly* (www.metroweekly.com) and the *Washington Blade* (www.washingtonblade.com).

Apex

1415 22nd Street, NW, between O & P Streets, Dupont Circle (1-202 296 0505, www.apex-dc.com). Dupont Circle Metro. **Open** 5pm-2am Mon-Wed, Sun; 9pm-2am Thur; 9pm-3am Fri, Sat. **Admission** $1-$6. **Credit** MC, V. **Map** p250 G4.
Apex keeps things tight and intimate but not claustrophobic. There are seven bars and two levels; head upstairs for mellow music and conversation.There's lots of action both on and off the dancefloor, but if you're still bored then the music video bar in the back of the club will help to keep you entertained. The weekend drag shows are a lot of fun.

★ Blowoff

9:30 Club, 815 V Street, NW, at 9th Street, Shaw; U Street/14th Street Corridor (1-202 393 0930, www.930.com, www.blowoff.us). U Street/African-American Civil War Memorial/Cardozo Metro. **Dates** see website. **Admission** varies. **Credit** AmEx, MC, V. **Map** p251 J3.

Housed in the main room of the 9:30 Club, Bob Mould and Rich Morel's 'diva-free' dance party pumps some real muscle into the District's nightlife. Expect anything from Black Legend to Madonna to Secret Machines to Mould and Morel's own remixes and compositions. Check the website for dates and times.
▶ *For more on the 9:30 Club, see p186.*

DC Eagle

639 New York Avenue, NW, between Sixth & Seventh Streets, Downtown (1-202 347 6025, www.dceagle.com). Mount Vernon Square/7th Street-Convention Center Metro. **Open** 4pm-2am Mon, Tue-Thur, Sun; 4pm-3am Wed, Fri, Sat. **Admission** free. **Credit** MC, V. **Map** p253 J5.
Those familiar with the Eagle standard, set in clubs across the country, will know what to expect. DC's version of the popular club offers the usual trappings – pool, pinball and a rock/industrial dance mix. However, what the unfamiliar might find most surprising is the lack of pretence and attitude among the bar's patrons. A great, but dimly lit, club for those who love men in leather (or just the smell of them).

The Fireplace

2161 P Street, NW, at 22nd Street, Dupont Circle (1-202 293 1293, www.fireplacedc.com). Metro Dupont Circle. **Open** 1pm-2am Mon-Thur, Sun; 1pm-3am Fri, Sat. **Admission** free. **Map** p250 G4.
It's very much a case of upstairs and downstairs at this place; upstairs is for dance and attracts a younger African American crowd, while downstairs, where the actual fireplace is, attracts an older, racially mixed clientele. Some say its cliquey and seedy, others love it. In any case, it's a DC fixture.

Green Lantern

1335 Green Court, NW, behind lot at 1335 L Street, between 13th & 14th Streets, Downtown (1-202 347 4533, www.greenlanterndc.com). McPherson Square Metro. **Open** 4pm-2am Mon-Thur, Sun; 4pm-3am Fri, Sat; 1pm-2am Sun. **Admission** free. **Credit** MC, V. **Map** p252 H5.
The Green Lantern still draws the same burly types that it always has, especially on Thursday nights

---

INSIDE TRACK
CENSORSHIP CONTROVERSY

In late 2010, the Smithsonian came under fire for bowing to conservative pressure to remove a four-minute video from the National Portrait Gallery's Hide/Seek: Difference and Desire in American Portraiture, an exhibition examining sexual identity in art. The video, by artist David Wojnarowicz, was intended as a metaphor for AIDS. Complaints were received about a scene in which ants were seen crawling over a crucifix.

---

when 'shirtless men drink free'. Second Sunday tea dances and trailer park parties on Friday nights add variety to the regular entertainment provided by pool tables, karaoke, the dancefloor and video screens. The real action is the cruising, though.

JR's

1519 17th Street, NW, at P Street, Dupont Circle (1-202 328 0090, www.jrswdc.com). Dupont Circle Metro. **Open** 2pm-2am Mon-Thur, Sun; 2pm-3am Fri, Sat. **Admission** free. **Map** p250 G4.
Bar staff move at lightning speed to serve customers in this tight space. Nightly happy-hour specials and and singalongs on Mondays, not to mention occasional seasonal events (such as the annual Easter bonnet contest), keep the crowd entertained. Videos and pool tables are the main entertainment – aside from cruising, that is – as there's no dancefloor.

Lace

2214 Rhode Island Avenue, NE, at South Dakota Avenue. (1-202 832 3888, www.lacedc.com). Rhode Island Avenue Metro then 83, 84, 86 bus. **Open** 6pm-3am Fri, Sat; 6pm-midnight Sun. **Admission** free. **Credit** AmEx, MC, V.
Linda McAllister arrived in Washington expecting to find a plethora of lesbian bars, but instead encountered a rather barren nightlife scene. She opened Lace in late 2008, as a restaurant and lounge. The clientele is mostly (but not exclusively) African-American, and if your brother is straight, he's welcome too. Decor is umistakably feminine, though. After all, as the website puts it, here 'every night is ladies' night'.

MOVA

1435 P Street, NW, between 14th & 15th Streets, Logan Circle (1-202 797 9730, www.movalounge. com). Dupont Circle Metro. **Open** 5pm-1.45am Mon-Thur, Sun; 5pm-2.45am Fri, Sat. **Credit** AmEx, MC, V. **Map** p250 H4.
On the site where Halo used to be, MOVA is a smart, sleek cocktail bar (its cucumber ginger martini came top in a *Washington Blade* readers' poll for best cocktail in 2010). DJs turn up the volume later in the evening, and weekly events include a Latin Party on Wednesday and Homolicious on Thursday. On Saturdays – aptly enough – it's Saturday Night Fever, with sounds from the 1970s and '80s.

★ Nellie's

900 U Street, NW, at 9th Street (1-202 332 6355, www.nelliesdc.com). U Street/African-American Civil War Memorial/Cardozo Metro. **Open** 5pm-1am Mon-Thur; 3pm-2am Fri; 11am-2am Sat; 11am-1am Sun. **Credit** MC, V. **Map** p251 J3.
A gay-friendly sports bar? Mais oui – with drag bingo on Tuesdays, Trivia Night on Wednesdays, board games galore, and a roof patio; along with ten HD TVs and one giant screen for game days – in the more traditional, sports-bar sense of the word. Nellie's, named after the owner's great- and great-great grandmothers,

Nellie's.

One of the city's most popular and packed dance clubs, with two floors and multiple rooms, Town also has a performance space hosting drag shows every weekend, plus a comfortable lounge. Occasional theme parties ('superheroes' was a recent one) are a popular draw.

Ziegfields/Secrets

1824 Half Street, SW, at T Street (1-202 863 0670, www.secretsdc.com). Navy Yard Metro. **Open** *Secrets* 9pm-2am Wed, Thur, Sun; 9pm-3am Fri, Sat. *Ziegfields* 9pm-2am Fri, Sat. **Credit** MC, V. Resurrected from the dead in 2009 – it was closed to make way for construction of the ballpark – Zeigfields is now back to doing what it does best: regular, uproarious drag nights with hostesses Ella Fitzgerald and Kristine Kelly. Upstairs, Secrets has DJs and occasional amateur dance contests.

GYMS

Bodysmith

1622 14th Street, NW, at Corcoran Street, Logan Circle (1-202 939 0800, www.bodysmithdc.com). Shaw-Howard University Metro. **Open** varies. **Credit** AmEx, MC, V. **Map** p250 H4.
Bodysmith's personal trainers are well qualified and, judging by the look of the patrons, they do their job well. Best to book ahead, however, as appointments go fast at this small personal training facility. There are no independent workouts here, only clients and their trainers.If you like a challenge you could always sign up for the ominously named 'Boot camp series'. **Other locations** 2200 Wisconsin Avenue, NW Upper Northwest, (1-202 333 7703).

Crew Club

1321 14th Street, NW, between N Street & Rhode Island Avenue, Logan Circle (1-202 319 1333, www.crewclub.net). McPherson Square Metro. **Open** 24hrs daily. **Rates** Day membership $10.5-day membership $30. Extra charges for some rooms & lockers. **Credit** AmEx, MC, V. **Map** p250 H4.
A licensed nudist facility, Crew Club caters to those looking for a workout that's uninhibited – or at least undressed. Showers, lockers and towels are all available, as are condoms. There's a TV room too.

Results, The Gym

1612 U Street, 1101 Connecticut Avenue NW, between 16th & 17th Streets, Shaw: U Street/14th Street Corridor (1-202 518 0001, www.resultsthegym.com). U Street/African-American Civil War Memorial/Cardozo Metro. **Open** 5am-10pm Mon-Fri; 7am-7pm Sat, Sun. **Rates** Day membership $20. **Credit** MC, V. **Map** p250 H3.
Results used to be the gym of choice for the gay community. The facility is still better than most, but the posing and chatting boys can bring your workout to a standstill during peak hours (6pm onwards). If it's a social scene you want, with patrons as steely

has all the accoutrements of a regular sports bar (wings, nachos, burgers), along with a mixed crowd, a serious take on sports, and Latin-themed *arepas* and *empanadas* from the Venezualan co-owner.

Phase One

525 8th Street, SE, between F & G Streets (1-202 544 6831). Eastern Market Metro. **Open** 7pm-2am Thur, Sun; 7pm-3am Fri, Sat. **Admission** free. **No credit cards. Map** p253 M8.
Phase One has done its best to overcome its image of a rough-gurl hangout where fist-flying bar brawls were the norm, though you're still most likely to find the place packed out when the Redskins game is projected on to a gigantic screen. The bar recently celebrated its 40th anniversary, no mean feat in a business where operations come and go with alarming regularity. Phase One now hosts occasional open mic events, jello wrestling every second Wednesday and even the occasional dance night. It also stands alone in presenting drag king shows.

Remington's

639 Pennsylvania Avenue, SE, between 6th & 7th Streets, Capitol Hill (1-202 543 3113, www.remingtonswdc.com). Eastern Market Metro. **Open** 4pm-2am Mon-Thur, Sun; 4pm-3am Fri, Sat. **Admission** $2-$5. **No credit cards. Map** p253 L7.
As the District's only gay country music venue, Remington's is still a draw for those who like to Roll the Rug and do the Tush Push. The club itself is one of the cleanest and friendliest environments in the city. Dance lessons, especially line dancing, are available at the beginning of most nights.

Town Danceboutique

2009 8th Street, NW, at U Street (1-202 234 8696, www.towndc.com). Shaw-Howard University Metro. **Open** 9pm-4am daily (last admission 2.30am). **Credit** MC, V (admission only). **Map** p251 J3.

ARTS & ENTERTAINMENT

and polished as the equipment, you'll be ecstatic. If it's a serious workout you're looking for, hit Results.

RESTAURANTS & CAFÉS

There really aren't any restaurants that are exclusively gay in the District. But there are joints where the community tends to congregate as much for the scene as for the sustenance.

Annie's Paramount Steak House

1609 17th Street, NW, between Q & Corcoran Streets, Dupont Circle (1-202 232 0395). Dupont Circle Metro. **Open** 11.30am-11.30pm Mon-Wed; 11.30am-1.30am Thur; 11.30am Fri-11pm Sun. **Main courses** $10-$22. **Credit** AmEx, Disc, MC, V. **Map** p250 G4.

A DC institution: having served DC's gay community for more than 50 years, it's worth grabbing a burger at Annie's just to say 'I was there'. There's nothing remarkable about the decor or the service – or the food, for that matter. Many of the patrons seem to come to reminisce about the glory of their youth, giving the restaurant even more of a neighborhood feel. Midnight brunch is served at weekends and holidays, and the kitchen remains open round the clock from Friday night until Sunday night.

Duplex Diner

2004 18th Street, NW, at Vernon Street, Adams Morgan (1-202 265 7828, www.duplexdiner.com). Dupont Circle Metro then 42 bus. **Open** 6-11pm Mon, Sun; 6pm-12.30am Tue, Wed; 6pm-1am Thur; 6pm-1.30am Fri, Sat. **Main courses** $9-$15. **Credit** AmEx, Disc, MC, V. **Map** p250 H3.

The Duplex Diner, or the 18th & U as it's also known, has the casual feel of the 1950s eateries it emulates and a reputation for *au courant* cocktails. Some nights attract more patrons than others; for instance, the Thursday night bar and club crowd often relies on the Duplex as its opening act. The menu lists diner favorites – burgers and fries, natch – but the real draw is the neighborhood feel.

Dupont Italian Kitchen (DIK)

1637 17th Street, NW, at R Street, Dupont Circle (1-202 328 3222, www.dupontitaliankitchen.com). Dupont Circle Metro. **Open** 11am-11pm Mon-Thur; 11am-1am Fri; 10.30am-1am Sat; 10.30am-11pm Sun. **Main courses** $6-$13. **Credit** AmEx, Disc, MC, V. **Map** p250 H4.

It's not the food that keeps this place in business, but rather the prime vantage point it offers for viewing the 17th Street fauna and flora. The meals are modestly priced and the mood is casual. It's a great place to spend a lazy afternoon outside, or to socialize in a warm summer night. But note that when patrons get a seat here, they're not likely to give it up in a hurry, and table turnovers can be few and far between. Upstairs is a favourite hang of those of a certain age who don't fancy the loud, late club scene.

L'Enfant Café

2000 U Street, NW, at corner of U Street & Florida Avenue, Adams Morgan (1-202 319 1800, www.lenfantcafe.com). Dupont Circle Metro then 42 bus. **Open** 6pm-midnight Mon-Thur; 6pm-1am Fri; 10am-1am Sat; 10am-midnight Sun. **Main courses** $12-$21. **Credit** AmEx, Disc, MC, V. **Map** p250 H3.

L'Enfant does its best to deliver decent French stalwarts, like boeuf bourguignon, at a reasonable price with reasonable speed. Dimly lit but welcoming and warm, it's an ideal spot to spend a winter afternoon.

Toyland

421 H Street, NE, at Fifth Street (1-202 450 4075). Union Station Metro. **Open** 5pm-midnight Mon-Thur; 5pm-2am Fri, Sat; 11.30am-11pm Sun. **Main courses** $11-$16. **Credit** AmEx, MC, V. **Map** p253 L5.

This place is all about cool kitsch, great cocktails and fun. The name harks back to the premises' earlier incarnation as a toyshop, but Toyland also lives up to its name with stacks of board games on the bar. The comfort food, ice-cream sodas, memorabilia, blue vinyl bar and '60s decor combine to great effect.

Duplex Diner.

Music

Diverse city, diverse sounds.

At various times, Washington has been known for bluegrass, hardcore punk and the syncopated funk known as go-go. But the local music 'scene' has always actually been a patchwork of scenes. How could the hometown of Al Jolson, Duke Ellington, John Philip Sousa, Marvin Gaye and Henry Rollins be limited to any one sound?

Punk no longer dominates, but the subculture it created – with its preference for easygoing all-ages clubs – still defines the live rock scene. While the National Symphony Orchestra has never been considered one of the country's best, the city has

an unusually active schedule of choral and chamber music concerts, and a growing array of venues. And the area's large Central American, Indian, Caribbean and African (especially Ethiopian) communities make 'world' music a local phenomenon.

VENUES

Washington has venues for practically every musical taste. The **Kennedy Center**, DC's landmark arts center, still plays host to those artists who require a more refined setting, though its Millennium Stage series is casual (and free). Mammoth acts head for the **Verizon Center** (*see p72*), while outdoor pop concerts and all-day rock festivals use such suburban venues as Maryland's **Merriweather Post Pavilion** (www.merriweathermusic.com) and **Fedex Field** (www.fedex-field.com); Virginia's **Jiffy Lube Live** (www.nissanpavilion.com); and occasionally DC's own **RFK Stadium** (*see p201*).

Yet there is no shortage of smaller stages around the District and acts like La Roux, the Roots, Lyle Lovett and My Chemical Romance can all be heard – and seen – in relatively intimate settings, rather than cavernous arenas. Many of these venues are in the **U Street Corridor**.

LISTINGS AND INFORMATION

The free weekly *Washington City Paper* has good music listings. The *Washington Post* has an extensive 'Weekend' section on Fridays. *Express*, a free commuter paper owned by the *Washington Post* and available at most Metro and bus stops, offers entertainment previews on Thursdays. (It's also at www.readexpress.com.)

Websites can lead your ears to music too. For a little bit of everything (including tons of non-music options and news), try www.dcist.com, www.cityguide.aol.com/washington or the City Guide at www.washingtonpost.com. For indie and punk, www.heresahint.org and www.bigyawn.net will help. For dancehall and reggae, check www.bashmentlinkup.com. For go-go, try www.tmottgogo.com.

Tickets for most performances can be bought direct from the venue. Ticket agencies such as **Ticketmaster** (www.ticketmaster.com) allow you to order online but add high surcharges.

Rock, roots & R&B

From small rooms to large arenas, DC's stages host every type of rock and pop performance imaginable, including the pretty bog standard. As well as venues listed below, some clubs and lounges, such as the **Eighteenth Street Lounge** (*see p195*) also host live music.

Folk, country and bluegrass music acts are now generally booked into rock clubs as well, although the **Birchmere**, **Iota Club & Café** and **Jammin' Java** have more than their share of unplugged acts.

Whatever you're going to see, get tickets well in advance. Younger punters should check venues' admissions policies: many require patrons to be 21 or over, though **9:30 Club**, **Black Cat** and smaller punk-rooted venues admit any age group (no alcoholic drinks served to under-21s).

★ 9:30 Club
815 V Street, NW, at 9th Street, Shaw: U Street/
14th Street Corridor (1-202 265 0930, 393 0930,
www.930.com). U Street/African-American Civil
War Memorial/Cardozo Metro or 66, 68, 70, 71,
90, 92, 93, 96, 98 bus. **Open** varies. **Admission**
varies. **Credit** AmEx, MC, V. **Map** p251 J3.
Once a tiny art-scene dive on F Street, renowned for
its heat (and smell), the 9:30 relocated in 1996. It now
boasts state-of-the-art sound and ventilation, as well
as a healthy slate of microbrews. A few long-lived
(or reunited) punk and post-punk bands have played
both incarnations, among them Wire, the Feelies and
Mission of Burma, but these days you're as likely to
see Gogol Bordello, Damian Marley or Spoon (not on
the same bill, of course) as the Decemberists, MF
Doom and Sean Paul. The open floor and balcony
layout is supposed to guarantee unrestricted viewing of the stage from anywhere in the club, and for
the most part it succeeds. However, arriving early,
scoping out the best vantage point and then standing your ground for the rest of the night is the best
way to ensure a good view.

Birchmere
3701 Mount Vernon Avenue, between W Reed
Avenue & Russell Road, Alexandria, VA (1-703
549 7500, www.birchmere.com). Pentagon Metro
then 10A or 10E bus. **Open** from 6pm on gig
nights. **Admission** $15-$45. **Credit** AmEx, MC, V.
Originally a bluegrass, folk, and country institution,
the Birchmere is one of those venues artists can't
bear to outgrow. Patty Loveless might play a couple
of nights here in the fall before heading to Wolf Trap
in the spring, and Merle Haggard's annual gigs
always sell out. Now the Birchmere also serves up
the kind of pop, smooth jazz, world music and that

appeals to an over-30s crowd. The Band Stand area
has a dancefloor, but most of the shows are in the
larger Music Hall. This is a listeners' club, not some
chicken-wire honky-tonk, and a few house rules
apply in the table-service Music Hall: no standing,
no smoking, no recording, no talking. Rowdier
patrons can head for the bar and the pool tables.

★ Black Cat
1811 14th Street, NW, between S & T Streets,
Shaw: U Street/14th Street Corridor (1-202 667
7960/www.blackcatdc.com). U Street/African-
American Civil War Memorial/Cardozo Metro.
Open 8pm-2am Mon-Thur, Sun; 7pm-3am Fri, Sat.
Red Room Bar 8pm-2am Mon-Thur, Sun; 7pm-
3am Fri, Sat. **Admission** $8-$20. **No credit**
cards (ATM in club). **Map** p250 H3.
As famous for having Foo Fighter Dave Grohl as a
backer as it is for the bands it books, the Black Cat
has picked up where the old 9:30 left off when it comes
to hosting less mainstream acts. Opened in 1993, the
Black Cat began with the Fall, Stereolab and Slant 6
and has been continuing pretty much along those
lines ever since. The vibe is dark and homey. A downstairs area – Back Stage – hosts greener local and out-
of-town bands, as well as DJ nights that range from
'80s retro to bhangra. The indie regulars here can
make for a rather undemonstrative crowd, but such
bands as No Age and the Joy Formidable recently
inspired outbursts of slam dancing.

Comet Ping Pong
5037 Connecticut Avenue, NW, at Nebraska
Avenue, Upper Northwest (1-202 364 0404).
Van Ness/UDC Metro, then L2, L4 bus. **Open**
10.30pm-2am Fri, Sat. **Admission** free-$8.
Credit AmEx, MC, V.

Rock & Roll Hotel. *See p188.*

INSIDE TRACK
DON'T FORGET YOUR ID

If you're going to a (non-classical) music venue, always carry ID. Most places will card you no matter how old you may look. Even venues that admit under-21s are strict about not serving them alcohol.

The underground rock scene that bounced around several funky downtown venues – some legal, some maybe not – has now landed at this gourmet pizza joint in an affluent residential neighborhood not famed for nightlife. Music begins as the pizza ovens start to cool, most Fridays and Saturdays, with the focus on indie rock, mostly touring acts. Funk, reggae and electronica can sometimes be heard. DJ nights feature such DC luminaries as Ian Svenonius (once of Nation of Ulysses) and Kid Congo Powers (the Cramps, Gun Club). All shows are all ages. *Photo p187.*
▶ For a restaurant review of Comet Ping Pong, see p131.

Crossroads

4103 Baltimore Avenue (Alternate Route One), north of Annapolis Road (Route 202), Bladensburg, MD (1-301 927 1056/www. crossroadsclub.com). Cheverly Metro then F1, F8 bus. **Open** Wed-Sun; door times vary. **Admission** varies. **Credit** AmEx, MC, V.
The area's premier club for Caribbean music, from roots reggae and dancehall to soca and steel bands, Crossroads is a mixture of concert venue, restaurant and social club for the area's West Indian diaspora. The music is loud and the vibe is usually casual. Most evenings feature DJs, but the club averages about four to six concerts every month.

DC9

1940 9th Street, NW, at U Street, Shaw: U Street/ 14th Street Corridor (1-202 483 5000, www.dc nine.com). U Street/African-American Civil War Memorial/Cardozo Metro. **Open** 8pm-2am Mon-Thur, Sun; 7pm-3am Fri, Sat. **Admission** $5-$15. No advance tickets. **Credit** MC, V. **Map** p251 J3.
This club's long, thin, vintage-looking first-floor bar leads to an oddly shaped upstairs performance space. It showcases the same sort of local and touring indie bands that play Galaxy Hut, Velvet Lounge and the Red & the Black, but has a larger capacity. Mostly alt-rock, although the Very Best made its DC debut to a packed house here.

Galaxy Hut

2711 Wilson Boulevard, between Danville & Edgewood Streets, Arlington, VA (1-703 525 8646, www.galaxyhut.com). Clarendon Metro. **Open** 5pm-2am daily. **Music** Mon, Sun. **Admission** $5.

This petite bar offers up-and-coming acts (mostly indie-rock) for a small cover charge. With a capacity of only 48, the place fills up easily, but in good weather you can watch the bands from outside, through the picture window.

Hole in the Sky

2110 5th Street, NE, at Rhode Island Avenue, Northeast (no phone, holeintheskydc.tumblr.com). Rhode Island Avenue Metro. **Open** 8pm-midnight on show nights. **Admission** $1-$10 donation. No advance tickets. **No credit cards.**
The latest place to enter the storied history of DC artspaces/punk venues is this multi-purpose, second-story loft in a light-industrial neighborhood. The non-profit collective hosts five to ten shows a month, mostly various forms of punk. Local bands predominate, although Brooklyn's Shellshag and San Francisco's Street Eaters were there recently. Enter through the alley between 4th and 5th Streets, and if you expect to be thirsty, bring your own beverage.

IOTA Club & Café

2832 Wilson Boulevard, between Edgewood & Fillmore Streets, Arlington, VA (1-703 522 8340, www.iotaclubandcafe.com). Clarendon Metro. **Open** 5pm-2am daily. **Admission** $10-$15. **Credit** AmEx, MC, V.
IOTA has an intimate atmosphere that makes it an excellent place in which to hear singer-songwriters such as the child-friendly Dan Zanes or the all-grown-up Ron Sexsmith. Unfortunately, the surroundings can be a little too intimate and it's not unknown for patrons to be asked to shut up or leave the premises – sometimes by the performers themselves – as even the slightest whisper can interfere with the music. The artist-comes-first policy has its benefits: Norah Jones and John Mayer played their first DC shows here. The layout of the tiny club doesn't provide many optimum vantage points, so early arrival is advised.

Jammin' Java

228 Maple Avenue, East Vienna, VA (1-703 255 1566, www.jamminjava.com). **Open** 7am-11pm Mon-Thur; 7am-midnight Fri; 8am-midnight Sat; noon-10pm Sun. **Admission** $10-$22. **Credit** AmEx, MC, V.
A Christian coffeehouse bought out and turned secular, Jammin' Java has earned a place on the folk, blues and roots circuits, with fare ranging from Bert Jansch, Pegi Young and the Mekons to a regular Monday-night open mic. Owners Luke and Daniel Brindley also occasionally take the stage as pop-rock duo the Brindley Brothers.

Jaxx

6355 Rolling Road, at Old Keene Mill Road, Springfield, VA (1-703 569 5940, www.jaxx roxx.com). **Open** times vary. **Admission** $6-$30. **Credit** AmEx, MC, V.

A hard-rock has-been haven par excellence, Jaxx is the room of choice for diehards who would see a Sebastian Bach-less Skid Row and a Glenn Danzig-less Misfits on back-to-back nights. Year after year, bands you didn't think still existed (WASP, Dokken, Warrant) crank it up to 11 and dust off the Gibsons for the long-haired faithful. Jaxx also books a regular schedule of renowned death metal acts like Cryptopsy and Napalm Death. It has great sound and lights, which gives the up-and-coming local groups that fill out the schedule a chance to jam in a professional environment. All this in a suburban shopping plaza.

Red Palace
1212 H Street, NE, at 12th Street, NE Street Corridor (1-202 399 3201, www.redandblack bar.com). McPherson Square or Gallery Place/Chinatown Metro then X2 bus. **Open** 5pm-2am Mon-Thur; 5pm-3am Fri, Sat. **No credit cards**. **Map** p84.
This recently revamped venue compounded the Red & the Black, a small rock bar, with its next-door-neighbor, Palace of Wonders, a club that celebrated circus sideshows and burlesque. You can still see bur-lesque performances here, but the emphasis is on alt-rock, indie-pop and singer-songwriters, often local.
For a review of the bar, see p142.

★ Rock & Roll Hotel
1353 H Street, NE, between 13th & 14th Streets (1-202 399 3201/www.rockandrollhoteldc.com). McPherson Square or Gallery Place/Chinatown Metro then X2 bus. **Open** 6pm-2am Mon-Thur; 6pm-3am Fri, Sat. **No credit cards**. **Map** p84.
Downstairs, this is a basic rock bar, but the upper floor plays on the hotel theme with private rooms that can be rented by small groups. (No beds; it's not that kind of hotel.) Since opening in 2006, the 400-capacity club has scored numerous booking coups, including utterly sold-out shows by Sleigh Bells, Best Coast and Phoenix (whose next DC gig was at the 3,700-set Constitution Hall). DJs rule upstairs, and occasionally below. *Photo p186.*

State Theatre
220 N Washington Street (Lee Highway/Route 29), Falls Church, VA (1-703 237 0300/www.the statetheatre.com). East Falls Church Metro then 2A, 3A bus. **Open** 7pm on show nights; closing time varies. **Credit** AmEx, Disc, MC, V.
Another converted movie theater, the State is a favorite haunt of jam bands, blues, and reggae artists – and classic-rock tribute bands – from near and far. Recent acts include Johnny Winter, the Church and Wu-Tang Clan. The club has ample seat-

City Sounds: Indie

The distinctive sound of Dischord – and much more.

Beginning with Minor Threat's first tour in 1981, Washington indie rock's reputation centered on Dischord Records and its bands – especially the ones featuring charismatic frontman (and Dischord co-owner) Ian MacKaye. The label and his best-known band, Fugazi, established an ethos of fierce independence, social activism and anti-commercialism that continues to influence local musicians, DC's all-ages clubs and the city's punk-rooted indie labels.

Even at the peak of Dischord's influence, however, its brand of lean, vehement post-punk was not the whole story. The city has also spawned such diverse musical phenomena as the jazzy 'downtempo' music of Thievery Corporation and its label, ESL; such country-tinged acts as Le Loup, Shortstack and Junior League; and singer-songwriters Brandon Butler, Benjy Ferree and Xyra Harper. There's also a growing prog-rock scene – think Battles, not Yes – that includes Hume and Imperial China (both affiliated with the Sockets label), as well as Bellflur and Tone.

These days, Dischord deals mostly in reissues, while distributing music released by other small labels. Fugazi has been on hiatus since late 2002, and few '80s punk scene's veterans perform regularly. MacKaye plays occasionally with the Evens, his folk-punk duo with partner Amy Farina. The most conspicuous Dischord-related acts are Title Tracks (fronted by Q and Not U's John Davis) and Medications; both released fine albums in 2010.

Ian Svenonius (once of Nation of Ulysses) mostly DJs now, but the Dismemberment Plan played a series of reunion gigs that may lead to something more. Jawbox's J. Robbins fronts Office of Future Plans, which adds cello to DC-style punk. Among the more widely touted young bands are the retro-rocking US Royalty, the New Order-ish Ra Ra Rasputin and the edgily eclectic True Womanhood.

Likely venues for such acts include the Black Cat, Comet Ping Pong, Red Palace, and the Velvet Lounge. Check fliers and websites for shows at occasional and non-commercial venues; in the summer, local bands play for free outdoors at Fort Reno Park (www.fortreno.com).

ing in the back and upstairs, plus a raked floor for good sightlines throughout the room. It may feel like a hike to get out there, but it's only a 10-minute bus journey from the East Falls Church Metro station.

Velvet Lounge
915 U Street, NW, between Vermont Avenue & 9th Street, Shaw: U Street/14th Street Corridor (1-202 462 3213, www.velvetloungedc.com). U Street/African-American Civil War Memorial/ Cardozo Metro. **Open** 8pm-2am Mon-Thur, Sun; 8pm-3am Fri, Sat. **Admission** $5-$15 **Credit** MC, V. **Map** p251 J3.

Often the province of local bands and their friends whooping them on from the audience, the Velvet Lounge also books indie-rockers from far outside the Beltway, including such cult acts as Damo Suzuki and the Homosexuals. The place still has the feel of a neighborhood bar that just happens to have a small stage upstairs. A good place to drop in after attending a show at the nearby 9:30 Club (*see p186*).

Comet Ping Pong. *See p186.*

Jazz

Washington has a rich jazz history, claiming the legendary likes of Duke Ellington and Shirley Horn as its own, though you wouldn't know it from the relatively few clubs hosting the music. But with jazz enshrined as 'American classical music', the **Kennedy Center** (*see p190*), particularly its KC Jazz Club, and the **Smithsonian** (*see p191*) help pick up the slack.

Blues Alley
1073 Wisconsin Avenue, NW, at M Street, Georgetown (1-202 337 4141, www.blues alley.com). Foggy Bottom-GWU Metro then 31, 32, 36, 38B, Circulator bus. **Open** 6pm-12.30am daily. **Admission** $16-$50. **Credit** AmEx, DC, MC, V. **Map** p249 E5.

Some patrons consider the cover charges here outrageously high, especially as there is also a two-drink minimum per person for each set, which usually lasts just under an hour. Others are just so thankful that they have a small space where first-rate acts such as Mose Allison or Pieces of a Dream will perform that money is not an object. Acoustics are as top-notch as the talent on the stage.

Bohemian Caverns
2003 11th Street, NW, between U & V Streets, Shaw: U Street/14th Street Corridor (1-202 299 0800, www.bohemiancaverns.com). U Street/ African-American Civil War Memorial/Cardozo Metro. **Open** 6pm-1am Tue; 8pm-2am Wed; 9pm-2am Thur; 9.30pm-3am Fri, Sat. **Credit** AmEx, MC, V. **Map** p250 J3.

After being shuttered for 30 years, the legendary Bohemian Caverns reopened in 2000. While it has not quite restored the glory days of U Street – it's

not even the best jazz club in the immediate area – it has found a place among the revitalised nightlife in the historic African-American corridor. Most of the acts are local, but the club recently hosted the DC debut of Brazilan chanteuse Luisa Maita.

HR-57
816 H Street, NE, between 8th & 9th Streets, H Street Corridor (1-202 667 3700/www.hr57.org). McPherson Square or Gallery Place/Chinatown Metro then X2 bus. **Open** phone for details. **Admission** varies. **No credit cards.**

This unassuming club has just relocated to the H Street strip, and is in the process of expanding its food and drink options (lunch is planned.) But the principal attraction will continue to be music, specifically jazz and blues; the place is named after the US House of Representatives' resolution recognizing jazz as a national treasure.' You won' find big names here, unless they stop in to jam after local concert-hall gigs, but you will find huge talent. The cover charge is usually only a few dollars, and a plate of greens and beans can be had for around the same price. Hit it on a good night, and you've got the best dinner-and-a-show value in town.

Twins Jazz/Twins Lounge
Twins Jazz *1344 U Street, NW, between 13th & 14th Streets, Shaw: U Street/14th Street Corridor (1-202 234 0072, www.twinsjazz.com). U Street/ African-American Civil War Memorial/Cardozo Metro.* **Open** 6pm-midnight Tue-Thur, Sun; 6pm-1am Fri, Sat. **Credit** AmEx, MC, V. **Admission** $10-$30. **Map** p250 H3.
Twins Lounge *5516 Colorado Avenue, NW, at Longfellow Street (1-202 882 2523, www.twins jazz.com). McPherson Square Metro then S2, S4 bus.* **Open** 6pm-2am Wed, Fri, Sat. **Admission** $10-$30. **Credit** AmEx, Disc, MC. V.

The twins here are owners Kelly and Maze Tesfaye, though their jazz/supper club also has dual locations. Both rooms regularly feature local (Lenny Robinson,

Michael Thomas) and national (David 'Fathead' Newman, Eddie Henderson) players, though the bigger names usually appear Downtown; the lounge is almost literally a hole in the wall. The headlining cuisine is that of the twins' native Ethiopia, with Caribbean and American dishes rounding out the menu. Like with most jazz clubs, there's a cover charge and a two-drink minimum.

Utopia
1418 U Street, between 14th & 15th Streets, Shaw: U Street/14th Street Corridor (1-202 483 7669, www.utopiaindc.com). U Street/African-American Civil War Memorial/Cardozo Metro. **Open** *Music* 9.30pm-1am Tue; 9pm-1am Wed; 9.30pm-1.30am Thur, Sun; 11pm-2.30am Fri, Sat. **Tickets** $7-$10. **Credit** AmEx, Disc, MC, V. **Map** p250 H3.
One of the first places to open as part of the regeneration of the Shaw neighborhood, this small space has settled into a regular schedule of local jazz and blues. Exhibits by local artists and a international cuisine (lunch and dinner) all go towards making Utopia a sophisticated but relaxed local joint.

Classical & Opera

Washington DC's classical music and opera scene can reflect the 'by the book' mentality of the city when it comes to the arts. Everything is professional and top-notch, of course, but there's not a lot that could be considered daring. Still, there are numerous embassies here with active cultural departments, offering an incredible number of opportunities to hear musicians from around the world. Many such events – held in the embassies or in venues around town – can be found at www.embassy series.com, www.embassyevents.com and www.culturaltourismdc.org. If you're around in June, be sure to catch a few of the concerts put on by the volunteer-run Washington Early Music Festival (www.earlymusicdc.org).

COMPANIES

Choral Arts Society
1-202 244 3669, www.choralarts.org. **Tickets** $17-$50. **Credit** AmEx, Disc, MC, V.
Under the direction of Norman Scribner, this 190-member chorus has a very popular subscription series for its performances at the Kennedy Center. Occasional international appearances are also part of its itinerary, and it routinely performs locally with the National Symphony Orchestra. Not bad for a bunch of volunteers.

National Symphony Orchestra
1-202 416 8100, www.kennedy-center.org/nso. **Tickets** $40-$75. **Credit** AmEx, DC, MC, V.

The National Symphony, which performs mainly in the Kennedy Center Concert Hall, tries to live up to its name by offering something for everyone. Music director Christoph Eschenbach, a German whose previous gig was in Philadelphia, arrived in 2010, so it's too soon to say how he'll transform the orchestra's style and repertoire. Former leader Leonard Slatkin focused on making the music more accessible, gearing some concerts towards children and naming Marvin Hamlisch as Principal Pops Conductor. Overall, the NSO delivers a variety of engaging performances throughout the year, including composer-themed festivals.

Washington National Opera
1-202 295 2400, www.dc-opera.org. **Tickets** $45-$290. **Credit** AmEx, MC, V.
The Washington Opera, resident at the Kennedy Center Opera House, is one of the city's best national performing arts groups. Placido Domingo has been the director since 1996, but has announced his mid-2011 departure. Recent productions include *Salome* and *Madama Butterfly*. The season usually sells out to subscribers but there is the chance that a call to the KenCen's box office will result in a lucky score of tickets. All productions have English subtitles.

MAIN VENUES

Folger Shakespeare Library
201 East Capitol Street, SE, Capitol Hill (1-202 544 7077, www.folger.edu). Capitol South or Union Station Metro. **Open** *Library* 10am-4pm Mon-Sat. **Performances** times vary. **Tickets** vary. **Credit** AmEx, MC, V. **Map** p253 L7.
The Globe this isn't, though the convincing back-lit canopy does manage to convey the appearance of an outdoor theatre from Shakespeare's time. The Folger Consort ensemble presents period recitals of medieval, Renaissance and baroque chamber music. Interesting for the casual fan and a must for anyone with a passion for lyres and lutes.

★ Kennedy Center
2700 F Street, NW, at New Hampshire Avenue & Rock Creek Parkway, Foggy Bottom (tickets & information 1-800 444 1324, 1-202 467 4600, office 1-202 416 8000, www.kennedy-center.org). Foggy Bottom-GWU Metro (free shuttle 9.45am-midnight Mon-Fri; 10am-midnight Sat; noon-midnight Sun). **Box office** 10am-9pm Mon-Sat; noon-9pm Sun. **Peformances** times vary. **Tickets** vary. **Credit** AmEx, MC, V. **Map** p252 F6.
The John F Kennedy Center for the Performing Arts – the national cultural centre of the United States – hosts a great variety of music, particularly on its free Millennium Stage. However, its primary focuses are classical and jazz. A welcome addition is the slate of intimate KC Jazz Club shows scheduled in the Terrace Gallery. The Center has five auditoriums. The Concert Hall is where the National Symphony Orchestra and Washington Chamber Symphony (among others)

City Sounds: Go-go

DC's very own brand of funk lives on.

Washington is not a hip hop desert: the city and its more urban suburbs are home to such rappers as Tabi Bonney, Wale and DJ Kool. But the beat of black Washington remains go-go, the heavily syncopated big-band funk pioneered in the 1970s by Chuck Brown and the Soul Searchers. This style has scored a few national hits, notably EU's 1988 'Da Butt', and has a cult following in Europe. But most Americans have heard go-go only in the samples beneath such hits as Nelly's 'It's Hot in Here' and Beyonce's 'Crazy in Love'.

Go-go and hip hop have grown closer over the years. Today's go-go bands rely more on keyboards and samplers, and less on the horn sections and multiple percussionists of such classic go-go outfits as EU, Rare Essence and the recently reunited Troublefunk. But go-go retains

such distinctive (and African-rooted) elements as chattering polyrhythms, call-and-response shout-outs to the audience and grooves that can extend for hours.

It's fundamentally live music, which is why few go-go acts release studio recordings anymore. (The venerable Chuck Brown, who had a street named for him in 2009, is an exception.) When Wale records, he works with such producers as British hitmaker Mark Ronson; but when he plays live, he's usually backed by a go-go band.

Go-go is an insular scene, whose shows are not publicized to outsiders, and whose venues can be sketchy. Listings for local shows can be found at www.gogobeat.com and www.TMOTTGoGo.com, but the safest course would be to experience the music at more mainstream hall, such as the 9:30 Club (*see p186*).

perform; its acoustics are first class. The Opera House hosts dance and ballet, Broadway-style musical performances, and is the home of the Washington Opera. Productions in the Eisenhower Theater tend to have more of an edge, while the Theater Lab and Terrace Theater are the Center's most intimate spaces.

FREE National Academy of Sciences

2100 C Street, NW, at 21st Street, The Northwest Rectangle (1-202 334 2436, www7.national academies.org/arts/). Foggy Bottom-GWU Metro. **Performances** times vary. **Tickets** free. **Map** p252 G6.

A favourite of chamber ensembles, this space hosts groups such as the Jupiter Symphony Chamber Players and the Mendelssohn String Quartet. The performances are free but the seating is on a first-come, first-served basis. Navigating the one-way streets around the Academy can be tricky so either take a cab or study your map before you set out.

OTHER VENUES
Museums & galleries

Corcoran Gallery of Art

500 17th Street, NW, at New York Avenue, The White House & around (1-202 639 1700, www.corcoran.org). Farragut West Metro. **Performances** times vary. **Tickets** vary. **Credit** AmEx, MC, V. **Map** p252 G5.

Music at the Corcoran Gallery is best enjoyed in the setting of the modest Hammer Auditorium, where

cabaret singers and jazz groups have taken over from chamber ensembles. The Sunday Gospel Brunch, which is held in the main lobby, is very popular, but if you're expecting an environment where the music is in the background, be warned: it can be extremely loud, irritatingly so depending on your taste and the performers concerned, and the musicians are often placed opposite the ticket/information desk, making for awkward transactions.

Phillips Collection

1600 21st Street, NW, at Q Street, Dupont Circle (1-202 387 2151, www.phillipscollection.org). Dupont Circle Metro. **Performances** Oct-May 5pm. **Tickets** concert included with museum admission. **Credit** AmEx, Disc, MC, V. **Map** p252 G4.

The Phillips, as it's known locally, carries with it a certain status that seems to lift it above the other smaller venues in Washington. Its Sunday afternoon concerts are thus fittingly first-rate as well. If it's name-recognition you're looking for, however, you won't always find it on the bill. But if it's an excellent performance of chamber music in an environment where such things are truly appreciated that you're seeking, then you won't be disappointed.

Smithsonian Institution

Various buildings of the Smithsonian Institution (1-202 357 2700/www.si.edu).

As part of its varied program, the Smithsonian regularly sponsors music events that can range from jazz performances and chamber music recitals to the two-week Folklife Festival that takes place in late June and

Eighteenth Street Lounge. *See p195.*

early July. Call ahead for the locations as they can change depending upon the seating required. Also of interest to music-lovers are the performances on the early instruments that are part of the permanent collection in the Museum of American History (*see p49*) and the Friday evening IMAX Jazz Café at the Museum of Natural History (*see p51*).

Churches

Several of the city's churches, cathedrals and synagogues open their doors for special performances. Others are known for the calibre of the choirs at their weekend services. In addition to those listed below, the **Church of the Epiphany** (1317 G Street, between 13th & 14th Streets, NW, Downtown, 1-202 347 2635) has an outstanding lunchtime musical program.

FREE Basilica of the National Shrine of the Immaculate Conception
400 Michigan Avenue, NE, at 4th Street, Northeast (1-202 526 8300/www.nationalshrine.com). Brookland-CUA Metro. **Performances** times vary. **Tickets** free. **Map** p251 L1.
Occasional choral performances, or carillon and organ recitals, which are healthily attended.

FREE St Augustine's Church
1419 V Street, NW, at 15th Street, Shaw: U Street/ 14th Street Corridor (1-202 265 1470, www.saint augustine-dc.org/music.html). U Street/African-American Civil War Memorial/Cardozo Metro. **Map** p250 H3.
As the Mother Church of the local African-American Roman Catholic community, St Augustine's is best known for its wonderful Easter vigil service. The Sunday 12.30pm mass is also popular. Led by the more sedate choir and choral group, the latter complete with ensemble accompaniment of bass, guitar and drums, the service becomes a mix of Gospel, old-time revival and traditional mass.

Multi-use venues

Atlas Performing Arts Center
1333 H Street, NE, between 13th & 14th Streets (1-202 399 7933/www.atlasarts.org). McPherson Square or Gallery Place/Chinatown Metro then X2 bus. **Tickets** vary. **Credit** AmEx, DC, MC, V.
Opened in 2006, this four-theater venue incorporates the long-abandoned Atlas, an art moderne cinema built in 1938. The programing emphasizes drama and dance, but the center also hosts the Library of Congress's 'On LOCation' series, which recently offered Victoire, a modernist chamber quartet, and the Afro-jazz Lionel Loueke Trio.

Clarice Smith Performing Arts Center
University of Maryland, College Park, MD (1-301 405 2787). College Park/U of Maryland Metro, then University of Maryland shuttle bus. **Tickets** vary. **Credit** AmEx, DC, MC, V.
The center majors in 'the unfamiliar, the unpredictable and the developing'. There are all kinds of theatre, dance and music performances. Music programing includes lots of student performances, but also the likes of Laurie Anderson, the Kronos Quartet and the DC area's first Bang on a Can Marathon.

FREE Coolidge Auditorium, Library of Congress
Independence Avenue, between 1st & 2nd Streets, SE, The Capitol & around (1-202 707 5502, www. loc.gov). Capitol South Metro. **Performances** times vary; most begin 8pm. **Tickets** free. **Map** p253 L7.
The problem with some Washington venues is that standards of architecture and acoustics don't always match – with monumental structures yielding muffled sound. But this auditorium in the Jefferson Building rises to the occasion on both counts. Programing is intriguing and intimate, running from classical to country to world music, with recent bookings ranging from the Utrecht String Quartet and Eighth Blackbird to country-harmony group Little Big Town.

George Mason University Center for the Arts
Roanoke Lane & Mason Drive, Fairfax, VA (1-703 993 8888, www.gmu.edu/cfa). Vienna/ Fairfax Metro then Cue Gold, Cue Green bus. **Tickets** $17.50-$84. **Credit** AmEx, Disc, MC, V.

It's a shame that one of the area's best concert facilities is located so far out of the District. Until the issue is addressed, however, folks will have to travel to the George Mason campus for some of the best in music, experimental drama and modern dance. The main hall seats nearly 2,000 and has hosted artists from the Canadian Brass to Dr John to the Dresden Philharmonic. The university's 10,000-seat stadium, the Patriot Center, hosts basketball games but also big-name musical acts, from REM to AR Rahman.

Lincoln Theatre
1215 U Street, NW, between 12th & 13th Streets, Shaw: U Street/14th Street Corridor (1-202 328 6000/www.thelincolntheatre.org). U Street/African-American Civil War Memorial/Cardozo Metro. **Tickets** $10-$50. **Credit** AmEx, MC, V. **Map** p250 H3.

Washington's one-time answer to Harlem's Apollo Theatre, this magnificent structure is most often the site of neo-'Chitlin Circuit' theater. The underused Lincoln is frequently dark, but over the years it has hosted Paul Weller, King Sunny Ade and the Smithsonian Jazz Orchestra.

Lisner Auditorium
730 21st Street, NW, at H Street, Foggy Bottom (1-202 994 6800, www.lisner.org). Foggy Bottom-GWU Metro. **Tickets** vary. **No credit cards.** **Map** p252 G5.

Located in George Washington University, Lisner hosts dance troupes, Latin music, and the Gay Men's Chorus of Washington. Author readings are scheduled as well, sometimes on the same night, as when Dave Eggers split the bill with They Might Be Giants. This is the most likely DC site for shows by prominent African performers, including Youssou N'Dour, Salif Keita and Ladysmith Black Mambazo.

INSIDE TRACK H STREET

The rebirth of H Street, NE – also known as the Atlas District – as a social and arts hub has brought some good new music venues, with the **Rock & Roll Hotel** (*see p188*), **Red Palace** (*see p188*) and **HR-57** (*see p189*) joining the multi-use **Atlas Performing Arts Center** (*see left*). The reopening of the Atlas in 2006 was a major step on the street's road to revival. For more on the street's bars and restaurants, *see p84* **A Taste of H Street.**

Sixth & I Historic Synagogue
601 I Street, NW, at 6th Street, Chinatown (1-202 408-3100, www.sixthandi.org). Gallery Place-Chinatown Metro. **Tickets** vary. **Credit** MC, V.

Rededicated as a synagogue in 2004 after five decades as a church, this Byzantine Revival temple is non-denominational and has no permanent congregation. While many of the activities here are religious, the striking, intimate two-story sanctuary has also become a significant concert venue. The musical bookings tend toward jazz, chamber music and such hushed indie-pop acts as Joanna Newsom and Antony and the Johnsons.

Strathmore
5301 Tuckerman Lane, North Bethesda, MD (1-301 581 5100, www.strathmore.org). Grosvenor-Strathmore Metro. **Tickets** vary. **Credit** AmEx, Disc, MC, V.

This suburban competitor to the Kennedy Center Concert Hall features a blond-wood interior that suggests a huge sailing ship. Part of a larger arts complex, Strathmore books jazz, rock and contemporary music, from Randy Newman and Bauhaus to Kenny G and the American première of Steve Reich's *2x5*. But it's designed for acoustic music, best heard in performances featuring such visiting classical soloists as Joshua Bell and Hilary Hahn. Initially, the venue was a second home for the Baltimore Symphony; it still appears there, but reduced its schedule after its first season drew modest crowds.

Warner Theatre
13th & E Streets, NW, The Federal Triangle (1-202 783 4000, www.warnertheatre.com). Metro Center Metro. **Tickets** vary. **Credit** AmEx, Disc, MC, V. **Map** p252 H6.

Built in 1924, the Warner Theatre has seen a variety of acts on its stage. The early deco design of the auditorium gives it either a decadent gaudiness or a stately individuality, depending on the performance. Comedians, dance troupes and Broadway plays dominate, but music acts still surface now and then.

Wolf Trap
1645 Trap Road, Vienna, VA (1-703 255 1900, www.wolf-trap.org). West Falls Church Metro then Wolf Trap shuttle bus. **Tickets** $10-$70. **Credit** AmEx, Disc, MC, V.

Calling itself 'America's National Park for the Performing Arts', Wolf Trap consists of two essentially separate performance spaces – the Barns and the Filene Center. Don't let the name 'Barns' fool you. Yes, the space is rustic, but that doesn't mean you'll be sitting on a milking stool. The acoustics here are top-notch, as are the seating and facilities. The Filene Center is the sprawling outdoor concert facility with lawn and pavilion seating. The scope of the performances at both spaces is broader than that at many venues in the District that also use the name 'national'. Note that the shuttle bus runs only in summer.

ARTS & ENTERTAINMENT

Nightlife

And the beat goes on.

Vibrant nightlife may not be something that you would immediately associate with Washington DC. The city is an activist's dream, with a swirl of political activity. But if you forget politics and instead focus on DC as a young, energetic and cosmopolitan city, with a creative drive and a distinctive indigenous music scene, then it's easier to imagine why its nightlife might be memorable. Here we list some of the city's best dance clubs, along with lounges with DJs and live music.

For bars with music, see **Bars**, *pp134-42*.
For live music venues, see **Music**, *p185-93*.

Information on club nights and parties can be found in the *Washington City Paper* and the *Washington Post*'s 'Night Watch' column in Friday's 'Weekend' section. Natural-born scruffs should note that some of the DC scene operates a dress code: think smart. Access to upscale joints will be denied those wearing jeans, sneakers or hats. The legal drinking age in the US is 21 and it is strictly enforced in DC. Though many clubs will let under-21s in, they can't buy booze, so it's a good idea to carry ID.

CLUBS & LOUNGES

Bravo! Bravo!
1001 Connecticut Avenue, NW, between K & L Streets, Downtown (1-202 223 5330, www. bravobravodc.com). Farragut North Metro. **Open** 11am-9pm Mon, Tue, Thur; 11am-3am Wed, Fri, Sat. **Admission** $10-$15. **Credit** AmEx, DC, Disc, MC, V. **Map** p252 G5.
For over ten years this unassuming nightclub three blocks from the White House has been attracting upwards of 400 polished dancers on Wednesday and Saturday (Latin) and Friday (world music) nights,

with salsa and bachata lessons on Wednesdays too. The mood is flirty; the music is a combination of Spanish-language club hits and up-tempo remixes. This is one of the few 18-and-over dance nights in the city. Lighting is harsh and security tight.

Bukom Café
2442 18th Street, NW, between Belmont & Columbia Roads, Adams Morgan (1-202 265 4600, www.bukom.com). Dupont Circle then 42 bus. **Open** 4pm-2am Mon-Thur; 4pm-3am Fri, Sat. **Admission** free. **Credit** AmEx, Disc, MC, V. **Map** p250 G3.
The crowd is West African and African-American but everyone's welcome to get lost in the sway. The Ghanaian menu is reason alone to visit, but arrive after 10pm and it's standing room only: be prepared to dance with whoever's next to you. Nightly bands play reggae, soca and funk.

Chi-Cha Lounge
1624 U Street, NW, between 16th & 17th Streets (1-202 234 8400). Dupont Circle or U Street/African-American Civil War Memorial/Cardozo Metro. **Open** 5.30pm-1.30am Mon-Thur, Sun; 5.30pm-2.30am Fri, Sat. **Admission** usually free. **Map** p250 H3.
Ecuadorean entrepreneur Mauricio Fraga-Rosenfeld has taught DC to relax to a Latin beat. Since opening Chi-Cha, he's expanded to Dupont Circle (Gazuza), Georgetown (Mate) and Arlington (Gua-Rapo). All follow the same formula: deep velvet couches, candlelight, Andean tapas, sangría, Latin jazz and hookah pipes filled with honey-cured tobacco. Chi-Cha hosts live bands from Sunday to Thursday; on these nights there's a $15 minimum consumption fee. No hats, ties or sportswear. That's right, no ties.

Eighteenth Street Lounge

*1212 18th Street, NW, between M Street &
Jefferson Place, Dupont Circle (1-202 466 3922,
www.eighteenthstreetlounge.com). Farragut North
or Dupont Circle Metro.* **Open** 5.30pm-2am Tue-
Thur; 5.30pm-2.30am Thur, Fri; 9.30pm-2.30am
Sat. **Admission** $5-$10. **Credit** AmEx, MC, V.
Map p250 G5.

Love it or hate it, ESL remains the city's trendiest
and most exclusive lounge, widely renowned (or
notorious) for its strict door policy. Should your
attire (or your connections) please the notoriously
fickle doormen and you're granted entrance through
the unmarked wooden door, you'll find hipsters mingling and dancing to live jazz or down-tempo electronic music spun by the city's best DJs.

Fly Lounge

*1802 Jefferson Place, NW, at 18th Street,
Dupont Circle (1-202 828 4433,
www.theflylounge.com/dc). Farragut North or
Dupont Circle Metro.* **Open** 5.30pm-2am
Tue-Thur; 10pm-3am Fri-Sat 10pm-2am Sun.
Admission free most nights, but reservations
up to $100 on weekends. **Credit** AmEx, MC, V.
This underground club has been designed to resem-
ble a jetliner's fuselage. Stainless steel tables simu-
late jet engines, with built-in ice buckets modeled on
F-15 Eagle afterburners. One of the club's owners is
Chuck Koch, aka local DJ Dirty Hands, and hip hop
and house music dominate the playlist. Capacity is
only 140 people, so lines can be long at weekends.

Fur

*33 Patterson Street, NE, at North Capitol Street,
Northeast (1-202 542 3401, www.furnightclub.
com). New York-Florida Avenue/Gallaudet U
Metro.* **Open** 8pm-2am Thur; 9pm-3am Fri, Sat.
Admission $10-$25. **Credit** AmEx, Disc, MC, V.
Map p253 K5.

Dress up and wait in line at the city's latest super-
club. What makes Fur different from DC's other
multi-level venues? All boast chic interiors, VIP
rooms, leading names and vast dance spaces. But
what sets Fur apart is its intimate lounges, which
provide a haven from the audio-visual show pulsat-
ing from the dancefloors. They have louche names
like the Mafia Room and the Mink Room. Theme
nights are frequent so check the website in advance.

Heaven & Hell

*2327 18th Street, NW, at Kalorama Road, Adams
Morgan (1-202 667 4355). Dupont Circle Metro
then 42 bus.* **Open** 7.30pm-2am Mon-Thur, Sun;
7pm-3am Fri, Sat. **Admission** $5 (includes 1 drink).
Credit AmEx, DC, Disc, MC, V. **Map** p250 G3.
If the 1980s were your idea of heaven, then head here
on Thursday nights for the best party in town. After
getting your glow-in-the-dark halo at the door, head
up to Heaven and immerse yourself in retro land. If
you're looking for a young singles meat market and
a trite but fun theme night, this is the place to be.

Love

*1350 Okie Street, NE, at New York Avenue,
Northeast (1-202 636 9030, www.welcometo
dream.com).* **Open** 9pm-3am Thur-Sat.
Admission $10-$40. **Credit** AmEx, MC, V.
Love is still one of the hottest dance clubs in town,
but it's a nightmare to reach (best to drive or take a
cab, as there's no Metro nearby and the area can be
dangerous). A refurbished four-storey warehouse in
an industrial neighborhood off New York Avenue,
the club is an evening's commitment. But dress to
impress and it's worth it. Inside are myriad bars,
rooms pumping hip hop, world music, salsa, house
and trance. Catch live shows Friday nights from the
likes of DMX and Busta Rhymes. At the time of writing rumor had it that Love might not be long for this
world, so check before visiting.

ARTS & ENTERTAINMENT

Patty Boom Boom. *See p196.*

Mie N Yu

3125 M Street, NW, between 31st Street &
Wisconsin Avenue, Georgetown (1-202 333 6122,
www.mienyu.com). Foggy Bottom-GWU Metro
then 31, 34, 36, 38B, Circulator bus. **Open**
5-10pm Mon-Thur; 4pm-2.30am Fri; 11am-2.30am
Sat; 11am-10pm Sun. **Admission** free. **Credit**
AmEx, DC, Disc, MC, V. **Map** p249 E5.
If you have the patience and the cash, a trip down
the Silk Road can be a kick. Launched as a restaurant, the bar culture all but takes over after 11pm at
weekends. Skip the fussy food and camp out in any
of the overdressed oriental theme areas. The fun here
lies in the people-watching.

Modern

3287 M Street, NW, between 33rd & Potomac
Streets, Georgetown (1-202 338 7027, www.
modern-dc.com). Foggy Bottom-GWU Metro then
31, 34, 36, Circulator bus. **Open** 9pm-2am Thur;
9pm-3am Fri, Sat. **Admission** varies. **Credit**
AmEx, MC, V. **Map** p249 E5.
Another of John Boyle's successes (Five, Mie N Yu),
this lounge is popular with young Georgetown. Of
the places to chill out, the favorite has to be the ring
of leather cubes around the sunken bar. Order into
the well and the bartenders hand up your bevs. The
hanging bubble chair is the best seat in the house.

Patty Boom Boom

1359 U Street, NW, at 14th Street, U Street
(1-202 629 1712, www.pattyboomboomdc.com).
U Street/African-American Civil War
Memorial/Cardozo Metro. **Open** noon-2am Mon-
Thur, Sun; noon-3am Fri, Sat. **Admission** free.
Credit AmEx, MC, V. **Map** p250 H3.
The latest outpost of the Eighteenth-Street Lounge/
Thievery Corporation empire is dedicated to two
Jamaican products: patties (spiced meat or veggies
in pastry) and reggae. Live bands perform at this
laid-back venue, but DJs dominate; they pump roots,
rock steady, dub and dancehall through a 21-speaker
sound system that doesn't stint on the bass. The food
and music draw a Jamaican clientele. The place
opens for lunch; the music starts at 9pm. *Photo p195.*

Pure

1326 U Street, NW, between 13th & 14th Streets,
U Street/14th Street Corridor (1-202 290
7058, www.pur. loungevip.com). U Street/
African-American Civil War Memorial/
Cardozo Metro. **Open** 7pm-2am Mon; 8pm-2am
Tue-Thur; 6pm-3am Fri; 9pm-3am Sat.
Admission free, except for special events.
Credit AmEx, DC, MC, V. **Map** p250 H3.
Formerly the Bar Nun, this place now has a sleek,
space-age look. The two levels feature different DJs,
with music that ranges from hip hop, house and soul
to soca, Afropop and reggae. The venue draws a
diverse clientele. There are open-mic sessions on
Mondays; salsa lessons on Wednesdays.

U Street Music Hall

1115 U Street, NW, between 11th & 12th Streets,
U Street (1-202 588 1880, www.streetmusichall.
com). U Street/African-American Civil War
Memorial/Cardozo Metro. **Open** 10pm-2am
Mon-Thur, Sun; 10pm-3am Fri, Sat. **Admission**
free-$10. **Credit** AmEx, MC, V. **Map** p250 J3.
This bare-bones basement club, which emphasizes
music over luxury, arrived just in time for the economic downturn. The vibe is closer to a rock club
than a 'bottle service' lounge, and rock bands perform live. But the club's founders, local DJs Will
Eastman and Jesse Tittsworth, built the room for
dancing: the 1,200sq ft hardwood dancefloor floats
on a cork foundation, and the 20,000-watt sound system is modeled on those in top London clubs. Recent
guest DJs include Simian Mobile Disco, Tensnake
and Richie Hawtin. Ages 18 and over.

Ultrabar

911 F Street, NW, between 9th & 10th Streets,
Downtown (1-202 638 4663, www.ultrabardc.com).
Gallery Place-Chinatown or Metro Center
Metro. **Open** 10pm-2am Thur-Sat; 10pm-3am
Sun. **Admission** $10-$15; sometimes free by
signing up via the website. **Credit** AmEx,
MC, V. **Map** p253 J6.
The last club standing on what a decade ago was a
bustling late-night block, Ultrabar is an upscale,
four-level venue in a former bank building. The management promises 'a slice of Miami', with different
styles of dance music on each level, and Persian/
Arabic sounds on Saturdays. Seats at tables require
bottle service ($100 and up), and a 'dress to impress'
code is enforced. Ages 18 and over only.

Zengo

781 7th Street, NW, at H Street, Downtown
(1-202 393 2929). Chinatown/Gallery Place Metro.
Open 5-10pm Mon-Thur, Sun; 5pm-12.30am Fri,
Sat. **Admission** free. **Credit** AmEx, MC, V.
Map p253 J5.
One of the few DC hot spots where the pricey cocktails are actually worth the money (try the Mojito De
Mango), Zengo's drinks, vibrant atmosphere and
food from renowned chef Richard Sandoval make it
a favourite among the trendy crowd. The one draw-
back to this sleek Latin-Asian lounge is that it closes
early – 12.30am – even at weekends.

COMEDY & CABARET

Improv

1140 Connecticut Avenue, NW, between L & M
Streets, Downtown (1-202 296 7008/www.dc
improv.com). Farragut North Metro. **Open** *Shows*
8.30pm Tue-Thur; 8pm, 10.30pm Fri, Sat; 8pm
Sun. **Admission** $15-$35. **Credit** AmEx, MC, V.
Map p252 G5.
The most common assessment of Improv is that the
service is disappointing but the material hysterical.

Sport & Fitness

Get out and play – or watch the professionals.

There's one big-news item in the world of Washington sports: the city has a brand-new ballpark, home to its major league baseball team, the Washington Nationals. But this city isn't all about baseball, of course, not with the Washington Redskins on the football field and the Wizards on the basketball court, both teams with great track records and devoted fans.

Away from professional sports and big stadiums, the superb natural resources surrounding the city provide a perfect environment for outdoor activities. Some of the Washington area's most famous city sights and beautiful rural spots can best be seen while rollerblading, biking, boating – or even on a Segway. Or check out the National Mall or Rock Creek Park in the spring and summer for pick-up games. So grab a baseball glove, kayak or football, and go out and play.

Participation Sports

BOATING & FISHING

In March and April, when the cherry blossoms are in peak bloom, a popular way to see the sights is on a peddleboat on the calm Tidal Basin. **Tidal Basin Peddle Boats** (1501 Maine Avenue, SW, 1-202 479 2426, www.tidalbasinpeddleboats.com) rents out peddleboats from mid March to mid October. It's $12 an hour for a two-seater and $19 for a four-seater.

Annapolis (*see p218*), about a 45-minute drive from DC, is on the Chesapeake Bay, the largest estuary in the US. **South River Boat Rentals** (Sunset Drive, Edgewater, MD, 1-410 956 9729, www.annapolisboatrental.com) rents out sailing boats and power boats for a day on the bay. **J World Annapolis** (213 Eastern Avenue, 1-410 280 2040, www.jworldannapolis.com) and the **Annapolis Sailing School** (7001 Bembe Beach Road, 1-800 638 9192, www.annapolissailing.com) both offer sailing classes.

Annapolis is also a great place to go sea-fishing. **Rod & Reel Charters** (4160 Mears Avenue, Chesapeake Beach, 1-301 855 8450, www.rodnreelinc.com, www.cbresort spa.com) is among several companies that offer fishing excursions for groups in the spring, summer and autumn. It's best to call several days in advance in order to be sure of reserving yourself a spot. Below are companies hiring boats in DC and the immediate area.

Fletcher's Boat House

4940 Canal Road, NW, at Reservoir Road, Upper Northwest (1-202 244 0461, www.fletchersboathouse.com). **Open** *early Mar-Nov* 7am-5pm daily (boats returned by 6pm). **No credit cards. Map** p248 B3.
Fletcher's rents out boats, canoes, bicycles and fishing equipment, and is convenient for the Potomac River and the C&O Canal.

Jack's Boathouse

3500 K Street, NW, under Francis Scott Key Bridge, Georgetown (1-202 337 9642, www.jacksboathouse.com). Rosslyn Metro. **Open** noon-5pm Mon-Fri; 8am-5pm Sat, Sun (boats returned by 6pm). **Credit** MC, V. **Map** p249 E5.
Canoes, kayaks and tandem kayaks are hired for $12 per person per hour (children aged 6-12 pay $6 per hour). Maximum three hours on river.

Thompson Boat Center

2900 Virginia Avenue, NW, at Rock Creek Parkway, Foggy Bottom (1-202 333 9543, www.thompsonboatcenter.com). Foggy Bottom-GWU Metro. **Open** *Mar-Oct* 8am-5pm daily (boats returned by 6pm). **Credit** MC, V. **Map** p252 H7.

Canoes and kayaks for rent from spring to autumn, and cycle hire available until mid November. Rowing lessons are available elsewhere too, from early May until late September.

Washington Sailing Marina
1 Marina Drive, off George Washington Memorial Parkway, Alexandria, VA (1-703 548 9027, www. washingtonsailingmarina.com). **Open** *Summer* 9am-6pm daily. *Winter* 10am-5pm daily. **Credit** MC, V.
This outfit hires out two types of sailboats: the smaller Aquafin, which comfortably accommodates two people ($15 per hour or $40 for three hours) and the 19ft Flying Scot, which costs $23 per hour (minimum two hours, maximum five people). You must be certified or pass a written test to hire.

CYCLING

Paved bicycle trails abound in Washington. They're easy to spot, being marked clearly with a green sign that has a picture of a bike on it. But for rougher terrain you'll have to leave the city environs. Check out Scott Adams's *Washington Mountain Bike Book* – available at local bicycle shops. Trail maps and on-street bike route maps can be found at bike shops. Also, the **Washington Area Bicyclist Association** (1803 Connecticut Avenue, NW, 1-202 518 0524, www.waba.org) has an informative website with maps and other resources for cycling enthusiasts. Metro riders note that you can take your bicycle on the trains only during off-peak hours – between 10am and 2pm and after 7pm during the week, and all day at weekends and holidays. Below are a list of popular cycling trails.

C&O Canal Towpath
A 184-mile gravel path that starts at the corner of the Pennsylvania Avenue, NW, ramp of the Rock Creek Parkway (which is near the Foggy Bottom Metro stop) and finally ends up in Cumberland, Maryland. For a popular biking trip, take the trail 19.9 miles to Great Falls Park in Virginia.

Capital Crescent Trail
This trail makes its way from the Thompson Boat Center on the Potomac River in Georgetown all the way up to Silver Spring in Maryland. The 11-mile trail also links with the Mount Vernon Trail (*see below*). The paved part of the trail terminates in Bethesda, Maryland, but more advanced cyclists can take the crushed stone Georgetown Branch Trail to Silver Spring.

Mount Vernon Trail
An asphalt trail that takes riders along the Potomac River. It starts out on Theodore Roosevelt Island in Rosslyn, Virginia (near the Rosslyn Metro stop), and travels 18.5 miles through Old Town Alexandria, ultimately terminating, as the name suggests, at George Washington's historic home.

Rentals & tours

Big Wheel Bikes
1034 33rd Street, NW, at Cady's Alley, Georgetown (1-202 337 0254, www.bigwheel bikes.com). Bus 38B. **Open** 11am-7pm Tue-Fri; 10am-6pm Sat, Sun. **Credit** AmEx, MC, V. **Map** p249 E5.
A basic bicycle is $5 an hour or $25 a day (the minimum rental time is three hours). A range of different models is available.
Other locations 3119 Lee Highway, Arlington, VA (1-703 522 1110); 6917 Arlington Road, Bethesda, MD (1-301 652 0192); 2 Prince Street, Alexandria, VA (1-703 739 2300).

Bike & Roll
Tour starts at the Old Post Office Pavillion, 1100 Pennsylvania Avenue, NW, Downtown (1-202 842 2453, www.bikethesites.com). Federal Triangle Metro. **Open** 9am-6pm Mon-Sat; 9.30am-6pm Sun. **Rates** phone for details. **Credit** AmEx, MC, V. **Map** p252 H7. .

See Washington on two wheels. Tours are typically three or four hours and from four to eight miles, usually costing $40 for adults and $30 for children, including bike and helmet hire.
Other locations Union Station, 50 Massachussetts Avenue, NE (1-202 962 0206); 1 Wales Alley, Alexandria, VA (1-703 548 7655).

GOLF

There are three public golf courses in the area. Golf equipment can be hired at the clubs, which are all open from dawn to dusk daily.

Langston Golf Course
2600 Benning Road, NE, at 26th Street (1-202 397 8638, www.golfdc.com). **Rates** (including cart hire) *9 holes* $20-$25; *18 holes* $30-$35.

East Potomac Golf Course
972 Ohio Drive, SW, between 15th Street & I-395 (1-202 554 7660, www.golfdc.com). **Rates** *9 holes* $10-$21; *18 holes* $27-$31. **Cart hire** *9 holes* $9; *18 holes* $14.

Rock Creek Golf Course
1600 Rittenhouse Street, NW, at 16th Street, Upper Northwest (1-202 882 7332, www. golfdc.com). **Rates** *9 holes* $16-$21; *18 holes* $21-$28. **Cart hire** *9 holes* $9; *18 holes* $14.

GYMS

Many hotels have fitness centres; *see p94-110.*

Gold's Gym
409 3rd Street, SW, between D & E Streets, Southwest (1-202 554 4653, www.goldsgym.com). Federal Center SW Metro. **Open** 5am-11pm Mon-Thur; 5am-10pm Fri; 8am-8pm Sat; 9am-6pm Sun. Introductory 1wk complimentary pass available. **Credit** AmEx, Disc, MC, V. **Map** p253 J7. Gold's has branches throughout DC and its suburbs; this location offers classes. Call ahead to register.

National Capital YMCA
1711 Rhode Island Avenue, NW, at 17th Street, Dupont Circle (1-202 862 9622, www.ymca nationalcapital.org). Farragut North Metro. **Open** 5.30am-10.30pm Mon-Fri; 8am-6.30pm Sat; 9am-5.30pm Sun. **Rates** YMCA members $10 per day. Non-members admittance only with a free 1wk 'good neighbor' pass downloadable from www.ymcadc.org. **Credit** MC, V. **Map** p250 G5.
Good equipment, a pool and fitness classes.

Washington Sports Clubs
1835 Connecticut Avenue, NW, at Florida Avenue, Dupont Circle (1-202 332 0100, www.mysportsclubs.com). Dupont Circle Metro.
Open 5.30am-11pm Mon-Thur; 5.30am-10pm Fri; 7am-8.30pm Sat, Sun. **Rates** phone for details. **Credit** AmEx, MC, V.
Popular with locals, this sports club offers classes, machines, weights and squash courts.

HIKING

Virginia and Maryland's sumptuous scenery makes for popular hiking territory, and the District has its own expanse of green in Rock Creek Park (which stretches into Maryland). A few well-known trails are listed below, but see www.trails.com or *60 Hikes Within 60 Miles: Washington, DC* by Paul Elliott for more.

Appalachian Trail
www.patc.net.
The AT, as it is known, stretches 2,168 miles from Georgia to Maine, making it a biy long for a day trip. But there are lots of shorter walks that take you along parts of the trail in Virginia and Maryland.

Catoctin Mountain Park
www.nps.gov/cato.
Tucked away in Thurmont, Maryland, the park has 25 miles of trails with scenic mountain views. Check out the 78-ft plummet at Cunningham Falls.

Rock Creek Park
www.nps.gov/rocr.
A good starting point for the park's 25 miles of trails is the seven-mile hike from the Meadowside Nature Center (5100 Meadowside Lane, Rockville, MD, 1-301 258 4030). You can also pick up trails at Lake Needwood (15700 Needwood Lake Circle, Rockville, MD, 1-301 924 4141) or on Beach Drive.

SKATING

For ice skaters, parks and area town centres often set up ice rinks in the winter months, usually from late October through to March. In DC, the popular rink with added scenic value is in the sculpture garden at the **National Gallery of Art** (*see p47*).

While many of the bike paths listed above are fair game also for in-line skaters, they're often too narrow and crowded. As an alternative, try Beach Drive, north of Blagden Road in Rock Creek Park, on weekends when it's closed to traffic. Visit www.skatedc.org for more information on where to roller skate.

PICK-UP GAMES

Evenings and weekends, Washingtonians of all ages enjoy playing in amateur sports teams and in pick-up games – impromptu events where anyone is welcome. The Mall is the most popular location but the Ellipse, south of the

White House, and the fields around the Lincoln Memorial are also hotspots. Track the games via the following websites:
basketball: http://infinitehoops.com
soccer: www.acromedia.com/soccer/pickup.html
hockey: www.pickuphockey.net
ultimate frisbee: http://sports.groups.yahoo.com/group/DCPickup/ultimate.

For listings of local clubs and events get a copy of *MetroSports Magazine* (free in street boxes, or see www.metrosportsdc.com).

SEGWAY TOURS

Segway Human Transporters are like self-balancing scooters that automatically respond to your body's movements. Try out one on a Segway tour of DC. City Segway Tours (624 9th Street, NW, at G Street, 1-877 734 8687, www.citysegwaytours.com/washington-dc) offers three-hour, day and night tours. They can be booked in advance online or by phone.

SWIMMING

Cooling off on a hot day in DC is easy – there are nearly three dozen indoor public swimming pools in the area, as well as public outdoor pools. Outdoor pools are usually open from Memorial Day (late May) to Labor Day (early September). The best are the **Capitol East Natatorium** (635 North Carolina Avenue, SE, 1-202 724 4495) and **Francis Pool** (25th & N Streets, NW, 1-202 727 3285). For more options, check out the government listings (blue-edged) in the Yellow Pages under 'District of Columbia, Parks and Recreation'. Some local gyms have pools that are open to the public for a fee.

TENNIS

Aside from these public facilities, check out parks and schools for outdoor-only courts. It's first come, first served, so be prepared to wait for a spot and cut your playing time to 30 minutes to an hour if others are in line.

East Potomac Tennis Center

1090 Ohio Drive, SW, at Buckeye Drive, Southwest (1-202 554 5962, www.eastpotomactennis.com). Smithsonian Metro then 20min walk. **Open** 7am-10pm daily. **Rates** check website for revised rates. **Credit** MC, V. **Map** p284 H8.
A public facility at Hains Point that has 24 courts, including ten clay and 14 hard. There's also a pro shop and you can call in advance to set up a lesson.

Rock Creek Tennis Center

16th & Kennedy Streets, NW, Upper Northwest (1-202 722 5949, www.rockcreektennis.com). Bus S1, S2, S3, S4, S5. **Open** 7am-11pm Mon-Thur;

7am-8pm Fri-Sun. **Rates** (for up to 4hrs, court 9) $28-$38 Mon-Fri; $38 Sat, Sun. **Credit** MC, V.
The club has 25 outdoor courts, five of which can be covered. Racquets and a ball machine are for hire.

Spectator Sports

Tickets for nearly all professional sporting events in Washington are sold by **Ticketmaster** (1-301 808 4300, www.ticketmaster.com). There is a service charge for all ticket purchases.

BASEBALL

Washington Nationals

Nationals Park, 1500 South Capitol Street, SE (1-202 640 7000, www.washington.nationals.mlb.com). Navy Yard Metro. **Tickets** vary. **Map** p253 K9.
See right **Hitting in the Major League**.

BASKETBALL

Both men's and women's basketball are popular in DC. The **Washington Wizards** of the NBA made it to the playoffs in 2005 and 2006, and the women's **Washington Mystics**, with stars like Alana Beard in their line-up, made it to the 2009 season playoffs. Tickets are usually relatively easy to get hold of and cost $10-$775 for the Wizards, or as little as $5 for the Mystics. The men play from November to May, the women from May to September.

Verizon Center

601 F Street, NW, at 7th Street, Downtown (1-202 628 3200, www.mcicenter.com). Gallery Place-Chinatown Metro. **Map** p253 J6.
This multi-use arena cost $200 million to build and seats nearly 20,000 fans.

FOOTBALL

Three-time Super Bowl winners the **Washington Redskins** play in Landover, Maryland at FedEx Field. All tickets at FedEx Field are season tickets, so you can't just walk up, buy tickets and watch a game – there's a decades-long waiting list. If you're keen to see a match, try the Ticketmaster website (*see p161*). There are tickets for sale direct from season-ticket holders on its NFL Ticket Exchange facility. Alternatively, try Craigslist.org or eBay.

If you travel to Baltimore, you have a better chance of seeing some American football action. The **Baltimore Ravens'** season tickets go on sale in August. Phone 1-410 261 7283 or check www.baltimoreravens.com for information. The football season runs from August to January.

ICE HOCKEY

American ice hockey is now well and truly back in the picture as one of the big four North American spectator sports after the catastrophic National Hockey League strike that canceled the entire season back in 2004-5. The **Washington Capitals** have had award-winning attendances at their games but it should be possible to obtain tickets at short notice, though early booking keeps the price down. Tickets cost $25-$355. Phone or check the website of the Verizon Center (*see p72*) for match information. Tickets are available from Ticketmaster (*see p161*).

SOCCER

Washington's **DC United** have proved themselves as a talented squad, refreshed by new arrivals such as Joseph Ngwenya.

RFK Stadium

22nd & East Capitol Street, NE, Northeast (office 1-202 547 9077, DC United office 1-202 587 500, www.dcsec.com). Stadium-Armory Metro. **Open** 8.30am-5.30pm Mon-Fri. **Tickets** vary. **Credit** MC, V.

Tickets are available from DC United (1-202 587 5000, www.dcunited.com) or through the ubiquitous services of Ticketmaster (*see left*).

Hitting in the Major League

Everyone loves the new ballpark, but not the Nationals' recent record.

Washington has a new, all-American landmark. Dominating the previously neglected Southeast waterfront and adjacent to Navy Yard, **Nationals Park** is an exuberantly modern take on a ballpark, in steel, glass and pre-cast concrete. Inside, there's state-of-the-art video and audio, including a 4,500 square foot high-definition scoreboard, as well as over 600 feet of LED ribbon board. Some seats have stunning views of the riverfront or city landmarks.

Seating over 41,000 and with around 3,5000 pieces of steel in its bowl structure, the stadium cost $611 million dollars to build and opened in March 2008, just in time for the 2008 season.

Since then, however, things have not quite gone to plan. Despite the presence of a shiny new stadium, the Nationals will find it hard to engage the fans if they continue to field teams like the 2010 iteration. During the season, almost everything that could have gone wrong went wrong: at the team's home opener against Philadelphia, the locals were outnumbered by fans of the rival Phillies; following a phenomenal start to his major-league career, young pitcher Stephen Strasburg tore an elbow ligament and was ruled out of action until 2012; and as the season progressed, crowds began to fall to sometimes embarrassing levels. Desperate to impress, the team signed Phillies outfielder Jayson Werth to a massive seven-year contract before the 2011 season. But in a competitive division, the immediate future of the Nationals looks less than bright.

Tickets can be bought on the website (*see left*), and stadium tours are also available.

ARTS & ENTERTAINMENT

Theater

It's all about the drama.

Like any theater town worth its greasepaint, Washington can point to posh troupes with a roster of distinguished directors as well as scrappy little outfits that get by on foundation grants and volunteer sweat. The stage scene here is in a state of rude health – it's the second healthiest after New York, if you believe the Helen Hayes Awards Society, which hands out the local equivalent of the UK's Oliviers or New York's Tonys. And while the museums and monuments still draw the biggest swarms of out-of-town visitors, locals have for the past few years been seeing a newer species of seasonal migrant: the theatrical tourist.

Glittering, glass-fronted new halls for the **Shakespeare Theatre Company** and **Arena Stage** represent both fresh landmarks on the map of a classical-theater mecca and new challenges for the companies that inhabit them. And the **Kennedy Center** – that cultural Bigfoot on the Potomac – sent musical-theater geeks rushing to book airline tickets when it announced a lavish 2011 revival of Stephen Sondheim's *Follies,* starring Bernadette Peters, Elaine Paige and Linda Lavin.

The biggest players are hardly the only ambitious outfits, though. The **Signature Theatre** took home a regional Tony Award in 2009 – despite making a place for itself in the famous-flop annals a year earlier by sending the would-be teen-musical sensation *Glory Days* to Broadway for a one-night-only run. (Wags immediately dubbed it *Glory Day.*) On Capitol Hill, the **Folger Theatre** plays host to Shakespearean oddities (a stirring *Henry VIII* in 2010), star performers (Lynn Redgrave performed her solo show *Rachel and Juliet* there barely a year before her death), and the occasional adventurous première (including, memorably, a thrilling modern-day rework of *The Winter's Tale* from dramatist Craig Wright).

About the author

Trey Graham is an arts editor at NPR and a theater critic for the Washington City Paper. He won the George Jean Nathan Award for drama criticism in 2004.

A tiny, ambitious bunch of Irish-oriented contemporary-theater specialists calling themselves **Solas Nua** have dazzled DC over the last half-decade by introducing the town to a motley chorus of modern voices, including Mark O'Rowe, Enda Walsh and Rosemary Jenkinson. And, back in 2006, two transplanted veterans of the Philadelphia Fringe asked why there was no equivalent of that festival in the nation's capital. Hey presto: the inaugural **Capital Fringe** sold 17,000 tickets to 400-plus performances by 96 acts – from a 'ukulele operetta' to a play about drowned French prostitutes, staged in a municipal swimming pool. Five years later, Capital Fringe (www.capfringe.org) has become a bona fide tent-pole on the DC performingarts calendar. Now billed as the second-largest unjuried fringe fest in the United States, it runs for 17 days, and in 2010 moved 28,000 tickets to 715 performances of 137 productions – featuring more than 2,000 artists from Washington and well beyond.

LISTINGS AND INFORMATION

For comprehensive information on dates, times and venues, check the *Washington City Paper* (www.washingtoncitypaper.com), the *Washington Post* (www.washington post.com), or the Helen Hayes Awards site (www.helenhayes.org). And for lively discussions of the local theatrical landscape, browse http://DCTheatreScene.com. For serendipitous discoveries, look for fliers in coffeehouses, theatres and bookshops.

MAJOR VENUES

Arena Stage

1101 6th Street, SW, at Maine Avenue,
Southwest (1-202 488 3300, www.arena
stage.com). Waterfront-SEU Metro. **Box**
office 10am 8pm Mon-Sat; noon-8pm Sun.
Tickets $30-$85. **Credit** AmEx, Disc, MC, V.
The city's theatrical grande dame and a pioneer in
the American resident theater movement, Arena
may be emerging from more than a decade of torpor.
Blessed (and cursed) with an affluent establishment
audience, artistic director Molly Smith has disappointed some critics by programing unchallenging
audience-pleasers. But there have been a few bold
ventures nonetheless: an epic trilogy of one-acts
(Sarah Ruhl's vividly imagined *Passion Play*) and the
archival excavation of a protofeminist rarity
(*Intimations for Saxophone,* from *Machinal* author
Sophie Treadwell) are just two. A two-season exile,
with shows in a suburban Virginia basement and
the echoing expanses of the U Street Corridor's landmark Lincoln Theatre, made the company's work
feel more uneven still, but Broadway transfers for
the musicals *33 Variations* and *Next to Normal* have
burnished Arena's reputation recently, and a triumphant homecoming to a glamorously rehabbed
facility, complete with a lovely 200-seat new-play
incubator space, has hopes high.
▶ *For more on the new theater building, see p206*
Crystal Palaces.

Kennedy Center

2700 F Street, NW, at New Hampshire Avenue
& Rock Creek Parkway, Foggy Bottom (1-800 444
1324, 1-202 467 4600, www.kennedy-center.org).
Foggy Bottom-GWU Metro then free shuttle
9.45am-midnight Mon-Fri; 10am-midnight
Sat; noon-midnight Sun. **Box office** 10am-9pm
Mon-Sat; noon-9pm Sun. **Tickets** $25-$150.
Credit AmEx, DC, MC, V. **Map** p252 F6.
As part of its broad-spectrum programming, the
national cultural center puts on a full theater season
each year. It's tilted toward imports and tours – not
since the 1980s has the house had a resident company – but now and again the imports are remarkable. (Dublin's Gate Theatre brought its celebrated
Waiting for Godot; Declan Donnellan staged *Twelfth
Night* and *Three Sisters,* both in Russian, for a 2010
Chekhov festival; an Edinburgh Fringe sampler
brought BLOOLIPS' Bette Bourne to DC with *A Life
in Three Acts.*) Home-grown productions are picking
up too: a full-throated *Ragtime* revival transferred
to Broadway in 2009, and the handsome Kennedy
Center Family Theater space hosts originals and
adaptations by the likes of movie star Whoopi
Goldberg and Japanese-American dramatist Naomi
Iizuka. And with ex-Covent Garden guru Michael
Kaiser at the helm, the center has sponsored a series
of ambitious festivals celebrating artists from
Shakespeare to Sondheim.

National Theatre

1321 Pennsylvania Avenue, NW, between 13th
& 14th Streets, The Federal Triangle (1-202
628 6161, www.nationaltheatre.org). Metro
Center or Federal Triangle Metro. **Box office**
When show is playing 10am-9pm Mon-Sat. *In*
weeks preceding show 10am-6pm Mon-Sat; noon-
6pm Sun. **Tickets** $15-$75. **Credit** AmEx, DC,
Disc, MC, V. **Map** p252 H6.
One of the city's oldest theatres (it dates from 1835),
the National has a history as a Broadway tryout
house – productions have included the flamingly
awful jukebox musical *Hot Feet,* which went on to
an ignoble 97 New York performances in 2006. But

Arena Stage.

in recent decades it has been home mostly to touring fluff – when it doesn't sit empty, that is. The high point in a disgracefully long spell of mediocrities was the tour of *Doubt* with the magnificent Cherry Jones, but that was back in 2007.

★ Shakespeare Theatre Company

450 7th Street, NW, between D & E Streets, Penn Quarter (1-202 547 1122, www.shakespeare theatre.org). Gallery Place-Chinatown Metro. **Box office** *Performance days* 10am-6pm Mon; 10am-6.30pm Tue-Sat; noon-6.30pm Sun. *Non-performance days* 10am-6pm Mon-Sat; noon-6pm Sun. **Tickets** $12-$120. **Credit** AmEx, Disc, MC, V. **Map** p253 J6.

Led for 25 years by noted director Michael Kahn and hailed by the *Economist* as 'one of the world's three great Shakespearean theatres', the Shakespeare Theatre is unquestionably the top classical company in the US – and now it's added an $85 million second house to its portfolio, the better to produce plays in rep and host visiting troupes. (Helen Mirren's *Phèdre*, the Tricycle Theatre's *The Great Game: Afghanistan* and National Theatre of Scotland's *Black Watch* have all played at the company's sleek new Sidney Harman Hall.) The STC stages its own season of major works, of course, serving up not just intelligent, inventive Bardolatry (its go-go-booted 1960s update of *Love's Labour's Lost* was a guest at the RSC's complete-works marathon in August 2006), but classics from the likes of Ben Jonson (an uproarious *Silent Woman*), Eugene O'Neill (a titanic *Mourning Becomes Electra*) and Aeschylus (a shattering new translation of *The Persians*). The company also makes a speciality of Tennessee Williams and Oscar Wilde, while experimenting with rarities by the likes of Alfred de Musset (a lusty *Lorenzaccio*) and Pierre Corneille (a fleet 2010 update of the 400-year-old comedy *The Liar,* courtesy of David Ives) – which is why it regularly attracts big-name directors (Chicago's Mary Zimmerman, Australian Gale Edwards, rising American light Ethan McSweeny, who launched his career here) and actors (Keith Baxter, Kelly McGillis, Marsha Mason, Hal Holbrook). It's even made a foray into musical theater recently, teaming up with Chicago's Goodman Theatre to co-produce a 2010 *Candide* that positively glittered.

▶ *For more on the new theater building, see p206* **Crystal Palaces**.

Studio Theatre

1501 14th Street, NW, at P Street, Shaw: Logan Circle (332 3300, www.studiotheatre.org). Dupont Circle or U Street/African-American Civil War Memorial/Cardozo Metro. **Box office** *Performance days* 10am-6pm Mon, Tue; 10am-9pm Wed-Sat; noon-8pm Sun. *Non-performance days* 10am-6pm Mon-Fri. **Tickets** $35-$75. **Credit** AmEx, Disc, MC, V. **Map** p250 H4.

INSIDE TRACK CHEAP TICKETS

Try **Ticketplace** (1-202 638 2406, www.ticketplace.org), at 407 Seventh Street, NW, for last-minute half-price tickets; check theatre-company websites for all kinds of cheap-seat offers, from rush tickets to hefty under-35 discounts.

Slick productions, smart directors and substantial plays (occasional cerebral musicals, too) make the Studio Theatre a serious player on the capital city's dramatic scene. In the Bush era, it was home to the first DC production of the docudrama *Guantanamo* (then-Defense Secretary Donald Rumsfeld didn't attend); a chamber-sized *Caroline, or Change* (the brooding, bittersweet Tony Kushner/Jeanine Tesori musical) was a 2006 highlight; bright young playwriting lights from Tarell Alvin McCraney to Annie Baker have been introduced to DC audiences in the three intimate 200-seat spaces here. (There's a cozy black box, too, and an acting conservatory.) Co-founder and artistic director Joy Zinoman retired in 2010, handing off an almost absurdly healthy organization – astonishingly, it ran a half-million-dollar surplus in fiscal 2009 – to the gifted, cerebral young director David Muse, whose earlier work for the house had included a rapturously reviewed production of Bryony Lavery's *Frozen*.

OTHER THEATERS & COMPANIES

Folger Theatre

201 East Capitol Street, SE, between 2nd & 3rd Streets, The Capitol & Around (1-202 544 7077, www.folger.edu). Capitol South Metro. **Box office** noon-4pm Mon-Sat. **Tickets** $15-$45. **Credit** AmEx, MC, V. **Map** p253 L7.

When the Shakespeare Theatre decamped for Downtown in the early 1990s, the Folger lay fallow for a year or two. But it has since revived, and its stable of regular directors (including British actor Richard Clifford) produces solid, intelligent fare. It was here that Lynn Redgrave developed what became the Broadway hit *Shakespeare For My Father,* and here that mischievous DC Shakespearean Joe Banno dramatized Hamlet's internal debates by splitting the title role into four parts – and casting women in three of them.

Ford's Theatre

511 10th Street, NW, between E & F Streets, Downtown (1-202 347 4833, www.fordstheatre. org). Metro Center or Gallery Place-Chinatown Metro. **Box office** 10am-6pm Mon-Fri. **Tickets** $27-$50. **Credit** AmEx, Disc, MC, V. **Map** p252 J6. President Abraham Lincoln's assassination – in 1865, during a performance of *Our American Cousin* –

shuttered this house for a century, but crusading producer Frankie Hewitt helped bring its stage back to life in the late 1960s. For decades, much of what Ford's offered was easy-to-swallow fare, but now and again producers surprise theatergoers with an edgy imported offering (Anna Deavere Smith's *Twilight: Los Angeles, 1992* had its DC run here). Since Hewitt's death in 2003, Alley Theatre veteran Paul Tetreault has steered the house gingerly in the direction of more substantial fare – including an admirable 2007 production of August Wilson's devastating *Jitney* and (to reopen the house in 2009 after a major renovation) an ambitious Lincoln commission called *The Heavens Are Hung in Black*. The surprise of DC's 2010 season was Ford's charming, handsomely upholstered revival of the 1950s romantic comedy *Sabrina Fair*.

Olney Theatre Center

2001 Olney-Sandy Spring Road (Route 108), Olney, MD (box office 1-301 924 3400, information 1-301 924 4485, www.olney theatre.org). Glenmont Metro then Y5, Y7, Y8, Y9 bus. **Box office** 10am-6pm Mon-Fri; noon-5pm Sat, Sun. **Tickets** $26-$54. **Credit** MC, V.

It's a hike, but the hour-long drive to this suburban Maryland house can be worth the trouble. Founded as a summer theater in the 1930s, it saw performances by a startlingly starry roster over the decades: Helen Hayes, Tallulah Bankhead, Olivia de Havilland, Hume Cronyn, Jessica Tandy, Uta Hagen and Ian McKellen are just a few of the names who've toured there. More recently, Olney's season has been largely subscriber-friendly fluff, and a fiscal crisis that nearly bankrupted the place in 2009-10 hasn't helped. But now and again artistic director Jim Petosa will offer up something gratifyingly bold: a gorgeous *Camille*,

David Hare's agonized *Racing Demon*, the hypnotic Calderón adaptation *Sueño*, a bracingly blunt staging of that reliably irascible Ibsen fellow. (*An Enemy of the People*, coming just after government leakers exposed domestic spying programs in 2006, seemed especially apt, and David Hare's *Stuff Happens* was a tonic in 2008.) A newish 440-seat main-stage completes a campus with no fewer than four performance spaces — one of them a casual outdoor stage.

Round House Theatre

Bethesda *7501 Wisconsin Avenue, at Waverly Street, Bethesda, MD. Bethesda Metro.* **Box office** noon-5pm Mon-Fri. **Tickets** $25-$60.
Silver Spring *8641 Colesville Road, between Georgia Avenue & Fenton Street, Silver Spring, MD (1-240 644 1099, www.roundhouse theatre.org). Silver Spring Metro.* **Box office** noon-5pm Mon-Fri. **Tickets** $15.
Both *Box office 1-240 644 1100, information 1-240 644 1099, www.roundhousetheatre.org.* **Credit** AmEx, MC, V.

An established company successful enough to have opened not one but two new spaces in recent years, Round House was home to the world premiere of *Columbinus*, a thoughtfully disturbing response to the Colorado school massacre. (It went on to get a well-received production off-Broadway.) Its main home is in the close-in suburb of Bethesda, but it also offers a regular slate of performances (including a cabaret series) near the other end of the Metro's Red Line, in a black-box space at the AFI Silver complex in Silver Spring. Its portfolio these days is heavy on literary adaptations. On the 2010-2011 bill: stage versions of Madeleine L'Engle's *A Wrinkle in Time* and Alice McDermott's *Charming Billy*.

Shakespeare Theatre Company

ARTS & ENTERTAINMENT

ARTS & ENTERTAINMENT

Crystal Palaces

Bold and beautiful new theaters herald a brave future.

Arena Stage.

When they made the announcement, the city arched an eyebrow: **Arena Stage** (*see p203*), that cornerstone of the Washington theater establishment, wouldn't be relocating to one of DC's resurgent downtown neighborhoods. Instead, it would sit tight in the capital's Southwest quadrant, down on the Potomac waterfront, in a woebegone district that hadn't had much life since a botched urban renewal scheme turned it into a beige concrete wasteland back in the 1950s.

But Arena wouldn't simply be sitting still. Instead, the company would gut its two vintage theaters, the in-the-round Fichandler and the smaller, proscenium-stage Kreeger, and enclose them in a curvaceous glass wrapper under a soaring, swooping sail of a roof. The architect's model was breathtaking.

And then, for years, the project went nowhere. Announced back in 2000, Arena's new campus wouldn't actually welcome its first patrons until a decade later. In the interim, the **Shakespeare Theatre Company** (*see p204*) had planned and then opened the gleaming, glass-fronted Sidney Harman Hall, an $85 million second home for the city's second-largest troupe, around the corner from its Lansburgh Theatre in the Penn Quarter neighborhood. And

across the river, the **Signature Theatre** (*see right*) proposed, funded and built a $16 million, two-theater space; if its own glass curtainwall looks out on to one of those prefabricated suburban 'downtowns' that have been popping up across the American landscape, it's still a pleasing, sophisticated gathering place, and one that represents a step into the big leagues for a company that got its start in a grotty industrial garage.

Arena's plans – laid as the dot-com boom of the late 1990s collapsed in the bust of the early 2000s, and clung to tenaciously even as the capital shuddered in the wake of the September 11 terrorist attacks – took longer to realize. For a while, observers wondered if they'd happen at all. But then the fundraising effort got a jolt in 2006, when philanthropists Gilbert and Jaylee Mead bumped up their original giving plans to an eye-popping $35 million. And once ground was broken in 2008, construction went swimmingly, with the complicated $135 million undertaking coming in on time and, astonishingly, under budget.

And the result? Worth the wait: a dream of a space, airy and substantial at once. Massive wooden columns, tall as yews and slanted like a ship's bowsprit, hold up that 450-foot blade of a roofline, and a surprising wickerwork basket of a new theater — a 200-seater called the Cradle, designed specifically to provide shelter for the development of plays too risky for Arena's bigger houses — provides a focus for it all. The lobby has that excellent and elusive quality, flow; it draws audiences in, up a wide stair, across a sloping expanse and up another stairway to a terrace with splendid views of trees and river and sky. Architecture critics greeted it ecstatically, anointing its creator, Vancouver-based Bing Thom, with their choicest adjectives. Theater critics pronounced themselves delighted with both the feel of the new Cradle and the way the renovation addressed long-standing acoustical anxieties in the four-sided Fichandler.

The **Mead Center for the American Theater**, the whole package is called, and it's a capstone on more than a decade of theatrical monument-making in the nation's capital. It's a material statement, too: like Harman Hall and the Signature space – the glass atrium at the center of the Studio Theatre complex, completed in 2004 – the jewel-box that is Arena Stage's new home speaks of openness, invitation and occasion all at once. They're event buildings, all of them, not just performance spaces; they're reminders that theaters were once shrines. They're public comments, too, on the maturity and substance of the Washington theater scene.

The challenge for all these grandly housed companies now, of course, is earning enough to keep the lights on. Their buildings may be bigger, but will their audiences grow? The Mead Center flung its doors open in October 2010, in a stagnant economy as dispiriting as the one that prevailed when it was conceived. Ticket prices have ticked higher everywhere, even as Americans have had to tighten their belts.

But if Washington's headline-making theaters make work that lives up to the ambition of their homes, it may convince their audiences – and their neighborhoods – that art shouldn't be an optional extra, but one of life's essentials – much like the light and air that inspired those dazzling crystal palaces. A dream of a space is just the start. Dreams *for* the space – that's what's going to be key.

Signature Theatre

3806 South Four Mile Run Drive, at Oakland Drive, Arlington, VA (1-703 820 9771, www. sig-online.org). Pentagon Metro then 7A (daily), 7F, 7H, 17F, 17G, 22A, 22B, FC306 bus (weekdays only). **Box office** 10am-6pm Mon-Fri; noon-6pm Sat, Sun. *During performances* 10am-6pm Mon-Fri; 10am-8.30pm Tue-Fri; noon-8.30pm Sat, Sun. **Tickets** $15-$85. **Credit** AmEx, Disc, MC, V.

Signature's signature is first-rate Sondheim, and if its instincts for straight plays aren't as keen, it's still an ambitious outfit: Sarah Kane's *Crave* and a Hebrew version of *Hamlet* were both on the house's 2007 calendar, as if a move into a $16-million, two-theatre complex weren't enough of a challenge that year. Landmark productions in other past seasons have included the first *Assassins* to be staged outside New York, a *Passion* that put the house on the map with national critics, and a world-première Van Gogh musical (*The Highest Yellow*) from Tony-nominated composer Michael John LaChiusa. More recent efforts include showy mountings of *Chess* and *Sunset Boulevard* in 2010, and the noble failure that was LaChiusa's musical adaptation of *Giant* in 2009.

▶ *For more on the Signature's new building, see left* **Crystal Palaces**.

Woolly Mammoth Theatre Company

649 D Street, NW, at 7th Street, Penn Quarter (1-202 393 3939, www.woollymammoth.net). Archives/Navy Memorial or Gallery Place/Chinatown Metro. **Box office** 10am-6pm Mon-Fri. *Performance weeks* 10am-6pm Mon-Fri; noon-6pm Sat, Sun. **Tickets** from $35. **Credit** AmEx, MC, V. **Map** p253 J6.

This brash and often-brilliant company has been pushing boundaries (both theatrical and personal) for a quarter-century, most recently in a superb new $7 million, 265-seat downtown home. Notable playwrights who've called Woolly home include *Six Feet Under* scribe Craig Wright, Pulitzer Prize finalist Sarah Ruhl (*The Clean House*) and that poet of neurosis, Nicky Silver.

SMALL COMPANIES

Washington is a terrific theatre town: there are far too many fringey, flaky, fearless small companies to list here. But look for anything involving the **Forum Theatre** (smart, politically aware stuff from contemporary writers and 20th-century giants, www.forum theatre.org), **Longacre Lea** (fearsomely intelligent, and fun to watch, www.longacre lea.org), **Synetic Theater** (gorgeous movement-based theater, www.synetic theater.org), **WSC** (scrappy) and **Solas Nua** (the swimming-pool nutters mentioned earlier in this chapter).

For the following companies, fixed addresses are given where possible; for information about performances by roving companies, call the number listed. Note that box office hours have not been given; it's generally a case of leaving a message on the answerphone for the company to call you back.

African Continuum Theatre Company

Information 1-202 529 5763, www.african continuumtheatre.com. **Tickets** $20-$35. **Credit** AmEx, MC, V.

A solo hip hop odyssey, solid forays into the tough territories charted by August Wilson and Athol Fugard, and rousing takes on Zora Neale Hurston's *Spunk* and Endesha Ida Mae Holland's *From the Mississippi Delta* – they were once all in a season's work (or maybe two) for this 15-year-old outfit devoted to the African-American experience. A lacerating look at Fugard's *Blood Knot* and a fine, snappy staging of *The Story* (a fictionalized take on a 1980s *Washington Post* scandal involving a black reporter and a made-up story) have perhaps been the company's finest hours so far. Leadership changes and fiscal challenges have all but killed the company more than once in recent years, though, and its future may be in doubt. (Shocking, that, in a capital still called Chocolate City by some.) The big events on its 2010-11 season were a new-play readings series and a revival of Pearl Cleage's *Blues for an Alabama Sky*.

GALA Hispanic Theatre

3333 14th Street, NW, between Park Street & Monroe Street, Columbia Heights (1-202 234 7174, www.galatheatre.org). Columbia Heights Metro. **Tickets** $30-$50. **Credit** AmEx, MC, V. **Map** p250 H1.

Ensconced in the rehabilitated Tivoli Theatre in Columbia Heights, Teatro GALA stages Spanish-language classics like Calderón de la Barca's *La Dama Duende* and García Lorca's *Blood Wedding*, plus modern plays by writers such as Venezuela's Gustavo Ott (*Evangélicas, Divorciadas y Vegetarianas*) and the occasional Latin-flavoured musical. Performances are generally in Spanish with a supertitled translation.

Rorschach Theatre

Information 1-202 452 5538, www.rorschach theatre.com. **Tickets** $12. **No credit cards**.

Itinerant as of the winter of 2010-11, the rambunctious Rorschach company finds interesting plays and intriguing spaces, applying its nervy vision to both. For the most part, it's a success; the company serves up everything from Serbian wunderkind Biljana Srbljanovic (*Family Stories: A Slapstick Tragedy*) to the sprightly Amy Freed (*The Beard of Avon*). Other outings have included a solid staging of Tony Kushner's Nazi-era fever-dream *A Bright Room Called Day* and a smart take on *The Arabian Nights*, the sexy, swoony fable by German playwright Roland Schimmelpfennig.

Theater Alliance

H Street Playhouse, 1365 H Street, NE (www.theateralliance.com). Gallery Place-Chinatown Metro then X2 bus. **Map** p84.

Once the sort of company that would take a playfully kinetic pass at Salman Rushdie's *Haroun and the Sea of Stories* or introduce Washington audiences to the hugely ambitious writer Naomi Wallace (with 2003's gob-smackingly bold *Slaughter City*), the Theater Alliance grew less ambitious as it went through leadership changes and the broader economy went south. By 2010-11, the troupe's season had shrunk to three plays, one of them a booked-in solo show, and its prospects seemed uncertain.

Washington Shakespeare Company

Artisphere, 1101 Wilson Boulevard, Arlington, VA (1-703 418 4808/www.washington shakespeare.org). Rosslyn Metro. **Tickets** $25-$35. **Credit** AmEx, MC, V.

Not to be confused with the deep-pocketed Shakespeare Theatre, this highbrow-on-a-shoestring troupe has 20-plus seasons of the Bard – not to mention Beckett, Marlowe, Stoppard, Albee and more – under its scruffy belt. It's sometimes quite good (a 2004 *Waiting for Godot* unearthed all the prodigious tenderness in that bleak play) and always ambitious: what company with a barebones budget tackles *The Royal Hunt of the Sun* and *Death and the King's Horseman* within a twelvemonth? A naked *Macbeth* drew worldwide attention in 2007. A new county-run arts venue has recently supplanted the troupe's beloved, dilapidated former warehouse home, and a more ambitious board of directors seems poised to capitalize on the opportunity. Even the BBC has taken notice: at press time, Stephen Fry was planning to pop in to participate in a gala 2011 fundraiser: *Hamlet*, performed partly in Klingon.

Washington Stage Guild

The Undercroft Theater at Mount Vernon Place United Methodist Church, 900 Massachusetts Avenue, NW, between 9th & 10th Streets (1-240 582 0050/www.stageguild.org). Mount Vernon Square or Gallery Place Metro. **Tickets** $40-$50. **No credit cards. Map** p250 H3.

Forced out of its longtime lodgings by DC's downtown redevelopment, and then rocked by the death of its much-loved founding artistic director, this tight-knit 25-year-old ensemble went dark for a couple of seasons, but resurrected itself and has found a new home. In an over-educated city where knotty dramas play out in each day's headlines, it draws a loyal crowd with smart stagings of Shaw (a politically well-timed *On the Rocks* in 2004 is remembered as a high point) and other literary-minded fare. The 2010-11 season lineup included Crispin Whittell's *Darwin in Malibu* and GK Chesterton's *Magic*, along with *The Apple Cart*, from GBS himself.

Escapes & Excursions

Chesapeake. *See p218.*

Escapes & Excursions   **210**
Presidential Homes   216

Escapes & Excursions

Stunning scenery and a historic city.

Head out of the city in almost any direction and you'll find something worth seeing. To the north is **Baltimore**, a city where redevelopment has made a mark on a gritty reputation, and which is host to a number of first-class museums. To the south are the **Shenandoah Valley** and the **Blue Ridge Mountains**, where the natural beauty is staggering and outdoor activities abound. And to the east is **Chesapeake Bay**, America's sailing capital and, at 7,000 square miles, the largest estuary in the United States.

This chapter offers a guide to the best sights and experiences in these three destinations, and also explores the area's historic homes that were once owned by America's Founding Fathers (*see p216* **Homes of the Presidents**).

TRANSPORT

The best (and just about only) way to visit Shenandoah and Chesapeake Bay is by car. Traffic can be extremely heavy during commuting hours, especially on I-66 or the Beltway that circles the city. The national car rental companies all have chains in Washington, both in the city and at major airports (*see p222*). Baltimore is more friendly to people without cars; trains depart daily from Union Station (50 Massachusetts Avenue, NE, at North Capitol Street). For more information, see the Getting There section for each destination.

Spirit of Washington Cruises (Pier 4, Water Street, SW, at Sixth Street, SW, 1-202 554 8000, 1-866 211 3811, www.spiritofwashington.com) operates boat trips from the city to Mount Vernon, site of George Washington's historic home, between March and October. Departure is at 8.30am and the trip takes about six hours, including three and a half hours to tour Mount Vernon ($38, $31-$36 reductions, free under-6s, price includes the admission to Mount Vernon).

BALTIMORE

Baltimore is one of the earliest true cities in America, a thriving port from the very beginning of the country and later an important manufacturing center. It was even briefly the seat of government of the fledgling nation. Things went wrong, however, and not so long ago it was known mostly for crime and post-industrial grit, and lived very much in the shadow of the nation's capital 40 miles to the south. But since the 1980s, the 'Charm City', as Mayor William Donald Schaefer dubbed it back in the 1970s, has been undergoing a resurgence. Washingtonians not only visit Baltimore for its many attractions; many have made the Charm City their home, commuting each day to jobs in the nation's capital.

Inner Harbor

Baltimore's revitalization is nowhere more apparent than around the Inner Harbor. No longer a depressing urban jungle of run-down factories and warehouses, the Inner Harbor has been transformed into Harborplace, a lively civic center bursting with interesting shops and restaurants. Glass-walled offices in the new high-rise business district form a bright, modern backdrop. For a view of the city from above, take the lift to the 27th-floor observation deck of the **World Trade Center** (aka the Top of the World); at 423

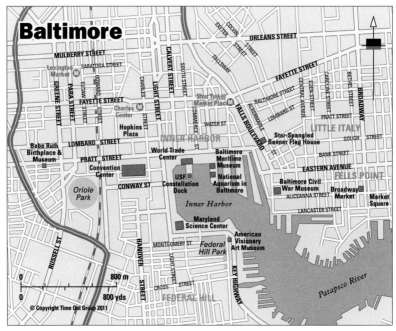

feet it's the world's tallest pentagonal building (401 East Pratt Street, 1-410 837 8439).

For a trip in the opposite direction visit the world-class **National Aquarium in Baltimore**, with aquatic delights including a daily dolphin show (501 East Pratt Street, 1-410 576 3800, www.aqua.org).

The **Baltimore Maritime Museum** (Pier 3, East Pratt Street, 1-410 396 3453, www.historicships.org) is the mooring place for two veterans of World War II, the Coast Guard cutter *Taney*, the last survivor of Pearl Harbor, and the submarine that fired the last torpedo of the conflict.

The USS *Constellation* (Pier 1, 301 East Pratt Street, www.constellation.org) is the last Civil War-era vessel still afloat. It patrolled the African coast near the mouth of the Congo River between 1859 and 1861 and intercepted ships that were illegally engaged in the slave trade (the US made the importation of slaves illegal in 1808). The fourth historic ship, the *Light Ship*, served as the floating lighthouse that for many years marked the entrance to Chesapeake Bay.

Americana

Baseball is the national pastime, and no one looms larger in the history of the game than the legendary Babe Ruth. The **Babe Ruth**

Birthplace & Museum (216 Emory Street, 1-410 727 1539, www.baberuthmuseum.com) is a cramped rowhouse in the scruffy neighborhood that was home to the young 'Sultan of Swat', a hero to American men and boys during the 1920s and '30s for his home run-hitting prowess on the field. (He was a legendary boozer and lecher off it.) It sits in the shadow of **Camden Yards**, a beautiful Major League baseball stadium where the Baltimore Orioles play their home games. The museum stays open until 7.30pm on game days.

For the history behind the American national anthem, which kicks off every baseball game, visit **Fort McHenry** (end of East Fort Avenue, 1-410 962 4290, www.nps.gov/fomc). During the War of 1812, Americans fought off the British attempt to take the fort, which guards the entrance to Baltimore harbor. Bombarded throughout the day and night of 14 September 1814, the fort held out and the British ships eventually withdrew. Francis Scott Key, a young lawyer who happened to be aboard one of the British ships to negotiate the release of a captured friend, was inspired by the sight of his country's badly torn flag still flying at dawn on the 14th and wrote the lyrics of 'The Star-Spangled Banner' (*see p25* **Profile**). The expanded fort now on the site dates from the Civil War.

Baltimore.

It was Mary Pickersgill who stitched the stars and the stripes on to the huge flag that flew tattered over Fort McHenry during the 1814 British bombardment. Her 1793 home is now the **Star-Spangled Banner Flag House** (844 East Pratt Street, 1-410 837 1793, www.flaghouse.org). There are guided tours of the house, furnished with appropriate Federal-period antiques and a museum. The actual banner underwent painstaking restoration at Washington's Smithsonian Institution before it was returned to public display at the National Museum of American History in 2006.

While not the birthplace (Boston was), Baltimore is the burial site of **Edgar Allan Poe**, the master of the macabre who first won national acclaim with his poem 'The Raven'. He died in 1849 at age 40. His final resting place is Westminster Hall & Burying Ground, the cemetery of the First Presbyterian Church (West Fayette Street & Greene Street). Visit the churchyard on your own, or call for a guided tour of the catacombs conducted on the first and third Friday of each month from April to November (1-410 706 2072, www.eapoe.org/balt/poegrave.htm).

The **Reginald F Lewis Museum of Maryland African American History & Culture** (830 East Pratt Street, 1-443 263 1800, www.africanamericanculture.org, closed Mon) is the largest African-American museum on the East Coast. Exhibits are divided into three major areas: community; slavery and labor; and art and intellect. Call or visit the website for information about special exhibitions. Exhibits

at the **Baltimore Civil War Museum** (601 President Street, open 10am-5pm Sat, Sun) highlights the city's ambivalent role in the bitter 1861-65 struggle between North and South. Baltimore was a station on the 'underground railroad' by which fugitive slaves escaped to the North, but it was also home to many Confederate sympathizers. There were riots when Union troops passed through the city. The museum closed in 2007 but has since reopened on a part-time basis with limited weekend hours, with the help of volunteers from a group of interested museum supporters, the Friends of President Street Station.

Art

The **Walters Art Museum** (600 North Charles Street, 1-410 547 9000, www.thewalters.org, closed Mon, Tue) is one of the best fine art museums in the US, with a collection including medieval, Renaissance, 18th- and 19th-century, Islamic and Asian art. Works on show include Raphael's *Madonna of the Candelabra*, Bernini's statue of the *Risen Christ* and El Greco's depiction of *St Francis Receiving the Stigmata*. The **Baltimore Museum of Art** (10 Art Museum Drive, 1-443 573 1700, www. artbma.org, closed Mon, Tue) has a notable collection of modern paintings and sculpture from Van Gogh to Warhol and Rodin to Nevelson. At the **American Visionary Art Museum** (800 Key Highway, 1-410 244 1900, www.avam.org, closed Mon) across the harbor in South Baltimore, the focus is on untrained but inspired artists working outside the norms.

Where to eat & drink

Phillips (301 Light Street, 1-410 685 6600, www.phillipsseafood.com, main courses $17-$30) is a large and popular restaurant with a great harbor view, terrace dining in season and seafood. **Rusty Scupper** (402 Key Highway, 1-410 727 3678, main courses $19-$50), across Inner Harbor from Harborplace, also does seafood, plus prime rib and the like.

Though in a rather bleak location, **Della Notte** (801 Eastern Avenue, 1-410 837 5500, $22-$39) is highly rated. Finally, the area of Fells Point is known not only for its antiques shops but its drinking establishments. Head to the funky Point for a drink or dinner.

Resources

Hospital
Johns Hopkins, 600 North Wolfe Street (1-410 955 5000, www.hopkinsmedicine.org). **Open** *Accident & Emergency 24hrs daily.*

Internet
Koba Café, 644 East Fort Avenue (1-410 986 0366). **Open** 6am-6pm Mon-Fri; 7am-7pm Sat, Sun. Free Wi-Fi with your coffee.

Police station
601 East Fayette Street (1-410 396 2525).

Post office
900 East Fayette Street (1- 800 275 8777).

Tourist information
Baltimore Area Convention & Visitors Association, 401 Light Street (1-877 225 8466, www.baltimore.org). **Open** 9am-6pm daily.

Babe Ruth statue, **Camden Yards.** See p211.

Getting there

By car
Baltimore is about an hour's drive from Washington. Take I-95 north to I-395, exit 53, which quickly becomes Howard Street (take care not to shoot off to the left on Martin Luther King Jr Boulevard). Continue north on Howard a short distance (a football stadium and the Camden Yards baseball stadium are on your left) to Pratt Street. Turn right and continue past Charles and Light Streets to Harborplace.

By train
Amtrak (1-800 872 7245, www.amtrak.com) and **Marc** (1-410 539 5000, www.mtamaryland.com) both run services to Baltimore from Washington's Union Station. Amtrak trains to Baltimore's Penn Station take 35-45mins and run until after midnight (most last trains depart Penn Station at 12.40am); Marc trains run into Penn Station and Camden Station, and take a little over an hour. Last trains are at 10.45pm and as this is a commuter service there is no service at weekends.

SHENANDOAH

More than a million people pass through **Shenandoah National Park** (1-540 999 3500, www.nps.gov/shen) and the surrounding area each year, making it the undisputed outdoor playground for Washingtonians. Straddling Virginia's Blue Ridge Mountains for more than 100 miles, the park takes its name from the valley and river just to its west. Skyline Drive follows the crest of the mountain range for the entire length of the park. There are 75 overlooks where motorists can take in the valley views.

The crowds begin to descend on the park in the spring, as the azaleas and dogwoods bloom. By summer, Skyline Drive can begin to feel like a clogged freeway. But the busiest time may be in the final weeks of October, when the changing foliage adorns the park in a resplendent display of color. Current accessible areas and other information can be picked up at park entrances and several visitors' centers along Skyline Drive.

Taking to the trails

A visit to Shenandoah is not complete without setting foot on one of the national park's 500 miles of trails. Trail maps published by the Potomac Appalachian Trail Club can be purchased ($6) when entering the park. (Some maps can be downloaded at www.nps.gov/shen/planyourvisit/mapshiking.htm.) From **Skyline Drive**, there are an endless number of hikes. Many include sections of the **Appalachian Trail**, an idea first conceived by a conservationist named Benton MacKaye

Discover the city from your back pocket

Essential for your weekend break, over 30 top cities available.

POCKET SIZED
from £6.99 / $11.95

as an antidote to the rapid urbanization and hectic pace of life in the northeastern US. Completed in 1937, the trail extends 2,174 miles from Maine to Georgia. Of these 101 run through **Shenandoah National Park**. Waterfalls are Shenandoah's feature attraction. The challenging nine-mile **Whiteoak Canyon Trail** (mile 45.6 off Skyline Drive) passes six of them and is one of the most popular routes. For a shorter hike, try the four-mile **Rose River Loop** (mile 49.4), which runs past a waterfall that drops more than 60 feet.

Vistas are another reason to take to the trails. The **Mary's Rock** (mile 31.6) trail climbs 1,210 feet and ends at a rock outcropping with a view of Thornton Gap. Legend has it that Mary Thornton, a 15-year-old former park resident, hiked the two miles to the top and returned with a bear cub under each arm. For a shorter hike with a big payoff, try **Stony Man** (mile 41.7). It's less than a mile to the 4,011-foot summit, the second highest in the park. If you can, take in the valley at sunset.

Shenandoah's most popular hike is **Old Rag Mountain**. At 3,200 feet it offers a breathtaking view of the valley. Near the summit of the mountain, the trail gives way to massive boulders. Scaling these rocks (or sliding between or under them) requires a sturdy pair of hiking boots and, on occasion, a friend's helping hand. The non-adventurous need not apply. Be forewarned: arrive at sunrise on weekends. Parking spaces fill up quickly, and in some cases you may need to hike before you even reach the trail.

To avoid the crowds, nearby **George Washington National Forest** (1-888 265 0019, www.fs.fed.us/r8/gwj) is less visited but has great scenery and hundreds of miles of trails. **Signal Knob Trail** leads to the top of a mountain that Confederate forces used to send messages during the Civil War. There are two overlooks before the summit – Buzzard Rock and Fort Valley. The ten-mile loop marked with yellow blazes starts just north of Elizabeth Furnace Campground off State Road 678.

A shorter option is the **Big Schloss Trail**, which starts at Wolf Gap Campground off State Road 675. The hike is about two miles one way and leads to a rock outcropping, which offers a panoramic view of the forest below. Peregrine falcons have been released in the wild here. Go to www.fs.fed.us/r8/gwj/lee/recreation/hiking/popular_hikes.shtml for directions.

Going underground

Shenandoah is home to hundreds of caves, where summer temperatures hover around a cool 55 degrees – a great way to beat the heat. Many are accessible to the public. **Luray Caverns** (970 US Highway 211 West,

1-540 743 6551, www.luraycaverns.com) has paved, well-lit walkways and a Disneyland feel. Its main feature is a stalacpipe organ. Outside the caverns is a garden maze where the children can have fun getting lost ($6, $5 reductions, free under-6s).

Other options include **Endless Caverns** (1800 Endless Caverns Road, New Market, 1-800 544 2283, www.endlesscaverns.com), where the fossilized tooth of a woolly mammoth was found in 1996, and **Shenandoah Caverns** (261 Shenandoah Caverns Road, 1-540 477 3115, www.shenandoah caverns.com), which has a calcite crystal formation called the Diamond Cascade. Some crystal caverns were closed at the time of writing because of a fungus affecting bats, so it might be a good idea to check before visiting.

Civil War soldiers during a break in the fighting autographed the walls of **Grand Caverns** (Grand Caverns Drive, Grottoes, 1-888 430 2283), and locals hosted dances in a 5,000-square-foot chamber called the Grand Ballroom. **Skyline Caverns** (10344 Stonewall Jackson Highway, Front Royal, 1-800 296 4545, www.skylinecaverns.com) has rare white-spiked ceiling formations called anthodites.

Reel talk

Herbert Hoover, the 31st president (1928-32), was one of the first Washingtonians to flee the humidity of the nation's capital for Shenandoah.

Shenandoah National Park.

ESCAPES & EXCURSIONS

Homes of the Presidents

Four of the first five US presidents were Virginians.

Monticello

Thomas Jefferson's **Monticello** (State Route 53, 1-434 984 9822, www.monticello.org, open Mar-Nov 9am-5pm daily, Dec-Feb 10am-4pm daily) is a two-and-a-half-hour drive from Washington, but worth the journey. To understand Jefferson – the author of the Declaration of Independence and third president (1801-09) – you must first understand Monticello, or so the saying goes. Jefferson was a Renaissance man, an architect and inventor who dabbled in archaeology, paleontology and astronomy. All of his pursuits are on display here. Jefferson designed and oversaw the construction of the house, a neo-classical gem befitting a Founding Father. He selected all the furnishings, many of which he purchased while serving as a diplomat in France. Tours of the three-storey, 21-room house are conducted continuously

each day. In the entrance hall, Jefferson created a mini-museum of European art and artifacts from explorers Lewis and Clark's celebrated Western expedition, which he commissioned as president. Tours also include Jefferson's sitting room, book room, bedroom, dining room and a guest bedroom. Visitors can wander through the wine and beer cellars in the basement on their own.

Seasonal tours are also available. Jefferson had a lifelong interest in botany and agriculture; his restored gardens can be explored in daily tours betwen October and April. 'Answering the Bell' is a house tour that explores the lives of enslaved men and women who worked at Monticello. The tour runs during February. 'Plantation Community' tours examine the lives of those slaves who worked on Jefferson's plantation (Sat, Sun in Feb, Mar; daily Apr-Oct).

If you visit Monticello, be sure to drop in on Jefferson's former neighbours. **Montpelier** (11407 Constitution Highway, State Route 20, 1-540 672 2728, www.montpelier.org, open Apr-Oct 9am-5pm daily; Nov-Mar 9am-4pm daily) is the former home of James Madison, the fourth president. Also designed by Jefferson, the house embodied his classical vision. Later owners, including the immensely wealthy Du Pont family, expanded and significantly altered the original structure. An extensive restoration that began in 2003 sought to

He chose for his presidential retreat a spot along the Rapidan River, largely because he loved to relax with rod and reel. Fishing, he wrote, 'is the chance to wash one's soul with pure air, with the rush of a brook, or with the shimmer of the sun on the blue water'.

Hoover had 13 cabins, three of which have been restored to their former glory, including the president's grand abode. Hike two miles down to the cabins along the Mill and Laurel Prong loop (mile 52.7) and meet up with a tour, or catch a van from the Harry F Byrd visitor center at Big Meadows. Tours are three hours long and have a 13-person limit. Check the schedule and make reservations by phone on 1-540 999 3500 or in person at the Byrd Visitor Center.

If Hoover inspires you, grab a reel and rod yourself (the president loved trout, particularly with bacon and eggs for breakfast). Brook trout,

smallmouth bass, brown trout; fly-fishing or conventional fishing; the options are well-nigh limitless. Guides provide equipment and can find the best holes. Harry Murray of **Murray's Fly Shop** (121 Main Street, Edinburg, 1-540 984 4212, www.murraysflyshop.com) and his son Jeff grew up fishing Stoney Creek, which flows by his store in the valley and into the North Fork of the Shenandoah River.

You'll need a Virginia fishing license, which you can purchase and print out online (www.dgif.virginia.gov/licenses). It's $11 for a freshwater license for five consecutive days.

Riding the river

Take your pick – canoe, kayak, raft or tube – numerous outfitters are ready to set you up for a whitewater adventure or a leisurely float.

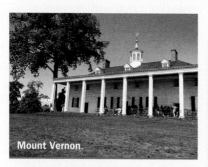

Mount Vernon.

restore the house to its original size and Federal-period appearance. It was completed in 2008.

James Monroe, the fifth US president (1817-1825), owned **Ash Lawn-Highland** plantation (Route 795, 1-434 293 9539, www.ashlawnhighland.org, open Apr-Oct 9 am-6pm daily, Nov-Mar 11am-5pm daily). Though without the size or scope of Monticello, it too has breathtaking views.

Just 14 miles south of DC along the George Washington Memorial Parkway (which ends at the visitors' entrance), **Mount Vernon** (1-703 780 2000, www.mountvernon.org, open Apr-Aug 8am-5pm daily, Mar, Sept, Oct 9am-5pm daily, Nov-Feb 9am-4pm daily) is the most celebrated and visited historic home in the country. George Washington has gone down in history as a soldier and statesman,

but he devoted the greater part of his life to improving the estate he had inherited from an older half-brother, seeking to recreate an English manor house on the banks of the Potomac. The faithfully restored plantation house contains original furniture and many of the first First Family's belongings. The gardens have been planted in colonial style, and Washington's Upper Garden is currently being renovated to make it more accurate for his era.

A major project in recent years has been the re-creation of a colonial-era farm where crops of Washington's day are raised using the simple implements of the time. It includes an ingenious octagonal threshing barn he devised, revealing him as a true agricultural innovator. An orientation center and museum, tactfully concealed under a meadow, further fleshes out Washington – literally, in the case of a forensically reconstructed statue of him at age 19. Traditional treasures shine alongside, notably Jean-Antoine Houdon's terracotta bust from life – the most accurate likeness of Washington ever created.

There are a couple of appealing ways to reach the estate: by car down the elegant George Washington Parkway (which set the scenic-drive standard in 1932); or by traditional excursion boat, with regular departures from Washington and Alexandria. An alternative route is by Huntington Metro station and then Fairfax Connector bus 101 or 102.

ESCAPES & EXCURSIONS

Reservations are essential; trips can fill up quickly. Front Royal bills itself as the 'Canoe Capital of Virginia'. Head to **Front Royal Canoe Company** (8567 Stonewall Jackson Highway, 1-800 270 8808, www.frontroyal canoe.com). In Luray, try **Shenandoah River Outfitters** (6502 South Page Valley Road, 1-540 743 4159, www.shenandoah-river.com). And in Bentonville, there is **Downriver Canoe Company** (884 Indian Hollow Road, 1-800 338 1963, www.downriver.com).

Where to eat

Thornton River Grille (3710 Sperryville Pike, Sperryville, 1-540 987 8790, www.thorntonriver grille.com, closed Mon, mains $10-$29) can fill up quickly for dinner thanks to its delicious burgers and crab cakes. Make a reservation. The **Joshua**

Wilton House (412 South Main Street, Harrisonburg, 1-888 294 5866/-540 434 4464, www.joshuawilton.com, closed Mon, Sun, mains $21-$30) is more upscale. The outdoor patio is a good place to wind down a day of outdoor fun. The menu is seasonal and reservations are recommended. To stock up on a few treats before hiking, head to **Cranberry's Grocery & Eatery** (7 South New Street, Staunton, 1-540 885 4755).

Where to stay

Skyland Resort (Mile 41.7, Skyline Drive, 1-800 778 2851, closed Dec-Feb, doubles $142-$186) is located at the highest point (3,680 feet) on Skyline Drive. It has lodge suites, rustic cabins, a decent restaurant and spectacular views. **Big Meadows Lodge** (Mile 51.2,Skyline

State Capitol building, **Annapolis**.

CHESAPEAKE

Sailboats dotting the bay, gentle bay breezes, life at a languid pace. There is no shortage of reasons to visit picturesque Chesapeake Bay and embark on a vacation from your vacation. **Annapolis** is the jewel of the Chesapeake and has been Maryland's capital since 1695. A modern city has grown up around the colonial core, but the historic city is largely preserved. The narrow streets surrounding the old harbor are lined with what is claimed to be the largest concentration of Georgian houses in the country. Annapolis is no longer the busy port it once was, but the sea remains very much part of its identity. Marinas, sailing schools and charter services make it a recreational center. Several tours, self-guided and otherwise, of the whole Annapolis historic area are also available. Check at the City Dock information booth for details.

South of Annapolis, the Chesapeake's less publicized West Shore stretches more than 100 miles to Point Lookout, where the Potomac River flows into the bay. Cross over the Bay Bridge from Annapolis to reach the Chesapeake's Eastern Shore.

Naval gazing

Annapolis is the home port of the **US Naval Academy**, which was founded in 1845 and educates future naval and marine officers. The academy appeared in *Patriot Games*, the 1992 movie that starred Harrison Ford as Professor Jack Ryan. The 4,000 students (or midshipmen, as they're known) stride around town conspicuously in their white uniforms. Despite heightened security at military installations since 9/11, the academy remains open to the public. Picture identification is required to enter the campus for anyone over 16. Visiting hours are generally 9am-5pm. Visitors may observe the noon formation of midshipmen held Monday to Friday, weather permitting, during the academic year. Guided tours are available at the **Armel-Leftwich Visitor Center** (52 King George Street, 1-410 293 8687). The visitor center also has naval and astronautical memorabilia, such as the *Freedom 7* space capsule and an exhibit on John Paul Jones.

Jones is America's preeminent naval hero from the Revolutionary War, best known for the words he uttered on 23 September 1779. As Jones fought the HMS *Serapis* on the North Sea off Flamborough Head, his ship, the *Bonhomme Richard*, came under fire and began to sink. When the opposing captain called for Jones to surrender, he allegedly responded, 'I have not yet begun to fight!' Jones then proceeded to board the *Serapis* and captured it. In 1792, Jones died in Paris. But in 1905, his remains were unearthed,

Drive, 1-800 778 2851, doubles $149-$188) has traditional-style rooms, some with fireplaces, in the beautifully panelled main lodge and another 72 in multi-unit lodges and rustic cabins. Its restaurant offers 'ladies high tea' ,which still uses the recipes dating from the era when the likes of Eleanor Roosevelt visited.
Lewis Mountain Cabins (Mile 57.5, Skyline Drive, 1-800 778 2851, doubles $ 82.25 -$117) is a more outdoorsy option.

Resources

Tourist information
Woodstock *Shenandoah County Tourism, Suite 101, 600 North Main Street (1-540 459 6227, 1-888 367 3965, www.shenandoahtravel.org).* **Open** 8.30am-5pm Mon-Fri.
New Market *Shenandoah Valley Travel Association, 277 West Old Cross Road, PO Box 1040 (1-540 740 3132).* **Open** 9am-5pm daily.
Edinburg *George Washington National Forest – Lee Ranger Forest District, 109 Molineu Road, (1-540 984 4101/933 6171).* **Open** 8am-4.30pm Mon-Fri.

Getting there

By car
Of the several entrances to the park, the most convenient from Washington is at its northern tip, 90mins or less via I-66 to exit 6, then south three miles on US 340 to Front Royal.

and he was reburied in a crypt in the basement of the Naval Academy's chapel. Today, the crypt is surrounded by artifacts from Jones's life, such as the gold medal Congress awarded him in 1787.

A collection of 108 ship models is one of the highlights of the **United States Naval Academy Museum** (Preble Hall, 1-410 293 2108). The museum also has artifacts from the USS *Constitution* and other ships, artwork depicting naval battles and memorabilia from significant naval figures.

Bay breezes

Annapolis has been called the 'sailing capital of the world', which should be incentive enough to take to the water. Call ahead for reservations and prices. Two-hour cruises usually run for around $30 per person. The *Woodwind* (1-410 263 7837, www.schoonerwoodwind.com), a 74-foot schooner, departs from the Annapolis Marriott Waterfront Hotel and offers two-hour rides. On Tuesdays, the captain offers up a selection of beer from microbreweries for tasting. He'll even let you take the wheel or help hoist the sails. If power boating is more your speed, **Watermark Cruises** (1-410 268 7601, www.watermarkcruises.com) has 90-minute and full-day tours. Full-day tours head to St Michaels or the fishing village of Rock Hall. Ninety minutes will get you to Thomas Point Lighthouse, a National Historic Landmark, among other destinations.

Chesapeake Bay was once filled with so many oysters that Maryland and Virginia fishermen actually resorted to violence as they argued over where the rightful boundary was between the two states. To revisit the bay when the oyster was king, set sail for a two-hour cruise on the *Rebecca T Ruark* (1-410 829 3976, www.skip jack.org), built in 1886 and currently the bay's oldest working skipjack. Captain Wade Murphy will demonstrate how skipjacks dredged for oysters before he does some dredging of his own.

Captain Ed Farley offers two-hour cruises on skipjack *HM Krenz* (1-410 745 6080, www oystercatcher.com). Farley helped author James Michener in his research for *Chesapeake*, the epic historical novel about the bay. Check beforehand as many river trip operators are closed out of season.

Beach life

Chesapeake's strands may not rival Miami's South Beach or Southern California's Laguna Beach, but they do attract a faithful following because of the many different activities on offer. More than a million visitors each year descend on Annapolis's **Sandy Point State Park** at the western terminus of the Bay Bridge (1100 East College Parkway, 1-410 974 2149, www.dnr.state.md.us/publiclands/southern/sandypoint.html). The site of a pre-Civil War resort, the park has a mile-long beach and offers the chance to swim, fish, go crabbing, rent a row-boat or motorboat (call the marina for prices and availability, 1-410 974 2772), have a picnic, or hike along nature trails. But maybe the best attraction is watching traffic back up on the Bay Bridge. For those not interested in this perverse pleasure, there are sailing regattas and sea-bound ships to ogle.

Sandy Point.

Calvert Cliffs State Park (Lusby, 1-301 743 7613, www.dnr.state.md.us/publiclands/southern/calvertcliffs.html) features 100-foot cliffs that loom over a small beach. More than 600 species of fossil have been discovered on the beach and cliffs, including the teeth of various sharks. From the parking lot, the hike to the beach is about two miles. **Point Lookout State Park** (11175 Point Lookout Road, Scotland, 1-301 872 5688, www.dnr.state.md.us/publiclands/southern/pointlookout.html) is nothing if not picturesque. A beach three-quarters of a mile long overlooks the point where the Potomac River flows into Chesapeake Bay. Rent motorboats or canoes, go fishing, hiking or swimming. A museum explains the park's history as a Civil War prison camp for more than 50,000 Confederate soldiers.

Getting crabby

Forget fancy napkins, highbrow wine lists and a maitre d' in tails. Maryland crab houses are all about the crab. The tables are paper-covered and the utensil of choice is a wooden mallet. No trip to Chesapeake is complete without tasting the local delicacy, but be warned: this isn't fast food. There's lots of labor necessary to get at the succulent meat.

Maryland's blue crabs spawn in southern Chesapeake Bay once the brackish water starts to warm in June, moving up the bay and its 150 tributaries, periodically shedding their shells as they grow. A crab caught during the first few hours between shedding its old shell and growing a new one is called 'softshell', capable of being cooked and devoured in its entirety. 'Hardshells' over the legal minimum size are a decidedly different dish. The cycle ends in late autumn. Don't be afraid to ask for a tutorial in how to open and slice up your crab, but whatever you do, don't eat its organs. Most crab shacks also offer a selection of shrimp, clams, mussels, calamari and fish, for those who are not crab crazy.

Jimmy Cantler's Riverside Inn (458 Forest Beach Road, 1-410 757 1311, www.cantlers.com) is a short drive from downtown Annapolis and the local favorite. Set against Mill Creek, Cantler's has outdoor seating. For another local favorite visit **Mike's Bar & Crab House** (3030 Riva Road, Riva, 1-410 956 2784, www.mikescrabhouse.com, mains $15-$31). Established in 1958, Mike's has a deck with views of the South River. **Cheshire Crab Restaurant** (1701 Poplar Ridge Road, Pasadena, 1-410 360 2220, www.cheshire crab.com, closed Jan-Mar and Mon all year round, mains $13-$22) has an outdoor deck that overlooks the Pleasure Cove marina, where watermen can tie up and head inside for a quick bite to eat before returning to the waves. On the east side of the Bay Bridge is **Harris Crab House** (433 Kent Narrows Way N, Grasonville, 1-410 827 9500, www.harriscrabhouse.com, mains $13-$26), which has a rooftop deck with a view of the Kent Narrows. Housed in an 1830s building first used as an oyster shucking shed (check out the authentic bar ceiling joints), **St Michaels Crab House** (305 Mulberry Street, St Michaels, 1-410 745 3737, www.stmichaelscrabhouse.com, mains $15-$25) has a waterfront patio that overlooks a marina off the Miles River. Finally, **Waterman's Crab House** (Sharp Street Wharf, Rock Hall, 1-410 639 2261, www.rockhallmd.com/watermans) has a deck that overlooks Rock Hall Harbor and the Bay Bridge. The sunsets from here can be pretty spectacular.

Resources

Tourist information
Annapolis & Anne Arundel County Conference & Visitors Bureau *26 West Street (1-888 302 2852, www.visit-annapolis.org).* **Open** 9am-5pm daily.
Maryland Department of Natural Resources *580 Taylor Avenue (1-410-260-8367, www.dnr.state.md.us).* **Open** 9am-5pm Mon-Fri. This office can provide hiking, camping and fishing information.

Jimmy Cantler's Riverside Inn.

Directory

Getting Around	222
Resources A-Z	226
Travel Advice	226
The Local Climate	233
Further Reference	234
Index	235
Advertisers' Index	242
Escapes & Excursions	245

Getting Around

ARRIVING & LEAVING

By air

Three airports serve Washington. **Washington Dulles International Airport**, 25 miles out in the suburbs of Virginia, handles the longer flights into the region, including most international flights. **Baltimore-Washington International Airport** (or BWI) is a lot closer to the first half of its name but easily accessible from Washington by public transport, and is popular for its cheaper fares and more bearable traffic. **Ronald Reagan Washington National Airport** (most people still use the old name 'National') is the closest to DC, located just across the Potomac River from Downtown, and gives a great view of the monuments as you fly in; it's used mostly for short- and medium-haul flights within the US and Canada.

The airports have their own official websites, but for general information, including ground transport, shops and services, hotels and maps, go to www.quickaid.com or www.metwashairports.com.

Major airline contact details

Air Canada 1-888 247 2262, www.aircanada.com.
American Airlines 1-800 433 7300, www.aa.com.
British Airways 1-800 247 9297, www.britishairways.com.
Continental Airlines Domestic 1-800 523 3273, international 1-800 231 0856, www.continental.com.
Delta Air Lines 1-800 221 1212, www.delta.com.
Southwest Airlines 1-800 435 9792, www.southwest.com.
United Airlines 1-800 241 6522, www.united.com.
US Airways 1-800 428 4322, www.usair.com.
Virgin Atlantic 1-800 862 8621, www.virgin-atlantic.com.

To & from Dulles Airport

1-703 572 2700, www.metwashairports.com.
The quickest and cheapest way to downtown DC is by getting the **Washington Flyer Bus** (1-888 927 4359, www.washfly.com), which operates between Dulles and the West Falls Church Metro stop (20- to 30-minute ride) at the

western end of the Orange Line. It costs $10 one way, $18 round trip, and runs at least every half-hour (5.45am-10.15pm Mon-Fri, and between 7.45am and 10.15pm Sat, Sun). From here you can continue your journey into the city on the Metro.

The **Washington Flyer Taxi Service** (1-703 661 6655) has the sole concession to operate out of Dulles (unless incoming passengers have a prearranged pick-up with another cab company). A ride from Dulles to downtown DC costs about $55-$65 plus tip. All Washington Flyer cabs are metered and take credit cards.

Super Shuttle (1-800 258 3826, 1-202 296 6662, www.super shuttle.com) offers door-to-door shared van service between all three airports and anywhere in the area. Price quotes can be obtained online; from Dulles to downtown DC hotels is $28. It's helpful to know the zip code of your final destination.

To & from BWI

1-800 435 9294, 1-410 859 7111, www.bwiairport.com.
Getting to Washington from BWI can often be expensive, a hassle, or both. A cheap combination (best if you have little to haul) to downtown DC is the shuttle-train-Metro option. Take the free shuttle bus (marked BWI Rail, 1-410 672 6169) from the BWI terminal to the train station about a mile away, then catch a Marc ($5 one way) or Amtrak (from $20) train (www.mtmaryland.com) south 25 minutes to Union Station, from where you can get on the Metro.

BWI is also served by cabs, private car companies and the Super Shuttle (*see above*), but beware of the long waits for the latter. You can get complete BWI ground transport information from the booth in Pier C or by calling 1-800 435 9294.

A cab from BWI to downtown DC costs about $60 plus tip.

To & from Reagan National Airport

1-703 417 8000, www.metwashairports.com.
National Airport is served by the Metro subway system (Yellow and Blue lines). It's about a 20-minute ride to Downtown. Going by cab is

another option: signs outside each baggage claim area will direct you to the taxi stand. The taxi operator will point you to a particular cab depending on whether you're going to DC, Virginia or Maryland. Virginia-licensed cabs can take you anywhere; DC- and Maryland-licensed cabs can't serve Virginia. Since Reagan National Airport is in Virginia, only cabs registered there will take you to the Downtown area.

The fare for Maryland, Virginia and DC cabs is determined by meter. All pick-ups from National Airport add a $1.75 surcharge. A cab to downtown Washington costs about $15-$20 plus tip (Virginia Yellow Cabs, 1-703 522 2222).

Reagan is also served by Super Shuttle (*see above*).

By rail

A train from New York City (Penn Station) to Washington DC takes roughly three hours. Fares vary, costing from around $76 each way for a reserved ticket on the slower Northeast Regional train (journey time around three and a half hours). For a reserved seat on the Acela Express service, which takes only two and a half hours, a one-way ticket is approximately $158-$203.

For more information on trains, call Amtrak on 1-800 872 7245 or go to www.amtrak.com. All trains to DC arrive at Union Station, which has its own Metro station.

By bus

The bus journey from New York around five hours, but it's really cheap – around $38 standard fare each way (reductions for online bookings). Greyhound buses (1-800 231 2222, www.greyhound.com) leave from a terminal in a rather grim area north of Union Station, and arrive at the Port Authority Bus Station in New York.

By car

Washington is served by several major highways, including Interstates 270, 66 and 95. At Washington, the 95 splits into the 495-95 and 95, looping the metropolitan area as the Capital Beltway.

DC's western border is the Potomac River. It is surrounded by Maryland on all other sides. However, the metropolitan area spreads into the neighboring states.

The city is divided into four quadrants – NW, NE, SE and SW – which meet at the US Capitol, the geographical center of Washington before the 1846 land retrocession to Virginia. North, South and East Capitol Streets, and the National Mall to the west, radiate out from the Capitol and serve as quadrant dividing lines. On one level, the District is completely rational in its layout. Numbered streets run north and south on both sides of the Capitol, with intersecting lettered streets and a few named streets tossed in, running east to west, for about 50 square blocks. The higher the number, and the further on in the alphabet the letter, the further away the street is from the Capitol. This grid system fades when the alphabet ends (when words beginning with A through Z replace the lone letters). But as straightforward as this seems, there is a crucial nuance. Because the naming system radiates from a central point, there are two First Streets (and Second, etc), one on either side of North/South Capitol Street – and ditto for lettered streets, one north and one south of the Mall (aside from A and B Streets, which don't appear in all four quadrants). This means that there can be four different places – one in each quadrant – where, say, a 4th Street and a G Street intersect, so you need to know which quadrant you're aiming for. This is why we have given the quadrant after every address in our listings, and this is also how you should give directions to a taxi driver (say 'Northwest' not 'NW'). Northwest is by far the biggest quadrant.

Street numbers correspond to cross streets; thus 800 C Street will be on C Street at 8th Street (or rather, the eighth block from the US Capitol); 890 C Street will be on the 800 block but closer to 9th Street. For addresses on numbered streets, you can also work out the location. For instance, 400 8th Street will be at the fourth block from the US Capitol. In practice this means you can count up the alphabet – ie 400 8th Street will be at D Street. There are some exceptions to this rule, however: the letter 'B' (or, strictly speaking, the 200 block) is counted even though there are no B Streets in central Washington (there are

named streets in their places – Constitution Avenue in NE and NW and Independence Avenue in SE and SW). Note also that there is no J Street, so it's ignored. For locating yourself, it's useful to remember that E Street is at 500, K is 1000, P is 1500, and U is 2000. Above W Street, the counting depends on the number of blocks, regardless of what the streets are named, although they are generally in alphabetical order. Woven into the grid of lettered and numbered streets are diagonal avenues, all named after American states – Pennsylvania Avenue, Massachusetts Avenue, and so on – that can easily cause drivers and walkers severe disorientation. Some diagonals can be a fast way across town, but most hit confusing traffic circles designed more for horse-and-buggy contraptions than modern travel, or run into parks or important buildings (such as the White House) that cause them to dogleg disconcertingly. Note that I Street is often written 'Eye' Street in order to avoid confusion with 1st/First Street.

PUBLIC TRANSPORT

The **Washington Metropolitan Area Transit Authority** runs the entire DC-area public transport network. For information on the Metrorail subway system and buses, call 1-202 637 7000 (6am-8.30pm Mon-Fri; 7am-8.30pm Sat, Sun) or go to its website at www.wmata.com, which features real-time alerts on delays.

Metrorail

The Metrorail (or, more commonly, Metro) subway system is a clean, safe and reliable public transport system. Trains run from 5am Monday to Friday and from 7am on Saturday and Sunday. The system closes at midnight Sunday to Thursday and at 3am on Saturday and Sunday mornings, but the last trains from the suburbs may depart before that. Holiday schedules vary. At busy times, trains come as often as two minutes apart. But even if everything is running on time, the scheduled waits at nights and weekends can be up to 20 minutes. Most signs and announcements use the line's final station as the identifier for platforms and trains – though not all trains go as far as the last station, so you need to know which direction you're heading.

You'll find a Metrorail map on page 256; also use the handy TripPlanner on the Metro website (www.wmata.com), or pick up the *Metro Pocket Guide*, which usefully lists the nearest Metro station to the monuments and other points of interest. Station entrances are marked on the street by square columns with a big white 'M' on top. Throughout this guide, we've listed the Metro stop nearest to each destination. If the Metro station is some distance away, a bus number is also listed. Metro lines can run deep and the escalators can be very long. The network is, however, wheelchair-accessible via elevators. If the elevators are broken at a particular station, a bus service will run from a nearby station.

Fares & passes

Fares depend on when and how far you travel and can almost double for some rides during rush hours. The minimum price of an off-peak Metro trip is $1.60, the maximum is $2.75; in peak hours journeys cost $1.95 to $5. Fares are printed on a big board on the information kiosk in each station. Up to two under-4s travel free with a full fare-paying adult; each additional child must pay full fare. Payment is by Farecard, SmarTrip® or Rail Pass.

Farecard

Insert your credit card or cash up to the value of $45 into a machine, this will then pop out a flimsy card with a magnetic stripe on the front. Use the card to enter and exit the Metro turnstiles. The price of each trip is subtracted and the remaining amount printed on the card until there's not enough value left to go anywhere. You can then transfer the remaining amount to a new card using the same machines you buy cards from. You can't get into the Metro without at least $1.60 on your card. If you don't have enough to get out at a particular station, use the Exit Fare machines just before the exit turnstiles, which take only $1 or $5 bills. The farecard is usable only on Metrorail.

SmarTrip card

This is a permanent, rechargeable plastic fare card like a credit card that can be purchased for $5 or $10 (with $5 value loaded), through Metro sales offices, vending machines, commuter stores, retail outlets and online at www.wmata.com or www.commuterdirect.com. You can then top up the card with

DIRECTORY

extra money. It is embedded with a special computer chip that keeps track of the amount available on the card. They are usable on either bus or Metro services and are cheaper and more flexible than other passes. It is likely that this will become the main, integrated system for Metro and buses. For further information, contact SmarTrip Helpline 1-888 762 7814.

There are Metro sales offices at Metro headquarters, 12th & F Street, NW (open 9am-3pm Mon-Fri) and Metro Center station (open 8am-6pm Mon-Fri).

Rail Passes

The **One-Day Pass**, $9, is valid for unlimited trips. It can used from 9.30am Mon-Fri, and all day at weekends.

The seven-day, **Short-Trip Pass**, $32.35, is valid for seven consecutive days for Metrorail trips costing up to $3.05 made 5-9.30am and 3-7 pm on weekdays. If the trip costs more than $3.05, you must use the Exit Fare machine to pay the additional fare. The pass is valid for any rail trip at other times.

The seven-day **Fast Pass**, $47, is valid for seven consecutive days of unlimited Metrorail travel.

Passes are sold at most Metro stations, online at www.wmata.com, some hotels and large grocery stores.

Transit Link Cards

This card offers unlimited Metrorail and Metro bus journeys for a month. It also includes anywhere the Metro runs in Maryland, Virginia and the District of Columbia as well as the use of Maryland and Virginia commuter rail lines.TLC cards are available online but not available at Metro Sales Offices. They cost $102.

The lines

Red Line: serves the Maryland suburbs north of DC and runs through the Downtown business district. The Zoo, Union Station and UDC (University of the District of Columbia) are on this line.
Green Line: serves Anacostia, the U Street district, Howard University and the eastern Mall area.
Blue Line: serves Arlington, Alexandria, National Airport, the RFK Stadium and most downtown memorials and museums. It parallels much of the Orange Line and some of the Yellow.
Yellow Line: serves Fairfax County (Virginia) via Alexandria to the Mall. Includes National Airport.

Orange Line: serves the suburbs from western Virginia to eastern Maryland. Parallels the Blue Line through most major tourist sights.

An extension to the system is currently under construction. The new line will run to Dulles International Airport and Tysons Corner, with 29 stations from Route 772 in Loudoun County, Virginia, to Stadium-Armory in DC. The first phase of the new line is set to open in 2013. A new system of streetcars, set to begin operation in 2012, has also been approved. The most useful for visitors will run from Downtown along H Street, NE.

Metrobuses

The bus system, also run by the Washington Metropolitan Area Transit Authority, covers the city well and is heavily used by locals. Bus stops are marked by three horizontal stripes in blue, white and red. A good timetable and route tool is available on the Metro website (www.wmata.com/timetables/default .cfm). The greater Washington area is served by different local bus systems. Alexandria and Fairfax Counties in Virginia and Montgomery, Prince George's and Prince William Counties in Maryland each run their own public transport or ride-share systems. To reach these services, call Metro (1-202 637 7000) for phone numbers and information.

Fares

The bus fare system has changed from paper tickets and passes to SmarTrip cards, the prepaid top-up travel cards also used on Metrorail.

The Metrobus fare for regular routes is $1.50 using SmarTrip or $1.70 using cash.The fare for express routes is $3.65 using SmarTrip or $3.85 using cash. Senior/Disabled fare is 75¢ for regular routes, $1.80 on express routes.

Bus passes

The weekly seven-day regional bus pass costs $15 ($7.50 seniors and disabled). It is uploaded to your SmarTrip card and activated once you start to use the card.

Useful bus routes

One popular area served better by bus than Metro is Georgetown: catch a **30**, **32**, **34**, **35** or **36** bus marked 'Friendship Heights' running west on Pennsylvania Avenue. The same buses serve the Upper Northwest area along Wisconsin Avenue. For Adams Morgan, including busy 18th Street,

take the **90**, **92** or **93** (U Street/ Garfield line) bus from Woodley Park-Zoo/Adams Morgan Metro, or the **42** (Mount Pleasant line) bus from Dupont Circle Metro. (Adams Morgan is also within walking distance of Columbia Heights Metro).

As its name suggests, the **Circulator** bus operates on circulatory routes; there are six of these, all incorporating downtown Washington DC. It is a useful system for visitors as it links cultural and entertainment centers to Downtown. Fares are $1 (50c seniors or disabled). Free transfers from Circulator to Circulator, valid for three hours, are available with a SmarTrip card; transfers are not available for cash tickets. For route maps and other information visit www.dccirculator.com.

The Circulator has a 'Where's My Bus' service that uses GPS data for bus arrival information and can be accessed from any mobile device with internet access: www.circulator.dc.gov.

Trains

Both Amtrak and Marc (Maryland Rail Commuter Service) operate out of DC's Union Station. **Amtrak** connects with cities all over the US, including Baltimore, and also has stops at Alexandria in Virginia and at Rockville and New Carrollton in Maryland. There are several trains daily to New York, Philadelphia and Boston, including Metroliner services, on which you're allowed to reserve seats.

Marc is a commuter train running from Union Station to parts of West Virginia and Maryland (including Baltimore). The Penn line goes to Baltimore's northern suburbs and runs from 4.45am to 11.40pm on weekdays (every 30 minutes during rush hour, every hour otherwise). It does not run at weekends. The Camden line stops at Camden Yards (Baltimore's baseball stadium) and runs only during morning and evening rush hours (6.42-8.05am and 4.13-7.35pm). Marc stops at some Metro stations in Maryland. Fares between DC and Baltimore are $7 each way. Both Amtrak and Marc serve the BWI Airport station, from where you take a free shuttle bus for the short journey to the terminal.

Union Station *50 Massachusetts Avenue, NE, at North Capitol Street (Amtrak 1-800 872 7245, www.amtrak.com, Marc 1-866 743 3682/www.mtamaryland.com).* **Map** p253 L6.

Taxis

As elsewhere in the States, driving a taxi is a typical job for recent immigrants, so it's not uncommon to get a driver who needs directions.

There are no taxi ranks but you can usually find cabs outside hotels and it's easy to flag down a DC-licensed cab around most central parts of the city. Cabs for hire have a light on top and the company name on the door. To call a cab in the District, try Diamond (1-202 387 2221, 6200) or Yellow Cab (1-202 544 1212). Cab fares are now metered based on how many miles you travel, with extra charges for additional passengers, rush-hour travel, calling for a cab, and traveling during designated snow emergencies. Bear in mind when traveling during rush hour, that time consumed while the taxicab is stopped (or traveling at less than 10mph for longer than 60 seconds) is charged (an extra $15 per hour with Yellowcabs). Baggage charges are usually $1 for each fairly large, grocery-sized bag handled by the driver, after the first one, and $2.50 for each big bag. In reality, some cabbies charge, some don't, depending, it seems, on their mood.

To give an idea of cost, one person, flagging the cab, with no bags, not at rush hour nor in the snow, will probably pay $14-$15 plus tip to travel from Capitol Hill to Dupont Circle.

In Maryland and Virginia, cabs also run on meters. Cabs licensed for these areas can legally only pick up fares in DC on a pre-arranged basis – and only take them to the jurisdiction in which they are licensed. That might be why, no matter how hard you're waving on a DC street, that empty cab goes right on by.

Driving

The Washington area (especially between DC and Virginia) is not a great place to drive. The traffic circles are confusing and some streets, notably Rock Creek Parkway, change direction in rush hours. Read carefully the times posted in the middle of 'Do Not Enter' and 'No Turns' signs; at other times, entrance is allowed. Unless there's a sign saying otherwise, you can make a right turn when the lights are red.

Parking

There are plenty of off-street pay parking lots around town: Monument Parking (1-202 833 9357)

has seven locations; Parking Management Incorporated (PMI, 1-202 785 9191) has many more. Street parking ranges from difficult to impossible, especially near the Mall, Downtown and in popular nightlife areas such as Georgetown and Adams Morgan. The parking police are notoriously pedantic. Add to this the regular street shutdowns for presidential motorcades and you'll see why nearly a third of District residents don't own a car.

For up-to-the-minute traffic conditions, check the live cameras on www.trafficland.com. Tune into WTOP (103.5 FM) for traffic reports every ten minutes.

Car hire

For getting right out of town, driving is often the best option. Almost every rental agency will require a credit card and matching driving license, and few will rent to anyone under 25. The price quoted won't include tax, liability insurance or collision damage waiver (CDW). If you already have an insured car in the US, your own liability insurance may cover the rental. Ask about discounts, available to members of the AAA (as well as British AA members), AARP (American Association of Retired Persons) and other organizations.

Zip Car (1-202 737 4900, www.zipcar.com) is a car sharing/rental company that has cars in many locations around the city, available on an hourly or daily basis. Foreign visitors will also be required to join the scheme, which has a fee of $50-$60 for membership plus an application fee of $25 (a drivers' license and paperwork with information about the prospective member's driving history is required). Once a member, the actual hiring fees are low – around $7 an hour. Metro Rail has linked up with Zip Car to situate car pick-up points at certain rail stations. Call 1-800 745 7433 for information.

The following national car rental companies have DC offices:
Alamo 1-800 462 5266, www.alamo.com.
Avis 1-800 331 1212, www.avis.com.
Budget 1-800 527 0700, www.budget.com.
Dollar 1-800 800 4000, www.dollarcar.com.
Hertz 1-800 654 3131, www.hertz.com.
National 1-800 227 7368, www.nationalcar.com.
Thrifty 1-800 847 4389/ www.thrifty.com.

Cycling

DC is a great place to cycle. Much of the city, including most of the Mall and Downtown, is flat (though there's Capitol Hill at the eastern end of the Mall). A web of bike paths take you to out-of-center spots, and riding from museum to monument will save your feet hours of ache (though you'll have to lock your bike to a signpost or railings). For more information on biking in and around DC, get in touch with the Washington Area Bicyclist Association (1-202 518 0524, www.waba.org).

Capital Bikeshare

Since the launch of the Capital Bikeshare Scheme in September 2010, the bright red aluminum bikes are increasing in number and are expected to become a real city presence with over 1,100 bikes and 110 stations. This scheme has replaced the 2008 SmartBike DC program, of which a few remnants exist. The service area includes Washington DC, with 100 stations, and two neighborhoods – Pentagon City and Crystal City – with 14 rental stations. Other areas, like Rosslyn, are set to follow. Each station will begin the day with about ten bikes and five empty docking spaces. Members can check on the website, www.capital bikeshare.com, how many bikes are available and how many docking stations are open for returning bicycles at any given moment. The pricing structure is designed to encourage short journeys rather than longer leisure trips.
Membership: $5 for 24 hours, $25 for 30 days, $75 for a year.
Rates: first 30mins free. The next half-hour (31-60mins) is $1.50. The following 30mins is $3. Thus total cost for 61-90mins is $4.50.

Thereafter, cost rises to $6 per half-hour, capping at six and a half hours for a total fee of $70.50. At this point you can then use it for up to 24 hours for no extra fee. If the bike isn't returned within 24 hours, it will be considered stolen and will incur a replacement fee of $1,000.

Walking

Walking is a great way to get around, but remember that summers are hot and muggy, and while the Mall might look like a nice gentle stroll, it's actually two miles long, with a hill at the Capitol end.

DIRECTORY

Resources A-Z

DIRECTORY

ADDRESSES

See p223 **Navigation**.

AGE RESTRICTIONS

You have to be 21 to drink alcohol in DC, Maryland and Virginia. Note that the law is very strictly enforced, with severe penalties. Be sure to carry ID with you (*see p228*).

ATTITUDE & ETIQUETTE

Washington is unquestionably a major tourist destination, so if you wear jeans, trainers and carry a small rucksack you should feel right at home. It is also, of course, a major business center, and walking around Downtown you'll see lawyers in suits and other members of a well-dressed workforce.

DC residents usually inhabit their own little niches. They read the *Washington Post* on the Metro, mind their own business on the sidewalk and get upset when tourists stand on the left side of the escalator instead of the right. But if you do stop someone on the street to ask for directions, they will generally be happy to oblige.

BUSINESS

There was a time, not that long ago, when the business scene in Washington could pretty much be covered in one word: government. Not only was the federal presence far and away the dominant industry, but dealing with it was the primary purpose of most private-sector activity. Government is still the 800lb gorilla of the DC jungle, but a number of A-list corporations now have their

headquarters in the Washington area. A high-tech industry has established itself along the so-called Dulles Corridor, turning the expressway linking the city with Dulles International Airport in the Virginia suburbs into something of a Silicon Valley East. The business epicentre is Downtown's K Street, lined with glassy office buildings. DC now has more office space than any other American city aside from New York.

That said, while Washington may have made the big time, standard operating procedures are lower-key than in comparable cities. There are similarities, such as the ubiquitous power lunch, but the overall style is less frenetic. In fact, as viewed from the vantage of New York, Washingtonians have no style. The idea is to dress down: dark (preferably blue) suits, and ties with a touch of red. In summer, when the heat and humidity threaten to reach meltdown levels, light-hued poplin and seersucker suits are almost a uniform. Year-round, the preferred accessory is a neck chain from which dangles a photo-ID card – it's virtually a badge of belonging.

Conventions

Walter E Washington Convention Center
801 Mount Vernon Place, NW, between 7th & 9th Streets, Downtown (1-202 249 3000, www.dcconvention.com). **Map** p253 J5.
The largest single building in the city, its 52,000sq ft ballroom and $4 million art collection make it worth a peek for casual visitors, many of whom stop in at the restaurants and retail outlets on-site.

Couriers

All the major international couriers, in addition to several locally based enterprises, are active in DC. For others, check the Yellow Pages under 'Air Cargo & Package Express Service', 'Delivery Service', or, for local deliveries, 'Messenger Services'.
Federal Express *1-800 463 3339, www.fedex.com.* **Credit** AmEx, Disc, MC, V.

Skynet Worldwide Courier
1-786 265 4830, www.skynet.net. **No credit cards**.

United Parcel Service *1-800 742 5877, www.ups.com.* **Credit** AmEx, MC, V.

Useful organizations

District of Columbia Chamber of Commerce *506 9th Street, NW, at E Street, Downtown (1-202 347 7201, www.dcchamber.org). Gallery Place Metro.* **Open** 8.30am-5.30pm Mon-Fri. **Map** p252 H5.

Greater Washington Board of Trade *Suite 300, 2101 L Street, NW, between 20th & 21st Streets, Downtown (1-202 857 5900, www.bot.org). Foggy Bottom or Farragut West Metro.* **Map** p252 G5.
The Board of Trade functions as a regional co-ordinating organization for DC, northern Virginia and suburban Maryland.

US Department of Commerce *14th Street & Constitution Avenue, NW, The Federal Triangle (1-202 482 2000, www.doc.gov). Federal Triangle Metro.* **Open** 8am-5.30pm Mon-Fri. **Map** p252 H6.

CONSUMER

Whenever possible, pay with a major credit card so you can cancel payment or get reimbursed if there is a problem (be sure to keep receipts or a form of documentation). Consider travel insurance that includes default coverage to protect yourself against financial loss.

CUSTOMS

A visa waiver form (I-94W) is generally provided by the airline during check-in or on the plane and must be presented to Immigration at the airport of entry to the US. International visitors should allow about an hour in the airport to clear Immigration. For more on visas, *see p233*.

A customs declaration form (6059B) is also provided on international flights into the US; this must be filled out and handed to a customs official after Immigration (keep it handy). Current US regulations allow foreign visitors to import the following duty-free: 200 cigarettes or 50 cigars (Cuban cigars are generally not allowed), 1 litre of wine or spirits (over-21s only), and a maximum of $100 in gifts. You can take up to $10,000 in cash, travellers' cheques or endorsed bank drafts in or out of the country. Anything above that you must declare on a customs form, or it risks seizure. It is illegal to transport most perishable foods and plants across international borders. If you are carrying prescription drugs, make sure they are labeled, and keep a copy of your prescription with you. The Customs and Border Patrol website (www.cbp.gov) contains information.

DISABLED

Washington is good at providing facilities for all types of tourists, including the disabled and elderly. Most museums, monuments and memorials are accessible to visitors using wheelchairs and many have other facilities to help disabled travelers. Nearly all streets in the Downtown area have wide sidewalks with kerb cuts for greater accessibility. The Metro has excellent facilities for those with visual and auditory impairments, or mobility problems. All stations are theoretically wheelchair-accessible, although lifts are not always in service. In these cases, a shuttle service is provided.

Information

An extremely useful website is www.disabilityguide.org, which rates DC's hotels, restaurants, malls and sights according to accessibility. It's run by **Access Information** (1-301 528 8664). The New York-based **Society for Accessible Travel & Hospitality** (1-212 447 7284, www.sath.org) offers advice for disabled travelers throughout the US.

DRUGS

Hard and soft drugs are illegal in Washington, as in the rest of the US. In practice, however, arresting people for the possession of small amounts of soft drugs is not a high priority for DC police.

ELECTRICITY

The US electricity supply is 110-120 volt, 60-cycle AC, rather than the 220-240 volt, 50-cycle AC used in Europe. Plugs are standard two-pins. An adaptor and, in some cases, a voltage converter (available at airport shops and hardware stores) are necessary to use foreign appliances. Check www.voltage valet.com to answer questions about electricity.

EMBASSIES & CONSULATES

Note that most visa offices keep shorter hours than the embassy hours listed. For other embassies and consular services, see the Yellow Pages or internet.

Australia *1601 Massachusetts Avenue, NW, at 16th Street, Dupont Circle (1-202 797 3000, www.austemb.org). Dupont Circle Metro.* **Open** 8.30am-5pm Mon-Fri. **Map** p250 H4.

Canada *501 Pennsylvania Avenue, NW, at 6th Street, Penn Quarter (1-202 682 1740, www.canadian embassy.org). Archives-Navy Memorial or Judiciary Square Metro.* **Open** 9am-5pm; consular services 9am-noon Mon-Fri. **Map** p252 J6.

Ireland *2234 Massachusetts Avenue, NW, at Sheridan Circle, Dupont Circle (1-202 462 3939, www.irelandemb.org). Dupont Circle Metro.* **Open** 9am-1pm, 2-4pm Mon-Fri. **Map** p250 F4.

New Zealand *37 Observatory Circle, NW, at Massachusetts Avenue, Upper Northwest (1-202 328 4800, www.nzembassy.com).* **Open** 8.30am-5pm Mon-Fri. **Map** p249 E3.

United Kingdom *3100 Massachusetts Avenue, NW, at Whitehaven Street, Upper Northwest (1-202 588 6500, www.britain usa.com). Dupont Circle Metro then N2, N4, N6 bus.* **Open** 9am-5.30pm Mon-Fri. **Map** p250 F3.

EMERGENCIES

The number to call for fire, police, ambulance and other emergency services is **911** (free from cellphones and public phones).

GAY & LESBIAN

Washington is home to a thriving, well-established gay and lesbian community. For information about groups and what's on, consult the *Washington Blade* (its excellent website is www.washblade.com).

For further information on the local scene, *see pp181-84*.

HEALTH

Accident & emergency

You will be billed for emergency treatment, although emergency rooms are legally only allowed to turn patients away if their injuries are not considered an emergency. However, hospitals will do all they can to ensure they receive payment for treatment. Taking out full medical insurance before you travel is imperative; it's a good idea to call your company before seeking treatment to find out which hospitals accept your insurance.

Children's National Medical Center *111 Michigan Avenue, NW, at First Street (1-202 884 2327, 1-888 884 2327, www. childrensnational.org). Brookland-CUA Metro then H2, H4 bus.* **Map** p251 K2.

Georgetown University Hospital *3800 Reservoir Road, NW, between 38th & 39th Streets, Georgetown (1-202 444 2000, www.georgetownuniversity hospital.org). Dupont Circle Metro then D6 bus, or Dupont Circle or Rosslyn Metro, then hospital shuttle, every 15-30mins.* **Map** p249 E4.

DIRECTORY

DIRECTORY

George Washington University Hospital *900 23rd Street, NW, between I Street & Washington Circle, Foggy Bottom (1-202 715 4000, www.gwhospital.com). Foggy Bottom Metro.* **Map** p252 G5.

Howard University Hospital *2041 Georgia Avenue, NW, at V Street (1-202 865 6100, www. huhealthcare.com) Shaw-University Metro then hospital shuttle bus, bus 70, 71, 90, 92, 96.* **Map** p251 J3

Contraception & abortion

Several branches of the CVS chain (*see p158*; or call 1-888 607 4287) are open 24 hours a day. Like other pharmacies, they sell condoms and can fill out prescriptions for other contraceptives. If you need advice about abortion, call Planned Parenthood on 1-202 347 8512 or go to its website, www.planned parenthood.org. It has a center in the Downtown area.

Dentists

DC Dental Society *1-202 547 7613, www.dcdental.org.* The DC Dental Society can refer you to a local dentist for treatment.

Dental Emergency *Howard University Hospital Dental Clinic (1-202 865 6100). For listing, see above.* Ask for the Dental Resident on duty.

Doctors

Doctors Referral *1-800 362 8677, www.1800doctors.com.* Can recommend a local doctor.

HIV & AIDS

Elizabeth Taylor Medical Center *1701 14th Street, NW, between R Street & Riggs Place, Shaw: Logan Circle (1-202 745 7000, www.wwc. org). McPherson Square Metro.* **Open** 8am-8pm Mon-Thur, 8am-5pm Fri. **Map** p250 H4. Part of the Whitman Walker Clinic – a pioneering institution offering services to people with HIV and other sexually transmitted diseases – the Elizabeth Taylor Medical Center provides counseling to AIDS patients and their families. The excellent website contains a wealth of useful information.

National HIV/AIDS Hotline *1-800 342 2437, www.thebody.com.* Will give information about the nearest HIV testing centers.

Pharmacies

See p158.

HELPLINES

Alcoholics Anonymous 1-202 966 9115, www.aa-dc.org.
Auto Impound 1-202 727 5000.
Mental Health 24hr Access Helpline 1-888 793-4357.
Poison Center 1-800 222 1222.
Rape Crisis Center 1-202 333 7273.
Substance Abuse Hotline 1-800 784 6776.
Suicide Prevention Center 1-800 784 2433.

ID

Unless you're driving or drinking alcohol, there isn't any law that says you must carry identification with you, but it makes sense to do so. Keeping your passport with you is risky, but a driver's license is usually a good idea, as everyone under the age of 40 seems to get carded – for entry to nightclubs, in particular – in DC.

INSURANCE

Non-nationals should arrange baggage, trip-cancellation and medical insurance before they leave home (but first check what your existing home and medical insurance covers). Medical centers and hospitals will ask for details of your insurance company and policy number if you require treatment, so it's a good idea to keep this information with you.

INTERNET

Most hotels and cafés have Wi-Fi access, sometimes free and sometimes for a small fee.
Branches of DC public libraries are great places to get online free, offering both Wi-Fi access and computers. For the Martin Luther King Jr Memorial Library, *see below*. For other DC libraries, see www.dclibrary.org.

LEFT LUGGAGE

All three of the area's major airports have effectively done away with luggage storage at their facilities in light of the US Homeland Security Department's new regulations following 9/11. The airport may be able to advise you on other facilities that may be available.

LEGAL HELP

In the legal capital of the country, more than one person in seven is a lawyer. If you can't afford a local lawyer, stop by the Legal Aid Society of the District of Columbia, where legal aid lawyers can provide free legal assistance.

Legal Aid Society *Suite 350, 1331 H Street, NW, between 14th Steet & New York Avenue, Downtown (1-202 628 1161, www.legalaiddc.org).McPherson Square or Metro Center Metro.* **Open** Initial interview hours 12.30-6pm Mon; 12.30-4pm Thur. **Map** p252 H3.

Libraries

Washington is home to a range of sites from the endless shelves of the Library of Congress to specialized libraries in each of the Smithsonian museums. Many national and international organizations also have their headquarters in DC, complete with archives. The city's universities all have excellent libraries, and the public library system (see www.dclibrary.org) has 27 branches.

Library of Congress *1st Street & Independence Avenue, SE, The Capitol & Around (operator 1-202 707 5000, visitor information 1-202 707 8000, www.loc.gov). Capitol South Metro.* **Open** varies. **Map** p253 L7.
As the central library for the US, the Library of Congress makes it its business to have a copy of almost everything printed. However, it may take a very long time to find one small book among the nearly 100 million items on 535 miles of shelves, even when the staff do the search for you. The library is open to the public, but you must first wait in line for a library card and an extensive security check. Take at least one photo ID. Note that opening times vary for the different buildings within the complex.

Martin Luther King Jr Memorial Library *901 G Street, NW, at 9th Street, Downtown (Mon-Fri 9.30am-4pm 1-202 727 0321, after 4pm Mon-Fri & weekends 1-202-727-1111, www.dclibrary. org/mlk). Gallery Place-Chinatown Metro.* **Open** noon-9pm Mon,Tue; 9.30am-5.30pm Wed-Sat; 1-5pm Sun. **Map** p253 J6.

LOST PROPERTY

If you leave something on the bus or subway, the chances are you won't see it again, but it's worth calling the Washington Metro Transit Authority Lost & Found on 1-202 962 1195 or submitting a claim online at www.wmata.com. It's also worth checking at the nearest police station to see if it's been handed in.

MEDIA

Washington is the one American city where many people actually watch the political chat shows run every Sunday by the main television networks and offered every day by the growing ranks of cable news channels – notably, the abrasive Fox News cable channel, which has been winning viewers at the expense of such polite operations as CNN (now part of Washington's multimedia superpower AOL Time Warner). There's even a local radio station that carries an audio version of the C-SPAN cable channel's Congressional coverage (WCSP, 90.1 FM). With all the major American news organizations and many foreign ones in residence in DC, news crews are a common sight around town. Newsmakers frequently appear at the National Press Club (13th Floor, 529 14th Street, NW, 1 202 662 7500, http://press.org), although only some of these events are open to the public.

Newspapers & magazines

Dailies

The Godzilla of local print journalism is the *Washington Post*, whose clout is the object of some awe and much resentment. Nonetheless, the *Post* has the highest market penetration of any major US daily, although its executives fret, with reason, that its power is waning with younger Washingtonians. The *Post*'s coverage exemplifies the inside-the-Beltway mentality, with heavy emphasis on politics and policy, and a poorly concealed scepticism that anything else really matters. By the standards of US newspapers, international coverage is strong, and over recent years the paper has greatly expanded its online presence as well as coverage of business and technology. By contrast, genuinely local news and the arts are often treated with

indifference. On Fridays, however, the *Post* publishes its 'Weekend' section, with extensive arts and entertainment listings.

This, along with the *Washington City Paper* (*see below*), is what most Washingtonians turn to for current entertainment information.

Owned by cronies of the Rev Sun Myung Moon, the *Washington Times* offers a right-wing view of events, with front-page stories that are often amusingly partisan. Although some commend its sports coverage, the paper is read principally by paleo-conservatives and people who really, really hate the *Post*.

Although it offers little specifically for Washingtonians, the *New York Times* has a significant DC readership. The paper is most popular on Sundays, when its arts and feature writing trounces the *Post*'s. Most large US newspapers are available in local street boxes.

USA Today, the country's only national general-interest daily, is produced at Tysons Corner, Virginia, but its terse stories, graphics-heavy presentation and middle-American mindset are not much to local taste.

Weeklies

Geographical or cultural subdivisions of the metropolitan area are served by many weekly tabloids, including some suburban ones owned by the *Post*, but the only such weekly of regional significance is *Washington City Paper* (www.washingtoncitypaper.com). Founded in 1981 and owned by the *Chicago Reader*, this 'alternative' free weekly has softened its approach over the years. Although it covers local politics, the paper is read mostly for its arts coverage, listings and adverts.

The District's gay community is served by the weekly *Washington Blade* (www.washingtonblade.com), which is a good source of local and national news. *MW* (Metro Weekly, www.metroweekly.com) includes listings for bars, clubs, guest DJ spots and parties. It also takes a more gossipy tone than the *Blade*. Both are free and readily available.

Monthlies

The *Washingtonian* is professional but seldom provocative, specializing in consumer journalism and profiles. Two locally published magazines with global agendas are *National Geographic* and

Smithsonian, which are circulated to members of their respective organisations and are also sold at newsstands. Their articles on science, history and other subjects of enduring importance – and *National Geographic*'s exceptional photography – exemplify the side of DC that is not consumed by the latest poll numbers.

Outlets

Washington has more newspaper and magazine outlets than you might at first think. Many large office buildings have newsstands, often concealed in their lobbies so that only workers and regular visitors are aware of them. Outdoor newsstands (along with sidewalk cafés) were illegal in Washington for much of the 20th century, and since the ban was lifted in the 1960s most attempts to establish them have failed – which explains why the sidewalks at major intersections are overwhelmed by newspaper vending machines. Among the larger newsstands – and the ones with the best selection of foreign publications – are **News World** (1001 Connecticut Avenue, NW) and **Metro News Center** (1200 G Street, NW). The city's numerous Borders and Barnes & Noble outlets have extensive periodical .

Television

Washington's airwaves carry all the usual suspects: **NBC** (WRC, Channel 4); **Fox** (WTTG, Channel 5); right-wing firebrand **Fox News**, **ABC** (WJLA, Channel 7); **CBS** (WUSA, Channel 9) and the WB- and UPN-merged **CW** Network. These offer the familiar sitcoms, cop and hospital dramas, and growing numbers (because they're cheap to produce) of news magazine shows. The local news programs on Washington's commercial TV outlets are supposedly less lurid than in most American cities, although that's hard to imagine. There are also three local public TV stations featuring the customary line-up of *Sesame Street*, British drawing-room dramas and highlights from *Riverdance*: **WMPT** (Channel 22), **WETA** (Channel 26) and **WHUT** (Channel 32). The latter also runs some Spanish-language shows, while a fourth public station, **WNVC** (Channel 56), along with the local cable network **MHZ**, specialize in international programming, from classic Japanese films to

DIRECTORY

the day's news in Mandarin, Polish and French.

On cable, the fare is also commonplace, although it varies slightly among local jurisdictions. National channels based in Washington include **BET** (Black Entertainment Television) and the latter's documentary offspring – **Animal Planet**, the **Learning Channel** and the **History Channel**. Washingtonians watch more **C-SPAN** and **C-SPAN 2** (with live coverage of Congress and other public affairs programming) than most Americans; channels seen only locally include the extensive local news coverage of **NewsChannel 8**.

Radio

World events can change Washington's daily climate rapidly, so visitors would be well advised to keep on top of daily headlines via the city's excellent all-news station, **WTOP** (103.5 FM), which also offers traffic and weather updates every ten minutes. Beyond that, the city is upscale, urban and has a large African-American population, so local radio stations play more classical and hip hop, and less country music than in most parts of the US. Since the Federal Communication Commission weakened regulations restricting the number of stations that could be owned by large corporations, however, regional diversity in US radio programming is dwindling. Increasingly, stations are tightly formatted to attract a chosen demographic, often with a carefully test-marketed subset of oldies: 'classic rock' (**WARW**, 94.7 FM), 'classic hits' (**WBIG**, 100.3 FM) and 'adult contemporary' (**WMMJ**, 102.3 FM). **WWDC** (101.1 FM) is the area's only 'alternative' station left. 'Urban contemporary' (hip hop and soul) music is heard on **WKYS** (93.9 FM), **WPGC** (95.5 FM) and **WHUR** (96.3 FM). Of the three, **WPGC** is the rowdiest, while **WHUR** goes for a somewhat older audience. The leading Top 40 station is **WIHT** (99.5 FM). **WGMS** (104.1 FM) is the city's commercial classical station. The top two public radio stations, **WETA** (90.9 FM) and **WAMU** (88.5 FM), broadcast much of the news and arts programming of Washington-based National Public Radio (**NPR**). The former also plays classical music; the latter offers public-affairs talk shows

and weekend folk and bluegrass music. The once-radical **WPFW** (89.3 FM) still mixes jazz and politics, but has become tamer. The *Post* has started a station (107.7 FM) that mixes in-depth stories, feedback from writers and Washington Nationals baseball broadcasts.

College radio, a free-form catalyst in many markets, is insignificant here; the University of Maryland's **WMUC** (88.1 FM) can be received only in the north-eastern suburbs. Washington is also the home of **XM**, the country's first digital satellite radio service. It broadcasts 100 channels of CD-quality music programming for those who have purchased the special receivers.

MONEY

The United States' monetary system is decimal-based: the US dollar ($) is divided into 100 cents (¢). Coins and dollars are stamped with the faces of US presidents and statesmen. Coin denominations are the penny (1¢ – Abraham Lincoln on a copper-coloured coin); nickel (5¢ – Thomas Jefferson); dime (10¢ – Franklin D Roosevelt); quarter (25¢ – George Washington); the less common half-dollar (50¢ – John F Kennedy) and the 'golden' dollar (depicting Sacagawea, a Native American woman who acted as a guide to 19th-century explorers Lewis and Clark). You may also come across the smaller 'Susan B Anthony' dollar coin, a failed attempt to introduce dollar coins.

Bills, or notes, are all the same size and come in $1 (George Washington); $5 (Abraham Lincoln); $10 (Alexander Hamilton); $20 (Andrew Jackson); $50 (Ulysses S Grant); and $100 (Benjamin Franklin) denominations.

Credit cards

As elsewhere in the US, credit cards are virtually a necessity in Washington. If you want to rent a car or book a ticket over the phone, you will need a major credit card. They are accepted almost universally in hotels, restaurants and shops, though occasionally you will find a gas station, small store or cinema that only takes cash. Visa and MasterCard are the most widely accepted cards, with American Express a distant third. Credit cards are also useful for extracting instant cash advances from ATMs and banks. However, where US account holders pay a flat service charge for getting cash this

way, UK companies' charges vary – and you pay interest, of course. Debit cards are also accepted at many shops.

ATMs

Automated Teller Machines (cashpoints) are located outside nearly all banks, inside all malls and major shopping areas, and now in many bars and restaurants. They are the most convenient and often the most cost-effective way of obtaining cash – but remember that most charge at least a $2 service fee on top of any charges levied by your home bank. All you need is an ATM card (credit or debit) – and your usual PIN number. Check with your bank before leaving home to find out what the fees will be.

Banks

Bank of America *1501 Pennsylvania Avenue, NW, at 15th Street, White House & Around (1-202 624 4253). McPherson Square Metro.* **Open** 9am-5pm Mon-Thur; 9am-6pm Fri. **Map** p252 H6.

PNC Bank *Corcoran Branch, 1503 Pennsylvania Avenue, NW, at 15th Street, White House & Around (1-202 835 4502). McPherson Square Metro.* **Open** 9am-2pm Mon-Fri. . **Map** p252 H6.

Currency exchange

Some – but not many – banks will exchange cash or travelers' checks in major foreign currencies. You will need photo ID, such as a passport, to exchange travelers' checks. The most convenient place for exchange is at the airport when you arrive – but banks often give better rates. Travelex and American Express also exchange currency. Most hotel desks will do the same – handy if you're stuck late at night without any cash and don't want to go out to an ATM.

American Express Travel *The Investment Building, 1501 K Street, NW, at 15th Street. (1-202 457 1300). MacPherson Square Metro.* **Open** 9am-5.30pm Mon-Fri. **Map** p252 H5.
Call 1-202 457-1300 for the purchase or refund of travelers' checks.

Travelex *Suite 103, 1800 K Street, NW, at 18th Street, Foggy Bottom (1-202 872 1428, www.travelex. com). Farragut North Metro.* **Open** 9am-7pm Mon-Fri. **Map** p284 G5.

DIRECTORY

Travelex also has branches at Union Station and Dulles and National airports. The central number is 1-800 287 7362.

Lost/stolen credit cards

In the event of a lost or stolen card, call the company immediately to deactivate it and also to request a replacement. Travelers' checks can be replaced via a local office.
American Express cards
1-800 528 4800.
American Express travellers cheques 1-800 221 7282.
Diners Club
1-800 234 6377.
1-866 535 1362.
Discover
1-800 347 2683.
MasterCard
1-800 627 8372.
Visa
1-800 847 2911.

Tax

The general consumer DC sales tax is 6.5 per cent; it's six per cent in Maryland and five per cent in Virginia. The tax on restaurant meals is ten per cent and is added later to the advertized menu price, while the tax on hotel rooms is 14.5 per cent.

OPENING HOURS

Business hours in DC are generally 9am to 5pm Monday to Friday. Most shops are open 10am to 5pm or 6pm Monday to Saturday and noon to 6pm on Sunday. Even in the business-heavy Downtown area, most shops are open at the weekend. From Monday to Saturday, mall stores usually stay open until 9pm. On the whole, banks open at 9am and close at about 3pm on weekdays only. Restaurants are usually open for lunch from 11am to 2pm and for dinner from 5pm to 10pm, but many are open all day. In Adams Morgan, Georgetown and Dupont Circle, some bars and eateries don't close until 2am or 3am.

POLICE

There are two phone numbers you should know in case you need to reach the police. The first number, **911**, is used in cases of emergencies: if a crime is in progress or has just occurred, or if you see a fire or medical emergency or a major vehicle crash; it is also the number for violent crimes.

The police non-emergency number, **311**, is for minor vehicle crashes, property crimes that are no longer in progress and animal control problems. The 311 number service has been extended to cover other city services.

A good resource for information on police hotlines and other city services is http://dc.gov.

POSTAL SERVICES

Call 1-202 636 2270 or check the phone book to find your nearest post office. They are usually open 8am-5pm on weekdays; some open for limited hours on Saturdays. Mail can be sent from any of the big blue mailboxes on street corners, but if you are sending a package overseas that is heavier than 16oz, it must be sent directly from a post office and accompanied by a customs form. American Express (*see p231*) provides a postal service for its clients.

General Mail Facility *900 Brentwood Road, NE, at New York Avenue (1-202 636 2270). Rhode Island Avenue Metro.* **Open** 9am-5pm Mon-Fri; 9am-4pm Sat;.
Credit AmEx, MC, V.
The city's main postal facility, but it's located quite a way from Downtown. A letter sent Poste Restante (called 'General Delivery' in the US) will end up here; better to have it sent to a specific post office (you'll need the zip code). Mail is held for 30 days.

National Capitol Station Post Office *City Post Office Building, North Capitol Street & Massachusetts Avenue, NE, Union Station & Around (1-202 523 2368). Union Station Metro.* **Open** 9am-7pm Mon-Fri; 9am-5pm Sat, Sun. **Credit** AmEx, MC, V. **Map** p253 K6.

RELIGION

Adas Israel Congregation *2850 Quebec Street, NW, Cleveland Park (1-202 362 4433, www.adas israel.org). Cleveland Park Metro.* **Map** p250 F1.
Conservative Jewish.

Basilica of the National Shrine of the Immaculate Conception *400 Michigan Avenue, NE, at 4th Street (1-202 526 8300, www. nationalshrine.com). Brookland-CUA Metro.* **Map** p251 L1.
The largest Roman Catholic church in North America, and one of the ten largest churches in the world.

Foundry Methodist Church
1500 16th Street, NW, at P Street, Dupont Circle (1-202 332 4010, www.foundryumc.org). Dupont Circle Metro. **Map** p250 H4.

Islamic Center *2551 Massachusetts Avenue, NW, at Belmont Road, Adams Morgan (1-202 332 8343, www.theislamic center.com). Dupont Circle Metro then N2, N4, N6 bus.* **Map** p250 F3.

New York Avenue Presbyterian Church *1313 New York Avenue, NW, between 13th & 14th Streets, Downtown (1-202 393 3700, www.nyapc.org). McPherson Square Metro.* **Map** p252 H5.

St John's Episcopal Church
1525 H Street, NW, at Lafayette Square, White House & around (1-202 347 8766, www.stjohns-dc.org). McPherson Square Metro. **Map** p252 H5.

Washington Hebrew Congregation
3935 Macomb Street, NW, at Massachusetts Avenue, Cleveland Park (1-202 362 7100, www.whctemple.org). Cleveland Park Metro. **Map** p249 D1.
Reformed Jewish.

Washington National Cathedral *Massachusetts & Wisconsin Avenues, NW, Upper Northwest (1-202 537 6200/www.cathedral.org/ cathedral). Tenley Town metro & then bus 30, 31, 32, 34, 35, 36, 37 going south on Wisconsin Avenue.* **Map** p249 E2.
Episcopal.

SAFETY & SECURITY

Apart from the large-scale security concerns and restrictions that come from being the capital of the United States, the areas of DC that are notorious for crime are parts of the Southeast and Northeast quadrants, far from the main (and even most of the secondary) tourist sights. The threat of crime near the major visitor destinations is generally small.

The area around the Capitol is very heavily policed, and Metro trains and stations are also well patrolled and virtually crime-free. Adams Morgan and the U Street/ 14th Street Corridor are much too heavy with traffic to be considered dangerous, but the sidestreets surrounding them can be dodgy after dark, as can some streets near Union Station and around Capitol Hill and H Street, NE. Stick to the heavily populated, well-lit thoroughfares when walking in these areas at night. Generally, as in any big city, you should take the usual security precautions. Be wary of pickpockets, especially in crowds. Look like you know what you're doing and where you're going – even if you don't. Use common sense and follow your intuition about people and situations. If someone does approach you for money in a threatening manner, don't resist. Hand over your wallet, then dial 911 or hail a cab and ask the driver to take you to the nearest police station where you can report the theft and get a reference number to claim insurance and travelers' check refunds.

SMOKING

It is illegal to smoke in a public space indoors.

STUDY

While not a full-blown university town like Boston, DC does have its share of colleges and universities. The major ones are listed below, but there are many smaller institutions, branch universities and schools in suburban Virginia and Maryland. Most of these schools conduct summer courses in politics, international relations and other programs directly relating to the city's weighty political scene. For Washington's libraries, *see p228.*

American University *4400 Massachusetts Avenue, NW, at Nebraska Avenue, Upper Northwest (1-202 885 1000, www.american. edu). Tenleytown-AU Metro then M4 bus.* **Map** p248 C1.
Over 11,000 students attend this university in residential Washington. It has strong arts and sciences programs, and a law library.

Catholic University of America *620 Michigan Avenue, NE, at Harewood Road, Northeast (1-202 319 5000, www.cua.edu). Brookland -CUA Metro.* **Map** p251 L1.
Catholic University received a papal charter in 1887. Its diverse programs include architecture, engineering and law.

Georgetown University *37th & O Streets, NW, Georgetown (1-202 687 0100, www.georgetown.edu). Dupont Circle Metro then G2 bus.* **Map** p249 D4.

Georgetown attracts students from all over the world to its prestigious international relations, business, medical and law schools.

George Washington University *I & 22nd Streets, NW, Foggy Bottom (1-202 994 1000, www. gwu.edu). Foggy Bottom-GWU Metro.* **Map** p252 G5.
GWU houses law and medical schools, and has strong programs in politics and international affairs.

Howard University *2400 6th Street, NW, at Georgia Avenue, Shaw (1-202 806 6100, www. howard.edu). Shaw-Howard University Metro.* **Map** p251 J2.
About 10,000 students attend this historically black university, studying medicine, engineering, dentistry, social work and communications.

University of the District of Columbia *4200 Connecticut Avenue, NW, at Van Ness Street, Upper Northwest (1-202 274 5000, www.udc.edu). Van Ness-UDC Metro.*
UDC was formed in 1974 as a land-grant institution with an open admissions policy. Not as prestigious as most of its neighbors, it nonetheless has a variety of programs, including arts, sciences and law.

TELEPHONES
Dialling & codes

The area code for DC is 202. To make a call within the District, you need only dial the seven-digit local number, not the 202 area code. Maryland and Virginia are more complicated. The area codes for the city of Alexandria and the counties of Arlington and Fairfax in Virginia are 1-703 and 1-571. In Maryland, Prince George's County and Montgomery County both use 1-301 and 1-240 area codes. Calls from any one of these area codes to another, as well as within one area code, are classed as local, but you must dial the area code, even if you're dialling from DC. Some calls are treated as local, others long distance. Non-Washingtonians will probably not know which is which, but you will always get through by dialling the '1' first, and if it is a local call you will only be charged for a local rate. For this reason we have included the 1 prefix before all numbers.

Numbers to other parts of the US always require the 1 prefix before the area code. This is also the case for numbers beginning 1-800, 1-888 and 1-877, which are all toll free within the US, though note that your hotel may still bill you a flat fee. Most are also accessible from outside DC and – at the usual international rates – from outside the US.

Operators & assistance

For local directory assistance within the DC metro area, dial 411. For national long-distance enquiries, dial 1 + [area code] + 555 1212 (if you don't know the area code, dial 0 for the operator). For international calls, dial 011 then the country code (UK 44; New Zealand 64; Australia 61 – see the phone book for others). For collect (reverse charge) calls, dial 0 for the operator. If you use voicemail, note that the pound key is the one marked # and the star key is *. On automated answering systems, 0 often gets you through to a real-life operator.

Mobile phones

US readers with mobile phones should contact their mobile phone operators about using their phone in Washington. All five UK mobile phone operators have roaming agreements with major US operators, so you should be able to use your mobile in Washington – as long as your phone is a tri-band (and modern phones generally are). All you need do is ensure that the roaming facility is set up before you travel.

Public phones

You'll still find public pay phones, and some of them even work. Phones take any combination of silver coins. To call long-distance or to make an international call from a pay phone you need to go through a long-distance company, such as AT&T. Make the call by either dialling 0 for an operator or dialling direct, which is cheaper. To find out how much it will cost, dial the number and a computerized voice will tell you how much money to deposit. You can pay for calls using your credit card. The best way to make long-distance calls is with a phone card, available from any post office branch and many newsagents and general stores.

Time

Washington DC operates on Eastern Standard Time (the same time zone as New York and Miami), which is five hours behind Greenwich Mean Time (London) and three hours ahead of Pacific Standard Time (Los Angeles). Clocks go forward one hour on the first Sunday in April to daylight saving time and back one hour on the last Sunday in October. To find out the exact time, call 1-202 844 2525.

TIPPING

Cab drivers and waiters are generally tipped 15-20 per cent – more for exceptionally good service. Bartenders expect $1 per drink. Hairdressers get ten per cent, bellhops $1 per bag and hotel maids $1-$2 per day.

TOILETS

Malls, museums, bookstores and even some grocery stores have toilets; clothes shops almost always do not. In restaurants you may have to buy a drink in order to use them.

TOURIST INFORMATION

DC Chamber of Commerce Visitor information Center *506 9th Street, NW, at F. Street (1-866 324 7386, 1-202 638 7330, www. dcvisit.com). Gallery Place Metro, (exit at 9th & G Streets & walk one block south).* **Open** 8.30am-5.30pm Mon-Fri. **Map** p252 H6.
Part of DC Chamber of Commerce, this office supplies tourist maps, city guides, restaurant and hotel information and advice.

Destination DC *4th Floor, 901 7th Street, NW, entrance at*

I Street, Downtown (1-202 789 7000, www.destinationdc.com, www.washington.org). Metro Center Metro. Open 8.30am-5pm Mon-Fri. **Map** p253 J5.
Good for general information on the city, largely via the website, which has a calendar of events and many other suggestions for visitors.

Local weather *1-202 936 1212.*

National Park Service *1-202 208 6843, www.nps.gov.*

Smithsonian information *1-202 633 1000, www.si.edu/visit.*
Information on all the Smithsonian's museums.

Traveler's Aid *1-703 572 2536 1127, www.travelersaid.org.*
Network of travel support. This branch is at Dulles Airport; there are others at Union Station (1-202 371 1937) and Reagan National Airport (1-703 417 1806).

VISAS & IMMIGRATION

Some 27 countries currently particpate in the Visa Waiver Scheme. If you are a citizen of the United Kingdom, the Republic of Ireland, Australia, New Zealand, Japan or most western European countries (check with your local US embassy or consulate for the exact status of your nation), you do not need a visa for stays in the US shorter than 90 days (business or pleasure) as long as you have a machine-readable passport valid for the full 90-day period, a return ticket and authorization through the ESTA scheme. Visitors must fill in the ESTA form at least 24 hours before travelling (72 hours in advance is recommended); the form can be found on US embassy websites.

Canadians will only need visas under special circumstances.
Citizens of other countries or people who are staying for longer than 90 days or who need a work or study visa should contact their nearest US consulate or embassy well before the date of travel (note that visitors requiring visas will also have to submit biometric data).
The US embassy in London has a service (020 7499 9000) for all general visa enquiries. The website (www.usembassy.org.uk) also has information.

WHEN TO GO

Autumn is a great time to visit, avoiding the humidity and heat of summer and the colder winter weather. April is, in theory, a lovely time to come – early in the month, the cherry blossoms are in flower at the Tidal Basin. However, it's also one of DC's busiest months for tourism. In autumn, the trees turn brilliant shades of orange, red and yellow, and the weather is pleasant.
If you do visit in summer, be sure to drink plenty of water so you don't get dehydrated, and start sightseeing early to avoid long lines. Daytime summer temperatures average 86°F (30.2°C) but feel much hotter because of the high humidity; aim to be inside an air-conditioned building at midday.
Winters are fairly mild, but even a light snowfall can still bring the city to a halt. Don't be surprised if there are long periods of bitter weather. Otherwise, winter days can be bright and clear.
If you want to see government in action, remember that in addition to Christmas and Easter breaks, Congress is in recess during August and the Supreme Court from May to September.

NATIONAL HOLIDAYS

New Year's Day 1 January
Martin Luther King Jr Day third Monday in January
Presidents Day third Monday in February
Memorial Day last Monday in May
Independence Day 4 July
Labor Day first Monday in September
Columbus Day second Monday in October
Election Day first Tuesday in November
Veterans Day 11 November
Thanksgiving fourth Thursday in November
Christmas Day 25 December

THE LOCAL CLIMATE

Average temperatures and monthly rainfall in Washington DC.

	High (°C/°F)	Low (°C/°F)	Rainfall (mm/in)
Jan	5.6/42	-3.4/26	69/2.7
Feb	7.3/45	-2.8/27	69/2.7
Mar	13.4/56	2.8/37	81/3.2
Apr	19/ 66	7.8/46	69/2.7
May	24.6/76	13.4/56	94/3.7
June	29.1/84	19/66	96/3.8
July	31.3/88	25.2/71	96/3.8
Aug	30.2/86	21.2/70	99/3.9
Sept	26.9/80	16.8/62	84/3.3
Oct	20.7/69	10.1/50	76/3.0
Nov	14.5/58	5/41	79/3.1
Dec	8.4/47	0.56/31	79/3.1

DIRECTORY

Further Reference

DIRECTORY

BOOKS

Non-fiction

All the President's Men
Carl Bernstein & Bob Woodward
The story behind the Watergate scandal.

The Beat
Kip Lornell & Charles Stephenson, Jr
Go-go's fusion of funk and hip hop, DC's music.

Dance of Days
Mark Andersen & Mark Jenkins
Two decades of punk in DC.

Dream City: Race, Power and the Decline of Washington, DC
Harry Jaffe & Tom Sherwood
An in-depth look at how race and power-lust corrupted local politics over several decades.

Parliament of Whores
PJ O'Rourke
America's most scabrous commentator gets to grips with the US political system, as practised in Washington.

Personal History: Katherine Graham's Washington
Katherine Graham
The autobiography of the erstwhile publisher of the *Washington Post*.

Plan of Attack
Bob Woodward
The inside story of the George W Bush administration's planning for the 2003 invasion of Iraq, by the famous reporter.

Ronald Reagan
Dinesh D'Souza
A view from the right: commentator Dinesh D'Souza puts the case for viewing the presidency of conservative hero Ronald Reagan in a favorable light.

Shadow: Five Presidents & the Legacy of Watergate
Bob Woodward
A thought-provoking bestseller on how the Watergate affair affected subsequent presidential scandals.

Washington Goes to War
David Brinkley
The history of Washington during World War II.

Fiction

Drum-Taps
Walt Whitman
Whitman's war poems were directly influenced by his work in Civil War hospitals in Washington.

Echo House
Ward Just
The story of three generations of a powerful Washington family, written by a former *Washington Post* reporter.

Empire
Gore Vidal
A historical novel based on Theodore Roosevelt's Washington, Vidal's epic brings America during the Gilded Age into vivid focus.

King Suckerman
George P Pelecanos
Murder, drugs and the coolest music in this homage to blaxploitation.

Murder in the Map Room (and other titles)
Elliott Roosevelt
Series of White House murder mysteries written by FDR's son, with First Lady Eleanor Roosevelt as the problem-solving sleuth.

O: A Presidential Novel
Anonymous
Speculation is rife as to who wrote this *Primary Colors*-style novel. Set during the 2012 presidential election campaign, it features a familiar-sounding president. The person behind it supposedly has vast personal experience of the Obama White House.

Primary Colors
Anonymous (Joe Klein)
Guess who's who in this fictionalised retelling of Bill Clinton's run for the presidency.

The Tenth Justice
Brad Meltzer
Bestselling thriller based on the travails of an ambitious young clerk to a Supreme Court justice.

Thank You for Smoking
Christopher Buckley
Send-up of TV pundits and political special-interest groups.

Reference

AIA Guide to the Architecture of Washington, DC
Christopher Weeks
Concise descriptions and photos of DC's notable structures, including 100 built since the mid 1970s.

Buildings of the District of Columbia
Pamela Scott & Antoinette J Lee
Detailed architectural history of DC, from the Revolutionary War to post-World War II, with photos, drawings and maps.

The Guide to Black Washington
Sandra Fitzpatrick & Maria R Goodwin
Places and events of significance to DC's African-American heritage.

WEBSITES

The following are useful for information on different aspects of DC. Websites for venues in the guide are included in the listings.

Washington Post
www.washingtonpost.com.
The Post makes every word it prints available online, although the stories are moved after two weeks to the archives, access to which requires the payment of a fee.

Washington City Paper
www.washingtoncitypaper.com.
Much of this paper's content is not available online, but its listings and classifieds are there, however, in a searchable form.

WTOP News
www.wtopnews.com.
The city's leading all-news radio station's excellent website includes breaking news and helpful links to weather and traffic reports, as well as a listen-live option.

DCist
www.dcist.com.
Daily digest for the blog generation, committed to 'documenting the nation's capital and all its quirks, one small detail at a time'.

Craigslist
www.washingtondc.craigslist.org.
More than ten million people visit this exhaustive community clearing house of jobs, housing, products and information each month.

DC Watch
www.dcwatch.com.
For outsiders seeking a sense of the passion and perplexity of civic affairs in America's 'last colony', this site gives an exhaustive introduction.

Congress
http://thomas.loc.gov.
Links to lots of useful Congressional information, including days-in-session for the House and Senate, full text of the bills that are being considered and a listing of how congressmen and -women have voted on specific issues in the past.

Content Index

A

Abbatiello, Biagio 154
accident & emergency 227
Adams Morgan 78
Bars 140
Hotels 107-108
Restaurants 125-127
Adams Morgan Day 167
addresses 226
African American Museum 48
afternoon tea 83
age restrictions 137, 187, 226
airport 222
American Indian cuisine 50
Annual High Heel Race 168
Annual White House Easter Egg Roll 164
antique stores 158
Architecture 34-40
Arlington & Alexandria 88-91
Hotels 109-110
Restaurants 133
art museums 61
ATMs 230
attitude & etiquette 226

B

bakeries 152
Baltimore 210-213
banks 230
Bars 134-142
By Area:
Adams Morgan 140
The Capitol & Around 134-135
Cleveland Park 142
Downtown 137
Dupont Circle 138-140
Federal Triangle 135
Foggy Bottom/West End 137-138
Georgetown 142
H Street Corridor 142
Logan Circle 140
Union Station & Around 137
U Street/14th Street Corridor 140-142
The White House & Around 134
Features:
back to basics bars 141
bars with a view 142
hotel bars 138-139
baseball 200
basketball 200
Bethesda, MD
Hotels 110
Black Family Reunion 167
Black History Month 168
Black Pride 165
breakfast 95
boating & fishing 197
book & magazine stores 144-147
buses 222
business 226

C

Calendar 164-168
Capital Jazz Fest 166
Capital Pride 165
The Capitol & Around 56-59
Bars 134-135
Hotels 97
Restaurants 112
Capitol Hill 86-87
Restaurants 121-122
Caribbean Festival 166
cheap theater tickets 204
Cherry Blossom Festival 164
Chesapeake 218-220
Children 169-171
babysitting 169
entertainment 169-171
children's stores 147
Childs, Julia 125
Chinese New Year 168
cinemas 172-174
cleaning laundry & repairs 150
Cleveland Park 83
Bars 142
clothing hire 150
Cluss, Adolf 66-67
contraception & abortion 228
conventions 226
consumer 227
couriers 226
credit cards 230
currency exchange 230
customs 227
cycling 198, 225

D

DanceAfrica DC: The Annual Festival 166
DC Neighbourhoods 64-87
Areas:
Adams Morgan 78
Capitol Hill 86-87
Cleveland Park 83
Downtown 67-72
Dupont Circle 76-78
Foggy Bottom 64-67
Georgetown 78-80
Judiciary Square 73-76
Mount Pleasant/ Columbia Heights 78
Penn Quarter 72-73
Shaw 78
Southeast 87
Woodley Park 83
dentists 228
department stores 143
designer fashion stores 148
disabled 227
discount fashion stores 148
doctors 228
Downtown 67-72
Bars 137
Galleries 176
Hotels 100-104
Restaurants 115-117
drink stores 152-153
driving 222, 224
drugs 227
Dupont Circle 76-78
Bars 138-140
Galleries 178
Hotels 104-107
Restaurants 122-125
Dupont-Kalorama Museum Walk Weekend 166

E

eastern market 153
electricity 227
electronics & photography stores 147-148
embassies & consulates 227
emergencies 227
Escapes & Excursions 210-220
Baltimore 210-213
Chesapeake 218-220
Shenandoah 213-218
Features:
presidential homes 216-217
Exorcist, The 172

INDEX

F

Famous birthdays 168
fares & passes 223-224
fashion accessories & services 150-151
fashion stores 148-150
The Federal Triangle 60-62
  Bars 135
  Hotels 97-98
  Film 172-174
festivals 174
Foggy Bottom/West End 64-67
  Bars 137-138
  Hotels 99-100
  Restaurants 112-115
food & drink stores 152-154
football 200
Fort Reno Summer Concert Series 165

G

Galleries 175-180
  Features:
  car showroom gallery spaces 179
Gay & Lesbian 181-184, 227
gyms 183
restaurants & cafés 184
Georgetown 78-80
  Bars 142
  Galleries 179-180
  Hotels 108-109
  Restaurants 129-131
Georgetown Hoyas 198
Getting Around 222-225
gifts, stationery & souvenirs 154-156
golf 199
gyms 199

H

hairdressers & barbers 157

half-smokes 128
hat stores 150
health 227
health & beauty 156-158
  stores 158
helplines 228
hiking 199
History 16-28
HIV & AIDS 228
Hotels 94-110
  By Area:
  Adams Morgan/Woodley Park 107-108
  Alexandria, VA 109-110
  Arlington, VA 110
  Bethesda, MD 110
  The Capitol & Around 97
  Downtown 100-104
  Dupont Circle 104-107
  Federal Triangle 97-98
  Foggy Bottom/West End 99-100
  Georgetown 108-109
  Logan Circle 108
  Penn Quarter 104
  South of The Mall 98-99
  Southwest 109
  Union Station & Around 97
  The White House & Around 95-97
  Features:
  best historic hotels 96
  best style hotels 103
  hotel gyms 105
  hotel snacking 99
house & home 158-161
  stores 158-160
H Street Corridor 84-85, 193
  Bars 142
  Galleries 178-179

I

ice hockey 201
ID 228

Independence Day 166
insurance 228
International Spy Museum 171
internet 228

J

jewelry stores 151
Judiciary Square 73-76
  Restaurants 118-121

K

Kennedy Center Open House Arts Festival/Prelude Festival 167
Komen Global Race for the Cure 166

L

left luggage 228
legal help 228
local climate 233
Logan Circle 108
  Bars 140
  Galleries 176-178
  Hotels 108
  Restaurants 127-128
lost property 229
lost/stolen credit cards 231

M

the Mall, history of 51
Mall & Tidal Basin, the 42-52
malls 143-146
Marine Band's Summer Concert Series & Evening Parades 165
Marine Corps Marathon 168
markets 153
Martin Luther King Jr's Birthday Celebrations 168
media 229
Memorial Day 165
Memorial Day Jazz Festival 165
menswear stores 151

Metrobuses 224
Metrorail 26-27, 223
mint juleps 135
money 230
The Monumental Center 42-63
  Areas:
  Capitol & Around, the 56-59
  Federal Triangle, the 60-62
  Mall & Tidal Basin, the 42-52
  Northwest Rectangle, the 62
  South of the Mall 62-63
  Union Station & Around 59-60
  White House & Around, the 52-56
  Mount Pleasant/ Columbia Heights 78
  Restaurants 133
museum shops 160
Music 185-139
  classical & opera 190-193
  jazz 189-190
  rock, roots & R&B 195-189
  Features:
  go-go 191
  indie 188
music & entertainment stores 161

N

National Book Fair 167
National Capital Barbecue Battle 166
National Christmas Tree Lighting 168
national holidays 233
National Portrait Gallery 68-69
neighbourhood heritage trails 64
newspapers & magazines 229

Newseum 74-75
New Year's Eve
celebrations 168
Nightlife 194-196
  By Topic:
  clubs & lounges
    194-196
  comedy & cabaret
    196
Northwest Rectangle,
  the 62

O

opening hours 231

P

Penn Quarter 72-73
  Hotels 104
  Galleries 176
  Restaurants 118
pharmacies 158,
  228
Phillips Collection 77
pick-up games 199
police 231
postal service 231
presidential
  inauguration route
  54-55
public transport
  223-225

R

radio 230
religion 231
**Restaurants
  111-133**
  By Area:
  Adams Morgan
    125-127
  Capitol & Around
    112
  Capitol Hill
    121-122
  Downtown 115-117
  Dupont Circle
    122-125
  Foggy Bottom
    112-115
  Georgetown
    129-131
  Judiciary Square
    118-121
  Logan Circle
    127-128
  Mount Pleasant &
    north 133

Penn Quarter 118
Upper Northwest
  131-133
U Street/14th
  Street Corridor
  128-129
White House &
  Around 111
  Features:
  best restaurants
    121
  best hot hangouts
    131
  best fun
    restaurants 116
  Ethiopian cuisine
    132
  food trucks 123
  presidential
    favorites 119

S

safety & security 231
St Patrick's Day
  Celebrations 164
sales tax 147
secondhand &
  vintage fashion
  stores 150
segway tours 44,
  200
skating 199
Shaw 78
Shenandoah
  213-218
shoe stores 151
**Shops & Services
  143-161**
The Smithsonian 45
Smithsonian
  American Art
  Museum 68-69
Smithsonian Annual
  Kite Festival 164
Smithsonian Folklife
  Festival 166
Smithsonian
  Information Center
  46
smoking 232
soccer 201
South of The Mall
  62-63
  Hotels 98-99
Southeast 87
Southwest 87
  Hotels 109
spas & salons

156-157
specialist bookstores
  145
specialist food &
  drink stores
  153-154
**Sport & Fitness
  197-201**
  By Topic:
  participation sports
    197-200
  spectator sports
    200-201
  Features:
  Nationals Park
    201
sport stores 161
Star-Spangled
  Banner 20-21
study 232
summer opening
  hours 43
swimming 200

T

tax 231
taxis 225
telephones 232
television 229
tennis 200
Theater 202-208
  major venues
    203-204
  other theaters
    & companies
    204-207
  small companies
    207-208
  Features:
  new theaters
    206-207
Thievery Corporation
  194
ticket stores 161
tipping 233
toilets 233
tourist information
  233
toy stores 147
trains 222, 224
traveller's needs
  stores 161

U

Union Station &
  Around 59-60
  Bars 137
  Hotels 97

urban renewal 70
used & antiquarian
  bookstores 147
U Street/14th Street
  Corridor 78, 79
  Bars 140-142
  Restaurants
    128-129

V

Veterans' Day
  ceremonies 167
Vietnam Veteran
  Memorial 53
visas & immigration
  233

W

walking 225
walks
  Georgetown 81
Washington Today
  29-33
when to go 233
The White House &
  Around 52-56
  Bars 134
  Hotels 95-97
  Restaurants 111
Woodley Park 83
  Bars 140
  Hotels 107-108

INDEX

Venue Index

★ **indicates a
critic's choice**

1789 129
9:30 Club 186 ★

A

A Little Shop of
Flowers 154
A Mano 155
Adam's Inn 108
Addison/Ripley Fine
Art 179
AFI Silver Theatre &
Cultural Center 174
African Continuum
Theatre Company
208
Afterwords Café 122
Alexandria Black
History Museum 89
Allan Woods Florist
155
AMC Loews
Georgetown 173
AMC Loews Mazza
Gallerie 173
AMC Loews Uptown
173
American Visionary
Art Museum 212
Amsterdam
Falafelshop 125
Anacostia
Community
Museum 87
Annapolis & Anne
Arundel County
Conference &
Visitors Bureau 220
Annie Creamcheese
150
Annie's Paramount
Steak House 184
Apex 181
Appalachian Spring
155
Arena Stage 203
Arlington Arts Center
180
Arlington National
Cemetery 90

Arthur M Sackler
Gallery 43
Arthur M Sackler
Gallery/Freer
Gallery of Art 171
Artisphere 180
Atlas Performing Arts
Center 192
Austin Grill 115
Avalon 173 ★
Aveda 156
Axis 157

B

Backstage 150
Baltimore Civil War
Museum 212
Baltimore Maritime
Museum 211
Baltimore Museum
of Art 212
Baltimore Tourist
information 213
Bangkok Joe's 129
Bar Pilar 140
Bar Rouge 138
Basilica of the
National Shrine of
the Immaculate
Conception 192
Beacon Hotel 106
Bedrock Billiards 140
Ben's Chili Bowl
128 ★
Best Buy 147
Best Cellars 152
Betsy Fisher 148
Biagio Fine
Chocolate 153 ★
Bibiana 115 ★
Big Meadows Lodge
217
Big Planet Comics
145
Big Wheel Bikes 198
Bike & Roll 198
Birch & Barley 127 ★
Birchmere 186
Birreria Paradiso 142
Birthplace &
Museum 211
Bistro Bis 118

Black Cat 186 ★
Blowoff 181 ★
Blue Mercury 157
Blues Alley 189
Bodysmith 183
Bohemian Caverns
141
Bohemian Caverns
189
Bombay Club 115
BOSS Hugo Boss
151
Bourbon Steak 130
Bravo! Bravo! 194
Breadline 111
Brooks Brothers 151
Bukom Café 194
Bureau of Engraving
& Printing 62
Busboys & Poets 128

C

Café Asia 112
Café Atlántico 118
Café La Ruche 130
Café Milano 130
Café Saint-Ex 141
Calvert Cliffs State
Park 220
Calvert Woodley 152
Capital Q 115
Capitol Hill Books
147
Capitol Skyline 109
Carbon 151
Carlyle House
Historic Park 89
Carroll Square 176
Ceiba 116
Celadon 157
Central 118
Chapters Literary Art
Center & Bookstore
144
Cheshire Crab
Restaurant 220
Chevy Chase Pavilion
143
Chi-Cha Lounge 194
Christ Church 89
Christophe 157
ChurchKey 140 ★
City Bikes 161

Civilian Art Projects
176
Clarice Smith
Performing Arts
Center 192
Clyde's of
Georgetown 130
Collection at Chevy
Chase 144
Comet Ping Pong
131, 186
Comfort Inn
Downtown/Convent
ion Center 103
Commander
Salamander 148
Conner
Contemporary Art
178 ★
Contemporaria 158
Coolidge Auditorium,
Library of Congress
192
Copenhaver 155 ★
Coppi's Organic 128
Corcoran Gallery of
Art 191
Corcoran Museum
of Art 53
Cork Wine Bar 127
★
Cowgirl Creamery
153 ★
Crew Club 183
Cross/MacKenzie
Ceramic Arts 180
Crossroads 187
Curator's Office 176
CVS 158

D

David Adamson
Gallery 176 ★
Dawn Price Baby
147
DC Coast 116
DC Eagle 182
DC-3 121 ★
DC9 187
De Vinos 153 ★
Dean & Deluca 153
Decatur House 53

Degrees Bar & Lounge 142
Della Notte 213
Department of the Interior Museum 62
Diner 125
District of Columbia Arts Center (DCAC) 180
Donovan House 103
Donovan House Side Bar 137 ★
Drug Enforcement Agency Museum 91
Dumbarton Oaks Research Library & Collections 80
Duplex Diner 184
Dupont at the Circle 106
Dupont Italian Kitchen (DIK) 184

E

East Potomac Golf Course 199
East Potomac Tennis Center 200
Eastern Market 86
Eighteenth Street Lounge 195
Embassy Suites Hotel 99
L'Enfant Café 184
L'Enfant Plaza Hotel 98
Equinox 112 ★
Estadio 127 ★
Everard's Clothing 151
Evolve 157

F

Fairmont 100
Fairy Godmother 147
Fashion Centre at Pentagon City 144
Filene's Basement 148
Firefly 138 ★
Fleet Feet 161
Fletcher's Boat House 197
Fly Lounge 138
Fly Lounge 195
Folger Shakespeare Library 190

Folger Shakespeare Library 57
Folger Theatre 204
Fondo Del Sol 178
Ford's Theatre & Lincoln Museum 70
Ford's Theatre 204
Fort McHenry 211
Four Seasons 108
Franklin Delano Roosevelt Memorial 43
Fraser Gallery Bethesda 180
Frederick Douglass National Historic Site (Cedar Hill) 87
Freer Gallery of Art 174
Freer Gallery of Art 44
Friendship Fire House 89
Full Kee 118
Fur 195

G

G Fine Art 179
Gadsby's Tavern Museum 89
GALA Hispanic Theatre 208
Galaxy Hut 187
Gallery 10 Ltd 178
Gallery at Flashpoint 176
George Mason University Center for the Arts 193
George Washington Masonic National Memorial 89
Georgetown Formal Wear & Custom Tailor 150
Georgetown Suites 109
Georgetown Tobacco 155
Georgetown University 80
Georgia Brown's 116
Ginza 156
Glen Echo Park 171
Goethe-Institut 176
Gold's Gym 199

Good Stuff Eatery 121 ★
Goodwood 158
Gordon Biersch 137
Graffiti 148
Green Lantern 182
Grooming Lounge 157

H

H&M 150
Hamilton Crowne Plaza 103
Hamiltonian Gallery 176
Hampton Inn Washington, DC-Convention Center 103
Hank's Oyster Bar 122
Harris Crab House 220
Hawk & Dove 134
Hay-Adams Hotel 95
Heaven & Hell 195
Hemphill Fine Arts 176
Heritage India 122
Hillwood Museum & Gardens 83
Hillyer Art Space at International Art & Artists 178
Hirshhorn Museum & Sculpture Garden 44 ★, 174
Hole in the Sky 187
Home Rule 158
Homebody 158
Hostelling International Washington, DC 103
Hotel George 97
Hotel Harrington 104
Hotel Helix 108
Hotel Lombardy 100
Hotel Madera 106
Hotel Monaco 101
Hotel Monticello 109
Hotel Rouge 108
Howard University 78
HR-57 189
Hudson Trail Outfitter 161

Hyatt Regency Bethesda 110
Hyatt Regency Washington on Capitol Hill 97

I

Illuminations 158
Ilo 157
Imperial Valet 150
Improv 196
Industry Gallery 179 ★
International Spy Museum 73 ★
IOTA Club & Café 187
Ipsa 157
Irvine 177

J

J Paul's 142
Jack's Boathouse 197
Jaleo 118
Jammin' Java 187
Jaxx 187
Jefferson 101
Jefferson Memorial 46
Jewelerswerk Galerie 151
Jewish Historical Society of Greater Washington 76
Jimmy Cantler's Riverside Inn 220
Johnny's Half Shell 112
JR's 182
Junction 150
JW Marriott 96

K

Katzen Arts Center at American University 180
Katzen Arts Center at American University 82
Kaz Sushi Bistro 112
Kenilworth Aquatic Gardens 86
Kennedy Center (children) 171
Kennedy Center (theatre) 203

INDEX

INDEX

Kennedy Center 190 ★
Kennedy Center 65
Key Bridge Marriott 110
Kid's Closet 147
Kinkead's 112
Komi 122 ★
Korean War Veterans Memorial 46
Kramerbooks 145 ★
Kreeger Museum 82
Kushi 121

L

Lace 182
Landmark E Street Cinema 173
Langston Golf Course 199
Lauriol Plaza 124
Lebanese Taverna 131
Letelier Theatre 174
Lewis Mountain Cabins 217
Liaison Affinia Hotel 97
Library of Congress 57
Lincoln Memorial 46 ★
Lincoln Theatre 193
Lisner Auditorium 193
Lord & Taylor 143
Love 195
Love Café 128
Lyceum, Alexandria's History Museum 89

M

Macy's 143
Madame Tussauds 71
La Madeleine 152
Madison 100
Majestic Café 133
Mandarin Oriental 98
Mansion on O Street 104
Marcel's 112 ★
Marian Koshland Science Museum of the National Academy of Sciences 73
Market Lunch 121

Marriott Wardman Park 107
Marsha Mateyka Gallery 178
Martin Luther King Jr Memorial Library 71
Marvelous Market 152
Marvin 129 ★
Maryland Department of Natural Resources 220
Matchbox 116
Maurine Littleton Gallery 180
Mazza Gallerie 144
McLean Project for the Arts 180
Meep's & Aunt Neensie's 150
Melody Records 161
Mendocino Grill & Wine Bar 130
Michel Richard Citronelle 130
Mie N Yu 196
Mike's Bar & Crab House 220
Millennium Decorative Arts 158 ★
Miss Pixie's 158
Moby Dick House of Kabob 131
Modern 196
Monaco Alexandria 109
Monkey's Uncle 147
Montmartre 122
Morrison House 110
MOVA 182

N

Nana 148
Nanny O'Brien's 142
National Academy of Sciences 191
National Air & Space Museum 46
National Aquarium in Baltimore 211
National Archives 60
National Building Museum 76
National Capital YMCA 199

National Gallery of Art 47 ★, 174
National Geographic Museum 72
National Geographic Museum at Explorers Hall 170
National Inventors Hall of Fame & Museum 90
National Museum of African Art 48
National Museum of American History 49 ★
National Museum of Crime & Punishment 72
National Museum of Health & Medicine 82
National Museum of Natural History 51 ★
National Museum of the American Indian 50 ★
National Museum of Women in the Arts 71
National Postal Museum 170
National Postal Museum 59
National Theatre 203
National World War II Memorial 51
National Zoo 83 ★
Neiman Marcus 143
Nellie's 182 ★
Newseum 170 ★
Newseum 76 ★
Normandy Hotel 107

O

Obelisk 124
Oceanaire Seafood Room 116
Old Ebbitt Grill 134
Old Post Office 62
Olney Theatre Center 205
Omni Shoreham 107

P

Palena 131
Palomar 105
Parish Gallery 180

Park Hyatt 99
Pâtisserie Poupon 131
Patisserie Poupon 152 ★
Patty Boom Boom 196
Penn Camera 148
Perry's 127
Phase One 183
Phillips 213
Phillips Collection 191
Phillips Collection 77 ★
Phoenix Park Hotel 97
Pizzeria Paradiso 124
Plan b 177
Point Lookout State Park 220
Politics & Prose 145 ★
Poste 137 ★
Potenza 117
POV 134 ★
Project 4 178
Proof 117 ★
Proper Topper 150
Pulp 156 ★
Pure 196

R

Raku 124
Rasika 118 ★
Ray's the Steaks 133
Red Palace 142
Red Palace 188
Reef 140
Regal Gallery Place 173
Regent 124
Reginald F Lewis Museum of Maryland African American History & Culture 212
Reincarnations 160
Relish 148
Remington's 183
Renaissance Mayflower Hotel 101
Renwick Gallery of the Smithsonian American Art Museum 54

Residence Inn by Marriott Capitol 98
Restaurant Eve 133
Results, The Gym 183
Reyes+Davis 176
RFK Stadium 201
Rice 128
Ris 115 ★
Ritz-Carlton, Georgetown 109
Ritz-Carlton, Washington, DC 99
River Inn 100
Roche 157
Rock & Roll Hotel 188 ★
Rock Creek Golf Course 199
Rock Creek Nature Center & Planetarium 170 ★
Rock Creek Park 82
Rock Creek Tennis Center 200
Rodman's 153
Rorschach Theatre 208
Rosa Mexicano 137
Round House Theatre 205
Round Robin Bar 135 ★
Russia House Restaurant & Lounge 139
Rusty Scupper 213

S

Saks Fifth Avenue 143
Sandy Point State Park 219
Sankofa Video 161
Saturday Morning at the National 171
Science Club 137
Second Story Books 147
Sephora 158
Sequoia 142
Sette Osteria 124
Shakespeare Theatre Company 204 ★
Shops at Georgetown Park 144
Shops at Union Station 144

Signature Theatre 207
Sixth & I Historic Synagogue 193
Skyland Resort 217
Smithsonian American Art Museum/National Portrait Gallery (S) 70 ★
Smithsonian Information Center 45
Smithsonian Institution 191
Society of the Cincinnati, Anderson House Museum 77
Sofitel Lafayette Square 96
Sonoma 134
Soulier 151
Splash at the Sports Club/LA 157
Sports Zone 161
St Augustine's Church 192
St Gregory Luxury Hotel & Suites 100
St Michaels Crab House 220
St Regis Bar 137
Stabler-Leadbeater Apothecary Shop 90
Star-Spangled Banner Flag House 212
State Department Diplomatic Reception Rooms 62
State Theatre 188
Strathmore 193
Studio Theatre 204
Sullivan's Toy Store 147
Supreme Court 57
Sur La Table 160
Sushi Taro 124
Sushi-Ko 133
Swann House 106

T

Tabandeh 151 ★
Tabaq Bistro 129
Tabard Inn 106

Tabard Inn 125
Tabard Inn 140
Tabletop 160
Teaism 125
Textile Museum 77
Thaiphoon 125
The Fireplace 182
The Gibson 141 ★
The Octagon 65
The Passenger/ Columbia Room 137 ★
The Phoenix 156 ★
The Source 121 ★
The Source 135 ★
Theater Alliance 208
Thompson Boat Center 197
Thornton River Grille 217
Tiny Jewel Box 151
Tonic Restaurant 133
Topaz Hotel 106
Torpedo Factory Art Center 90
Torpedo Factory Arts Center 180
Touchstone Gallery 176
Town Danceboutique 183
Toyland 184
Transformer 177
Trio's Fox & Hounds 140
Tryst 127
Tune Inn 135
Twins Jazz 189
Twins Lounge 189
Tysons Corner Center 144

U

U Street Music Hall 196
Ugly Mug 122
Ultrabar 196
Union Pub 137
Union Station 59
United States Botanic Garden 58
United States Capitol 58 ★
United States Holocaust Memorial Museum 63 ★

United States National Arboretum 86
Urban Outfitters 150
US Navy Memorial & Heritage Center 73
Utopia 190

V

Vace 153 ★
Vastu 161
Velvet Lounge 141
Velvet Lounge 189
Verizon Center 200
Verizon Center 72
Vidalia 115
Vietnam Veterans Memorial 52

W

W 95
Walters Art Museum 212
Warner Theatre 193
Washington Monument 52
Washington National Cathedral 82
Washington Nationals 200
Washington Sailing Marina 198
Washington Shakespeare Company 208
Washington Sports Clubs 199
Washington Stage Guild 208
Waterman's Crab House 220
West End Cinema 173 ★
White House 55
Whole Foods 154
Willard InterContinental 97
Wilton House 217
Wolf Trap 193
Woolly Mammoth Theatre Company 207

Z

Zaytinya 117
Zengo 196
Ziegfields/Secrets 183

INDEX

Advertisers' Index

Please refer to the relevant pages for contact details.

Introduction

Newseum	**4**
MoneyGram	**6**

In Context

Trees for Cities	**14**

Consume

Shops & Services	
Premium Outlets	**146**

Arts & Entertainment

Oxfam	**162**

Maps

Human Rights Watch	**244**

INDEX

Maps

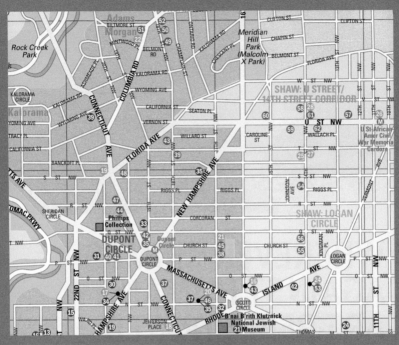

Legend

Major sight or landmark . . . .

Hospital or college . . . .

Railway station . . . .

Parks . . . .

River . . . .

Motorway . . . .

Main road . . . .

Main road tunnel . . . .

Pedestrian road . . . .

Steps . . . .

Airport . . . .   ✈

Church . . . .   ✚

Area name . . . .   SHAW

Escapes & Excursions	245
DC Overview	246
DC Neighborhoods: NW & Upper NW	248
DC Neighborhoods: NW & NE	250
Monumental Center/ DC Neighborhoods	252
Street Index	254
Metro Map	256

WHEREVER CRIMES AGAINST HUMANITY ARE PERPETRATED.

Across borders and above politics.
Against the most heinous abuses
and the most dangerous oppressors.
From conduct in wartime
to economic, social, and cultural rights.
Everywhere we go,
we build an unimpeachable case
for change and advocate action
at the highest levels.

HUMAN RIGHTS WATCH TYRANNY HAS A WITNESS

WWW.HRW.ORG

HUMAN
RIGHTS
WATCH

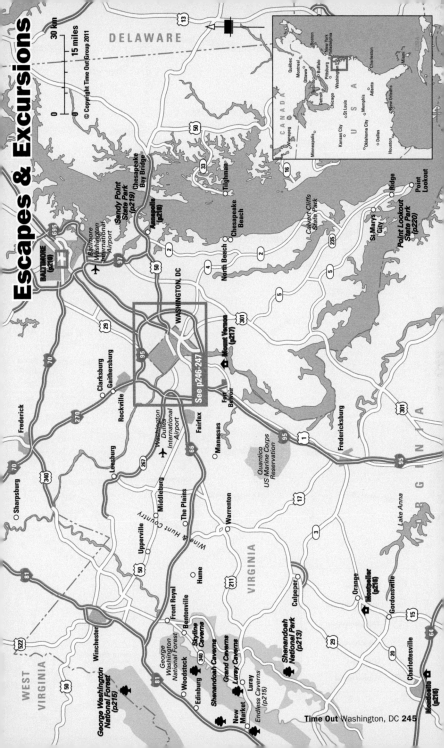

DELAWARE

© Copyright Time Out Group 2011

30 km

15 miles

CANADA

USA

Montreal
Quebec
Ottawa
Buffalo
Toronto
Boston
New York
Philadelphia
WASHINGTON
Pittsburgh
Detroit
Cleveland
Chicago
St Louis
Indianapolis
Charleston
Atlanta
Memphis
New Orleans
Houston
Dallas
Oklahoma City
Kansas City
Minneapolis
Winnipeg

13

50

33

Tilghman

Chesapeake Bay Bridge

Sandy Point State Park (p219)

Annapolis (p218)

Baltimore Washington International Airport

BALTIMORE (p210)

695

97

50

2

4

North Beach

Chesapeake Beach

2

Calvert Cliffs State Park

5

5

235

St Mary's City

Point Lookout State Park (p220)

Ridge

Point Lookout

29

WASHINGTON, DC

301

301

95

Mount Vernon (p217)

Fort Belvoir

See p246-247

Frederick

70

70

340

Sharpsburg

522

WEST VIRGINIA

81

50

George Washington National Forest (p215)

Winchester

Clarksburg

Gaithersburg

Rockville

270

Leesburg

267

Washington Dulles International Airport

Fairfax

Manassas

66

Middleburg

The Plains

Upperville

Wine & Hunt Country

50

Hume

211

Warrenton

17

3

VIRGINIA

Quantico US Marine Corps Reservation

1

95

Fredericksburg

Lake Anna

Monticello (p216)

Orange

Gordonsville

15

Culpeper

29

20

Charlottesville

64

Woodstock

81

Edinburg

340

Shenandoah Caverns

Grand Caverns

Luray Caverns

Luray

New Market

Endless Caverns (p215)

Front Royal

Bentonville

Skyline Caverns

George Washington National Forest

Shenandoah National Park (p213)

250

Waynesboro

Time Out Washington, DC **245**

DC Overview

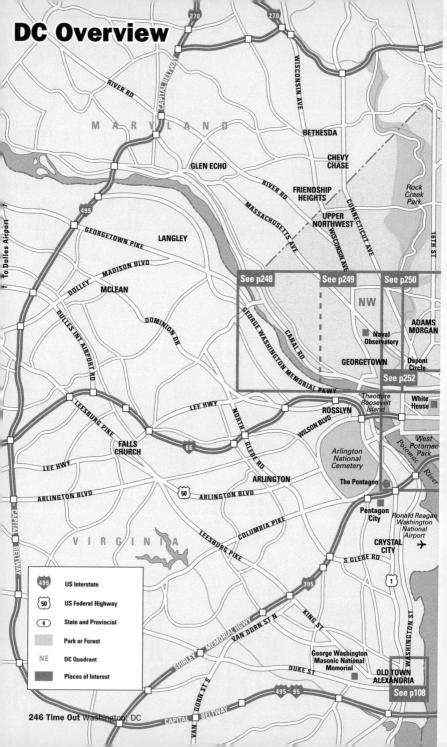

MARYLAND

VIRGINIA

270

270

RIVER RD

CAPITAL BELTWAY

WISCONSIN AVE

BETHESDA

CHEVY CHASE

GLEN ECHO

RIVER RD

FRIENDSHIP HEIGHTS

Rock Creek Park

UPPER NORTHWEST

MASSACHUSETTS AVE

WISCONSIN AVE

CONNECTICUT AVE

16TH ST

495

GEORGETOWN PIKE

LANGLEY

To Dulles Airport

DOLLEY

MADISON BLVD

MCLEAN

DOMINION DR

DULLES INT AIRPORT RD

See p248

See p249

See p250

NW

ADAMS MORGAN

Naval Observatory

GEORGE WASHINGTON MEMORIAL PKWY

CANAL RD

GEORGETOWN

Dupont Circle

See p252

White House

Theodore Roosevelt Island

ROSSLYN

LEE HWY

NORTH GLEBE RD

WILSON BLVD

West Potomac Park

Potomac River

FALLS CHURCH

66

LEESBURG PIKE

Arlington National Cemetery

LEE HWY

ARLINGTON

50

ARLINGTON BLVD

The Pentagon

ARLINGTON BLVD

COLUMBIA PIKE

Pentagon City

Ronald Reagan Washington National Airport

LEESBURG PIKE

CRYSTAL CITY

CAPITAL BELTWAY

395

S GLEBE RD

1

SHIRLEY MEMORIAL HIGHWY

VAN DORN ST N

KING ST

WASHINGTON ST

VAN DORN ST S

George Washington Masonic National Memorial

DUKE ST

OLD TOWN ALEXANDRIA

See p108

495 - 95

CAPITAL BELTWAY

Legend

495	US Interstate
50	US Federal Highway
4	State and Provincial
	Park or Forest
NE	DC Quadrant
	Places of Interest

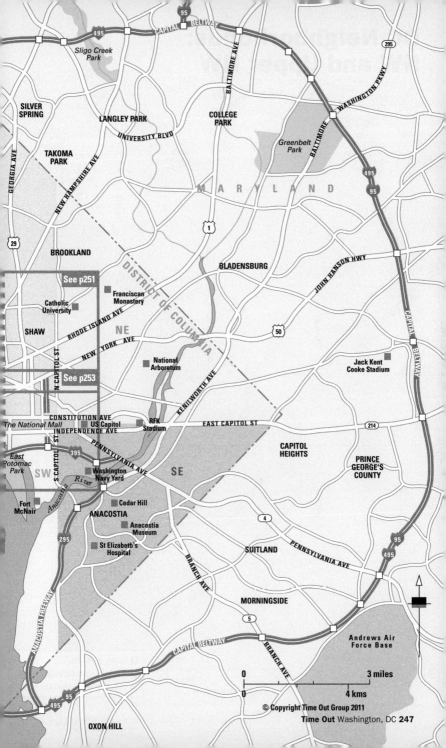

SILVER SPRING

LANGLEY PARK

COLLEGE PARK

Sligo Creek Park

Greenbelt Park

TAKOMA PARK

UNIVERSITY BLVD

GEORGIA AVE

NEW HAMPSHIRE AVE

BALTIMORE AVE

BALTIMORE WASHINGTON PKWY

BALTIMORE

M A R Y L A N D

BROOKLAND

DISTRICT OF COLUMBIA

BLADENSBURG

JOHN HANSON HWY

CAPITAL BELTWAY

See p251

Catholic University

Franciscan Monastery

SHAW

RHODE ISLAND AVE

NE

NEW YORK AVE

National Arboretum

KENILWORTH AVE

Jack Kent Cooke Stadium

N CAPITOL ST

See p253

CONSTITUTION AVE

The National Mall

US Capitol

INDEPENDENCE AVE

RFK Stadium

EAST CAPITOL ST

CAPITOL HEIGHTS

PRINCE GEORGE'S COUNTY

East Potomac Park

PENNSYLVANIA AVE

395

SW

S CAPITOL ST

Washington Navy Yard

Anacostia River

SE

Fort McNair

Cedar Hill

ANACOSTIA

295

Anacostia Museum

St Elizabeth's Hospital

ANACOSTIA FREEWAY

BRANCH AVE

SUITLAND

PENNSYLVANIA AVE

MORNINGSIDE

Andrews Air Force Base

BRANCH AVE

CAPITAL BELTWAY

OXON HILL

0   3 miles
0   4 kms

© Copyright Time Out Group 2011

Time Out Washington, DC **247**

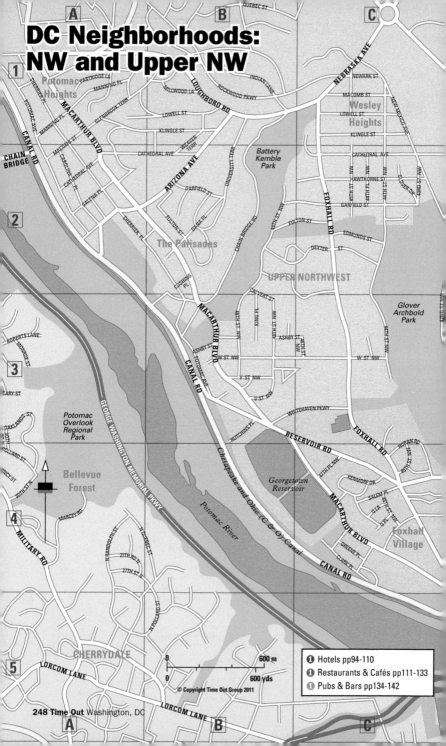

DC Neighborhoods:
NW and Upper NW

Potomac
Heights

Wesley
Heights

Battery
Kemble
Park

The Palisades

UPPER NORTHWEST

Glover
Archbold
Park

Potomac
Overlook
Regional
Park

Bellevue
Forest

Georgetown
Reservoir

Foxhall
Village

Potomac River

Chesapeake and Ohio (C & O) Canal

CHERRYDALE

0   600 m
0   600 yds

© Copyright Time Out Group 2011

LORCOM LANE

248 Time Out Washington, DC

- ❶ Hotels pp94-110
- ❶ Restaurants & Cafés pp111-133
- ❶ Pubs & Bars pp134-142

QUEBEC ST

NEBRASKA AVE

NEWARK ST

MACOMB ST

INDIAN LANE

ROCKWOOD PKWY

LOUGHBORO RD

MILLWOOD LA

PARTRIDGE LA

MANNING PL

GLENBROOK TERR

LOWELL ST

LOWELL ST

KLINGLE ST

KLINGLE ST

WEAVER TERR

CATHEDRAL AVE

CATHEDRAL AVE

HAWTHORNE ST

GARFIELD ST

GARFIELD ST

MACARTHUR BLVD

ARIZONA AVE

UNIVERSITY TERR

FULTON ST

FULTON ST

DANA PL

CHAIN BRIDGE RD

EDMUNDS ST

DEXTER ST

CUSHING PL

CALVERT ST

MACARTHUR BLVD

CANAL RD

ASHBY ST NW

W ST NW

W ST NW

POTOMAC AVE

V ST NW

U ST NW

WHITEHAVEN PKWY

HUTCHINS PL

RESERVOIR RD

FOXHALL RD

FOXHALL RD

HILL PL NW

KENMORE DR

SALEM PL

MACARTHUR BLVD

GREENE PL

CLARK PL

CANAL RD

CHAIN BRIDGE

CANAL RD

POTOMAC AVE

SHERRIER PL

GALENA PL

CAROLINE ST

MANNING PL

SHERRIER AVE

GEORGE WASHINGTON MEMORIAL PKWY

ROBERTS LANE

MONROE ST

LEARY ST

OAKLANDS ST

POLLARD ST

QUINCY ST

20TH ST N

MARCEY RD

MILITARY RD

RANDOLPH ST

TUCKERT ST

27TH RD N

27TH ST N

21ST ST N

LORCOM LANE

LOUGHBORO RD

16TH ST NW

A

B

C

1

2

3

4

5

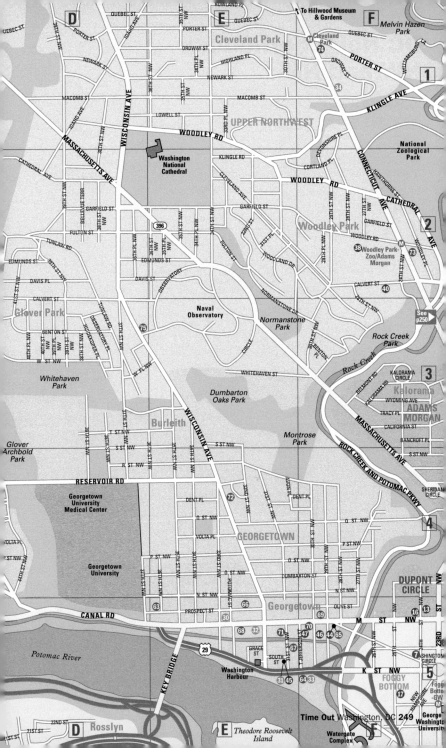

DC Neighborhoods: NW and NE

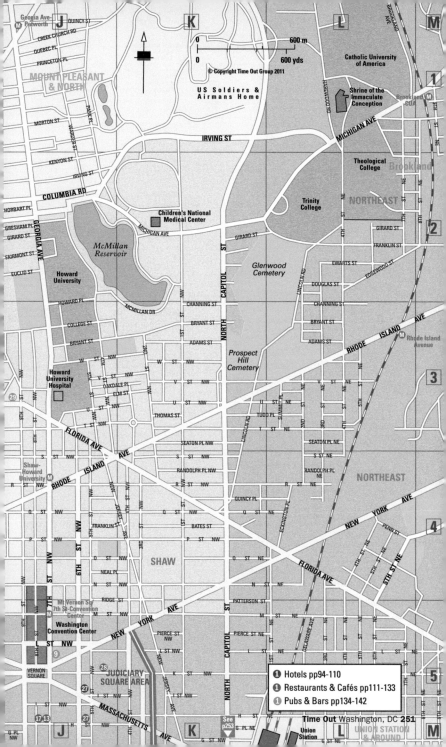

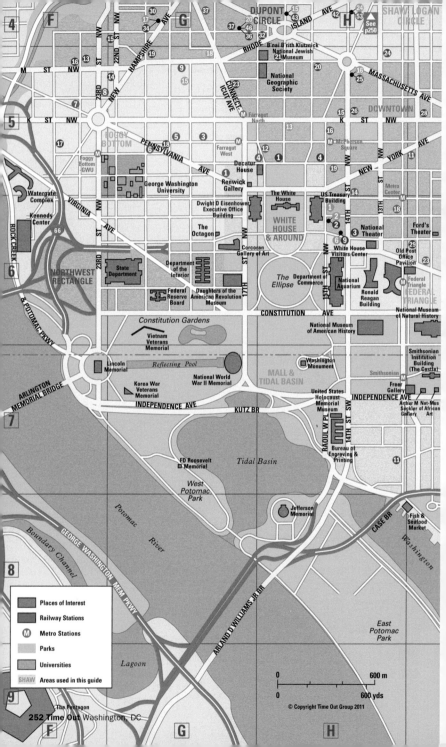

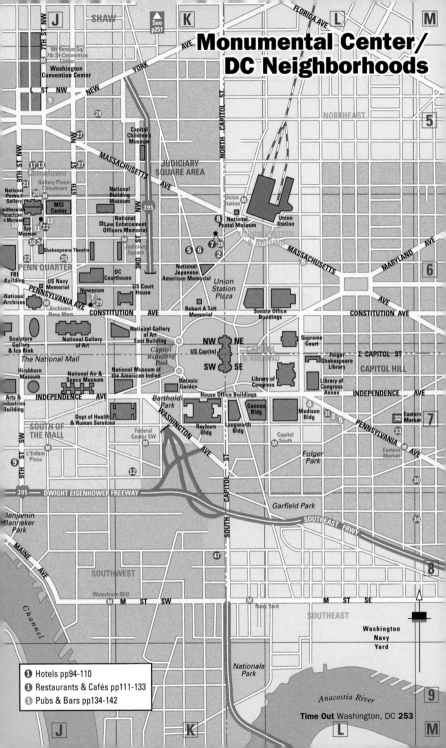

Monumental Center/ DC Neighborhoods

SHAW

FLORIDA AVE

NORTHEAST

Mt Vernon Sq/ 7th St-Convention Center

Washington Convention Center

Capital Children's Museum

JUDICIARY SQUARE AREA

Chinatown

Gallery Place-Chinatown

National Portrait Gallery

Smithsonian American Art Museum

Spy Museum

MCI Center

National Building Museum

National Law Enforcement Officers Memorial

Union Station

National Postal Museum

Union Station

Shakespeare Theatre

Judiciary Square

DC Courthouse

US Court House

National Japanese American Memorial

Union Station Plaza

Senate Office Buildings

PENN QUARTER

FBI Building

US Navy Memorial

Newseum

National Archives

PENNSYLVANIA AVE

Archives-Navy Mem'l

CONSTITUTION AVE

Robert A Taft Memorial

CONSTITUTION AVE

MASSACHUSETTS AVE

MARYLAND AVE

Sculpture Gallery & Ice Rink

National Gallery of Art

National Gallery of Art East Building

The National Mall

Hirshhorn Museum

National Air & Space Museum

National Museum of the American Indian

Capitol Reflecting Pool

NW NE

US Capitol

SW SE

Supreme Court

Folger Shakespeare Library

E CAPITOL ST

CAPITOL HILL

CAPITOL & AROUND

Library of Congress

Library of Congress Annex

Arts & Industries Building

INDEPENDENCE AVE

Botanic Garden

Bartholdi Park

House Office Buildings

INDEPENDENCE AVE

SOUTH OF THE MALL

Dept of Health & Human Services

Rayburn Bldg

Longworth Bldg

Cannon Bldg

Madison Bldg

Eastern Market

PENNSYLVANIA AVE

Eastern Market

Federal Center SW

Capitol South

Folger Park

Benjamin Banneker Park

DWIGHT EISENHOWER FREEWAY

L'Enfant Plaza

Garfield Park

SOUTHEAST FRWY

MAINE AVE

SOUTHWEST

Waterfront-SEU

Channel

Navy Yard

SOUTHEAST

Washington Navy Yard

Nationals Park

Anacostia River

Hotels pp94-110

Restaurants & Cafés pp111-133

Pubs & Bars pp134-142

Time Out Washington, DC **253**

Street Index

1st St NE – p251 L4/5, p253 L4-6
1st St NW - p251 K2-5
1st St SE - p253 L8/9/M7-9
1st St SW - p253 K8/9
2nd St NE - p251 L1-5, p253 L4-6
2nd St NW - p251 K3-5, p253 K4-K6
2nd St SE- p253 L7/8
2nd St SW- p253 K7
3rd St NE - p251 L1-5, p253 L4-6
3rd St NW - p251 K4/5, p253 K4-K6
3rd St SE- p253 L7/8
3rd St SW - p253 K78-9
4th St NE - p251 L1-5, p253 L4-6
4th St NW – p251 J3-5, K4/5, p253 K4-K6
4th St SE- p253 L7/8
4th St SW- p253 K6-8
5th St NE - p251 L1-5, p253 L4-6
5th St NW - p251 J3-5, p253 J4-J6
5th St SE- p253 L7/8
6th St NE - p251 L4, p253 L4-6
6th St NW - p251 J4/5, p253 J4-J6
6th St SW- p253 J7/8
7th St NE - p251 L1-5, p253 L4-6
7th St NW - p251 J4/5, p253 J4-J6
7th St SE- p253 L7/8
7th St SW - p253 J7/8
8th St NE - p251 M1-5, p253 M4-6
8th St NW - p251 J3-5, p253 J4-6
8th St SE - p253 M7/8
9th St NE - p251 M1/M5, p253 M4-6
9th St NW - p251 J3-5, p253 J4-J6
9th St SE - p253 M7/8
9th St SW - p253 J7
10th St NW - p250 J1-5, p252 J4-7
11th St NW - p250 J1-5, p252 J4-7
12th St NW - p250 H1-5, p252 H4-7
13th St NW - p250 H1-5, p252 H4-6
14th St NW - p250 H1-5, p252 H4-6
14th St SW - p252 H5-7
15th St NW - p250 H1-5, p252 H4-6
16th St NW - p250 H1-5, p252 H4/5
17th St NW - p250 G1, p250 G1/H1-5, p252 G4-7
18th St NW - p250 G3-5,

p252 G4-6
19th St NW - p250 G1-5, p252 G4-6
20th St NW - p250 G3-5, p252 G4-6
21st St - p249 D5
21st St NW - p250 G4/5, p252 G4-6
22nd St - p249 D5
22nd St NW - p250 G4/5
23rd St NW – p249 F4/5, p250 F4/5, p252 F4-6
24th St NW - p249 F2/F5, p250 F4/5, p252 F4/5
25th St NW - p249 F5, p250 F4/5, p252 F4/5
26th St N - p248 A4/5
26th St NW - p249 F5, p250 F4/5, p252 F5
27th Rd N - p248 A4
27th St N - p248 A4
27th St NW - p249 F2/4/5, p250 F4, p252 F4/5
28th St NW - p249 F2-5, p250 F4, p252 F4/5
29th Pl NW - p249 F2
29th St NW - p249 F2-5
30th Rd N - p248 A3/4
30th St N - p248 A4
30th St NW - p249 E1-5
31st Pl - p249 E2
31st St NW - p249 E4/5
32nd St - p249 E2
32nd St NW - p249 E4
33rd Pl NW - p249 E1
33rd St NW - p249 E4/5
34th Pl NW – p249 E1/2
34th St NW - p249 E2-5
35th Pl NW - p249 E2
35th St NW - p249 E1-5
36th Pl NW - p249 D2
36th St NW - p249 D3/E1-4
37th St NW - p249 D3-5
38th St NW - p249 D1-4
39th Pl NW - p249 D3
39th St NW - p249 D1-4
40th Pl NW - p249 D3
40th St NW - p249 D3
41st St NW - p249 D2/3
42nd St NW - p248 C3
43rd St NW - p248 C2
44th Pl NW - p248 C2
44th St NW - p248 C2/3, p249 D4
45th St NW - p248 C2/4
46th St NW - p248 C3
47th Pl NW - p248 C4
48th St NW - p248 B3
49th St NW - p248 B2/3
A St NE - p253 L6/M6
Acker Pl- p253 L6
Adams Mill Rd - p250 G1/2
Adams St - p251 K3
Alexander Hamilton Pl - p252 H6
Arizona Ave - p248 B1/2

Arland D Williams Jr Br - p252 G8/9/H8
Arlington Memorial Bridge - p252 F7
Ashby St - p248 B3/C3
Ashmeade Pl - p250 G3
Avon Pl - p249 E4
Bancroft St - p249 F3, p250 F3/G3
Bates St - p251 K4
Bellevue Terr - p249 D2
Belmont Rd - p249 F3, p250 F3
Belmont St - p250 H3
Benton Pl - p249 F3
Benton St - p249 D3
Biltmore St - p250 G3
Brookland Ave - p251 L1
Bryant St - p251 J3-K3
Buckeye Dr - p252 H8
C St NE- p253 K6-M6
C St NW - p252 F6-H6, p253 J6/K6
C St SE - p253 K7-M7
C St SW - p252 H7/J7, p253 J7/K7
California St - p249 F3, p250 F3/G3
Calvert St - p248 B2/3, p249 D2/3/F2, p250 F2/G2
Canal Rd – p248 A1/2/B3/ 4/C4, p249 D4
Carolina Pl - p248 A2
Caroline St - p250 H3
Case Br - p252 H8
Cathedral Ave - p248 A2-C2, p249 D2/F2, p250 F2
Chain Bridge - p248 A2
Chain Bridge Rd - p248 B1/2
Champlain St - p250 G3
Channing St - p251 K3
Chapin St - p250 H3
Church St - p250 G4/H4
Clark Pl - p248 C4
Cleveland Ave - p249 E2
Clifton St - p250 H2/3
College St - p251 J3
Columbia Rd - p250 G2/3/H2, p251 J2
Connecticut Ave – p249 F1-3, p250 F2/G3-5, p252 G4/5
Constitution Ave - p252 G6-H6, p253 J6-M6
Corcoran St - p250 G4
Cortland Pl - p249 F2
Creek Church Rd - p251 J1
Cushing Pl - p248 B2
D St NE - p253 K6-M6
D St NW - p252 G6/H6, p253 J6/K6
D St SE - p253 K7-M7
D St SW - p252 H7, p253 J7/K7
Dana Pl - p248 B2
Daniel French Dr - p252 F6-H6
Davis Pl - p249 D2

Davis St - p249 D2/E2
De Sales St - p250 G4, p252 G5
Delaware Ave - p251 L5, p253 K6-8/L5
Dent Pl - p249 E4/F4
Devonshire Pl - p249 F1/2
Dexter St - p248 B2/C2
Douglas St - p251 L2
Dumbarton St - p249 E4/F4
Dupont Circle - p250 G4
Dwight Eisenhower Freeway - p253 J7/K7
E Capitol St - p253 K7-M7
E St NE - p253 L6/M6
E St NW - p252 F6-H6, J6/K6
E St SE - p253 K7/L7
E St SW - p253 J7/K7
Eckington Pl - p251 L4
Edgewood St - p251 L2
Edmunds St - p248 C2, p249 D2/E2
Ellipse Rd - p252 H6
Elm St - p251 J3/K3
Euclid St - p250 G2-J2, p251 J2
Ewarts St - p251 L2
F St NE - p253 L6/M6
F St NW - p252 F6-H6, p253 J6/K6
F St SE - p253 K7-M7
Fairmont St - p250 H2/J2
Florida Ave - p250 G3/H3, p251 L4, p253 K5-M5
Foxhall Rd - p248 C1-4
Franklin Square - p250 H5
Franklin St NE- p251 L2/M2
Franklin St NW - p251 J4
Fuller St - p250 G2/H2
Fulton St - p248 B2/C2, p249 D2/E2
G Pl NE - p251 K5
G Pl NW - p251 J5
G St NE - p251 L5, p253 K5-M5
G St NW - p251 K5/L5, p252 F6-H6, p253 J6/K6
G St SE - p253 K8-M8
G St SW - p253 J8/K8
Galena Pl - p248 A2
Garfield St - p248 B2/C2, p249 D2-F2
George Mason Mem Brg - p252 G8
George Washington Memorial Pkwy - p248 A2/3/B4/5/C5, p252 F7/8/G8/9
Georgia Ave - p251 J1-3
Girard St - p250 H2/J2, p251 J2-L2
Glenbrook Rd - p248 B1
Glenbrook Terr - p248 A1
Glover Dr - p248 C2
Grace St - p249 E5
Greene Pl - p248 C4
Gresham Pl - p251 J2
H St NE - p251 K5-M5, p253 K5-M5

H St NW - p250 F4-H4, p251 J4-L5, p252 F5-H5, p253 J5/K5
H St SW - p253 J8/K8
Half St SE - p253 K8/9
Half St SW - p253 K8/9
Harewood Rd - p251 L1
Harvard St - p250 G2-J2
Hawthorne St - p248 C2, p249 F2
Henry Bacon Dr - p252 G6
Highland Pl - p249 E1
Hoban Rd - p248 C3/4
Hobart St - p250 G2/H2
Holmead Pl - p250 H1
Horbart Pl - p251 J2
Howard Pl - p251 J2/3
Huidekoper Pl - p249 D3
Hutchins Pl - p248 B3
I St NE - p251 L5, p253 K5-M5
I St NW - p250 F4-H4, p251 J4-L5/K5, p252 F5-H5, p253 J5/K5
I St SE - p253 K8-M8
I St SW - p253 J8/K8
Idaho Ave - p249 D1
Independence Ave - p252 F7-H7, p253 J7-M7
Indian Lane - p248 B1
Irving St - p250 G2-J2, p251 K1/L1
Ivy St- p253 K7
Jackson Pl - p250 H5, p252 H5
Jefferson Dr - p253 J7/K7
Jefferson Pl - p250 G5
Johnson Ave - p250 H4
Judiciary Square - p253 J6
K St NE - p251 J5/L5, p253 K5-M5
K St NW - p249 F5, p250 F5-J5, p251 K5, p252 F5-H5, p253 J5/K5
K St SE - p253 K8-M8
K St SW - p253 J8/K8
Kalorama Circle - p249 F3, p250 F3
Kalorama Rd - p249 F3, p250 F3-H3
Kansas Ave - p250 H1
Kenmore Dr - p248 C4
Kenyon St - p250 G2-J2, p251 J2
Key Bridge - p249 E5
Kilbourne Pl - p250 G2
King Pl - p248 B3
Kingman Pl - p250 H4
Klingle Ave - p249 F1
Klingle Rd - p249 E2
Klingle St - p248 B1/C1
Kutz Br - p252 G7/H7
L St NE - p251 K5/L5, p253 K5-M5
L St NW - p294 F5-J5, p251 J5-L5, p253 J5/K5, p252 F5-H5
L St SE - p253 K8-M8
L St SW - p253 J8/K8
Lafayette Square - p250 H5, p252 H5
Lamont St - p250 G1
Lanier Pl - p250 G2
L'enfant Promenade - p252 J7
Lexington Pl - p253 L6

Lincoln Rd - p251 K3/L3/4
Logan Circle - p250 H4
Lorcom Lane - p248 A5/B5
Loughboro Rd - p248 B1
Louisiana Ave - p253 K6
Lowell St - p248 B1/C1, p249 E1
M St NE - p251 K5/L5, p253 K4/L6
M St NW - p249 E5/F5, p250 F5-J5, p251 J4/K4, p252 F5-H5, p253 J5/K5
M St SE - p253 K8-M8
M St SW - p253 J8/K8
Macarthur Blvd - p248 A1/2/B3/C4
Macomb St - p248 A1/2/C1, p249 D1-F1
Madison Dr - p252 H6, p253 J6/K6
Madison Pl - p250 H5, p252 H5
Maine Ave - p253 J8
Manning Pl - p248 A1
Marcey Rd - p248 A4
Maryland Ave - p253 J7/K7
Massachusetts Ave - p249 D1/2/E2/3/F3/4, p250 F3/4/G4/5, p251 J5/K5, p252 H4/5, p253 J5/K5/6/L6
Maud St - p248 A1
McMillan Dr - p251 K3
Michigan Ave - p251 K2 /L1/2
Military Rd - p248 A4/5
Millwood La - p248 B1
Monroe St - p248 A3, p250 G1
Morris Pl - p253 L6
Morton St - p251 J1
Mt Pleasant St - p250 H1/2
N Oaklands St - p248 A3
N Peary St - p248 A3
N Pollard St - p248 B5
N Quebec St - p248 A4/B4
N Randolph St - p248 A4
N St NE - p251 K4/L4, p253 K4/L4
N St NW - p249 E4/F4, p250 F4-J4, p251 J4/K4, p252 F4-H4, p253 J4/K4
Neal Pl - p251 J4/K4
Nebraska Ave - p248 C1
New Hampshire Ave - p249 F5, p250 F5/G4/5, p252 F5g4/5
New Jersey Ave - p251 J4/K4/5, p253 K4-7/L8
New Mexico Ave - p248 C1/2
New York Ave - p250 H5/J5, p251 J5/K4/5/L4, p252 G6/H6, p253 J5/K4/5
Newark St - p248 C1, p249 D1/E1
Newton St - p250 G1/H1
Normanstone Dr - p249 E2/3/F3
North Capitol St - p251 K1-5, p253 K4-6
North Carolina Ave - p253 K7-M7
Norton St - p248 A1
O St NE - p251 K4, p253 K4

O St NW - p249 E4/F4, p250 G4-J4, p251 J4/K4, p253 J4/K4
O St SE - p253 K9/L9
O St SW - p253 J9/K9
Oakdale Pl - p251 J3/K3
Observatory Circle - p249 E2/3
Observatory Pl - p249 D3
Ogden St - p250 H1
Ohio Dr - p252 G7/8/H8/9
Olive St - p249 F4, p250 F5, p252 F5
Ontario Pl - p250 G2
Ontario Rd - p250 G2/3
Ordway St - p249 E1/F1
Otis Pl - p250 H1
P St NW - p249 D4-F4, p250 F4-J4, p251 J4-L4
P St SW - p253 J9/K9
Park Pl - p251 J1/2
Park Rd - p250 H1/2
Partridge La - p248 A1
Patterson St - p251 K5, p253 K4
Penn St - p251 L4
Pennsylvania Ave - p250 G5, p252 G5, p253 J6/L7/M7
Perry Pl - p250 H1
Pierce St NE - p251 K5, p253 K4
Pierce St NW - p251 K5
Piney Branch Pkwy - p250 G1
Pollard St - p248 A4
Porter St - p249 D1-F1, p250 F1
Potomac Ave - p248 A1/2/B3, p253 K9
Potomac St - p249 E4/5
Princeton Pl - p251 J1
Prospect St - p249 E5
Q La - p248 C4
Q Pl - p248 C4
Q St NE - p251 K4/L4
Q St NW - p249 E4/F4, p250 F4-J4, p251 J4-L4
Q St SW - p253 K9
Quebec Pl - p251 J1
Quebec St - p248 B1, p249 D1-F1
Quincy Pl - p251 K4/L4
Quincy St - p248 A4, p250 H1/J1, p251 J1
R St NE - p251 L4
R St NW - p249 D4/E4, p250 F4-J4, p251 J4-L4
R St SW - p253 K9
Randolph Pl NE - p251 L4
Randolph Pl NW - p251 K4
Raoul W Pl - p252 H7
Reservoir Rd - p248 B1/C4, p249 D4/E4
Rhode Is Ave - p252 H4
Rhode Island Ave - p250 H4/J4, p251 L3/M3
Ridge St - p251 J4, p253 J4
Riggs Pl - p250 G4
Roberts Lane - p248 A3
Rochambeau Mem Brg - p252 G8
Rock Creek & Potomac Pkwy - p250 F3-5, p252 F4-6
Rockwood Pkwy - p248 B1
Rowland Pl - p249 E1

S Carolina Ave - p253 L7/M7
S St NE - p251 L4
S St NW - p249 D3/E3, p250 F4-J4, p251 J4-L4
Salem Pl - p248 C4
School St - p253 J7
Scott Circle - p250 G4, p252 H4
Seaton Pl - p250 G3
Seaton Pl NE - p251 L3
Seaton Pl NW - p251 K3
Seward Square - p253 M7
Sheridan Circle - p250 F4
Sherrier Pl - p248 A1/2/B2
South Capitol St- p253 K7/8
South St - p249 E5
Southeast Frwy- p253 K8-M8
Spring Rd - p250 H1
State Pl - p252 G6/H6
Summit Pl - p251 L3
T Jefferson St - p249 F5
T St NE - p251 K3/L3
T St NW - p249 D3/E3, p250 H3/J3, p251 J3-K3
Thomas Circle - p250 H5, p252 H5
Thomas St - p251 K3
Todd Pl - p251 K3/L3
Tracy Pl - p249 F3, p250 F3
Tunlaw Rd - p249 D2/3
U St NE - p251 K3/L3
U St NW - p248 B3, p250 H3/J3, p251 J3-K3
University Terr - p248 B1/2
V St NE - p251 L3
V St NW - p248 B3, p250 H3/J3, p251 J3-K3
Vermont Ave - p250 H4/J3/4, p252 H5
Vernon Place - p253 L6
Vernon Square - p251 J5, p253 J5
Vernon St - p250 G3
Virginia Ave - p252 F5/6/G6, p253 K7-8/L8
Volta Pl - p249 D4/E4
W Pl NW - p249 D3
W St NW - p248 B3/C3, p249 D3, p250 H3/J3, p251 J3-K3
W Virginia Ave - p253 M5
Wallach Pl - p250 H3
Ward Pl - p250 G4/5
Warder St - p251 J1/2
Washington Ave - p253 K7
Washington Circle - p249 F5, p250 F5, p252 F5
Water St - p253 J8
Weaver Terr - p248 B1/2
Whitehaven Pkwy - p248 B3/C3
Whitehaven St - p249 E3
Willard St - p250 G3
Williamsburg La - p249 F1
Wisconsin Ave - p249 D1-3/E3-5
Woodland Dr - p249 E2
Woodley Rd - p249 E1/2/F2, p250 F2
Wyoming Ave - p249 F3, p250 F3/G3

Washington, DC Metro Map

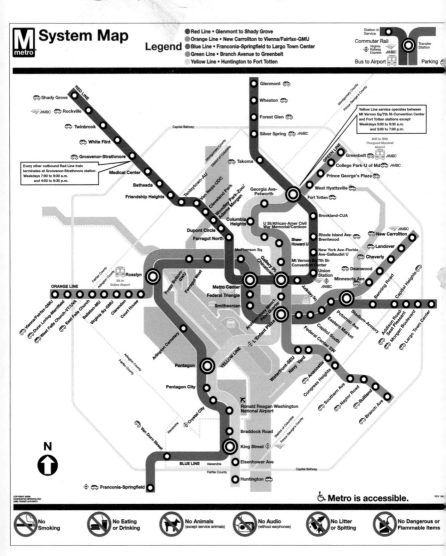